17.00 EC
01

Y0-BUB-607

THE

OXFORD REFORMERS

JOHN COLET, ERASMUS, AND THOMAS MORE.

AMS PRESS

NEW YORK

THE

OXFORD REFORMERS

JOHN COLET, ERASMUS, AND THOMAS MORE.

BEING A HISTORY OF THEIR FELLOW-WORK.

BY

FREDERIC SEEBOHM.

' Tu interea patienter audi ; ac nos ambo, collidentibus inter se silicibus, si quis ignis excutiatur, eum avide apprehendamus. *Veritatem* enim quærimus, non opinionis offensionem . . .' (*Colet*, Eras. Op. v. p. 1292).

' Take no heed what thing many men do, but what thing the *very law of nature,* what thing *very reason,* what thing *Our Lord himself* showeth thee to be done' (*Pico della Mirandola*, translated by More : More's English Works, p. 13).

' Cur sic arctamus Christi professionem quam Ille latissime voluit patere ? ' (*Erasmus,* Letter to Volzius, prefixed to the ' Enchiridion ').

REPRINTED FROM THE THIRD EDITION (1911)

REISSUE

LONGMANS, GREEN, AND CO.

39 PATERNOSTER ROW, LONDON
NEW YORK, BOMBAY, AND CALCUTTA

1913

Reprinted from the edition of 1911, London

First AMS edition published 1971

Manufactured in the United States of America

International Standard Book Number: 0-404-05696-2

Library of Congress Number: 70-147115

AMS PRESS INC.
NEW YORK, N.Y. 10003

PREFACE

TO

THE THIRD EDITION

—•—

SINCE this book was written, years ago, the works of Dean Colet have one after another been placed within reach of the public, ably edited by my friend Mr. Lupton, and now I understand that a biography by the same competent hand is also in the press.

Under these circumstances I have had some hesitation in allowing a Third Edition to be printed. I have yielded, however, to Mr. Lupton's pleading that this history of the fellow-work of the three friends, imperfect as it always was, and antiquated as it has now become, may live a little longer.

F. S.

THE HERMITAGE, HITCHIN: *March* 8, 1887.

PREFACE

TO

THE SECOND EDITION

———•◦•———

Two CIRCUMSTANCES have enabled me to make this Second Edition more complete, and I trust more correct, than its predecessor.

First : the remarkable discovery by Mr. W. Aldis Wright, on the blank leaves of a MS. in the library of Trinity College, Cambridge, of an apparently contemporary family register recording, *inter alia*, the date of the marriage of Sir Thomas More's parents, and of the birth of Sir Thomas More himself (see Appendix C), has given the clue, so long sought for in vain, to the chronology of More's early life. It has also made it needful to alter slightly the title of this work.

Secondly : the interesting MSS. of Colet's, on the ' Hierarchies of Dionysius,' found by Mr. Lupton in the library of St. Paul's School, and recently published by him with a translation and valuable introduction,[1]

---

[1] Mr. Lupton's volume (*Bell and Daldy*, 1869) has a double interest. Apart from the interest it derives from its connection with Colet, it is also interesting as placing, I believe, for the first time, before the Eng- lish reader, a full abstract of two of the Pseudo-Dionysian writings, to which attention has recently been called by Mr. Westcott's valuable article in the *Contemporary Review*.

have supplied a missing link in the chain of Colet's mental history, which has thrown much fresh light, as well upon his connection with the Neo-Platonists of Florence, as upon the position already taken by him at Oxford, before the arrival of Erasmus.

The greater part of the First Edition was already in the hands of the public, when I became aware of the importance of this newly discovered information; but, in October last, I withdrew the remaining copies from sale, as it seemed to me that it would hardly be fair, under the circumstances, to allow them to pass out of my hands. They have since been destroyed.

In publishing this revised and enlarged edition, I wish especially to tender my thanks to Mr. Lupton for his invaluable assistance in its revision, and for the free use he has throughout allowed me to make of the results of his own researches.

I have also to thank the Librarian of Emmanuel College, Cambridge, for the loan of a beautiful copy of Colet's MS. on ' I. Corinthians ; ' and Mr. Bradshaw, for kindly obtaining for me a transcript of the MS. on ' Romans ' in the University Library.

At Mr. Bradshaw's suggestion I have added, in the Appendix, a catalogue of the early editions of the works of Erasmus in my collection. It will at least serve as evidence of the wide circulation obtained by these works during the lifetime of their author.

HITCHIN: *May* 10, 1869.

PREFACE

TO

THE FIRST EDITION

SOME PORTIONS of this History were published in a somewhat condensed form in the course of last year in the 'Fortnightly Review,' and I have to thank the Editor for the permission to withdraw further portions, although already in type, in order that the publication of this volume might not be delayed.[1]

Having regard to the extreme inaccuracy of the dates of the letters of Erasmus,[2] the conflicting nature of the evidence relating to the chronology of More's early life,[3] and the scantiness of the materials for anything like a continuous biography of Colet, I should have undertaken a difficult task had I attempted in this volume, even so far as it goes, to give anything approaching to an exhaustive biography of Colet, Erasmus, and More. But my object has not been to

---

[1] To avoid any charge of plagiarism I may also state, that a portion of the materials comprised in this volume has been made use of in articles contributed by me to the North British Review, in the years 1859 and 1860.

[2] Where not otherwise stated, all references to these letters and to the collected works of Erasmus (Eras. Op.), refer to the Leyden edition.

[3] See note on the date of More's birth in Appendix C.

write the biography of any one of them. I have rather endeavoured to trace their *joint*-history and to point out the character of their *fellow-work*. And with regard to the latter the evidence is so full, so various, and so consistent as to leave, I think, little room for misapprehension, either as to whether their work was indeed *fellow-work*, or as to the general spirit and scope of the work itself.

I gladly take this opportunity of tendering my best thanks to those who have aided me in this undertaking.

My warmest thanks are due to the Rev. J. S. Brewer, M.A., as well for the invaluable aid afforded by his Calendars of the Letters, &c. of Henry VIII., and for the loan of the proof-sheets of the forthcoming volume, as for *the revision of the greater part of my translations* ; also to Mr. Gairdner for his ever ready assistance at the Public Record Office ; to Dr. Edward Boehmer, of the University of Halle, for his aid in the collection of many of the early editions of works of Erasmus quoted in this volume ; to the Senate and the late Librarian of the Cambridge University Library for the loan of the volume of MSS. marked Gg. 4, 26 ; and to Mr. Henry Bradshaw, of King's College, Cambridge, for much valuable assistance, most courteously rendered, in the examination of this and other manuscripts at Cambridge. I have also to thank the Rev. J. H. Lupton, of St. Paul's School, for the description given in Appendix C.[1] of a manuscript of Colet's in the Library of St. Paul's School which I had overlooked,

---

[1] Of the First Edition.   This has since been published by Mr. Lupton.

and which I am happy to find is likely soon to be printed by him.

In conclusion, I cannot refrain from adding a tribute of affectionate regard for the memory of two of my friends—the late Mr. William Tanner of Bristol, and the late Mr. B. B. Wiffen of Woburn—of whose interest in the progress of this work I have received many proofs, and of whose kindly criticism I have gratefully availed myself.

HITCHIN : *March* 30, 1867.

CONTENTS.

CHAPTER I.

CHAPTER II.

CHAPTER III.

CHAPTER IV.

CHAPTER V.

CHAPTER VI.

CHAPTER VII.

CHAPTER VIII.

Contents.

CHAPTER XIV.

CHAPTER XV.

CHAPTER XVI.

APPENDICES.

THE OXFORD REFORMERS:

COLET, ERASMUS, AND MORE.

CHAPTER I.

I. JOHN COLET RETURNS FROM ITALY TO OXFORD (1496).

It was probably in Michaelmas Term of 1496 [1] that the announcement was made to doctors and students of the University of Oxford that John Colet, a late student, recently returned from Italy, was about to deliver a course of public and gratuitous lectures in exposition of St. Paul's Epistles.

This was an event of no small significance and perhaps of novelty in the closing years of that last of the

---

[1] In a letter written in the winter of 1499–1500, Colet is spoken of as '*Jam triennium enarranti*,' &c. See *Erasmus to Colet*, prefixed to *Disputatio de Tœdio et Pavore Christi*, Eras. *Op.* v. p. 1264, A. Colet was in Paris, apparently on his way home from his continental tour, soon after the publication of the work of the French historian Gaguinus, *De Orig. et Gest. Francorum.* (See Eras. Epist. xi.) The first edition, according to Panzer and Brunet, of this work, was that of *Paris.* Prid. Kal. Oct. 1495. Colet may thus have returned home in the spring of 1496, and proceeded to Oxford after the long vacation. Erasmus states, ' Reversus ex Italia, mox ' relictis parentum ædibus, Oxoniæ ' maluit agere. Illic publice et ' gratis Paulinas Epistolas omnes ' enarravit.'—*Op.* iii. p. 456, B.

B

Middle Ages; not only because the Scriptures for some generations had been practically ignored at the Universities, but still more so because the would-be lecturer had not as yet entered deacon's orders,[1] nor had obtained, or even tried to obtain, any theological degree.[2] It is true that he had passed through the regular

academical course at Oxford, and was entitled, as a Master of Arts, to lecture upon any other subject.[3] But a degree in Arts did not, it would seem, entitle the graduate to lecture upon the Bible.[4]

It does not perhaps follow from this, that Colet was guilty of any flagrant breach of university statutes, which, as a graduate in Arts, he must have sworn to obey. The very extent to which real study of the Scriptures had become obsolete at Oxford, may possibly suggest that even the statutory restrictions on Scripture lectures may have become obsolete also.[5]

Before the days of Wiclif, the Bible had been free,

---

[1] He was ordained deacon December 17, 1497. Knight's *Life of Colet*, p. 22 (Lond. 1724), on the authority, doubtless, of Kennett, who refers to *Reg. Savage, Lond.*

[2] Erasmus Jodoco Jonæ : Eras. *Op.* iii. p. 456, C. 'In theologica 'professione nullum omnino grad- 'um nec assequutus erat, nec 'ambierat.'

[3] 'The degree of Master in Arts 'conferred also, and this was prac- 'tically its chief value, the right of 'lecturing, and therefore of receiv- 'ing money for lectures, at Oxford.' *Monumenta Academica*: Rev. H. Anstey's *Introduction*, p. lxxxix.

[4] One of the statutes decreed as follows :—' Item statutum est, ' quod non liceat alicui præterquam

'Bachilaris Theologiæ, legere bi- ' bliam biblice.'—*Ibid.* p. 394. That the word ' legere,' in these statutes, means practically to ' lecture,' see Mr. Anstey's *Introduction*, p.lxxxix.

[5] It is possible also that Colet's mode of lecturing did not come within the meaning of the technical phrase, ' legere bibliam *biblice*,' which is said to have meant ' read- 'ing chapter by chapter, with the ' accustomed glosses, and such ex- 'planations as the reader could add.' *Observations on the Statutes of the University of Cambridge* : by George Peacock, D.D., Dean of Ely. Lond. 1841, p. xlvi. *n.* See also Mr. Anstey's *Introduction*, p. lxxi, on the doubtful meaning of ' legere *cursorie*.'

and Bishop Grosseteste could urge Oxford students to
devote their *best morning hours* to Scripture lectures.[1]
But an unsuccessful revolution ends in tightening the
chains which it ought to have broken. During the
fifteenth century the Bible was *not* free. And Scripture
lectures, though still retaining a nominal place in the
academical course of theological study, were thrown
into the background by the much greater relative importance of the lectures on ' the Sentences.' What
Biblical lectures were given were probably of a very
formal character.[2]

---

[1] See the remarkable letter of Bishop Grosseteste to the ' Regents ' in Theology ' at Oxford—date 1240 or 1246—*Roberti Grosseteste Epistolæ*, pp. 346–7, of which the following is Mr. Luard's summary : ' Skilful builders are always care- ' ful that foundation stones should ' be really capable of supporting ' the building. The best time is the ' morning. Their lectures, there- ' fore, especially in the morning, ' should be from the Old and New ' Testaments, *in accordance with* ' *their ancient custom* and the ex- ' ample of Paris. Other lectures ' are more suitable at other times.' P. cxxix. •

[2] It would not be likely that sta- tutes, framed in some points speci- ally to guard against Lollard views, and probably early in the fifteenth century, should ignore the Scrip- tures altogether. Thus, before in- ception in theology, by Masters in Theology (see Mr. Anstey's *Intro- duction*, p. xciv), three years' at- tendance on biblical lectures was required, and the inceptor must have lectured on some canonical book of the Bible (*Monumenta Aca- demica*, p. 391), according to the statutes. They also contained the following provision :—' Ne autem ' lecturæ variæ confundantur, *et ut* ' *expeditius* in lectura bibliæ proce- ' datur, statutum est, ut bibliam bi- ' blice seu cursorie legentes quæs- ' tiones non dicant nisi tantum- ' modo literales.'—*Ibid.* p. 392. The regular course of theological train- ing at Oxford may be further illustrated by the following passage from Tindale's ' Practice of Pre- lates' Tindale, when a youth, was at Oxford during a portion of the time that Colet was lecturing on St. Paul's Epistles.

' In the universities they have ' ordained that no man shall look on ' the Scripture until he be noselled ' in heathen learning eight or nine ' years, and armed with false prin- ' ciples with which he is clean shut ' out of the understanding of the ' Scripture. . . . . And when he ' taketh his first degree, he is sworn ' that he shall hold none opinion ' condemned by the Church. . . . .

CHAP. I.

A.D. 1496.

Commencement of a new movement at Oxford.

The announcement by Colet of this course of lectures on St. Paul's Epistles was in truth, so far as can be traced, the first overt act in a movement commenced at Oxford in the direction of practical Christian reform —a movement, some of the results of which, had they been gifted with prescience, might well have filled the minds of the Oxford doctors with dismay.

They could not indeed foresee that those very books of ' the Sentences,' over which they had pored so intently for so many years, in order to obtain the degree of Master in Theology, and at which students were still patiently toiling with the same object in view—they could not foresee that, within forty years, these very books would ' be utterly banished from Oxford,' ignominiously ' nailed up upon posts ' as waste paper, their loose leaves strewn about the quadrangles until some sportsman should gather them up and thread them on a line to keep the deer within the neighbouring woods.[1] They could not, indeed, foresee the end of the movement then only beginning, but still, the announcement of Colet's lectures was likely to cause them some

---

' And then when they be admitted ' to study divinity, because the ' Scripture is locked up with such ' false expositions and with false ' principles of natural philosophy ' that they cannot enter in, they go ' about the outside and dispute all ' their lives about words and vain ' opinions, pertaining as much unto ' the healing of a man's heel as ' health of his soul. Provided yet ' . . . . that none may preach ' except he be admitted of the ' Bishops.' — *Practice of Prelates*, p. 291. Parker Society.

What the biblical lectures were it

is difficult to understand, for Erasmus wrote (Eras. Epist. cxlviii.) : 'Compertum est hactenus quosdam 'fuisse theologos, qui adeo nunquam ' legerant divinas literas, ut nec ' ipsos Sententiarum libros evol- ' verent, neque quicquam omnino ' attingerent præter quæstionum ' gryphos.'—P. 130, C.

[1] Ellis's *Letters*, 2nd series, vol. ii. pp. 61, 62. Letter of Richard Layton and his Associates to Lord Cromwell, upon his Visitation of the University of Oxford, Sept. 12, 1535.

uneasiness. They may well have asked, whether, if
the exposition of the Scriptures were to be really
revived at Oxford, so dangerous a duty should not be
restricted to those duly authorised to discharge it ?
Was every stripling who might travel as far as Italy
and return infected with the ' new learning ' to be
allowed to set up himself as a theological teacher,
without graduating in divinity, and without waiting
for decency's sake for the bishop's ordination ?

On the other hand, any Oxford graduate choosing to
adopt so irregular a course, must have been perfectly
aware that it would be one likely to stir up opposition,
and even ill-will,[1] amongst the older divines ; and it
may be presumed that he hardly would have ventured
upon such a step without knowing that there were at
the university others ready to support him.

II. THE RISE OF THE NEW LEARNING (1453–92).

In all ages, more or less, there is a new school of The old
thought rising up under the eyes of an older school and new
school of
of thought. And probably in all ages the men of the thought.
old school regard with some little anxiety the ways of
the men of the new school. Never is it more likely to
be so than at an epoch of sharp transition, like that on
which the lot of these Oxford doctors had been cast.

We sometimes speak as though our age were *par ex-* An age of
progress
cellence the age of progress. *Theirs* was much more so and trans-
if we duly consider it. The youth and manhood of ition.
some of them had been spent in days which may well
have seemed to be the latter days of Christendom.

---

[1] ' Provinciam sumsisti . . . (ne   'plenam.'—Eras. Coleto: Eras. *Op.*
' quid mentiar) et negotii et invidiæ   v. p. 1264, A.

They had seen Constantinople taken by the Turks. The final conquest of Christendom by the infidel was a possibility which had haunted all their visions of the future. Were not Christian nations driven up into the north-western extremity of the known world, a wide pathless ocean lying beyond ? Had not the warlike creed of Mahomet steadily encroached upon Christendom, century by century, stripping her first of her African churches, from thence fighting its way northward into Spain ? Had it not maintained its foothold in Spain's fairest provinces for seven hundred years ?

And from the East was it not steadily creeping over Europe, nearer and nearer to Venice and Rome, in spite of all that crusades could do to stop its progress ? If, though little more than half the age of Christianity, it had already, as they reckoned it had, drawn into its communion five times [1] as many votaries as there were Christians left, was it a groundless fear that now in these latter days it might devour the remaining sixth ? What could hinder it ?

A Spartan resistance on the part of united Christendom perhaps might. But Christendom was not united,
nor capable of Spartan discipline. Her internal condition seemed to show signs almost of approaching dissolution. The shadow of the great Papal schism still brooded over the destinies of the Church. That schism had been ended only by a revolution which, under the guidance of Gerson, had left the Pope the constitutional instead of the absolute monarch of the Church. The

---

[1] 'The Turks being in number 'five times more than we Christians.' And again, ' Which multitude is ' not the fifth part so many as they 'that consent to the law of Ma- 'homet.'—*Works of Tyndale and Frith*, ii. pp. 55 and 74.

great heresies of the preceding century had, moreover,
not yet been extinguished. The very names of Wiclif
and Huss were still names of terror. Lollardy had
been crushed, but it was not dead. Everywhere the
embers of schism and revolution were still smouldering
underneath, ready to break out again, in new fury,
who could tell how soon ?

It was in the ears of this apparently doomed genera- Defeat of
the Moors
in Spain,
and dis-
covery of
America.
tion that the double tidings came of the discovery of
the Terra Nova in the West, and of the expulsion of
the infidel out of Spain.

The ice of centuries suddenly was broken. The
universal despondency at once gave way before a spirit
of enterprise and hope ; and it has been well observed,
men began to congratulate each other that their lot had
been cast upon an age in which such wonders were
achieved.

Even the men of the old school could appreciate
these facts in a fashion. The defeat of the Moors was
to them a victory to the Church. The discovery of
the New World extended her dominion. They gloried
over both.

But these outward facts were but the index to an
internal upheaving of the mind of Christendom, to
which they were blind. The men who were guiding
the great external revolution—reformers in their way
—were blindly stamping out the first symptoms of this
silent upheaving. Gerson, while carrying reform over
the heads of Popes, and deposing them to end the
schism or to preserve the unity of the Church, was at
the same moment using all his influence to crush Huss
and Jerome of Prague. Queen Isabella and Ximenes,

Henry VII. and Morton, while sufficiently enlightened
to pursue maritime discovery, to reform after a fashion
the monasteries under their rule, and ready even to
combine to reform the morals of the Pope himself in
order to avert the dreaded recurrence of a schism,[1]
were not eager to pursue these purposes without the
sanction of Papal bulls, and without showing their zeal
for the Papacy by crushing out free thought with an
iron heel and zealously persecuting heretics, whether
their faith were that of the Moor, the Lollard, or the Jew.

The re-
vival of
learning.
The fall of Constantinople, which had sounded almost
like the death-knell of Christendom, had proved itself
in truth the chief cause of her revival. The advance
of the Saracens upon Europe had already told upon
the European mind. The West has always had much
to learn from the East. It was, for instance, by translation from Arabic versions that Aristotle had gained
such influence over those very same scholastic minds
to which his native Greek was an abomination.

This further triumph of infidel arms also influenced
Christian thought. Eastern languages and Eastern
philosophies began to be studied afresh in the West.
Exiles who had fled into Italy had brought with them
their Eastern lore. The invention of printing had
come just in time to aid the revival of learning. The

---

[1] See British Museum Library,
under the head ' Garcilaso,' No.
1445, *g* 23, being the draft of private
instructions from Ferdinand and
Isabella to the special English Ambassador, and headed, ' Year 1498.
' The King and Queen concerning
' the correction of Alexander VI.'
The original Spanish MS. was in the
hands of the late B. B. Wiffen, Esq.,
of Mount Pleasant, near Woburn,
and an English translation of this
important document was reprinted
by him in the Life of Valdes, prefixed to a translation of his *CX
Considerations.* Lond. Quaritch,
1865, p. 24.

printing press was pouring out in clear and beautiful
type new editions of the Greek and Latin classics. Art
and science with literature sprang up once more into
life in Italy ; and to Italy, and especially to Florence,
which, under the patronage of the splendid court
of Lorenzo de' Medici, seemed to form the most
attractive centre, students from all nations eagerly
thronged.

It was of necessity that the sudden reproduction Its effect
of the Greek philosophy and the works of the older on religion.
Neo-Platonists in Italy should sooner or later produce Revival
of Neo-
a new crisis in religion. A thousand years before, Platonism.
Christianity and Neo-Platonism had been brought
into the closest contact. Christianity was then in its
youth—comparatively pure—and in the struggle for
mastery had easily prevailed. Not that Neo-Platonism
was indeed a mere phantom which vanished and left
no trace behind it. By no means. Through the
pseudo-Dionysian writings it not only influenced profoundly the theology of mediæval mystics, but also
entered largely even into the Scholastic system. It
was thus absorbed into Christian theology though lost
as a philosophy.

Now, after the lapse of a thousand years, the same
battle had to be fought again. But with this terrible
difference ; that now Christianity, in the impurest form
it had ever assumed—a grotesque perversion of Christianity—had to cope with the purest and noblest of
the Greek philosophies. It was, therefore, almost a The
Platonic
matter of course that, under the patronage of Lorenzo Academy,
de' Medici, the Platonic Academy under Marsilio Ficino.
Ficino should carry everything before it. Whether
the story were literally true of Ficino himself or not,

that he kept a lamp burning in his chamber before a
bust of Plato, as well as before that of the Virgin, it
was at least symbolically true of the most accomplished
minds of Florence.

Questions which had slept since the days of Julian
and his successors were discussed again under Sixtus

Plato and
Chris-
tianity.
IV. and Innocent VIII. The leading minds of Italy
were once more seeking for a reconciliation between
Plato and Christianity in the works of the pseudo-
Dionysius, Macrobius, Plotinus, Proclus, and other
Neo-Platonists. There was the same anxious endeavour, as a thousand years earlier, to fuse all philosophies into one. Plato and Aristotle must be reconciled,
as well as Christianity and Plato. The old world was
becoming once more the possession of the new. It
was felt to be the recovery of a lost inheritance, and
everything of antiquity, whether Greek, Roman,
Jewish, Persian, or Arabian, was regarded as a treasure.
It was the fault of the Christian Church if the grotesque
form of Christianity held up by her to a reawaken-
ing world seemed less pure and holy than the aspira-
tions of Pagan philosophers. It would be by no merit
of hers, but solely by its own intrinsic power, if Christianity should retain its hold upon the mind of Europe,
in spite of its ecclesiastical defenders.

Christianity brought into disrepute by the conduct
of professed Christians, was compelled to rest as of
old upon its own intrinsic merits, to stand the test
of the most searching scientific criticisms which Florentine philosophers were able to apply to it. Men
versed in Plato and Aristotle were not without some
notion of the value of intrinsic evidence, and the
methods of inductive enquiry. Ficino himself thought

it well, discarding the accustomed scholastic interpreters, to turn the light of his Platonic lamp upon
the Christian religion. From his work, ' *De Religione
Christianâ,*' dedicated to Lorenzo de' Medici, and
written in 1474, some notion may be gained of the
method and results of his criticism. That its nature
should be rightly understood is important in connection with the history of the Oxford Reformers.

Ficino commences his argument by demonstrating
that *religion* is natural to man ; and having, on Platonic authority, pointed out the truth of the one common religion, and that all religions have something
of good in them, he turns to the Christian religion in
particular. Its truth he tries to prove by a chain of
reasoning of which the following are some of the links.

He first shows that ' the disciples of Jesus were not
' deceivers ; ' [1] and he supports this by examining, in a
separate chapter, ' in what spirit the disciples of Christ
' laboured ; ' [2] concluding, after a careful analysis of the
Acts of the Apostles and the Epistles, that they did not
seek their *own* advantage or honour but ' the glory of
' *Christ* alone.' Then he shows that ' the disciples of
' Christ were not *deceived* by anyone,' [3] and that the
Christian religion was founded, not in human wisdom,
but ' in the wisdom and power of God; ' [4] that Christ was
' no astrologer,' but ' derived his authority from God.' [5]
He adduced further the evidence of miracles, in which
he had no difficulty in believing, for he gave two in-
stances of miracles which had occurred in Florence only
four years previously, and in which he declared to

---

[1] Chap. v.   [2] Chap. vi.   [3] Chap. vii.
          [4] Chap. viii.   [5] Chap. ix.

Lorenzo de' Medici, that, philosopher as he was, he believed.[1] After citing the testimony of some Gentile writers, and of the Coran of the Mahometans, and discussing in the light of Plato, Zoroaster, and Dionysius, the doctrine of the 'logos,' and the fitness of the incarnation, he showed that the result of the coming of Christ was that men are drawn to love with their whole heart a God who in his immense love had himself become man.[2] After dwelling on the way in which Christ lightened the burden of sin,[3] on the errors he dispelled, the truths he taught,[4] and the example he set,[5] Ficino proceeds in two short chapters to adduce the testimony of the 'Sibyls.'[6] This was natural to a writer whose bias it was to regard as genuine whatever could be proved to be ancient. But it is only fair to state that he relies much more fully and discusses at far greater length the prophecies of the Ancient Hebrew prophets,[7] vindicating the Christian rendering of certain passages in the Old Testament against the Jews, who accused the Christians of having perverted and depraved them.[8] He concludes by asserting, that if there be much in Christianity which surpasses human comprehension, this is a proof of its divine character rather than otherwise. These are his final words. ' If these ' things be divine, they must exceed the capacity of any ' human mind. Faith (as Aristotle has it) is the founda- ' tion of knowledge. By faith alone (as the Platonists ' prove) we ascend to God. " I believed (said David) ' " and therefore have I spoken." Believing, therefore,

---

[1] Chap. x.
[2] Chap. xix.
[3] Chap. xx.
[4] Chap. xxii.

[5] Chap. xxiii.
[6] Chaps. xxiv. and xxv.
[7] Chaps. xxvi.–xxxiv.
[8] Chap. xxxvi.

' and approaching the fountain of truth and goodness
' we shall drink in a wise and blessed life.' [1]

Thus was the head of the Platonic Academy at Florence turning a critical eye upon Christianity, viewing it very possibly too much in the light of the lamp kept continually burning before the bust of Plato, but still, I think, honestly endeavouring, upon its own intrinsic evidence and by inductive methods, to establish a reasonable belief in its divine character in minds sceptical of ecclesiastical authority, and over whom the dogmatic methods of the Schoolmen had lost their power.[2] Nevertheless Ficino, as yet, was probably more of an intellectual than of a practical Christian, and Christianity was not likely to take hold of the mind of Italy—of re-awakening Europe—through any merely philosophical disquisitions. The lamp of Plato might throw light on Christianity, but it would not light up Christian fire in other souls. For Christianity is a thing of the heart, not only of the head. Soul is kindled only by soul, says Carlyle; and to teach religion the one thing needful is to find a man who *has* religion.[3] Should such a man arise, a man himself on fire with Christian love and zeal, his torch might light up other torches, and the fire be spread from torch to torch. But, until such a man should arise, the lamp of philosophy must burn alone in Florence. Men might come from far and near to listen to Marsilio Ficino—to share the patronage of Lorenzo de' Medici, to study Plato and

---

[1] Chap. xxxvii.

[2] *Villari*, in his ' Life and Times ' of Savonarola,' book i. chap. iv., does not seem to me to give, by any means, a fair abstract of the ' *De Religione Christianâ*,' though his chapter on Ficino is valuable in other respects. I have used the edition of Paris, 1510.

[3] ' Chartism,' chap. x. ' Impossible.'

Plotinus,—to learn how to harmonise Plato and Aristotle, to master the Greek language and philosophies,
—to drink in the spirit of reviving learning—but, of
true Christian *religion*, the lamp had not yet been lit
at Florence, or if lit was under a bushel.

Oxford
students
in Italy.

Already Oxford students had been to Italy, and
returned full of the new learning. Grocyn, one of
them, had for some time been publicly teaching Greek
at Oxford, not altogether to the satisfaction of the
old divines, for the Latin of the Vulgate was, in their
eye, the orthodox language, and Greek a Pagan and
heretical tongue. Linacre, too, had been to Italy and
returned, after sharing with the children of Lorenzo
de' Medici the tuition of Politian and Chalcondyles.[1]

These men had been to Italy and had returned, to
all appearances, mere humanists. Now five years
later Colet had been to Italy and had returned, *not* a
mere humanist, but an earnest Christian reformer,
bent upon giving lectures, not upon Plato or Plotinus,
but upon St. Paul's Epistles. What had happened
during these four years to account for the change?

III. COLET'S PREVIOUS HISTORY (1496).

Colet's
return
from Italy

John Colet was the eldest [2] son of Sir Henry Colet, a
wealthy merchant, who had been more than once Lord
Mayor of London,[3] and was in favour at the court of

---

[1] *Pauli Jovii Elogia Doctorum Virorum*: Basileæ, 1556, p. 145. The period of the stay of Grocyn and Linacre in Italy was probably between 1485 and 1491. They therefore probably returned to England before the notorious Alexander VI. succeeded, in 1492, to Innocent VIII. See Johnson's *Life of Linacre*, pp. 103–150. And Wood's *Athen. Oxon.* vol. i. p. 30. Also *Hist. et Antiq. Univ. Oxon.* ii. 134.

[2] Eras. *Op.* iii. p. 455, F.

[3] Erasmus Jodoco Jonæ : *Op.* iii. p. 455, F. Also Sir Henry Colet's Epitaph, quoted in Knight's *Life of Colet*, p. 7.

Henry VII. His father's position held out to him the prospect of a brilliant career. He had early been sent to Oxford, and there, having passed through the regular course of study in all branches of scholastic philosophy, he had taken his degree of Master of Arts.

On the return of Grocyn and Linacre from Italy full of the new learning, Colet had apparently caught the contagion. For we are told he ' eagerly devoured ' Cicero, and carefully examined the works of Plato ' and Plotinus.' [1]

When the time had come for him to choose a profession, instead of deciding to follow up the chances of commercial life, or of royal favour, he had resolved to take Orders.

The death of twenty-one [2] brothers and sisters, leaving him the sole survivor of so large a family, may well have given a serious turn to his thoughts. But inasmuch as family influence was ready to procure him immediate preferment, the path he had chosen need not be construed into one of great self-denial. It was not until long after he had been presented to a living in Suffolk and a prebend in Yorkshire, that he left Oxford, probably in or about 1494, for some years of foreign travel.[3]

The little information which remains to us of what Colet did on his continental journey, is very soon told.

He went first into France and then into Italy.[4]   On

---

[1] ' Et libros Ciceronis avidissime ' devorarat et Platonis Plotinique ' libros non oscitanter excusserat.' Eras. *Op.* iii. p. 456, A.

[2] Eras. *Op.* iii. p. 455, F. 'Mater, ' quæ adhuc superest [in 1520], in- ' signi probitate mulier, marito suo ' undecim filios peperit, ac totidem

' filias . . . , sed ex omnibus ille ' [Colet] superfuit solus, cum illum ' nosse cœpissem ' [in 1498].

[3] See list of Colet's preferments in the Appendix.

[4] ' Adiit Galliam, mox Italiam.' Eras. *Op.* iii. p. 456, A.

Colet
studies the
Scriptures
in Italy.

his way there, or on his return journey, he met with some German monks, of whose primitive piety and purity he retained a vivid recollection.[1] In Italy he ardently pursued his studies. But he no longer devoted himself to the works of Plato and Plotinus. In Italy, the hotbed of the Neo-Platonists, he '*gave himself up*' (we are told) '*to the study of the Holy Scriptures,*' after having, however, first made himself acquainted with the works of the Fathers, including amongst them the mystic writings then attributed to Dionysius the Areopagite. He acquired a decided preference for the works of Dionysius, Origen, Ambrose, Cyprian, and Jerome over those of Augustine. Scotus, Aquinas, and other Schoolmen had each shared his attention in due course. He is said also to have diligently studied during this period Civil and Canon Law, and especially what Chronicles and English classics he could lay his hands on ; and his reason for doing so is remarkable— that he might, by familiarity with them, polish his style, and so prepare himself for the great work of preaching the Gospel in England.[2]

What it was that had turned his thoughts in this direction no record remains to tell. Yet the knowledge

---

[1] Eras. *Op.* iii. p. 459, A.

[2] *Ibid.* p. 456, B. The words of Erasmus are the following :—' Ibi ' se totum evolvendis sacris auctoribus dedit, sed prius per omnium ' literarum genera magno studio ' peregrinatus, priscis illis potissi' mum delectabatur Dionysio, Ori'gene, Cypriano, Ambrosio, Hiero'nymo. Atque inter veteres nulli ' erat iniquior quam Augustino. ' Neque tamen non legit Scotum, ac ' Thomam aliosque hujus farinæ, si ' quando locus postulabat. In utri' usque juris libris erat non indili' genter versatus. Denique nullus ' erat liber historiam aut constitu' tiones continens majorum, quem ' ille non evolverat. Habet gens ' Britannica qui hoc præstiterunt ' apud suos, quod Dantes ac Petrar' cha apud Italos. Et horum evol' vendis scriptis linguam expolivit, ' jam tum se præparans ad præco' nium sermones Evangelici.'

of what was passing in Italy, while Colet was there,
surely may give a clue, not likely to mislead, to the
explanation of what otherwise might remain wholly
unexplained. To have been in Italy when Grocyn and
Linacre were in Italy—between the years 1485 and
1491—was, as we have said, to have drunk at the
fountain-head of reviving learning, and to have fallen
under the fascinating influence of Lorenzo de' Medici
and the Platonic Academy—an influence more likely
to foster the selfish coldness of a semi-pagan philosophy
than to inspire such feelings as those with which Colet
seems to have returned from *his* visit to Italy.[1]

But in the meantime Lorenzo had died, the tiara had
changed hands,and events were occurring during *Colet's*
stay in Italy—probably in 1495—which may well have
stirred in his breast the earnest resolution to devote
his life to the work of religious and political reform.

For to have been in Italy while Colet was in Italy Ecclesiastical
was to have come face to face with Rome at the time scandals.
when the scandals of Alexander VI. and Cæsar Borgia
were in everyone's mouth ; to have been brought into
contact with the very worst scandals which had ever
blackened the ecclesiastical system of Europe, at the
very moment when they reached their culminating
point.

On the other hand, to have been in Italy when Colet
was in Italy was to have come into contact with the
first rising efforts at Reform.

If Colet visited Florence as Grocyn and Linacre had Savonarola.
done before him, he must have come into direct contact with Savonarola while as yet his fire was holy and

---

[1] Savonarola's first sermon in the Duomo at Florence was
preached in 1491.—Villari, i. p. 122.

his star had not entered the mists in which it set in later years.

Recollecting what the great Prior of San Marco was —what his fiery and all but prophetic preaching was— how day after day his burning words went forth against the sins of high and low ; against tyranny in Church or State ; against idolatry of philosophy and neglect of the Bible in the pulpit ; recollecting how they told their tale upon the conscience of Lorenzo de' Medici and of his courtiers as well as upon the crowds of Florence ; —can the English student, it may well be asked, have passed through all this uninfluenced ? If he visited Florence at all he must have heard the story of Savonarola's interview with the dying Lorenzo ; he must have heard the common talk of the people, how Politian and Pico, bosom friends of Lorenzo, had died with the request that they might be buried in the habit of the order, and under the shadow of the convent of San Marco ; [1] above all, he must again and again have joined, one would think, with the crowd daily pressing to hear the wonderful preacher. Lorenzo de' Medici had died before Colet set foot upon Italian soil : probably also Pico and Politian.[2] And the death of these men had added to the grandeur of Savonarola's position. He was still preaching those wonderful sermons, all of them in exposition of Scripture, to which allusion has been made, and exerting that influence upon his hearers to which so many great minds had yielded.

---

[1] See Villari, i. 232. Anno 1494.
[2] Lorenzo de' Medici died in 1492 ; Pico and Politian in 1494. Colet left England early in 1494 probably, but as he visited France on his way to Italy, the exact time of his reaching Italy cannot be determined.

The man who *had* religion—the one requisite for teaching it—had arisen. And at the touch of his torch other hearts had caught fire. The influence of Savonarola had made itself felt even within the circle of the Platonic Academy. Pico had become a devoted student of the Scriptures and had died an earnest Christian. Ficino himself, without ceasing to be a Neo-Platonic philosopher, had also, it would seem, been profoundly influenced for a time by the enthusiasm of the great reformer.[1] And in the light of Colet's

---

[1] The influence of Savonarola on the religious history of Pico was very remarkable.

In a sermon preached after Pico's death, Savonarola said of Pico, ' He was wont to be conversant ' with me, and to break with me ' the secrets of his heart, in which ' I perceived that he was by privy ' inspiration called of God unto re-' ligion : ' i.e. to become a monk. And he goes on to say that, for *two years,* he had threatened him with Divine judgment ' if he fore-' sloathed that purpose which our ' Lord had put in his mind.'— More's *English Works,* p. 9. Pico died in November, 1494. The intimacy of which Savonarola speaks dated back therefore to 1492 or earlier.

` According to the statement of his nephew, J. F. Pico, the change in Pico's life was the result of the disappointment and the troubles consequent upon his ' vainglorious ' disputations ' at Rome in 1486 (when Pico was twenty-three). By this he was ' wakened,' so that he ' drew back his mind flowing in ' riot, and turned it to Christ ! '

Pico waited a whole year in Rome after giving his challenge, and the disappointment and troubles were not of short duration. They may be said to have commenced perhaps after the year of waiting, i.e. in 1487, when he left Rome. He was present at the disputations at Reggio in 1487, and this does not look as though as yet he had altogether lost his love of fame and distinction. There he met Savonarola ; and there that intimacy commenced which resulted in Savonarola's return, *at the suggestion of Pico,* to Florence. (J. F. Pico's *Vita Savonarolæ,* chap. vi. ; Harford's *Life of Michael Angelo,* i. p. 128 ; and Villari, i. pp. 82, 83.) In 1490, as the result of his first studies of Holy Scripture, according to J. F. Pico (being twenty-eight), he published his *Heptaplus,* which is full of his cabalistic and mystic lore, and betokens a mind still entangled in intellectual speculations rather than imbued with practical piety. He had, however, already burnt his early love songs, &c. ; and it is evident the change had for some time been going on.

return to Oxford from Italy, a lover of Dionysius and to lecture on St. Paul's Epistles, it is curious to observe

About the time when Savonarola commenced preaching in Florence, in 1491 (three years before his death, according to J. F. Pico), Pico disposed of his patrimony and dominions to his nephew, and distributed a large part of the produce amongst the poor, consulting Savonarola about its disposal (J. F. Pico's *Life of Savonarola,* chap. xi. ' *De mira Hieronymi lenitate et* ' *amore paupertatis* '), and appointing as his almoner *Girolamo Benivieni,* a devout and avowed believer in Savonarola's prophetic gifts. This was doubtless the time when Pico was wont to break to Savonarola ' the secrets of his ' heart;' the time also to which J.F. Pico alludes when he speaks of him as ' talking of the love of Christ ; ' and adding, ' the substance I have ' left, after certain books of mine ' finished, I intend to give out to ' poor folk, and fencing myself with ' the crucifix, barefoot, walking ' about the world, in every town ' and castle, I purpose to preach ' of Christ.'—Vide infra, p. 153. In 1492, a few weeks after Lorenzo's death, he wrote three beautiful letters to his nephew (Pici *Op.* pp. 231–236. Vide infra, pp. 153–156)— letters as glowing with earnest Christian piety as the *Heptaplus* was overflowing with cabalistic subtleties. His religion now, at all events, had the true ring about it. It belonged to his heart, not his head only. Then follow the remaining two years of his life when Savonarola exerted his influence

(but without success) to induce him to enter a religious order. On Sept. 21, 1494, he was present at Savonarola's famous sermon, in which he predicted the calamities which were coming upon Italy and the approach of the French army, listening to which Pico himself said that he ' was filled with horror, and ' that his hair stood on end ' (narrated by Savonarola in his *Compendium Revelationum*) ; and lastly in November, as Charles entered Florence, Pico was peacefully dying. He was buried in the robes of Savonarola's order and within the precincts of Savonarola's church of St. Mark. In the light of Savonarola's sermon, and the facts above stated, it can hardly be doubted that whilst, in one sense, brought about by the disappointment of his worldly ambitions, the change of life in Pico was at least, *in measure,* the result of his contact with the great Florentine reformer.

With regard to the history of Savonarola's influence on *Ficino's* religious character, the facts are not so easily traced. In early years he is said to have been more of a Pagan than a Christian. Before writing his *De Religione Christiandâ,* he seems to have become fully persuaded of the truth of Christianity. The book itself shows this. And there is a letter of his (Ficini *Op.* i. p. 640, Basle ed.), written while he was composing it, during an illness, in which he says that the words of Christ give him more comfort than philosophy, and his vows paid

that, shortly before Colet's visit to Italy, Ficino himself had published translations of some of the Dionysian writings,[1] and that apparently about the time of Colet's visit he was himself lecturing on St. Paul.[2]

If therefore Colet visited Florence, it may well be believed that he came into direct contact with Savonarola and Ficino. Whilst even if he did not visit Florence at all (and there appears to be no direct evidence that he did),[3] there remains abundant

---

to the Virgin more bodily good than medicine. He also says that his father, a doctor, was once warned in a dream, while sleeping under an oak tree, to go to a patient who was praying to the Virgin for aid.

But the religion of a man resting on dreams, and visions, and vows made to the Virgin, was not necessarily of a very deep and practical character. Superstition and philosophy were easily united without the heart taking fire. Schelhorn (in his *Amœnitates Literariœ,* i. p. 73) quotes from Wharton's appendix to Cave, the following statement, ' Rei philosophicæ nimium deditus, religionis et pietatis curam posthabuisse dicitur, donec Savonarolæ Florentiam advenientis eloquentiam admiratus, concionibus ejus audiendis animum adjecit, dumque flosculis Rhetorices inhiavit, pietatis igniculos recepit : reliquamque dein vitam religionis officiis impendit.' Wharton does not give his authority. Fleury (vol. xxiv. p. 363) makes a similar statement; also Brucker (*Historia critica Philosophiœ,* iv. p. 52); also Du Pin; also Harford in his *Life of Michael*

Angelo (i. p. 72) on the authority of Spondanus, who himself gives no contemporary authority. See also Mr. Lupton's *Introduction* to *Colet's Celestial and Ecclesiastical Hierarchies of Dionysius,* where the subject is discussed. I am informed, through the kindness of Count P. Guicciardini, of Florence, that in Ficino's *Apologia,* which exists in the MSS. *Stroziani* of *Libr. Magliabecchiana,* class viii. cod. 315, he says of himself that ' for five years he was one ' of the many who were deceived by ' the Hypocrite of Ferrara,' whom he calls ' Antichrist.' The truth therefore seems to be that he was profoundly influenced by Savonarola's enthusiasm, but only for a time.

[1] Ficino's editions of his translations of the Dionysian treatises on the ' Divine Names ' and the ' Mystic Theology ' seem to have been published at Florence in 1492 and 1496.—Fabricii *Bibliotheca Grœca,* vii. pp. 10, 11.

[2] Herzog's *Encyclopœdia,* article on ' Marsilius Ficinus.'

[3] Mr. Harford, in his *Life of Michael Angelo,* vol. i. p. 57, mentions Colet, among others, as studying at Florence, and cites

evidence, which will turn up in future chapters, that Colet had studied the writings of Pico,[1] of Ficino,[2] and of the authors most often quoted in their pages. He thus at least came directly under *Florentine* influence, at a time when the fire of religious zeal, kindled into a flame by the enthusiasm of the great Florentine Reformer, and fed by the scandals of Rome, was scattering its sparks abroad.

Spirit in which Colet returned to Oxford.

Be this as it may, whatever amount of obscurity may rest upon the history of the mental struggles through which Colet had passed before that result was attained, certain it is that he had returned to England with his mind fully made up, and with a character already formed and bent in a direction from which it never afterwards swerved. He had returned to England, not to enjoy the pleasures of fashionable life in London, not to pursue the chances of Court favour, not to follow his father's mercantile calling, not even to press

---

' *Tiraboschi*, vi. pt. 2, p. 382, edit. ' Roma, 4to. 1784.' But I cannot find any mention of Colet in Tiraboschi, after careful search.

In opposition to the likelihood of his having been at Florence it may be asked, why Colet never alludes to it in his letters or elsewhere ? In reply, it may be said that we have nothing of Colet's own writing relating to his early life. All we know of it is derived from Erasmus, and the only allusion by Colet to his Italian journey which Erasmus has preserved is the passing remark that he (Colet) had there become acquainted with certain *monks* of true wisdom and piety.—Eras. *Op.* iii. 459, A. ' Nar- ' rans sese apud Italos comperisse

' quosdam monachos vere prudentes ' ac pios.' Whether Savonarola's monks were amongst these is a matter of mere speculation.

[1] See marginal note on his ' Romans,' in the Cambridge University Library, MS. Gg. 4, 26, leaf 3*a*, in which he refers to him—' *Hec Mirandula*,' and cites a passage from Pico's *Apologia*, Basle edition of *Pici Opera*, p. 117. There is also a long and almost literal extract from Pico in the MS. on the ' Ecclesiastical Hierarchy,' in the St. Paul's School Library. See Mr. Lupton's translation, p. 161.

[2] See an extract from Ficino in Colet's MS. on ' Romans,' leaf 13*b*. Another is pointed out by Mr. Lupton, p. 36, *n*.

on at once towards the completion of his clerical
course ; but, unordained as he was, and without
doctor's degree, in all simplicity to begin the work
which had now become the settled purpose of his
life, by returning to Oxford and announcing this
course of lectures on St. Paul's Epistles.

IV. THOMAS MORE, ANOTHER OXFORD STUDENT (1492–6).

When Colet, catching the spirit of the new learning
from Grocyn and Linacre, left Oxford for his visit to
Paris and Italy, he left behind him at the University
a boy of fifteen, no less devoted than himself to the
study of the Greek language and philosophy.

This boy was *Thomas More.* He was the son of a Thomas
successful lawyer, living in Milk Street, Cheapside. More.

Brought up in the very centre of London life, he had
early entered into the spirit of the stirring times on
which his young life was cast. He was but five years
old when in April 1483 the news of Edward IV.'s
death was told through London. But he was old
enough to hear an eyewitness tell his father, that ' one
' Pottyer, dwelling in Redcross Street, without Cripple-
' gate,' within half a mile of his father's door, ' on the
' very night of King Edward's death, had exclaimed, His early
' " By my troth, man, then will my master the Duke history
' " of Glo'ster be king." ' [1] And followed as this was by

---

[1] ' Quem ego sermonem ab eo
' memini, qui colloquentes audi-
' verat, jam tum patri meo renun-
' ciatum, cum adhuc nulla prodi-
tionis ejus suspicio haberetur.'
—Thomæ Mori ' *Latina Opera,*'
Lovanii, 1566, fol. 46. As to the
authorship of the history of Richard
III. see Mr. Gairdner's preface to
*Letters of Richard III. and Henry
VII.* vol. ii. p. xxi. As More was
born in February, 1478, there is no
difficulty in accepting the authen-
ticity of this incident, which, when

Cardinal
Morton.

More's
genius.

Richard's murder of the young Princes, he never forgot
the incident. After some years' study at St. Anthony's
School in Threadneedle Street, his father placed him in
domestic service (as was usual in those times) with the
Archbishop and Lord Chancellor Morton,[1] a man than
whom no one knew the world better or was of greater
influence in public affairs—the faithful friend of
Edward IV., the feared but cautious enemy of Richard,
the man to whose wisdom Henry VII. in great measure
owed his crown. Morton was the Gamaliel at whose
feet young More was brought up, drinking in his
wisdom, storing up in memory his rich historic
knowledge, learning the world's ways and even something of the ways of kings, till a naturally sharp wit
became unnaturally sharpened, and Morton recognised
in the youth the promise of the future greatness of
the man. He was but thirteen or fourteen at most,
yet he would ' at Christmas time suddenly sometimes
' step in among the players, making up an extempore
' part of his own ; ' . . . and the Lord Chancellor ' would
' often say unto the nobles that divers times dined
' with him, "This child here waiting at table, whoso-
' " ever shall live to see it, will prove a marvellous
man." ' [2] It was Morton who had sent him to Oxford
' for his better furtherance in learning.' [3]

Colet probably had known More from childhood.
Their fathers were both too much of public men to be
unknown to each other, and though Colet was twelve
years older than young More when they most likely

1480 was assumed as the date of
More's birth, seemed quite impossible, as More would only have
been three years old when it
occurred, and could not have
remembered the conversation.

[1] Roper, Singer's ed. p. 3. Morton was not made a cardinal till
1493.

[2] Roper, p. 4.   [3] Ibid.

met at Oxford in 1492-3, their common studies
under Grocyn and Linacre were likely to bring them
into contact.[1] More's ready wit, added to great
natural power and versatility of mind, were such as
to enable him to keep pace with others much older
than himself, and to devote himself with equal zeal
to the new learning.

Whether it was thus at Oxford that Colet had first
formed his high opinion of More's character and
powers, we know not, but certain it is that he was long
after wont to speak of him as the *one genius* of whom
England could boast.[2] Moreover, along with great His
intellectual gifts was combined in the young student fascina-
a gentle and loving disposition, which threw itself into racter.
the bosom of a friend with so guileless and pure an ting cha-
affection, that when men came under the power of its
unconscious enchantment they literally *fell in love* with
More. If Colet's friendship with More dated back to
this period, he must have found in his young acquaintance the germs of a character somewhat akin to his
own. Along with so much of life and generous loveliness, there was a natural independence of mind which
formed convictions for itself, and a strength and
promptness of will whereby action was made as a
matter of course to follow conviction. There was, in
truth, in More's character a singular union of conservative and radical tendencies of heart and thought.

---

[1] Colet probably left Oxford for
the Continent about 1494. The
most probable date of More's stay
at Oxford was 1492 and 1493. This
leaves 1494 and 1495 for his studies
at New Inn, previous to his entry
at Lincoln's Inn, in February, 1496.

[2] Eras. *Op.* iii. p. 477, A. Speaking of More, Erasmus writes:
' Joannes Coletus, vir acris ex-
' actique judicii, in familiaribus
' colloquiis subinde dicere solet,
' Britanniæ non nisi unicum esse
' ingenium.'

But the intercourse between them at Oxford did not last long, for Colet, as already said, went off on his travels, leaving More buried in his Oxford studies under Linacre's tuition.

It was the father's purpose that the son at Oxford should be preparing for his future profession. Jealous lest the temptations of college life should disqualify him for the severe discipline involved in those legal studies to which it was to be the preparatory step, he kept him in leading-strings as far as he possibly could, cutting down his pecuniary allowance to the smallest amount which would enable him to pay his way, even compelling him to refer to himself before purchasing the most necessary articles of clothing as his old ones wore out. He judged that by these means he should keep his son more closely to his books, and prevent his being allured from the rigid course of study which in his utilitarian view was best adapted to fit him for the Bar.[1]

So far as can be traced, this stern discipline did not fail of its end ;[2] he worked on at Oxford, without getting into mischief, and certainly without neglecting his books. But there was another snare from which parental anxiety was not able wholly to preserve him.

Before he had been two years at Oxford, the father found out that he had begun to show symptoms of fondness for the study of the Greek language and

---

[1] Stapleton's *Tres Thomœ*, Colon. 1612 ed. chap. i. pp. 155–6. 'Hanc 'ob causam sic ei necessaria sub-'ministravit ut ne quidem terun-'cium in sua potestate eum habere 'permitteret, præter id quod ipsa 'necessitas postulabat. Quod adeò 'strictè observavit, ut nec ad re-'ficiendos attritos calceos, nisi à 'patre peteret, pecuniam haberet.' See also Eras. *Op.* iii. p. 475, A, respecting his father's motive.

[2] Stapleton's *Tres Thomœ*, Colon. 1612, p. 156.

literature,[1] and might even be guilty of preferring CHAP. I.
the philosophy of the Greeks to that of the School- A.D. 1496.
men. This was treading on dangerous ground, and
it seemed to the anxious parent high time that a stop
should be put to new-fangled and fascinating studies,
the use of which to a lawyer he could not discern.
So, somewhat abruptly, he took young More away
from the University, and had him at once entered as
a student at New Inn.[2] After the usual course of More
legal studies at New Inn, he was admitted in February enters
Lincoln's
1496,[3] just as Colet was returning from Italy, as a Inn.
student of Lincoln's Inn, for a few more years of hard
legal study, preparatory to his call to the Bar.

V. COLET FIRST HEARS OF ERASMUS (1496).

One other circumstance must be mentioned in this
chapter.

Whilst Colet was passing through Paris, on his Colet first
return journey from Italy, he became acquainted with hears of
Erasmus.
the French historian Gaguinus, whose work ' *De Ori-*
' *gine et Gestis Francorum* ' had been published shortly
before.[4] Colet was in the habit of reading every book
of history which came in his way,[5] and no doubt this

---

[1] ' Juvenis ad Græcas literas ac
' philosophiæ studium sese appli-
' cuit adeo non opitulante patre
' . . . ut ea conantem omni subsidio
' destitueret ac pene pro abdicato
' haberet, quod a patriis studiis de-
' sciscere videretur, nam is Brit-
' annicarum legum peritiam profi-
' tetur.'—Eras. *Op.* iii. p. 475, A.

[2] ' Sic voluit pater qui eum ad
' Græcarum literarum et philoso-

' phiæ studium omni subsidio de-
' stituit, ut ad istud (i.e. English
' Law) induceret.' — Stapleton's
Tres Thomæ, p. 168.

[3] XII. February,—11 HenryVII.
Foss's *Judges of England*, v. p. 207.

[4] Vide supra, p. 1, *n*.

[5] Eras. *Op.* iii. p. 456, B. ' Nullus
' erat liber, *historiam* aut constitu-
' tiones continens majorum, quod
' non evolverat.'

history of Gaguinus was no exception to the rule. Whilst he was at Paris, a letter was shown to him which the historian had received from a scholar and acquaintance of rising celebrity in Paris, in which the new history was reviewed and praised.[1] From the perusal of this letter, Colet formed a high estimate of the learning and wide range of knowledge of its accomplished writer.[2] But scholars were plentiful in Paris, and he was not personally introduced to this one in particular. He was not then, like Gaguinus, one of the lions of Paris, though he was destined to become one of the lions of History. Colet after reading his letter did not forget his name. Nor was it a name likely to be soon forgotten by posterity.

It was, ' *Erasmus.*'

---

[1] Eras. Epist. App. ccccxxxvii.   [2] Eras. Epist. xi.

CHAPTER II.

I. COLET'S LECTURES ON ST. PAUL'S EPISTLE TO THE ROMANS (1496-7 ?).

To appreciate the full significance of Colet's lectures, it is needful to bear in mind what was the current opinion of the scholastic divines of the period concerning the Scriptures, and what the practical mode of exposition pursued by them at the Universities.

The scholastic divines, holding to a traditional belief in the *plenary* and *verbal* inspiration of the whole Bible, and remorselessly pursuing this belief to its logical results, had fallen into a method of exposition almost exclusively *textarian*. The Bible, both in theory and in practice, had almost ceased to be a record of real events, and the lives and teaching of living men. It had become an arsenal of texts ; and these texts were regarded as detached invincible weapons to be legitimately seized and wielded in theological warfare, for any purpose to which their words might be made to apply, without reference to their original meaning or context.

Thus, to take a practical example, when St. Jerome's opinion was quoted incidentally that possibly St. Mark, in the second chapter of his Gospel, might by a slip of memory have written ' Abiathar ' in mistake for ' Abi-' melech,' a learned divine, a contemporary of Colet's at

Oxford, nettled by the very supposition, declared positively that ' that could not be, unless the Holy Spirit
' himself could be mistaken; ' and the only authority he
thought it needful to cite in proof of the statement was a
text in Ezekiel : ' Whithersoever the Spirit went, thither
' likewise the wheels were lifted up to follow Him.' [1] It
was in vain that the reply was suggested that ' it is not
' for us to define in what manner the Spirit might use
' His instrument.'   The divine triumphantly replied,
' The Spirit himself in Ezekiel *has* defined it.   The
' wheels were not lifted up, except to follow the Spirit.' [2]

Theory of
manifold
senses.
This Oxford divine did not display any peculiar
bigotry or blindness.   He did but follow in the well-
worn ruts of his scholastic predecessors.   It had been
solemnly laid down by Aquinas in the ' Summa,' that
' inasmuch as God was the author of the Holy Scrip-
' tures, and all things are at one time present to His
' mind, therefore, under their single text, they express
' several meanings.' ' Their literal sense,' he continues,
' is manifold ; their spiritual sense threefold—viz. alle-
' gorical, moral, anagogical.' [3] And we have the evidence
of another well-known Oxford student, also a contem-

---

[1] ' Ut tribuatur lapsui memoriæ
' in evangelista gravatim audio. Qui
' si spiritu sancto inspiratus scripsit,
' memoria falli non potuit, nisi et ille
' etiam falli potuerit, quo ductore
' scripsit. Dicit mihi Ezechiel : Quo-
' cunque ibat spiritus, illuc pariter et
' rotæ elevabantur sequentes eum.'
*Annotationes Ed. Leei in annota-
tiones Novi Testamenti Desiderii
Erasmi.* Basil. 1520, pp. 25, 26.
Lee studied at Oxford during a
portion of the time of Colet's residence there.   Knight states that

he was sent to St. Mary Magd.
College (the college where Colet is
supposed to have taken his degree
of M.A.) in 1499.—Knight's *Erasmus,* p. 286.

[2] ' Quod dicis (non est nostrum
' definire, quomodo spiritus ille
' suum temperârit organum) verum
' quidem est, sed spiritus ipse in
' Ezechiele definivit: Rotæ non ele-
' vabantur nisi sequentes spiritum.'
Annotationes Edvardi Leei, p. 26.

[3] Aquinas, *Summa,* pt. 1, quest.
i. article x.

porary with Colet at the University, that this was then
the prevalent view. Speaking of the dominant school
of divines, he remarks : ' They divide the Scripture into
' four senses, the literal, tropological, allegorical, and
' anagogical—the literal sense has become nothing at
' all. . . . . Twenty doctors expound one text twenty
' ways, and with an antitheme of half an inch some of
' them draw a thread of nine days long. . . . . They   Literal
' not only say that the literal sense profiteth nothing,   sense ne-
    glected.
' but also that it is hurtful and noisesome and killeth
' the soul. And this they prove by a text of Paul,
' 2 Cor. iii., " The letter killeth, but the Spirit giveth
' " life." Lo ! say they, the literal sense killeth, the
' spiritual sense giveth life.' [1] And the same student,
in recollection of his intercourse at the Universities with
divines of the traditional school in these early days,
bears witness that ' they were wont to look on no more
' Scripture than they found in their Duns ; ' [2] while at
another time he complains ' that some of them will
' prove a point of the Faith as well out of a fable of
' Ovid or any other poet, as out of St. John's Gospel
' or Paul's Epistles.' [3] Thus had the scholastic belief in
the verbal inspiration of the sacred text led men blind-   The Bible
fold into a condition of mind in which they practically   a dead
  book.
ignored the Scriptures altogether.[4]

---

[1] Tyndale's *Obedience of a Christian Man,* chap. ' On the Four ' Senses of the Scriptures.'

[2] Preface to the Five Books of Moses.

[3] Tyndale's *Obedience of a Christian Man,* chap. ' On the Four ' Senses of Scripture.' That Tyndale was at Oxford during Colet's stay there (i.e. before 1506), see the

evidence given by his biographers. It appears that he was born about 1484. Fox says ' *he was brought ' up from a child in the University ' of Oxford,*' and there is no reason to suppose that he removed to Cambridge before 1509. See Tyndale's *Doctrinal Treatises,* xiv. xv. and authorities there cited.

[4] Sir Thomas More in a letter to

Such was the state of things at Oxford when Colet commenced his lectures. The very boldness of the lecturer and the novelty of the subject were enough to draw an audience at once. Doctors and abbots, men of all ranks and titles, flocked with the students into the lecture hall, led by curiosity doubtless at first, or it may be, like the Pharisees of old, bent upon finding somewhat whereof they might accuse the man whom they wished to silence. But since they came again and again, as the term went by, *bringing their note-books with them,* it soon became clear that they continued to come with some better purpose.[1]

Colet already, at thirty, possessed the rare gift of saying what he had to say in a few telling words, throwing into them an earnestness which made every one feel that they came from his heart. ' You say what ' you mean, and mean what you say. Your words have ' birth in your heart, not on your lips. They follow ' your thoughts, instead of your thoughts being shaped ' by them. You have the happy art of expressing with ' ease what others can hardly express with the greatest ' labour.'[2] Such was the first impression made by Colet's eloquence upon one of the greatest scholars of the day,

---

the University of Oxford (Jortin's *Erasmus,* ii. App. p. 664, 4to ed.) complains of a Scotist preacher because ' *neque integrum ullum Scrip-* ' *turæ caput tractavit, quæ res in usu* ' *fuit veteribus* [this was the old method *revived* by Colet] ; neque ' dictum aliquod brevius e Sacris ' literis, qui mos apud nuperos ino- ' levit [the scholastic method] ; sed ' thematum loco delegit Britannica ' quædam anilia proverbia.' [The

practical result of the textarian method when pushed to its ultimate results.]

[1] Eras. Jodoco Jonæ : Eras. *Op.* iii.p.456, C. ' Nullus erat illic doctor ' vel theologiæ vel juris, nullus ' abbas, aut alioqui dignitate præ- ' ditus quin illum audiret, etiam ' allatis codicibus.'

[2] Eras. Coleto : Eras. *Op.* iii. p. 40, F. Epist. xli.

Chap. II.

A.D. 1496.

Colet's
method of
exposi-
tion.

who heard him deliver some of these lectures during another term.

From the fragments which remain of what seem to be manuscript notes of these lectures, written by Colet himself at the 'urgent and repeated request,' as he expressed it, ' of his faithful auditors,' [1] and now preserved in the Cambridge Libraries,[2] something more than a superficial notion may be gained of what these lectures were.

They were in almost every particular in direct contrast with those of the dominant school. They were not *textarian.* They did not consist of a series of wiredrawn dissertations upon isolated texts. They were no ' thread of nine days long drawn from an ' antitheme of half an inch.' Colet began at the beginning of the Epistle to the Romans, and went through with it to the end, in a course of lectures, treating it as a whole, and not as an armoury of

---

[1] ' Tamen certe multum ac diu ' rogatus a quibusdam amicis, et ' eisdem interpretantibus nobis ' Paulum fidis auditoribus, quibus- ' cum pro amicicia quod in superio- ' rem epistolæ partem scriptum est ' a nobis communicavi, adductus ' fui tandem ut promitterem, quod ' est ceptum modo me perrecturum, ' et in reliquam epistolam quod re- ' liquum est enarrationis adhibi- ' turum.'—Cambridge University Library MS. Gg. 4, 26, fol. 27*b*.

[2] A copy of Colet's exposition of ' Romans,' with corrections apparently in Colet's handwriting, is in the Cambridge University Library; MS. Gg. 4, 26. A fair copy, apparently by Peter Meghen, is in the Library of Corpus Christi College, Cambridge, MS. No. 355.

Amongst the ' Gale MSS.' in Trinity Library, Cambridge, is a MS. (O. 4, 44) said to be Colet's, containing short notes or abstracts of the Apostolic Epistles. Through the kindness of Mr. Wright I had a copy taken of this MS., but on close comparison of passages with the *Annotationes* of Erasmus, I was obliged to conclude that the writer had before him an edition of the latter not earlier than that of 1522. This MS. cannot, therefore, have been written by Colet. Possibly it may have been written by Lupset, Colet's disciple. The copy in the Trinity Library is in a later hand.

detached texts.[1] Nor were they on the model of the *Catena aurea*, formed by linking together the recorded comments of the great Church authorities. There is hardly a quotation from the Fathers or Schoolmen throughout the exposition of the Epistle to the Romans.[2]

Instead of following the current fashion of the day, and displaying analytical skill in dividing the many senses of the sacred text, Colet, it is clear, had but one object in view, and that object was to bring out the direct practical meaning which the apostle meant to convey to those to whom his epistles were addressed.

Colet points out the marks of St. Paul's own character.

To him they were the earnest words of a living man addressed to living men, and suited to their actual needs. He loved those words because he had learned to love the apostle—the *man*—who had written them, and had caught somewhat of his spirit. He loved to trace in the epistles the marks of St. Paul's own character. He would at one time point out, in his abruptly suspended words, that ' *vehemence of speaking* ' which did not give him time to perfect his sentences.[3] At another time he would stop to admire the rare prudence and tact with which he would temper his speech and balance his words to meet the needs of the different classes by whom his epistle would be read.[4] And again he would compare the eager expectations ex-

---

[1] This appears to have been the character also of the Expositions of Marsilio Ficino. See Fragment on ' Romans.'—*Ficini Opera*, ed. 1696, pp. 426–472.

[2] The *names* of Origen, Jerome, Chrysostom, and Augustine are mentioned, but incidentally, and without any quotations of any length being given from them.

[3] '—est ex vehementia loquendi ' imperfecta et suspensa sententia.' MSS. Gg. 4, 26, fol. 23, *in loco*. Rom. ix. 22.

[4] ' Ita Paulus mira prudentia et ' arte temperat orationem suam in ' hac epistola, et eam quasi librat ' tam pari lance, et Judeos et ' Gentes simul, etc.'—*Ibid.* fol. 26.

pressed in the Epistle to the Romans of so soon visiting Chap. II.
Rome and Spain, with the far different realities of A.D. 1496.
the apostle's after life ; recalling to mind the circumstances of his long imprisonment at Cæsarea, and his
arrival at last in Rome, *four years* after writing his Colet's
epistle, to remain a prisoner two years longer in the personal
interest in
Imperial city before he could carry out his intention of St. Paul.
visiting Spain.[1] He loved to tell how, notwithstanding
these cherished plans for the future, the apostle, being
a man of great courage, was prepared, ' by his faith,
' and love of Christ,' [2] to bear his disappointment, and
to reply to the prophecy of Agabus, that he was ready,
not only to be bound, but also to die at Jerusalem for
the name of his Master, if need be, instead of fulfilling
the plans he had laid out for himself.

And whilst investing the epistles with so *personal* an Circumstances of
the Roman
Chris-
tians.
interest, by thus bringing out their connection with
St. Paul's character and history, Colet sought also to
throw a sense of reality and life into their teaching,
by showing how specially adapted they were to the
circumstances of those to whom they were addressed.
When, for instance, he was expounding the thirteenth
chapter of the Epistle, he would take down his *Suetonius* in order to ascertain the state of society at
Rome and the special circumstances which made it
needful for St. Paul so strongly to urge Roman
Christians ' to be obedient to the higher powers, and
' to pay tribute also.' [3]

---

[1] MSS. Gg. 4, 26, fols. 59*b*, 61*a*.
[2] Ibid. fol. 60. ' Sed ille homo
'magno animo, fide, et amore Christi,
' fuit paratus non solum ligari,' &c.
[3] Ibid. fols. 42–45 (*in loco*, Rom.
xiii.). In these pages Colet com-

pares with great care the information to be collected from passages in the Epistle to the Romans
and in the Acts of the Apostles with
what is recorded by Suetonius, and
admires St. Paul's ' sapientissima

CHAP. II.

A.D. 1496.

Colet tries
to look at
all sides of
a doctrine.

It is very evident, too, how careful he was not to give a one-sided view of the apostle's doctrine—what pains he took to realise his actual meaning, not merely in one text and another, but in the drift of the whole epistle ; now ascertaining the meaning of a passage by its place in the apostle's argument ; [1] now comparing the expressions used by St. Paul with those used by St. John, in order to trace the practical harmony between the Johannine and Pauline view of a truth, which, if regarded on one side only, might be easily distorted and misunderstood. In expounding the Epistle to the Romans it was impossible to avoid allusion to the great question afterwards forced into so unhappy a prominence by the Wittemberg and Geneva Reformers, as it had already been by Wiclif and Huss—the question of the freedom of the Will. Upon this

question Colet showed an evident anxiety not to fall into one extreme whilst avoiding the other. His view seems to have been that the soul which is melted and won over to God by the power of *love* is won over *willingly*, and yet through no merit of its own. Probably his views upon this point would be described as ' mystic.' Certainly they were not Augustinian.[2] In concluding a long digression upon this endless and

---

' admonitio opportune sane adhibi-
' ta.'—Ibid.fols.42*b* and 43*a*. Again,
at fol. 44*a*, Colet says, ' Hæc autem
' refero ut magna Pauli consideratio
' et prudentia animadvertatur ;
' qui cum non ignoravit Claudium
' Cesarem tenuisse rempublicam,
' qui fuit homo vario ingenio et
' improbis moribus, &c.' . . . .

[1] In his exposition of Romans (chap. iv.) he says :—' Sed caute

' circumspicienda sunt omnia Pauli,
' antequam de ejus mente aliqua
' feratur sentencia. Nunquam enim
' censuisset revocandum ad eccle-
' siam fornicatorem illum, quem
' tradidit Sathanæ in prima Epi-
' stola ad Corinthios, si peccatoribus
' post baptismum nullum penitendi
' locum reliquisset.'—Ibid. fol. 6*b*.

[2] It would be difficult in short quotations to give a correct impres-

perplexing question, Colet apologises for the length to
which he had wandered from St. Paul, and excuses

sion of the doctrinal standpoint assumed by Colet in his exposition of
the Epistle to the Romans. But
it may be interesting to enquire,
whether any connection can be
traced between his views and those
of Savonarola, on this point.

Now *Villari* states that a 'funda-
'mental point' in Savonarola's
doctrine was his '*conception of love,*
' which he sometimes says is the
' *same as grace,*' and that it was
through this conception of love that
Savonarola, ' to a certain extent,'
explained the ' mystery of human
' liberty and Divine omnipotence.'
Villari's *Savonarola and his Times,*
bk. i. c. vii. p. 110.

Whether there be any real
connection between Savonarola's
teaching and the following passages
from Colet's exposition, I leave the
reader to judge.

' Wherefore St. Paul concludes,
' men are justified by faith, and
' trusting in God alone by Jesus
' Christ, are reconciled to God and
' restored into grace ; so that with
' God they stand, and remain them-
' selves sons of God. . . . . If He
' loved us when alienated from Him,
' how much more will He love us
' when we are reconciled ; and
' preserve those whom He loves.
' Wherefore we ought to be firm
' and stable in our hope and joy, and,
' nothing doubting, trust in God
' through Jesus Christ, by whom
' alone men are reconciled to God.'
—MS. fol. 5. After speaking of
that *grace* which where sin had
abounded did much more abound

unto eternal life, Colet proceeds :—
' But here it is to be noted that this
' *grace* is nothing else than the *love*
' of God towards men—towards
' those, i.e. whom He wills to love,
' and, in loving, to inspire with His
' Holy Spirit ; which itself is love
' and the love of God ; which (as
' the Saviour said, according to St.
' John's Gospel) *blows where it lists.*
' But, loved and inspired by God,
' they are also *called* ; so that ac-
' cepting this love, they may love in
' return their loving God, and long
' for and wait for the same love.
' This waiting and hope springs
' from *love. This love truly is ours*
' *because He loves us :* not (as St.
' John writes in his 2nd Epistle) as
' though we had first loved God,
' but because He first loved us, even
' when we were worthy of no love
' at all ; but indeed impious and
' wicked, destined by right to eter-
' nal death. But some, i.e. those
' whom He knew and chose, He
' also loved, and in loving called
' them, and in calling them justi-
' fied them, and in justifying them
' glorified them. This gracious love
' and charity in God towards men
' is *in itself* the calling and justifica-
' tion and glorification. . . . And
' when we speak of men as drawn,
' called, justified, and glorified by
' *grace,* we mean nothing else than
' that men *love in return God who*
' *loves them.*'—MS. Gg. 4, 26, fol. 6.

Again: 'Thus you see that things
' are brought about by a providing
' and directing God, and that they
' happen as He wills in the affairs

himself on the ground that ' his zeal and affection to-
' wards men '—his desire ' to confirm the weak and
' wavering '—had got the better of his ' fear of weary-
' ing the reader.' [1]

Connected with this habit of trying to look at all
sides of a doctrine, there is, I think, visible throughout,

' of men, not from any force from
' without (*illata*)—since nothing is
' more remote from force than the
' Divine action—but by the natural
' desire and will of man, the Divine
' will and providence secretly and
' silently, and, as it were, naturally
' accompanying (*comitante*) it, and
' going along with it so wonder-
' fully, that whatever you do and
' choose was known by God, and
' what God knew and decreed to be,
' of necessity comes to pass.'—MS.
fol. 18.

The following passage is from
Colet's exposition of the Epistle to
the Corinthians (MS. 4, 26, p. 80).
' The mind of man consists of *in-*
' *tellect* and *will*. By the *intellect* we
' know : by the *will* we have power
' to act (*possumus*). From the
' knowledge of the intellect comes
' faith : from the power of the will
' charity. But Christ, the power of
' God, is also the wisdom of God.
' Our minds are illuminated to faith
' by Christ, " *who illumines every*
' " *man coming into this world*, and
' " He gives power to become the sons
' " of God to whose who believe in
' " His name." By Christ also our
' wills are kindled in charity to love
' God and our neighbour ; in which
' is the fulfilment of the law. From
' God alone therefore, through
' Christ, we have both knowledge

' and power ; for by Him we are in
' Christ. Men, however, have in
' themselves a blind intellect, and
' a depraved will, and walk in dark-
' ness, not knowing what they do.
' . . . Those who by the warm rays
' of his divinity are so drawn that
' they keep close in communion with
' Him, are indeed they whom Paul
' speaks of as called and elected to
' His glory,' &c.

For the Latin of these extracts
see Appendix (A).

In further proof that Colet's views
(like Savonarola's) were not Augustinian upon the question of the
' freedom of the will,' may be cited
the following words of Colet (see
infra, chap. iv.) : ' But in especial is
' it necessary for thee to know that
' God of his great grace hath made
' thee his image, having regard to
' thy memory, understanding, and
' *free-will*.' Probably both Colet and
Savonarola, in common with other
mystic theologians, had imbibed
their views directly or indirectly
from the works of the Pseudo-Dionysius and the Neo-Platonists.

[1] ' Ex quodam nostro studio et
' pietate in homines . . . . non
' tam verentes legentium fasti-
' dium, quam cupientes confirma-
' cionem infirmorum et vacillan-
' tium.'—Fol. 22*b*.

an earnest attempt to regard it in its practical connection with human life and conduct rather than to
rest in its logical completeness.

If he quotes from the Neo-Platonic philosophers of Colet
Florence (and almost the only quotation of any length dwells
on the
contained in this manuscript is from the *Theologia* practical
Platonica of Marsilio Ficino [1]), it is, not to follow them aspects of
St. Paul's
into the mazes of Neo-Platonic speculation, but to doctrines.
enforce the practical point, that whilst, here upon Quotes
earth, the *knowledge* of God is impossible to man, the Marsilio
Ficino,
love of God is not so ; and that by how much it is
worse to *hate* God than to be ignorant of Him, by so
much is it better to *love* Him than to *know* Him.

And never does he speak more warmly and earnestly
than when after having urged with St. Paul, that ' rites
' and ceremonies neither purify the spirit nor justify the
' man,' [2] and having quoted from *Aristeas* to show how, and
Aristeas.
on Jewish feast days, seventy priests were occupied in
slaying and sacrificing thousands of cattle, deluging
the temple with blood, thinking it well pleasing to
God, he points out how St. Paul covertly condemned
these outward sacrifices, as Isaiah had done before
him, by insisting upon that *living sacrifice of men's*
hearts and lives which they were meant to typify.[3] He
urges with St. Paul that God is pleased with *living*
sacrifices and not dead ones, and does not ask for
sacrifices in cattle, but in *men*.   His will is that their
beastly appetites should be slain and consumed by
the fire of God's Spirit [4] . . . . ; that men should be
converted from a proud trust in themselves to an

---

[1] MS. Gg. 4, 26, fols. 13*b* to 15*a*.   [3] Ibid. fols. 28*b* and 29.
[2] Ibid. fol. 3*b*.   [4] Ibid. fol. 29.

CHAP. II.
A.D. 1496.

humble faith in God, and from self-love to the love of God. To bring this about, Colet thought was 'the chief cause, yes the sole cause,' of the coming of the Son of God upon earth in the flesh.[1]

Nor was he afraid to apply these practical lessons to the circumstances of his own times. Thus, in speaking of the collections made by St. Paul in relief of the sufferers from the famine in Judea (the same he thought as that predicted by Agabus), he pointed out how much better such voluntary collections were than 'money extorted by bitter exactions under the name of 'tithes and oblations.'[2] And, referring to the advice to Timothy, ' to avoid avarice and to follow after justice, ' piety, faith, charity, patience, and mercy,' he at once added that ' *priests of our time* ' might well be admonished ' to set such an example as this *amongst their* ' *own parishioners*,' referring to the example of St. Paul, who chose to ' get his living by labouring with his ' hands at the trade of tentmaking, so as to avoid even ' suspicion of avarice or scandal to the Gospel.'[3]

Colet points out the need of ecclesiastical reform.

One other striking characteristic of this exposition must be mentioned—the unaffected modesty which breathes through it, which, whilst not quoting authority, does not claim to be an authority itself, which does not profess to have attained full knowledge, but preserves throughout the childlike spirit of enquiry.[4]

On the whole, the spirit of Colet's lectures was in keeping with his previous history.

The passage already mentioned as quoted from

---

[1] MS. Gg. 4, 26, fol. 30*b*.

[2] Ibid. fol. 59*b*. ' Elicienda est ' dulci doctrina prompta voluntas 'non acerba exaccione extor-

' quenda pecunia nomine decimar-' um et oblacionum.'

[3] Ibid. fol. 60*a*.

[4] See particularly fol. 27 and 61*b*.

Ficino, the facts that, in a marginal note on the manuscript, added apparently in Colet's handwriting, there
is also a quotation from Pico,[1] and that the names
of Plotinus,[2] and ' Joannes Carmelitanus,'[3] are cited in
the course of the exposition—all this is evidence of
the influence upon Colet's mind of the writings of the
philosophers of Florence, confirming the inference
already drawn from the circumstances of his visit to
Italy.   But in its *comparative* freedom from references
to authorities of *any* kind, except the New Testament,
Colet's exposition differs as much from the writings
of Ficino and Pico as from those of the Scholastic
Divines.

In many peculiar phrases and modes of thought,
evident traces also occur of that love for the Dionysian
writings which Colet is said to have contracted in
Italy, and which he shared with the modern Neo-
Platonic school.

In the free critical method of interpretation and
thorough acknowledgment of the human element in
Scripture, as well as in the anti-Augustinian views
already alluded to, there is evidence equally abundant
in confirmation of the statement, that he had acquired
when abroad a decided preference for Origen and
Jerome over Augustine.

Lastly in his freedom from the prevailing vice of the
patristic interpreters—their love of allegorising Scripture—and in his fearless application of the critical
methods of the new learning to the Scriptures themselves, in order to draw out their literal sense, there is

margin notes:
CHAP. II.

A.D. 1496.

Colet
quotes
the Neo-
Platonists.

Marks of
his love for
Dionysius.

Origen
and
Jerome.

His in-
dependent
search for
truth.

---

[1] MS. Gg. 4, 26, fol. 3*a*.
[2] Ibid. fol. 7*b*.
[3] Ibid. fol. 15*b*. *Ioannes Baptista*

Mantuanus, general of the Carmelites, an admirer of Pico.—See
Pici *Opera*, p. 262.

striking confirmation of the further statement that, whilst in Italy, he had 'devoted himself wholly '[1] to their study. Colet's object obviously had been to study St. Paul's Epistle to the Romans for *himself,* and his whole exposition confirms the truth of his own declaration in its last sentence, that ' he had tried to the best ' of his power, with the aid of Divine grace, to bring ' out St. Paul's true meaning.' ' Whether indeed '(he adds modestly) ' I have done this I hardly can tell, ' but the greatest *desire* to do so I *have* had.' [2]

II. VISIT FROM A PRIEST DURING THE WINTER VACATION
(1496–7 ?).

Visit from a priest.

Colet, one night during the winter vacation, was alone in his chambers. A priest knocked at the door. He was soon recognised by Colet as a diligent attender of his lectures. They drew their chairs to the hearth, and talked about this thing and that over the winter fire, in the way men do when they have something to say, and yet have not courage to come at once to the point. At length the priest pulled from his bosom a little book. Colet, amused at the manner of his guest, smilingly quoted the words, ' Where your treasure is, ' there will your heart be also.' The priest explained

Conversation on the richness of St. Paul's writings.

that the little book contained the Epistles of St. Paul, carefully transcribed by his own hand. It was indeed a treasure, for of all the writings that had ever been

---

[1] ' Ibi se totum evolvendis sacris ' auctoribus dedit.'—Eras. *Op.* iii. p. 456 B.

[2] '. . . conatique sumus quoad ' potuimus divina gratia adjuti ' veros illius sensus exprimere.

' Quod quam fecimus haud scimus ' sane, voluntatem tamen habu- ' imus maximam faciendi.'—*ffinis argumenti in Epistolam Pauli ad Romanos.* Oxonie.

written, he most loved and admired those of St. Paul ;

and he added, in a politely flattering tone, that it was
Colet's lectures during the recent term, which had
chiefly excited in him this affection for the apostle.
Colet turned a searching eye upon his guest, and finding that he was truly in earnest, replied with warmth,
' Then, brother, I love you for loving St. Paul, for I,
' too, dearly love and admire him.' In the course of
conversation, which now turned upon the object which
the priest had at heart, Colet happened to remark how
pregnant with both matter and thought were the
Epistles of St. Paul, so that almost every word might
be made the subject of a discourse. This was just what
Colet's guest wanted. Comparing Colet's lectures with
those of the scholastic divines, who, as we have heard,
were accustomed ' out of an antitheme of half an inch
' to draw a thread of nine days long ' upon some useless
topic, he may well have been struck with the richness
of the vein of ore which Colet had been working, and
he had come that he might gather some hints as to his
method of study. ' Then,' said he, stirred up by this
remark of Colet's, ' I ask you now, as we sit here at
' our ease, to extract and bring to light from this
' hidden treasure, which you say is so rich, some of these
' truths, so that I may gain from this our talk whilst
' sitting together something to store up in the memory,
' and at the same time catch some hints as to how, fol-
' lowing your example, I may seize hold of the main
' points in the epistles when I read St. Paul by myself.'

' My good friend,' replied Colet, ' I will do as you
' wish. Open your book, and we will see how many
' and what golden truths we can gather from the first
' chapter only of the Epistle to the Romans.' Romans i.
taken
as an
example.

' But,' added the priest, ' lest my memory should fail ' me, I should like to write them down as you say them.' Colet assented, and thereupon dictated to his guest a string of the most important points which struck him as he read through the chapter. They were, as Colet said, only like detached rings, carelessly cut from the golden ore of St. Paul, as they sat over the winter fire, but they would serve as examples of what might be gathered from a single chapter of the apostle's writings.

The priest departed, fully satisfied with the result of his visit ; and from the evident pleasure with which Colet told this story in a letter to Kidderminster, Abbot of Winchcombe,[1] we may learn how his own spirits were cheered by the proof it gave, that he had not laboured altogether in vain.

The letter itself, too, apart from the story which it tells, may give some insight into his feelings during these months of solitary labour.   It reads, I think, like the letter of a man deeply in earnest, engaged in what he feels to be a great work ; whose sense of the greatness of the work suggests a natural and noble anxiety, that though he himself should not live to finish it, it may yet be carried forward by others ; whose ambition it is to die working at his post, leaving behind him at least the first stones laid of a building which others greater than he may carry on to completion.

After telling the story of the priest's visit, Colet writes thus :—

---

[1] Cambridge University Library, MSS. Gg. 4, 26, p. 62, *et seq.*, and printed in Knight's *Life of Colet*, App. p. 311.

Colet to the Abbot of Winchcombe.

.   .   .   .   .   .

' Thus, Reverend Father, what he [the priest] wrote
' down at my dictation I have wished to detail to you,
' so that you too, so ardent in your love of all sacred
' wisdom, may see what we, sitting over the winter
' fire, noted offhand in our St. Paul.

' In the first chapter only of the Epistle to the
' Romans, we found all the following truths. [Here
' follows a long list.] . . . These we extracted, and
' noted, venerable father, as I said, offhand, in this one
' chapter only. Nor are these all we might have noted.
' For even in the very address one might discover that
' Christ was promised by the prophets, that Christ is
' both God and man, that Christ sanctifies men, that
' through Christ there is a resurrection, both of the soul
' and of the body. And besides these there are num-
' berless others contained in this chapter, which any-
' one with lynx eyes could easily find and dig out, if
' he wished, for himself. *Paul*, of all others, seems to me
' to be a fathomless *ocean* of wisdom and piety. But
' these few, thus hastily picked out, were enough for
' our good priest, who wanted some thoughts struck
' off roundly, and fashioned like rings, from the gold
' of St. Paul. These, as you see, I have written out
' for you with my own hand, most worthy father, that
' your mind, in its golden goodness, might recognise,
' as from a specimen, how much gold lies treasured
' up in St. Paul.

' I want the Warden also to read this over with you,
' for his cultivated taste and love of everything good

Colet
wants his
friend to
see why
he admires
St. Paul's
writings.

' is such that I think he will be very much pleased
' with whatever of good it may contain.
    ' Farewell, most excellent and beloved father.

Yours, JOHN COLET.'

    ' When you have read what is contained on this
' sheet of paper, let me have it again, for I have no
' copy of it ; and, although I am not in the habit of
' keeping my letters, and cannot do so, as I send them
' off just as I write them, without keeping a copy ; yet
' if any of them contain anything instructive (*aliquid*
' *doctrinæ*), I do not like to lose them entirely. Not
' that they are in themselves worth preserving, but
' that, left behind me, they may serve as little memo-
' rials of me. And if there be any other reason why I
' should wish to preserve my letters to you, this is one,
' and a chief one—that I should be glad for them to
' remain as permanent witnesses of my regard for you.
    ' Again, farewell ! '

The sole survivor of a family of twenty-two, though
himself but thirty, Colet might well keep always in
view the possibility of an early death.

III. COLET ON THE MOSAIC ACCOUNT OF THE CREATION
(1497 ?).

It would seem that one of Colet's friends, named
Radulphus, had been attempting to expound ' *the dark
' places of Scripture,*' and that in doing so he had commenced with the words of Lamech in the fourth
chapter of Genesis, as though this were the first ' dark
' place ' to be found in the Bible !

Out of this circumstance arose a correspondence on the meaning of the first chapter of Genesis, which Colet thought required explanation as much as any other portion of Scripture. Four of Colet's letters to Radulphus, containing his views on the Mosaic account of the creation, have fortunately been preserved, bound up with a copy of his manuscript exposition on the Epistle to the Romans, in the Library of Corpus Christi College, Cambridge.[1] Colet seems to have thought them worth preserving, as he did the letter to the Abbot of Winchcombe ; and as any attempt to realise the position and feelings of Colet, when commencing his lectures at Oxford on St. Paul's epistles, would have been very imperfect without the story of the priest's visit, so these letters to Radulphus, apart from their intrinsic interest, are especially valuable as giving another practical illustration of the position which Colet had assumed upon the question of the inspiration and interpretation of the Scriptures ; as showing, perhaps, more clearly than anything else could have done, that the principles and method which he had applied to St. Paul's writings, were not hastily adopted, but the result of mature conviction,—that Colet was ready to apply them consistently to the Old Testament as well as to the New, to the first chapter of Genesis as well as to the Epistle to the Romans.

Colet begins his first letter by telling Radulphus how surprised he was that, whilst professing to expound the ' dark places of Scripture,' he should, as already mentioned, have commenced with the words of Lamech, leaving the first three chapters of Genesis

CHAP. II.

A.D. 1497.

Letters of Colet on the Mosaic account of creation.

First letter to Radulphus.

---

[1] In the volume of manuscripts marked 355.

untouched ; for these very chapters, so lightly passed over by Radulphus, seemed to him, he said, ' so ' obscure that they might almost in themselves be ' that " *abyss* " to which Moses alluded when he wrote ' that " darkness covered the face of the deep." ' [1]

Use of a knowledge of Hebrew.
After admitting the impossibility of coming to an accurate understanding of the meaning of what Moses wrote without a knowledge of Hebrew and access to Hebrew commentaries, ' which Origen, Jerome, and all ' really diligent searchers of the Scriptures have appre- ' ciated,' he goes on to say that, notwithstanding their extreme obscurity, and the possibility that Radulphus might be able to throw more light upon them than he himself could, he would nevertheless give him some of his notions on the meaning of the verses from ' In the ' beginning,' &c. to the end of the ' first day.'

He then began his explanation by saying that, though not unmindful of the manifold senses of Scripture, he should confine himself to rapidly following *one* ; [2] and this seems to be the only allusion in these letters to the prevalent theory of the ' manifold senses.' Taken in connection with the full expression of his views upon the subject on a future occasion, the words here made use of probably must be construed rather as showing that he did not wish at that moment to enter into the question with Radulphus, than as intended to give any indication of what his views were upon it.

Then he proceeds to state his conviction that the first few verses of Genesis contain a sort of summary of

---

[1] ' In quibus mihi videtur tanta ' caligo ut totus ille sermo con- ' tentus in ipsis tribus capitulis ' appareat esse ille abyssus super ' cujus faciem dicit Moises tenebras ' fuisse.'

[2] ' Non me latet plures esse sen- ' sus, sed unum persequar cursim.'

the whole work of creation. ' First of all, I conceive,'
Colet wrote, ' that in this passage the creation of the
' universe has been delivered to us in brief (*summatim*),
' and that God created all things *at once* in his eternity [1] All things
' —in that eternity which transcends all time, and yet created at
' is less extended than a point of time, which has no eternity.
' division of time, and is before all time.'

The world consists primarily of *matter* and *form*, and
the object of Moses was, Colet thought, to show that
both matter and form were created *at once* (*simul*).
And therefore Moses began with saying, ' In the be-
' ginning (i.e. in eternity) God created heaven (i.e.
' form) and the earth ' (i.e. matter).[2] Matter was never
without form, but that he might point out the order
of things, Moses added, that ' the earth (matter) was
' empty and void [3] (i.e. without solid and substantial
' being), and darkness covered the face of the deep '
(i.e. the matter was in darkness, and without life and
being).[4] Then the text proceeds, ' The Spirit of God
' moved upon the face of the waters.' ' See how beau-
' tifully ' (wrote Colet), ' he proceeds in order, showing
' at one view the creation and union of form with
' matter,[5] using the word " water " to express the un-
' stable and fluid condition of matter.' Then follow
the words, ' Let there be light ' (i.e. according to Colet,
things assumed form and definition [6]).

---

[1] ' . . universa simul creasse sua
' eternitate.'

[2] ' In principio (i.e. eternitate)
creavit Deus cœlum (formam) et
terram (materiam).'

[3] ' . . inanis et vacua.'

[4] ' Terra (materia) erat inanis et
' vacua (hoc est sine solida et sub-

' stantiali entitate) et tenebræ, &c.
' (i.e. tenebrosa fuit materia, &c.).'

[5] ' Vide quam bellè pergit ordine,
' significans summariam creaci-
' onem copulationemque formæ
' cum materia.'

[6] ' . . forma et terminacio
rerum.'

E

Having thus explained the opening verses of Genesis as a statement in brief—*a summary*—of the whole work of creation, Colet concluded this first letter by saying, ' What follows in Moses is a repetition and ' further expansion of what he has said above—a ' distinguishing in *particular* of what before was com- ' prehended in the *general*. If you think otherwise, ' pray let me have your views. Farewell.' [1]

Second letter.

Radulphus having, apparently in reply to this letter, requested Colet to proceed to explain the *other* days, Colet, in the *second* letter, takes up the subject where he left it in the first. Having spoken of form and matter, Moses proceeds, he says, in proper order, and treats of things in particular, ' placing before the eye ' the arrangement of the world ; which he does in this ' way, in my opinion ' (wrote Colet), ' that he may seem ' to have regard to the understanding of the vulgar and

Colet takes into account the rude multitude for whom Moses wrote.

' rude multitude whom he taught.' [2] Thus, as when try- ing to understand the Epistle to the Romans, Colet took down his ' Suetonius,' and studied the circumstances of the Roman Christians to whom the epistle was written, so, in trying to understand the book of Genesis, Colet seems to have regarded it as written expressly for the benefit of the children of Israel, and to have called to mind how rude and uncivilised a multitude Moses had to teach ; and he seems to have come to the conclusion that the object of Moses was not to give to the learned

---

[1] ' Quæ sequuntur in Moyse est ' repetitio et latior explicacio su- ' periorum, ac *speciatim* distinctio ' earum rerum quas primum *genera- ' tim* complexus est. Tu aliud si ' sentis fac nos te queso participes. ' Vale.'

[2] . . . ' Particulatim res aggre- ' ditur, et mundi digestionem ante ' oculos ponit, quod sic facit *meo ' judicio*, ut sensus vulgi et rudis ' multitudinis quam docuit racio- ' nem habuisse videatur.'

of future generations a scientific statement of the
manner and order of the creation of the universe, but
to teach a *moral* lesson to the people whom he was
leading out of the bondage and idolatry of Egypt.
And thus, in Colet's view, Moses, ' setting aside matters
' purely Divine and out of the range of the common ap-
' prehension, proceeds to instruct the unlearned people
' by touching rapidly and lightly on the order of those
' things with which their eyes were very palpably con-
' versant, that he might teach them what men are, and
' for what purpose they were born, in order that he
' might be able with less difficulty to lead them on after-
' wards to a more civilised life and to the worship of
' God—*which was his main object in writing.*[1] And that
' this was so is made obvious by the fact, that even
' amongst things cognisable to the senses, Moses passed
' over such as are less palpable, as *air* and *fire*, fearing
' to speak of anything but what can easily be seen, as
' land, sea, plants, beasts, men ; singling out from
' amongst stars, the sun and moon, and of fishes, " great
' " whales." Thus Moses arranges his details in such
' a way as to give the people a clearer notion, and he
' does this *after the manner of a popular poet*, in order
' that he may the more adapt himself to the spirit of
' simple rusticity, picturing a succession of things,
' works, and times, of such a kind as there certainly
' could not be in the work of *so great a Workman.*'[2]

CHAP. II.

A.D. 1497.

And that
his object
was to
give them
a moral
lesson,
not a
scientific
one.

---

[1] See quotation from Chrysostom
to a similar effect : *Summa*, prima
pars, lxvii. art. iv. conclusio. After
speaking of the views of Augustine
and Basil, Aquinas says :—
  ' Chrysostomus (Homil. 2 in Gen.
' circa medium illius tom. i.) autem

' assignat aliam rationem quia
' Moyses loquebatur rudi populo
' qui nihil nisi corporalia poterat
' capere, quem etiam ab idololatria
' revocare volebat,' &c.
  [2] ' . . . . Et hoc more poetæ ali-
' cujus popularis, quo magis consu-

Chap. II.

a.d. 1497.

Moses accommodated himself to the rude minds of the people.

This recognition by Colet of *accommodation*, on the part of Moses, to the limited understanding of the rude people whom he taught, occurs over and over again in these letters; *so* often, indeed, that in one letter he apologises to Radulphus for the repetition, being aware, as he says, that *he* is not addressing a ' muddle-headed He-' brew' (lutulentum Hebræum), but a most refined philosopher! Thus he explains the difficulty of the creation of the firmament on the second day by saying, ' This ' was made before, but that simple and uncivilised multi-' tude had to be taught in a homely and palpable way.' [1]

Third letter.

In the third letter Colet proceeds to speak of the third day—the separation of the waters from the dry land, and the creation of plants and herbs. Here again everything is explained on the principle of accommodation. ' Since the untutored multitude, looking round ' them, saw nothing but the sky above, and land and ' water here below, and then the things which spring ' from land and water, and live in them, so Moses suits ' his order to their powers of observation.'

The firmament or sky was spoken of in the second day; now, therefore, on the third day, Moses mentions and and water, and the things which spring from them. Plants and herbs are thus spoken of almost as though they were a part of land and water; and here Colet gives Radulphus what he speaks of as a notion of his own, hard, perhaps, for his friend to receive, but nevertheless his own conviction, that [instead of each element being separately created, as it were, out of nothing]

Colet believes in a sort of development of things.

' lat spiritui simplicis rusticitatis, ' fingens successionem rerum ' operum et temporum cujusmodi ' apud tantum Opificem certènulla

' esse potest.'
    [1] ' Crassiter et pingue docenda ' fuit stulta illa et macra multi-' tudo.'

' fire springs from ether, air from fire, water from air,
' and from water, lastly, earth.' And Moses probably
in speaking of the creation of plants &c. on the third
day, before he came to other things, intended thereby
to show, Colet thought, that the earth is spontaneously
productive of plants. He also thought that Moses
mentioned the creation of plants before the heavenly
bodies, in order to show that the germinating principle
is in the earth itself, and not, according to the vulgar
idea, in the sun and stars.

At the end of the third letter, Colet naturally
stumbles on the difficulty of explaining how, if all
things were created *at once* ' in the beginning,' before
all time, Moses could say at the end of each stage of
his description of the creation, ' and the evening and
' the morning were the first, second, third, &c. *day :* '
and, after fairly losing himself in an attempt to solve this
difficulty, he ends by urging Radulphus to leave these
obscure points, which are practically beyond our range,
and to bear in mind throughout what he had before
spoken of, viz. that whilst Moses wished to speak in
a manner not unworthy of God, he wished, at the same
time, in matters within the knowledge of the common
people, to satisfy the common people, and to keep to
the order of things ; above all things, to lead the people
on to the religion and worship of the one God.[1] ' The
' chief things known to the common people were sky,
' land and water, stars, fishes, beasts, and so he deals
' with them. He arranged them in six days ; *partly* Moses di-
' because the things which readily occur to men's minds vided the creation.

---

[1] ' (1) Moysen digna Deo loqui ' voluisse. (2) In rebus vulgo cog- ' nitis vulgo satisfacere. (3) Or- ' dinem rerum servare. In primis ' populum ad religionem et cultum ' unius Dei traducere.'

CHAP. II.

A.D. 1497.

into six
days,
after the
manner of
a poet, by
a useful
and most
wise
poetic
figment.

'are six in number : [1]—(1) What is above the sky, (2)
' sky itself, (3) land, surrounded by water, and produc-
' tive of plants, (4) sun and moon in the sky, (5) fish
' in the water, (6) beasts inhabiting earth and air, and
' *man*, the inhabitant of the whole universe ;—and
' *partly* and *chiefly*, that he might lead the people on
' to the imitation of God, whom, *after the manner of
' a poet*, he had pictured as working for six days and
' resting the seventh, so that they also should de-
' vote every seventh day to rest and to the contempla-
' tion of God and to worship.' [2] 'For, beyond all doubt,'
Colet proceeds to say, ' Moses never would have put
' forward a number of days for any other purpose than
' that, by this most useful and most wise poetic figment,
' the people might be provoked to imitation by an
' example set before them, and so ending their daily
' labours on the sixth day, spend the seventh in the
' highest contemplation of God.' [3]   Colet ends his third
letter by saying, ' Thus you have my notions upon the
' work of the third day, but what to make of it I
' know not. It is enough, as I have said, to have
' touched upon it lightly. Farewell.'

Fourth
letter.

From the commencement of the fourth letter it
would seem that Radulphus had been from home four
days, and Colet jokingly tells him that *he* had spent all
those four days in getting through *one* more of the

---

[1] ' Partim quia sex numero facile
' in rebus homini in mentem venire
' possunt.'

[2] ' Maxime . . . ut imitacio di-
' vina (quem, more poetæ, finxit sex
' dies operatum esse, septimo quie-
' visse) populum septimo quoque die
' ad quietem et contemplacionem
' Dei et cultum adduceret.'

[3] ' Nunquam dierum numerum
' statuisset, nisi ut illo utilissimo et
' sapientissimo figmento, quasi quo-
' dam proposito exemplari populum
' ad imitandum provocaret, ut sexto
' quoque die diurnis actibus fine
' imposito, septimo in summa Dei
' contemplatione persisterent.'

Mosaic days. 'And indeed whilst you have been
' working in the day under the sun, I, during this time,
' have been wandering about in the night and the dark-
' ness ; neither did I see which way to go, nor do I know
' at what point I have arrived.' And then he went on
to tell Radulphus that, while in this perplexity himself,
he seemed to have caught Moses also in a great mistake, for in concluding each day's work with the words,
' the evening and the morning were the second day,
' the third day,' and so on, he ought not to have said
day but *night*. What intervenes between the evening
and the morning must of necessity be *night* ! For a *day*
begins in the morning and ends with the evening!
And he went on jokingly to say that there was a still
more pressing reason why Moses, dividing his subjects
into days, might have rather called them *nights* ; viz.
that ' they are so overwhelmed with darkness that
' nothing could be more like *night* than these Mosaic
' *days* ! ' Then looking back upn his attempts to explain their obscurity, he was obliged to confess that
' perhaps while he had been trying to throw some light
' upon them, he might, after all, have increased the
' darkness ; ' and he entreated Radulphus ' to pour into
' the darkness some of his light, that he might be en-
' abled thereby to see Colet, and Colet together with
' him to see Moses.' [1]

Chap. II.
───
A.D. 1497.
Colet
confesses
his un-
certainty.

---

[1] ' Salve Radulphe, ac cum salute
' puto te rediisse quod tibi opto.
' Quatuor ut arbitror dies transiisti :
' ego interea vix unum Moysaicum
' diem transii. Immo tu elaborâsti
' in die sub sole ; ego hoc tempore
' in nocte et tenebris vagatus sum,
' nec vidi quo eundum esset : nec

' quo perveni intelligo. Sed incepto
' pergendum erat, ac tandem inveni
' exitum ut poteram. In quo diffi-
' cili errore, videor mihi apud
' Moysen magnum errorem depre-
' hendisse. Nam quum cujusque
' diei opus concluserat hiis verbis,
' *Et factum est vespere et mane dies*

CHAP. II.
———
A.D. 1497.

All things
must have
been
created
at once.

After this candid confession of uncertainty, Colet tried to explain the work of the fourth day, and the words, 'Let there be lights in the firmament of heaven;' but the only way he could do so was by resorting again to the principle of accommodation, which he did in these words: 'As we have said, all these were created at 'once. For it is unworthy of God, and unbecoming 'in us, to think of any one thing as created after any 'other, as though He had been unable to create them 'all at once. Hence in Ecclesiasticus, "He who dwells '" in eternity created all things *at once.*" But Moses,

Accommo-
dation on
the part
of God
to man.

'*after the manner of a good and pious poet,*[1] as Origen '(against Celsus) calls him, was willing to invent some 'figure, not altogether worthy of God, if only it 'might but be profitable and useful to men; which 'race of men is so dear to God, that God himself 'emptied himself of his glory, taking the form of a 'servant, that he might accommodate himself to the 'poor heart of man.[2] So all things of God, when given 'to man, must needs lose somewhat of their sublimity,[3] 'and be put in a form more palpable and more within

---

' *unus, secundus, tercius,* non addi-
' disset dies sed *nox* pocius *una,*
' *secunda,* et *tercia,* propterea quod
' inchoante vespere deinde mane se-
' quente, est necesse quod intercedat
' inter antecedens vesper et sub-
' sequens mane nox sit. Dies enim
' incipit mane, vesperi terminatur.
' Sed maxime profecto quæ Moyses
' scribens in dies distinxerat, noctes
' appellâsset magis, propterea quod
' offuse sint tantis tenebris ut nihil
' possit nocti videri similius quam
' dies Moysaicus. Quas nocturnas
' tenebras cum opinione aliqua lucis

' conati sumus discutere, fortasse
' nos quoque tenebrosi tenebras
' auximus, noctesque produximus.
' Attamen prestat nos recte facere
' voluisse, ac quicquid est quod
' egimus, si tibi obscurum videatur
' infunde tum aliquid luminis tui,
' ut et nos videas, utque nos eciam
' simul tecum Moysen videre
' possimus.'

[1] 'More boni piique poetæ.'

[2] 'Homunculorum cordi consu-
' leret.'

[3] . . . . 'A sua sublimitate de-
' generent.'

' the grasp of man. Accordingly, the high knowledge
' of Moses about God and Divine things and the crea-
' tion of the world, when it came to be submitted to
' the vulgar apprehension, savoured altogether of the
' humble and the rustic, so that he had to speak, not
' according to *his* own power of comprehension, but
' according to the comprehension of the multitude.
' Thus, accommodating himself to *their* comprehension,
' Moses endeavoured, by this most honest and pious
' poetic figure, at once to allure them and draw them
' on to the worship of God.' [1]

Moses
uses a
most
honest
and pious
poetic
figure.

Here the manuscript abruptly ends [2] in the middle of
a reference to the works of Macrobius, whose sanction

---

[1] ' Honestissimo et piissimo fig-
' mento simul inescare et trahere
' eos ut Deo inserviant.'

[2] For the above abstracts of these
interesting letters I am mainly indebted to the kind assistance of my
friend Henry Bradshaw, Esq., of
King's College, Cambridge, who has
also furnished me with the following description of the manuscript.

Letters to Radulphus.

1. Beginning (p. 195): ' Miror
' sane te optime Radulphe quum
' voluisti . . . . ;' ending (p. 199):
' . . . fac nos te queso participes.
' Vale.'

2. Beginning (p. 199) : ' Parum-
' per de reliquis diebus uti petis in
' calce Epistole. Facta mentione
' de materia et forma . . . . ;' ending (p. 207); ' . . . . scribendi
' paululum levaverim. Vale.'

3. Beginning (p. 207) : ' Tercium
' nunc deinceps diem aggrediamur,
' memores semper . . . ;' ending

(p. 222) : ' . . . leviter nos in hiis
' rebus lucubrasse. Vale.'

4. Beginning (p. 222) : ' Salve
' Radulphe, ac cum salute puto te
' rediisse quod tibi opto . . .'
breaking off at the end of the quire
(p. 226) : ' . . . . id licere facere
' docet Macrobius in Comen[tario
' edito] . . .'

*** These letters follow Colet's
Exposition of the Epistle to the
Romans, in the volume marked
355, in Corpus Christi College
Library.

The *Exposition* is written in the
handwriting of Colet's scribe, Peter
Meghen, the ' monoculus Brabanti-
' nus,' and there are corrections and
alterations throughout, evidently
by Colet himself.

The *letters to Radulphus* are
merely *bound with* the other. Only
two quires are now remaining : the
handwriting is not the same, but
similar.

Colet was apparently about to quote in support of his attempt to explain the first chapter of Genesis by reference to the principle of accommodation.[1]

Where Colet got these views.

The question may be asked :—' Whence came this 'doctrine of accommodation which Colet here used so ' boldly ? ' It was at least no birth of the nineteenth century, nor of the fifteenth. It belonged to a period a thousand years earlier, when men had (as in Colet's days and in ours) to reconcile reason and faith—to find a firm basis of *fact* for Christianity, instead of resting upon mere ecclesiastical authority.

It will have been noticed that the two authors cited by Colet in these letters were Origen and Macrobius. Traces of Dionysian influence are also apparent.[2]

---

[1] The following appears to be the passage Colet was about to quote : ' Aut sacrarum rerum notio, sub ' *figmentorum* velamine, *honestis* et ' tecta rebus et vestita nominibus ' enuntiatur ; et hoc est solum fig-'menti genus, quod cautio de divinis ' rebus admittit.'—*In Somnium Scipionis*, lib. i. c. 2. The ' aut ' with which the sentence begins refers to its being an alternative of two kinds of mythical writing, about which Macrobius has been speaking. I am indebted to Mr. Lupton for this reference.

[2] The following passage from Mr. Lupton's translation of Colet's abstract of Dionysius's *De celesti Hierarchiâ* (pp. 12, 13) will show that he may have derived some of his thoughts from that source. ' Thus led he forth those unin-' structed Hebrews, like boys, to ' school; in order that like children,

' playing with dolls and toys, they ' might represent in shadow what ' they were one day to do in reality ' as men : herein imitating little ' girls, who in early age play with ' dolls, the images of sons, being ' destined afterwards in riper years ' to bring forth real sons : . . . ' " When I was a child," says St. ' Paul, " I understood as a child ; ' " but when I became a man, I put ' " away childish things." From ' childishness and images and imi-' tations Christ has drawn us, who ' has shone upon our darkness, and ' has taught us the truth, and has ' made us that believe to be men, ' in order that we, " with open face ' " beholding as in a glass the glory ' " of the Lord, may be changed ' " into the same image from glory ' " to glory even as by the spirit ' " of the Lord." ' . . .

' In these foreshadowings and

It has already been pointed out, that when, after a
thousand years' interval of restless slumber, the spirit
of free enquiry was reawakened by the revival of
learning in Italy, the works of the pre-scholastic
fathers and philosophers were studied afresh. The
works of Origen, Macrobius, and, more than all, of
Dionysius, were constantly studied and quoted by such
men as Ficino and Pico. And thus it came to pass
that the doctrine of accommodation, with other apparently new-fangled but really *old* doctrines, floated, as
it were, in the air which Colet had recently been
breathing in Italy.

The immediate source of some of the views contained in the letters to Radulphus was evidently Pico's
' Heptaplus ' [1] on the six days' creation ; a work published in beautiful type, shortly before Colet's visit
to Italy, and dedicated to Lorenzo de' Medici.[2]

' signs, metaphors are borrowed
' from all quarters by Moses—a
' theologian and observer of nature
' of the deepest insight—inasmuch
' as there are not words proper to
' express the Divine attributes. For
' nothing is fitted to denote God
' Himself, who is not only unut-
' terable but even inconceivable.
' Wherefore he is most truly ex-
' pressed by negations ; since you
' may state what He is not, but not
' what He is ; for whatever positive
' statement you make concerning
' Him, you err, seeing that He is
' none of those things which you
' can say. Still because a hidden
' principle of the Deity resides in
' all things, on account of that faint
' resemblance, the sacred writers
' have endeavoured to indicate

' Him by the names of all objects,
' not only of the better but of
' the worse kind, lest the duller
' sort of people, attracted by the
' beauty of the fairer objects,
' should think God to be that very
' thing which He is called.'
The above is *Colet's amplification*
of the passage in Dionysius (chap.
ii.). The latter part of it is a pretty
close rendering of the original.

[1] ' Heptaplus Johannis Pici Mi-
' randulæ de Septiformi sex dierum
' Geneseos Enarratione.'

[2] The first edition is without
date, but the publisher's letter at
the commencement, to Lorenzo de'
Medici, shows that it was published
during the lifetime of the latter,
i.e. before 1492—probably in 1490.

Comparing this treatise of Pico's with Colet's letters, the small verbal coincidences are too striking to leave any doubt of the connection.

Nor does this tracing of Colet's thoughts to their source detract from his originality so much as might at first sight appear.

Colet found many different germs of thought in Pico. Falling into congenial soil, this one attained a vigorous growth in his mind, which it never attained with Pico. Other germs which flourished under Pico took no root with Colet. The result was, that the spirit of the letters to Radulphus had little in common with that of the ' Heptaplus.' Colet showed his originality and independence of thought by seizing one rational idea contained in Pico's treatise, and leaving the rest. He caught and unravelled one thread of common sense which Pico had contrived to interweave with a web of learned but not very wise speculation.

IV. COLET STUDIES AFRESH THE PSEUDO-DIONYSIAN WRITINGS (1497 ?).

The next glimpse of Colet and his labours at Oxford reveals him immersed in the study of the Pseudo-Dionysian writings : writing from memory an abstract of the ' Celestial' and 'Ecclesiastical ' Hierarchies,[1] and even composing short treatises of his own, based throughout upon Dionysian speculations.[2]

---

[1] The letter preceding the abstract of the ' Celestial Hierarchy,' in the Cambridge MS. Gg. 4, 26, is evidently a copy by the same hand as the letter to the Abbot of Winchcombe. Possibly the Abbot may be the person to whom it was addressed.

[2] These treatises were :—1. ' De ' Compositione Sancti Corporis ' Christi mistici.'—Camb. MS. Gg. 4, 26.

During the most part of the middle ages the Pseudo-Dionysian writings were accepted generally as the genuine productions of Dionysius the Areopagite—i.e. of a disciple of St. Paul himself. It is not surprising, therefore, that Colet, falling into this current view, should regard the writings of the disciple with some degree of that interest and reverence with which he regarded those of the master. For a time it is evident they exercised a strong fascination on his mind. CHAP. II.
——
A.D. 1497.
The
Pseudo-
Dionysian
writings.

It has already been mentioned, that the influence of the Dionysian writings upon the Neo-Platonists of Florence was natural, seeing that they were in fact the embodiment of the result of the effervescence produced by the mixture of Neo-Platonic speculations with the Christianity of a thousand years earlier.

But whilst it was their *Neo-Platonic* element which attracted the attention of Florentine philosophers, it was chiefly, as it seems to me, their *Christian* element which fascinated Colet.

Nor can we of the nineteenth century altogether afford to ignore these writings as forgeries. There must have been in them enough of intrinsic power, apart from their supposed authorship, to account for the enormous Their
intrinsic
power.

---

2. 'On the Sacraments of the 'Church,' printed with a very valuable introduction and notes, by the Rev. J. H. Lupton, M.A., from the MS. in the St. Paul's School Library. (Bell and Daldy, 1867.)

3. A short essay in the Camb. MS. Gg. 4, 26, commencing 'Deus 'immensum bonum,' &c.

Mr. Lupton is publishing Colet's abstracts of the 'Celestial' and 'Ecclesiastical' Hierarchy of Dionysius, from the MSS. at St. Paul's School; and it will be seen how much use I have made in this chapter of his admirable translation. I have expressed in the preface to this edition the obligations I am under to Mr. Lupton for bringing to light these interesting MSS., and thus materially assisting in restoring some lost links in the history of Colet's inner life and opinions.

influence exerted by them for centuries over the highest minds in the church, in spite of the wildness of speculation in which they seemed to revel; just as there was enough of intrinsic power in St. Augustine to account for *his* mighty influence, in spite of his narrow views upon some points. It is quite possible that, as the very dogmatism of St. Augustine may have increased his influence in a dogmatic age, so, inasmuch as the dogmatic theology of the Schoolmen aimed at a pan-theological settlement of every possible question, their very wildness of speculation may have aided the influence of the Dionysian writings. This may partly account for the remarkable extent to which the works of St. Augustine and Dionysius furnished, as it were, the weft and woof out of which Aquinas wove his scholastic web.[1] But nothing but some intrinsic power in these works themselves, apart from their dogmatism and speculation, could account for their double position as forming the basis, not only of the Scholastic Theology itself, but also of so many reactions against the results of its supremacy. These reactions were not always Augustinian. Some of them were mystic, and the supposed Dionysius was, so to speak, the prophet of the Mystics.

One main secret of the intrinsic power of the Dionysian writings, especially to such men as Colet, lay, undoubtedly, in the severe rebuke they gave to the ecclesiastical scandals of the times. The state of the

---

[1] Balthasar Corderius, in his prefatory observations to his edition of the works of St. Dionysius (Paris 1644), speaks of Dionysius as being the originator of the Scholastic Theology, and proves it by giving four folio pages of references to passages in the 'Summa' of Aquinas, where the authority of Dionysius is quoted.

church under Alexander VI. was such that earnest
men in Italy had practically either ceased to believe
in it, and in Christianity, as of divine institution ; or
were seeking a solution of their difficulties through
those Neo-Platonic speculations, out of which these
Pseudo-Dionysian writings had themselves sprung.

Colet doubtless, when he came to Italy, had the
same difficulties to fight. Could this ecclesiastical
system, so degraded, so vicious, so hollow and pernicious, be of God ? He could not, and probably
there was not anyone in Europe at that moment who
could, from his standing-point, wholly reject it, without rejecting Christianity along with it. The Dionysian writings presented a way of escape from this
terrible alternative. If they were genuine (and Colet
believed them to be so), then the hierarchical system
and its sacraments, however perverted, were yet of
apostolic origin. These writings apparently described,
in the words of a disciple of St. Paul, their apostolic
institution and their original intention and meaning.
But the notion gathered by Colet from Dionysius of
the apostolic intention presented an ideal so utterly
pure and holy, as compared with the hollowness and
wickedness of ecclesiastical practice, as he saw it in
Italy, that he must indeed have had a heart of stone
had he not been moved by it.

The following passage will show, in Colet's own
words, how, following the lead of such men as Pico
and Ficino (with whose writings, we have seen, he was
acquainted), he was led to regard the Jewish traditions
of the Cabala as genuine Mosaic traditions, committed
to writing by Ezra ; and, in like manner, to accept
the Pseudo-Dionysian traditions as genuine apostolic

traditions, committed to writing by a disciple of St. Paul; and, further, it will place in a clear light the connection between his faith in Dionysius, his grief over the scandals of the church, and his zeal for reform.

Colet sees
the differ-
ence be-
tween the
Dionysian
and the
Papal
rites.

'I know not by what rashness of bishops, in later 'ages, the ancient custom fell into disuse—a custom 'which, owing to its apostolic institution, had the 'highest authority. . . . And had not St. Dionysius '(who seems to me to be such in our church as was 'Ezra in the synagogue of Moses, who willed that the 'mysteries of the old law should be committed to 'writing, lest in the confusion of affairs and of men 'the record of so much wisdom should perish)—had 'not Dionysius, I say, in like manner, as though di-'vining the future carelessness of mankind, left written 'down by his productive pen what he retained in 'memory of the institutions of the apostle in arranging 'and regulating the church, we should have had no 'record of this ancient custom. . . . How it befel, '(Colet continued) without grievous guilt, that these 'became afterwards wholly changed, I know not; since 'we must believe that it was by the teaching of the 'Holy Spirit that they ordained all things in the church. 'For the words of our Saviour in St. John are these : '" Howbeit, when he, the Spirit of truth, is come, he '" will guide you into all truth : for he shall not speak '" of himself, but whatsoever he shall hear, that shall '" he speak ; and he will show you things to come." 'It is because their most holy traditions have been 'superseded and neglected, and men have fallen away 'from the Spirit of God to their own inventions, 'that, beyond doubt, all things have been wretchedly 'disturbed and confounded ; and, as I said before,

unless God shall have mercy upon us, all things will
' go to ruin.' [1]

The truth was that the Dionysian writings, though
not of apostolic origin as Colet supposed, presented,
nevertheless, a picture of the ecclesiastical usages of an
age a thousand years earlier than Colet's ; and putting
the earlier and the later usages in contrast, it was impossible for him not to perceive at once how much
more pure and rational in its spirit and tendencies was
the ancient Dionysian system than the more modern
Papal one.

Purity
of the
Dionysian
standard.

Both were sacerdotal and ritualistic ; but the sacerdotalism and ritualism of Dionysius were radically
opposed in spirit to those of the more modern system.
During the interval between the fifth and the fifteenth
century, sacerdotalism had had time to turn almost
literally upside-down, and ritualism with it. It was
thus quite natural that Colet, in the light of Dionysius,
should find ' all things wretchedly disturbed and con-
' founded.'

The Dio-
nysian
sacerdotal
and ritu-
alistic
system is
radically
different
from the
Papal.

The Dionysian theory, however speculative and
vicious as such, at least according to Colet's version
of it, did not, like the modern theory, tend towards
that grossest heathen conception of religion, according to which its main object is the propitiation of
the Deity, rather than the changing of the heart
of man.

The object
of religion
not to
propitiate
the Deity,
but to
change
the heart
of man.

Its gospel was not that Christ offered his sacrifice
to propitiate an unreconciled God—to reconcile God
to man. On the contrary, it told of a God who is

---

[1] Mr. Lupton's translation, pp. 135, 136.

F

' beautiful and good,' [1] who had created all things because He is good, because He is good recalling [2] all things to Himself, by the sacrifice of Himself redeeming them not from His own wrath, but from the power of Evil.

Cur Deus Homo ?

The following passage may be taken in illustration of this:—'When, directly after the creation, foolish human ' nature was allured by the seductive enticements of ' the enemy, and fell away from God into a womanish ' and dying condition, and was rolling headlong down ' with rapid course to death itself, then at length, in ' His own time, our good, and tender, and kind, and ' gentle, and merciful God, giving us all good things at ' once in place of all that was bad, willed to take upon ' Him human nature, and to enter into it, and rescue it ' from the power of the adversary, overthrowing and ' destroying his empire.   For, as St. Paul writes to the ' Hebrews, " Forasmuch as the children "—or servants ' —" are partakers of flesh and blood," . . . therefore ' also God himself " made himself of no reputation, ' " and took upon him the form of a servant," and ' " himself likewise took part of the same " flesh and ' blood—that is, human nature—" that through death ' " he might destroy him that had the power of death, ' " that is, the devil ; and deliver them who through ' " fear of death were all their lifetime subject to ' " bondage : " that he might destroy, I say, that ' enemy, not by force, but (as Dionysius says) by judg-

---

[1] ' God, who is one, beautiful ' and good—Father, Son, and Holy ' Ghost : the Trinity which created ' all things—is at once the purifica- ' tion of things to unity, their illu- ' mination to what is beautiful, and ' their perfection to what is good.'

Mr. Lupton's translation, pp. 15, 24.
[2] 'God created all things because ' He is good (p. 16); and because He ' is good, He also recalls to himself ' all things according to their capa- ' city, that He may bountifully com- ' municate himself to them.'

' ment and righteousness; which he calls a hidden thing
' and a *mystery*.[1] For it was a marvellous victory,
' that the Devil, though victorious, in the very fact of
' his conquering, should be conquered ; and that Jesus
' should conquer in the very fact of his being van-
' quished on the cross ; so that in reality, in the victory
' on each side, the matter was otherwise than it seemed.
' And thus when the adversary that vanquished man
' was himself vanquished by God, man was restored,
' without giving any just cause of complaint to the
' devil, to the liberty and light of God. There was
' shown to him the path to heaven, trodden by the
' feet of Christ, whose footsteps we must follow if we
' would arrive where he has gone. A suffering Christ,
' I say (most marvellous !), and dying as though van-
' quished, overcame. . . . By that death we have been
' rescued from the dead, and are the servants of
' God.'[2]

Quaint and curious as this view of the connection
between the sacrifice of Christ and the just conquest
of the power of Evil may seem to modern ears, it re-
flects faithfully the view most current amongst the

CHAP. II.
___
A.D. 1497.
Colet on
the ' mar-
vellous
victory '
of a
' suffering
Christ.'

Object of
Christ's
death.

---

[1] All after this is Colet's own
addition to what is said in Dionysius.

[2] Mr. Lupton's translation of
Colet's Abstract of the *Eccl. Hier.*
p. 92. In a short essay contained in
the MSS. Gg. 4, 26, of the Cambridge University Library, entitled
' De compositione sancti corporis
' Christi mistici, quæ est ecclesia,
' quæ sine anima ejus, Spiritu sci-
' licet, dispergitur et dissipatur.'
Colet, after showing how men, if
left to themselves, would wander
apart and become scattered ; and

that the purpose of God is, that
they should be united in one body
the church by the Spirit, as by a
magnet, goes on to say, ' Predesti-
' natum fuit hominem qui decidit
' a Deo retrahi ad Deum non posse
' quidem nisi per Deum factum ho-
' minem . . . Mortuus est ut liberos
' faceret homines ad talem vitam,
' ut debita cujusque hominum in
' illius morte soluta, nunc desi-
' nentes peccare deinceps liberi
' sint justiciæ, ut non amplius
' maneamus in peccato,' &c.—
Ff. 70*b*, 71*a*.

early Greek Fathers ; and it has at least this merit, that it cannot be translated into the language of the heathen doctrine of propitiation.

It followed that, as the Dionysian theory left no place for the notion that the sacrifice of Christ was offered to reconcile God to man (seeing that it upheld the doctrine that it was the sheep that had gone astray, and rejected the doctrine that the Shepherd had ever deserted the sheep), so it left no place for a sacerdotal order, according to the heathen notion of a priesthood. Its priests were not priests according to the modern definition. It did not—it could not—represent its priesthood as appearing as heathen priests did (and as some modern priests seem to think they do) [1] *on behalf of man* before God, presenting men's offerings to him. If Christ's office, according to Dionysius, were emphatically to *plead with men*, to bring *them* back, so the priest's office was to act in his stead in the same work.

The following passage from Colet's abstract presents these two dependent facts in their proper connection : ' Christ's office on earth the bishops [elsewhere he

Modern 'priests' act on behalf of man before God.

---

[1] Wilberforce, in his *Doctrine of the Incarnation*, third edition, 1850, thus expressed the modern sacerdotal theory. In the word *Priest*, in primitive languages, 'the ' notion of the setting apart those ' who should act *on man's behalf* ' *towards God* is everywhere visible.' P. 229.

'Now if Christ is still maintaining ' a real intercession (if He still pleads ' that sacrifice) then is there ample ' place for that sacerdotal system, by ' which some actual *thing* is still to ' be effected, and in which some ' agents must still be employed.' —P. 381. ' We put the Priestly ' office under the law in a line with ' the ministerial office under the ' Gospel ; we assert, that if the title ' of Priest could be given fitly to the ' first, it belongs also to the second.' —P. 383. ' Any persons who dis- ' charge an office which has refer- ' ence to God, and who present to ' Him what is offered by men, may ' be called Priests.'—P. 384.

CHAP. II.

A.D. 1497.

According
to Diony-
sius and
Colet,
priests act
on behalf
of God
towards
man.

' speaks of priests and bishops as identical] everywhere
' discharge, and in Him act as He acted, and with like
' zeal strive for the purification, illumination, and
' salvation of mankind by constant preaching of the
' truth and diffusion of Gospel light, even as He strove.
' St. Paul says, " God was in Christ, reconciling the
' " world unto himself, not imputing their trespasses
' " unto them, and hath committed unto us the word of
' " reconciliation. Now then we are ambassadors for
' " Christ." Acting in Christ's stead, they fan the fire
' which Christ came to send upon the earth. . . . (Luke
' xii. 49, 50.) He baptized, as John testifies," with the
' " Holy Ghost and with fire." For fire purifies, illu-
' mines, and perfects. That fire of the Spirit does
' this in the souls of men. For the increasing of this
' wholesome conflagration amid the forest of men, the
' bishops are vicars and ministers of Jesus, and they
' seek the kindling of mankind in God. Now this fire
' is, I doubt not, the holy love of God.[1] . . . And the
' messenger of this goodness, compassion, love, and
' tenderness of God was his lovely son Jesus Christ,
' who . . . . . . brought down love to men, that they
' being born anew by love, might in turn love their
' heavenly Father along with Him.' [2]

The Dionysian theory of sacerdotalism being thus,

---

[1] See the same views expressed
by Colet in his exposition of
' Corinthians.' — Emmanuel Col.
MS. 3, 3, 12, leaf g, 2.

[2] Colet's Abstract of the *Eccl.
Hier.* ch. ii. s. 2. Mr. Lupton's
translation, pp. 61, 62. Colet
writes a little further on :—' The

' office of the bishop is, like Christ,
' to preach constantly and diligently
' the truth he has received. For he
' is, as it were, a messenger midway
' between God and men, to announce
' to men heavenly things, as Christ
' did.'—Pp. 63, 64.

Chap. II.

A.D. 1497.

Modern
and Dio-
nysian
ritualism
very
different.

in its spirit and attitude, an exact inversion of the modern one, it might naturally be expected that the Dionysian ritualism would, in like manner, involve an inversion of modern ritualistic notions.

This was the case. Instead of idolizing the sacraments as of mystic power and virtue in themselves, the Dionysian theory represented them as divinely instituted ceremonies intended to draw mankind by types and shadows upward to God.

It did not, like modern ritualism, tend towards the view that the Eucharist is a *sacrifice* in the heathen sense—a continued offering by a human priesthood of the sacrifice of Christ.[1] On the contrary, it represented this sacrament as commemorative of the death of Christ, and as symbolic of the professed communion on the part of men with Christ, and with one another.[2] It did not set forth the sacrament of baptism as modern ritualists are so fond of doing, as effecting there and then the regeneration of the person baptized. But it

regarded baptism as a symbolic *profession* of change of heart—as the ceremony in which the believer openly takes his soldier's oath to Christ, and promises amended

---

[1] ' Through this bread and this ' cup, that which is offered as a true ' sacrifice in heaven is present as a ' real though immaterial agent in 'the church's ministrations. So that ' what is done by Christ's ministers 'below is a constitutent part of that ' general work which the one great ' High Priest performs in heaven : ' through the intervention of his ' heavenly Head, the earthly sacri- ' ficer truly exhibits to the Father ' that body of Christ which is the one ' only sacrifice for sins ; each visible ' act has its efficacy through those ' invisible acts of which it is the 'earthly expression, and things done ' on earth are one with those done in ' heaven.'—Wilberforce's *Doctrine of the Incarnation*, pp. 372, 373.

[2] Colet's abstract of the *Eccl. Hier.* ch. iii. Mr. Lupton's translation, pp. 78–94. Whilst not disapproving in *others* daily attendance ' ad mensam Dominicam,' Erasmus tells us that Colet did not make a *daily* habit of it himself.—Eras. *Op.* iii. p. 459, E.

life.[1] It did not represent the sponsors as promising or
professing *in the child's stead*, that he is then and there
regenerated, but promising that they themselves will do
all they can to bring him up as a child of God.[2] It did
not admit in any sacerdotal order, any power to remit
or retain sin, to bind or to loose. On the contrary,

Chap. II.

A.D. 1497.
Sponsors.
Priests
have no
power of
loosing
and
binding.

---

[1] *Eccl. Hier.* ch. ii. Colet speaks
in his abstract (Mr. Lupton's translation, p. 65) of the Christian being
'brought to the captain of the army,
'the bishop,' that by the soldier's
oath, &c. '*he may own himself a
'soldier of Christ.*' He concludes
this section as follows :—

'Such was the custom and cere-
'mony of baptism and the washing
'of regeneration in the primitive
'church, instituted by the holy
'apostles, *whereby the more excellent
'baptism of the inner man is signi-
'fied.* And this form differs very
'greatly from the one we make use
'of in this age. And herein I own
'that I marvel ! . . . The apostles
'being fully taught by Jesus Christ,
'knew well what are convenient
'symbols and appropriate signs for
'the mysteries. So that one may
'suspect either rashness or neglect
'on the part of their successors in
'what has been added to or taken
'from their ordinances.'

Then follows a section on the
'spiritual contemplation of bap-
'tism,' in which occurs the passage
beginning 'Gracious God ! ' &c.—
Infra, p. 73. *Eccl. Hier.* ch. ii.
s. 3, pp. 76, 77 of Mr. Lupton's
translation.

[2] 'Meanwhile the foster father,
'who has undertaken the rearing of
'the child in Christ, gives a pledge

'and sacred promise, on behalf of
'the infant, of all things that true
'Christianity demands, viz. a re-
'nouncing of all sin, &c. . . . And
'this he says, *not in the child's stead,*
'since it would be a fond thing for
'another to speak in place of one
'that was in ignorance ; but when,
'in his own person, he speaks of
'renouncing, he professes that *he
'will bring it to pass, so far as he can,*
'that the little infant, as soon as
'ever it is capable of instruction,
'shall in reality and in his life
'utterly renounce, &c. . . .

'When the bishop, I say, hears
'him saying, " I renounce," *which
'means, as Dionysius explains it* "I
'" *will take care that the infant* re-
'" nounce," &c. . . . Thus we see
'how in the primitive church, by the
'ordinance of the apostles, infants
'were not admitted unreservedly to
'the sacred rites, but on condition
'only that some one would be surety
'for them, that when they came to
'years of discretion they should
'thenceforward set before them in
'reality the pattern of Christ.

'Mark thus how great a burden
'he takes upon himself who pro-
'mises to be a godfather,' &c.—
Mr. Lupton's translation of Colet's
abstract of the *Eccl. Hier.* ch. viii.
pp. 158, 159.

it regarded the priests as God's ministers, who ought to keep in communion with Him, so that receiving intimation by the Spirit 'of what is already bound or loosed in heaven, they may disclose it on earth.[1]

If any sacerdotal theory could be believable, it must be confessed, there is an intrinsically rational and *Christian* tone about the Dionysian theory according to Colet's rendering of it, strangely lacking in that of modern sacerdotalists.

Forgetting for the moment the speculative adjuncts to the theory, the professed knowledge of mysteries unknown, which Colet's belief in Dionysius obliged him to accept, but which did not add any force to the theory itself, it will be seen at once how powerful a rebuke he must have felt it to be to the ecclesiastical scandals of the closing years of the fifteenth century. It assumed, as the essential attribute of any sacerdotal order laying claim to apostolic institution, the attribute of a really pure and personal holiness. No merely official sanctity imputed outwardly to a consecrated order, by virtue of its outward consecration, could possibly satisfy its requirements.[2]   And in the same way the sacraments were nothing apart from the personal spiritual realities which they were meant to symbolize.

---

[1] ' Men execute the previous de-cisions of God, and by the ministry of men that is at length disclosed 'on earth,' &c.—Mr. Lupton's translation, p. 149. ' It must be heedfully marked, lest bishops should be presumptuous, that it is not the part of men to loose the bonds of sins : nor does the power pertain to them of loosing or binding anything.' . . . ' And if they do not proceed according to revelation, moved by the Spirit of God . . . they abuse the power given to them, both to the blaspheming of God and the destruction of the Church.'—*Ibid.* 150.

[2] See Eras.*Op.*iii.p.459,C and D.

Underneath, therefore, the wild excess of symbolism and speculation which lay on the surface, and formed, as it were, the *froth* of the Dionysian theology, Colet seems to have found this basis of eternal truth, that religion is a thing of the heart, not of creed nor of ceremonial observances; that, in Colet's own rendering of the Dionysian theory :—' Knowledge leads not to ' eternal life, but *love.* Whoso loveth God is known ' of Him. Ignorant love has a thousand times more ' power than cold wisdom.' [1]

Colet's abstracts of the Dionysian treatises abound with passages expressive of the purity and holiness of heart required of the Christian, and of the necessity of his love not being merely of the contemplative kind, but an active love working for Christ and his fellow-men. The following extracts may be taken as illustrations of this.

In concluding the chapter on the meaning of baptism Colet exclaims :—' Gracious God ! here may one per-' ceive how cleansed and how pure he that professes ' Christ ought to be ; how inwardly and thoroughly ' washed ; how white, how shining, how utterly without ' blemish or spot ; in fine, how perfected and filled, ' according to his measure, with Christ himself. . . . .

---

[1] Mr. Lupton's translation of Colet's abstract of the *Eccl. Hier.* p. 83. This was a strictly Dionysian thought and one shared also by Pico. ' The little affection of an ' old man or an old woman to God-' ward (were it never so small), he ' set more by than all his own ' knowledge as well of natural ' things as godly.' . . . He writeth thiswise [to Politian], ' Love God ' (while we be in this body), we ' rather may than either know Him, ' or by speech utter Him.'—Life of Picus, E. of Mirandula, *Sir Thomas More's Works,* p. 7.

To the same purport is the passage from Ficino, quoted by Colet in his MS. on the ' Romans.'—Vide supra, p. 37.

' May Jesus Christ himself bring it to pass, that we who
' profess Christ may both be, and set our affections on,
' and do all things that are worthy of our profession.' [1]

Speaking of the anointing after baptism of the soldier
of Christ, Colet says :—' You must strive that you may
' conquer; you must conquer that you may be crowned.
' Fight in Him who fights in you and prevails—even
' Jesus Christ, who has declared war against death,
' and fights in all. . . . . . It is the rule of combat
' that we should imitate our leader. . . . . . We have
' no enemies except sin (which is ever against us), and
' the evil spirits that tempt to sin.   When these are
' vanquished in ourselves, then let us, armed with the
' armour of God, in charity succour others, even though
' they be not for suffering us, even though in their
' folly they see not their bondage, even though they
' would put their deliverers to death.   So to love man
' as to die in caring for his salvation is most blessed.' [2]

Self-
sacrifice
for others
a blessed
thing.

These passages may also be taken as evidence how
fully Colet had caught hold of the spirit, not merely
of the froth, of the Dionysian doctrine ; how he had
approached it in earnest search after practical religion,
and not merely in the love of speculation.   They will
also do much to explain how, drinking deeply at this
well of mystic religion, he came back from Italy,
not a mere Neo-Platonic philosopher or ' humanist,'
but a practical Reformer.   In Italy he had become
acquainted with the scandals of Alexander VI.   In his
abstract of Dionysius, in speaking of '*the highest Bishop*
' *whom we call " the Pope," '* he bursts out into these
indignant sentences :—' If he be a lawful bishop, he of

---

[1] Mr. Lupton's translation, pp. 76, 77.   [2] Ibid. p. 73.

' himself does nothing, but God in him. But if he do
' attempt anything of *himself*, he is then a breeder of
' poison. And if he also bring this to the birth, and
' carry into execution his own will, he is wickedly dis-
' tilling poison to the destruction of the Church. This
' has now indeed been done for many years past, and
' has by this time so increased as to take powerful hold
' on all members of the Church ; so that, unless that
' Mediator who alone can do so, who created and
' founded the church out of nothing for Himself (there-
' fore does St. Paul often call it a " creature ")—unless,
' I say, the Mediator Jesus lay to his hand with all
' speed, our most disordered church cannot be far from
' death. . . . Men consult not God on what is to be
' done, by constant prayer, but take counsel with men,
' whereby they shake and overthrow everything. All
' (as we must own with grief, and as I write with both
' grief and tears) seek their own, not the things which
' are Jesus Christ's, not heavenly things but earthly,
' what will bring them to death, not what will bring
' them to life eternal.' [1]

The following passage also burns with Colet's zeal
for ecclesiastical reform :—' Here let every priest ob-
' serve, by that sacrament of washing [before cele-
' bration of the eucharist], how clean, how scoured,
' how fresh he ought to be, who would handle the
' heavenly mysteries, and especially the sacrament of
' the Lord's body ; how such ought to be so washed
' and scoured and polished inwardly, as that not so
' much as a shadow be left in the mind whereby the
' incoming light may be in any wise obscured, and that

---

[1] Mr. Lupton's translation, pp. 150, 151.

CHAP. II.

A.D. 1497.
Colet
on the
wicked-
ness of
priests.

' not a trace of sin may remain to prevent God from
' walking in the temple of our mind. Oh priests! Oh
' priesthood! Oh the detestable boldness of wicked
' men in this our generation! Oh the abominable
' impiety of those miserable priests, of whom this age
' of ours contains a great multitude, who fear not to
' rush from the bosom of some foul harlot into the
' temple of the Church, to the altar of Christ, to the
' mysteries of God! Abandoned creatures! on whom
' the vengeance of God will one day fall the heavier,
' the more shamelessly they have intruded themselves
' on the Divine office. O Jesu Christ, wash for us,
' not our feet only, but our hands and our head!' [1]

In conclusion, I must remind the reader that it would
not be fair to take this sketch of Colet's abstract of the
Dionysian treatises as in any sense an abstract of the
treatises themselves. What I have tried to do is, to
show in what Colet's own mind was influenced by
them. The passages I have quoted are not passages
from Dionysius but from Colet. The radical conception
is most often due to Dionysius; the passages themselves
represent the effervescence produced by the Dionysian
conceptions in Colet's mind. The enthusiasm—the fire
which they kindled there they would not have kindled
in every one's breast. The fire was indeed very much
Colet's own. I find passages which *burn* in Colet's
abstract *freeze* in the original. Whilst, therefore, acknowledging the influence of the Dionysian writings
upon Colet's mind, it must not be forgotten that this

---

[1] Mr. Lupton's translation, pp.
90, 91. See also pp. 123–126, where
Colet inveighs warmly against the
nomination by secular princes of
worldly bishops.

influence was exerted upon the mind of a man not only already acquainted with the writings of the modern Neo-Platonists and of the Greek Fathers, but also already devoted to the study of the Scriptures, and bent upon drawing out for himself from themselves their direct practical meaning.

The truth is, that just as in the Greek Fathers, with all their tendency to allegorise Scripture, there was combined a rational critical element which formed the germ of a sounder and more scientific method of Scriptural interpretation—a germ which fructified whenever it fell into a soil suited to its growth, whether in the fifth and sixth or in the fifteenth and sixteenth centuries—so in the Pseudo-Dionysian philosophy, with all its unscientific tendency to revel in the wildest speculation, there were combined germs of true scientific thought, which in like manner were sure to fructify in such a mind as Colet's.

Thus in the Dionysian doctrine that God is inscrutable—that all human knowledge is relative—that man cannot rise to a knowledge of the absolute—that therefore no conceptions men can form of God can be accurate, and no language in which they speak of Him can be more than clumsy analogy—in this principle there is the germ of a rational understanding of the necessary conditions of Divine revelation involving the admission of the necessity of *accommodation* and the *human* element in Scripture. Again, in the doctrine that whilst, in this sense, the *knowledge* of God is impossible to man, the *love* of God is not so, there lies the basis of truth on which alone science can be reconciled with religion, and religion itself become a power of life.

Lastly, in the very attempt, so striking throughout

Dionysius, to find out in the sacerdotal and sacramental system a symbolic meaning, who does not recognise the attempt to find out a *rational intention* in its institution, which should make it believable in an age of reviving philosophy and science ?

V.   COLET LECTURES ON ' I. CORINTHIANS ' (1497 ?).

If the manuscript exposition of the 1st Epistle to the Corinthians preserved at Cambridge, apparently in Colet's own handwriting, with his own latest corrections,[1] may be taken as evidence of what his lectures on this epistle were, it may be of some value, apart from its own intrinsic interest, in enabling us to judge how far he adhered to the same leading views and method of exposition which he had before adopted, and how far, in preceding chapters, we have been able to judge rightly of what they were.

Colet's lectures on Corinthians. MSS. at Cambridge

I think it will be found that this exposition of the Epistle to the Corinthians is in perfect harmony with all which had preceded it, and that it shows evident traces of those phases of thought through which Colet had been passing since his arrival at Oxford.

Its striking characteristic, like that on the ' Romans,' would seem to be the pains taken to regard it throughout as the letter of a living apostle to an actual church.

Colet's love for St. Paul.

On the one hand, it teems with passages which show the depth of Colet's almost personal affection for St. Paul, and the clearness with which he realised the special characteristics of St. Paul's character ; his

---

[1] Camb. University Library, MS. Gg. 4, 26. There is a beautiful copy embodying these corrections in the hand of Peter Meghen, in the Library of Emmanuel College Cambridge, MS. 3, 3, 12.

extreme consideration for others,[1] his modesty,[2] his
tolerance, his wise tact and prudence,[3] his self-denial
for others' good.[4]

On the other hand, no less conspicuous is the attempt Colet
on Colet's part to realise the condition and peculiar studies
the cha-
character and circumstances of the Corinthians, to racter of
the Corin-
whom the apostle was writing, as the true key to the thians.
practical meaning of the epistle.

Thus Colet, in treating of the commencement of the
epistle—an epistle intended to correct the conduct of
the Corinthians in some practical points in which they
had erred—stops to admire the wisdom of St. Paul's
method in speaking first of that part of their conduct
which he could praise, before he proceeded to blame.
And this he did, Colet thought, ' that by this gentle
' and mild beginning he might draw them on to read
' the rest of his epistle, and lead them to listen more
' easily to what he had to blame in their conduct. For
' (Colet continues) had he at once at starting been
' rougher, and accused them more severely, he might
' indeed have driven away from himself and his exhor-
' tations minds as yet tender and inexperienced in
' religion, especially those of that Greek nation, so Pride of
' arrogant and proud, and prone to be disdainful.[5] Pru- the Greek
nation.
' dently, therefore, and cautiously had the matter to be
' handled, having due regard to persons, places, and

---

[1] Emmanuel Col. MS. leaf e, 5 :
' Homo unus omnium divinissimus
' et consideratissimus.' See also
leaf k, 6.

[2] Leaf a, 5. ' Quod tamen facit
' ubique modestissime homo piissi-
' mus.'

[3] ' Velit ergo prudentissimus

' Paulus.'—Leaf k, 3.

[4] Leaf k, 6, and p. 8.

[5] In another place Colet writes,
' Fuit illa græca natio illis argutiis
' versatilibus humani ingenii sem-
' per prompta ad arguendum et
' redarguendum.'—Leaf c, 2.

'seasons, in his observance of which Paul was surely
'the one most considerate of all men, who knew so well
'how to accommodate the means to the end, that while
'he sought nothing else but the glory of Jesus Christ
'upon earth, and the increase of faith and charity,
'this man with divine skill neither did nor omitted
'anything ever amongst any which should impede or
'retard these objects.' [1]

Colet
describes
the state
of the
Corin-
thian
Church.

The same method receives a further illustration from
the way in which Colet draws a picture of the condition of the Corinthian church, evidently feeling while
he did so, how closely in some points it resembled the
condition of the church in his own day. He surely
must have had the Schoolmen in his mind, as he
described some among the Corinthians, 'derogating
'from the authority of the Apostles, and especially of
'St. Paul, whose name ought to have had the greatest
'weight amongst them, setting up institutions in the
'church according to their own fancy and in their own
'wisdom, making the people believe that they knew
'all about everything which pertained to the Christian
'religion, and that they could easily solve and give an
'opinion upon every point of doubt that might arise.
'So that, in this infant church, many things had
'come to be allowed which were abhorrent from the
'institutions of Paul, wherefrom had arisen divisions
'and factions, between which were constant conten-
'tions and altercations, so that all things were going
'wrong.' [2]

Colet's almost personal affection for St. Paul enabled

---

[1] Emmanuel Col. MS. 3, 3, 12,
leaf a, 4, and Appendix (B, a).

[2] Abridged quotation. Leaf a,
5, and Appendix (B, a).

him also to realise how, being the 'first parent of the
' Corinthian church,' he was ' troubled ' at this state
of things, not so much at their having tried to undermine his own authority, as at the danger they were in
of making shipwreck of their faith, after all his pains in
piloting their vessel. ' Therefore, as far as he dared and
' could (writes Colet), ' he upbraided those who wished
' to seem wise, and who conducted the affairs of the
' Christian republic more according to their own fancies
' than according to the will of God. Which, however,
' he did everywhere most modestly; the most pious man St. Paul's
' seeking rather the reformation of the evils than the modesty
' blame of any.' And therefore it was (Colet thought), and tact.
that St. Paul in his whole epistle, and especially in the
first part of it, strove to assert that men of themselves
can know and do nothing, to eradicate the false foundation of trust in themselves, and to lead them to
Christ, who alone is the wisdom of God and the power
of God.[1]

And here again, after following St. Paul's statement, that the wisdom of man being foolishness, God
had chosen the foolish rather than the wise to hear
him and to preach his gospel, Colet was led off into
a train of thought which harmonises well with what
has been stated in previous chapters, in that it shows
how fully he had accepted the Dionysian writings as
the genuine writings of St. Paul's disciple, and how
closely he associated in his mind the name of the
disciple with that of the master.

For he exclaims, ' What if sometimes some men,
' endowed with secular wisdom such as Paul and his

---

[1] Emmanuel Col. MS. leaf a, 5, 6, and Appendix (B, a).

'disciple, Dionysius the Areopagite, and a few others,
'were chosen both to receive the truths of his wisdom,
'and to teach them to others, these indeed in teaching
'others what they had learned from God, took the
'greatest pains to appear to know nothing according
'to this world, thinking it unworthy to mix up human
'reason with Divine revelations. . . . Hence Paul, in
'wise and learned Greece, was not afraid to seem in
'himself a fool and weak, and to profess that he knew
'nothing but Jesus Christ and Him crucified.'[1]

Then follows a passage in which Colet states, in his
own language, what Paul meant when he preached
'Christ crucified;'[2] a passage very similar to that
already quoted from his abstract of Dionysius, and
bearing the same marks of the modes of thought of
a man who, as is affirmed of Colet, was more inclined
to follow Dionysius, Origen, and Jerome, than St.
Augustine.

Nor did Colet in this exposition show himself to be any
more inclined to follow Augustine upon the question
of election than he showed himself in his exposition of
'the Romans.' He is indeed ready enough to admit,
that men never could of themselves rise out of the
darkness of worldly wisdom to 'accept the wonderful
'miracle of Christ,'—'such is the miserable and lost
'condition of men;' and yet he does not fall into the
pitfall of Augustine's doctrine, that men were chosen
wholly without reference to their own characters. 'It
'would seem,' he said, 'that it was not without reason

---

[1] Leaf b, 4, and Appendix (B, b).
See a very similar remark with reference to St. Paul and Dionysius
in *Joan. Fran. Pici Mirand. De*
Studio Div. et Hum. Philosophiæ
lib. i. ch. iii. J. F. Pico was living
when Colet was in Italy.

[2] Appendix (B, c).

'that God chose, out of the crowd of men grovelling 'in the darkness of worldly wisdom, those who had not 'fallen so far into the depths of this darkness, and so 'could more easily be touched by the divine light. '. . . If God himself be nobility, wisdom and power, 'who does not see that Peter, John, and James, and 'others like them, even before the truth of God had 'shone in the world, surpassed others in wisdom and 'strength, in proportion as they were free from their 'foolishness and impotence, so that no wonder if God 'chose those *held* foolish and impotent, since indeed 'they were really the most noble of all the world, most 'separate, and standing out farthest from the vileness 'of the world ; so that just as that land which rises 'highest is touched by the rays of the rising sun most 'easily and most quickly, so in the same way it was of 'necessity that, at the rising of that light which lighteth 'every man coming into this world, it should first light 'up those who rose highest amongst men, and stood 'out like mountains in the valleys of men.' [1]

The striking characteristic of Colet's letters to Radulphus was the stress laid upon the principle of *accommodation* on the part of the teacher to the limited capacities of the taught. This is another point which crops up again in the MS. on Corinthians. When Colet turned to the practical teaching of St. Paul to the Corinthians, he seems to have been struck with the fact, that the rules which St. Paul laid down with reference to marriage and the like, were to be explained upon this principle.[2]

---

[1] Appendix (B, d). Emmanuel Coll. MS. leaf b, 6, and b, 8.

[2] 'In these matters regard must 'be had to condition and strength.

Carried away by the authority of the Dionysian
writings, Colet seems not only to have held the
doctrine of the celibacy of the clergy, but even to
have regarded marriage as allowed to the laity only
by way of concession to the weakness of the flesh.
He had expressed this view in his MS. treatise on
' the Sacraments,' and he repeated it, under cover of
St. Paul's allusions to marriage in the Epistle to the
Corinthians.

The influence of the Dionysian writings is indeed
very frequently evident. Again and again the phraseology used by Colet betrays it, and sometimes a Dionysian turn of thought leads to a long digression. As
might be expected, a notable example of this occurs
when Colet treats of the chapters in the epistle with
which the Dionysian theory of the celestial hierarchy
was intimately connected; in which St. Paul speaks, on
the one hand, of the church as one body with many

members, and, on the other, of celestial bodies and
bodies terrestrial, and their differing order of glory. It
was probably about the time that Colet was lecturing on
Corinthians that Linacre was translating the work of

' . . . It was thus that Moses
' taught the truth and justice of
' God, as it was brought down to
' the level of sensible things, and
' diluted for the ancient Hebrews.
' It was thus that Christ taught to
' the disciples what they were able
' to bear. It was thus, lastly, that
' Paul, both gently and sparingly
' gave to the Corinthians, as it
' were, milk instead of meat. . . .
' He spoke wisdom to the perfect,
' to the imperfect he accommodated
' as it were foolish, more humble
' and more homely things. With
' this design, also, he tolerated in-
' dulgently less perfect and less ab-
' solute morals for a time, dealing
' gently with them as far as was
' lawful, not thinking how much
' was lawful to himself, but what
' was expedient to others; not how
' much he himself could bear, but
' what was adapted to the Corin-
' thians.' . . .—Leaf c, 7. See also
leaf e, 6.

Proclus, a Neo-Platonist of the Alexandrian School,' De
' Spherâ ; ' and Grocyn writing a preface to Linacre's
translation in the form of a letter to Aldus, the great
printer at Venice, by whom it was afterwards published
in 1499, in an edition of the ' Astronomi veteres.' [1]
Astronomy was one of the sciences which the revival
of learning had brought into prominence.[2] At this very
moment Copernicus was pursuing in Italy those studies
which resulted in the overturning of the Ptolemaic
system. That system, however, which had become in-
separably interwoven with scholastic theology, was as
yet in undisputed ascendancy. Its crystalline spheres
had for generations been devoutly believed in by the
Schoolmen, and classed by them among ' things ce-
' lestial ; ' and as Luther stood in awe at their magic
motions, as ' no doubt done by some angel,' [3] so poor
Colet was led, by Dionysian influence, to draw strange
fanciful analogies between their ' differing order of
' glory ' and that of the ' celestial hierarchy.' [4] Thus
it came to pass that his exposition of the Epistle to
the Corinthians was even disfigured with diagrams
to illustrate these fancied analogies.

Whilst thus pointing out the evidence that Colet

---

[1] See Eras. *Op.* iii. p. 1263, and
Ibid. p. 184, E. ' 1499 was the date
' of the 1st edition, which is com-
' prised in eight pages, and forms
' the last treatise in a volume of an-
' cient writers on astronomy, edited
' by Aldus. It is intituled, " Procli
' " Diadochi Sphæra, Astronomiam
' " discere Incipientibus Vtilissima,
' " Thomâ Linacro Britanno Inter-
' " prete." '—Johnson's *Life of
Linacre,* p. 152.

[2] In a letter from Politian to
Franciscus Casa, there is a description of an ' orrery ' made at
Florence. The letter was written
1484.—*Illustrium Virorum Epistolæ ab Angelo Politiano,* n. 1523,
fol. lxxxiii.

[3] Luther's *Table Talk,* ' Of As-
' tronomy and Astrology.'

[4] So also in Pico's *Heptaplus*
the same kind of speculation is
much indulged in.

was led astray by his unsuspecting confidence in the genuineness of the Dionysian writings, into doubtful speculations of this kind, and notions upon even practical points, from which his own English common sense, if left to itself, might have protected him, it is but fair to point out also the evidence contained in this manuscript, of that zeal for ecclesiastical reform which the purity of the Dionysian ideal of the priest-hood at all events helped to inflame. There is one passage especially, in which he bursts out into an indignant rebuke of those ' narrow and small minds ' who do not see that constant contention and litigation about secular matters on the part of the clergy ' is a ' scandal to the church.' Their folly, he thinks, would be ridiculous, were it not rather to be wept over than laughed at, seeing that it so injures and almost destroys the church. ' These lost fools (he continues) ' of which this our age is full, amongst whom there ' are some who, to say the least, ought not to be clergy-' men at all, but who nevertheless are regarded as ' bishops in the church—these lost fools, I say, utterly ' ignorant of gospel and apostolic doctrine, ignorant of ' Divine justice, ignorant of Christian truth, are wont ' to say, that the cause of God, the rights of the church, ' the patrimony of Christ, the possessions of priests, ' *ought* to be defended by them, and that it would be ' a sin to neglect to defend them. O narrowness, ' O blindness of these men ! . . . with eyes duller ' than fishes ! ' Colet then points out how the church is brought into disrepute with the laity by their worldly proceedings ; whereas, if the clergy lived in the love of God and their neighbour, how soon would their ' true piety, religion, charity, goodness towards men,

'simplicity, patience, tolerance of evil . . . . conquer
'evil with good! How would it stir up the minds
'of men everywhere to think well of the church of
'Christ! How would they favour it, love it, be good
'and liberal towards it, heap gift upon gift upon it,
'when they saw in the clergy no avarice, no abuse of
'their liberality!'. . . . Finally, after saying that to
a priesthood seeking first the promotion and extension
of the kingdom of God upon earth, neither asking nor
expecting anything, all things would have been added;
and asking with what face those, who differ from the
laity only in dress and external appearance, can demand much from the laity, Colet exclaims, 'Good
'God! how should we be ashamed of this descent into
'the world, if we were mindful of the love of God
'towards us, of the example of Christ, of the dignity
'of the Christian religion, of our name and profession.'[1]

Passing from this one example of Colet's zeal for ecclesiastical reform, there remains only to be mentioned
one other feature of this exposition of Colet's which
must not be overlooked : a feature which might seem
to show that Colet was not wholly unacquainted with
the writings of men of the school of Tauler and Thomas
à Kempis, and which seems to connect itself with a remark of Colet's, reported by Erasmus, that he had met
on his travels with some German monks, amongst whom
were still to be found traces of primitive religion.[2]
I allude to the warmth with which Colet urges the
necessity of following the perfect but not impossible [3]
example of Christ, of Christians being bound in a

---

[1] Emmanuel Col. MS. 3, 3, 12,
leaves d, 3 to d, 5, and Appendix
(B, e). See also leaf n, 2.

[2] Eras. *Op.* iii. p. 459, A.
[3] Leaf g, 4.

CHAP. II.

A.D. 1497.

relationship with Him, so close that their joint love for Christ shall form a bond of brotherhood between themselves more close than that of blood:[1] so that what is for the good of the brethren will become the test of what is lawful in Christian practice[2]—the earnestness with which he tried to realise the secret of that wonderful example, concluding that it lay in Christ's keeping himself as retired as possible from the world—from the lust of the flesh, the lust of the eye, and the pride of life—and as close as possible to God—in his whole soul being dedicated to God. 'He was,' writes Colet, altogether 'pious, kind, gentle, merciful, patient 'of evil, bearing injuries, in his own integrity shunning 'empty popular fame, forbidding both men and demons 'to publish his mighty power, in his goodness always 'doing good even to the evil, as his Father makes His 'sun to rise on the just and on the unjust. . . . His 'body He held altogether in obedience and service to 'his blessed mind . . .; eating after long fasts, sleeping 'after long watching . . .; caring nothing for what 'belongs to wealth and fortune. His eye was single, so 'that his whole body was full of light . . . . . Such is 'the leader whom we have on the heavenly road . . .; 'whom, without doubt, if we do not follow with our 'whole strength toward heaven, as far as we are able, 'we shall never get there!'[3]

Character of Christ.

Colet's love for St. Paul, but greater love for Christ.

If Colet had risen out of Neo-Platonism to Dionysius and from Dionysius to St. Paul, it is evident that he did not rest even there. How in the following few words, overflowing as they do with his personal love

---

[1] Emmanuel Col. MS. Leaf i, 1 to leaf i, 3.

[2] Leaf k, 7 and 8.
[3] Leaves g, 5 to g, 7.

for St. Paul, does he give vent to a still more tender
love and reverence for *Christ!*

'Here I stand amazed, and exclaim those words of
'*my Paul,* " Oh the depth of the riches of the wisdom
'" and knowledge of God!" O wisdom! wonderfully
'good to men and merciful, how justly thy loving-
'kindness can be called the " depth of riches "!—
'Thou who commending thy love towards us hast
'chosen to be so bountiful to us that Thou givest thy-
'self for us, that we may return to Thee and to God.
'O holy, O kind, O beneficent wisdom! O voice,
'word, and truth of God in man! truth-speaking and
'truth-acting! who hast chosen to teach us humanly
'that we may know divinely; who hast chosen to be
'in man that we may be in God; who lastly hast
'chosen in man to be humbled even unto death—the
'death even of the cross—that we may be exalted
'even unto life, the life even of God.' [1]

It may safely be concluded, that if Colet's manuscript
expositions preserved at Cambridge may be taken as
evidence of the nature of his public lectures, they may
well have excited all the interest which they seem to
have done. Doctors of Divinity, coming to listen at
first that they might find something definite to censure,
might well indeed find something to learn. Amongst
the students, probably, the seed found a soil in some
degree prepared to receive it. But it must have required
an effort on the part of the most candid and honest
adherents of the traditional school to reach the standpoint from which alone Colet's method of free critical

[1] Emmanuel Col. MS. Leaf f, 6, and Appendix (B, f).

interpretation could be found to be in perfect harmony with his evident love and reverence for the Scriptures. *They* attributed an extent of Divine inspiration to the apostle which placed his words on a level in authority with those of the Saviour himself ; while Colet, we are told (and some of the passages last quoted seem to confirm the statement), was wont to declare, ' that ' when he turned from the Apostles to the wonderful ' majesty of Christ, their writings, much as he loved ' them, seemed to him to become poor, as it were, in ' comparison ' [with the words of their Lord].[1]

Yet they could hardly fail to see, whether they would or not, that while their own system left the Scriptures hidden in the background, Colet's method brought them out into the light, and invested them with a sense of reality and sacredness which pressed them home at once to the heart.

VI. GROCYN'S DISCOVERY (1498 ?).

Colet was not alone at Oxford in his regard for the Pseudo-Dionysian writings.

Grocyn discovers that the Pseudo-Dionysius was not the disciple of St. Paul.

Grocyn was so impressed with the genuineness and value of the ' Celestial Hierarchy,' that he consented to deliver a course of lectures upon it, about this time, in St. Paul's Cathedral.   But having commenced his course by very strongly asserting its genuineness, and harshly condemning Laurentius Valla and others who

---

[1] ' Plurimum tribuebat Epistolis ' Apostolicis, sed ita suspiciebat ' admirabilem illam Christi majes- ' tatem ut ad hanc quodammodo ' sordescerent Apostolorum scrip- ta.'—Eras. *Op.* iii. p. 459, F. See also this view supported by Eras- mus in his *Ratio Veræ Theologiæ.* ' Nec fortassis absurdum fuerit, ' in sacris quoque voluminibus ' ordinem auctoritatis aliquem con- ' stituere,' &c.—Eras. *Op.* v. p. 92, C ; and *Ibid.* p. 132, C.

had started doubts, it chanced that when he had pro- CHAP. II.
ceeded with his lectures for some weeks, he became A.D. 1498.
himself convinced, by strong internal evidence, that
the work was not written by a disciple of St. Paul;
and being an honest man seeking for truth, and not
arguing for argument's sake, was obliged candidly to
confess the unpleasant discovery to his audience.[1]

What effect this unexpected discovery of Grocyn's Effects
had upon the mind of Colet we are not distinctly of the discovery
informed. Whether Grocyn was able to convince him on Colet's
of the truth of his mature judgment does not directly mind.
appear.[2] He had so earnestly embraced the Dionysian
writings, and they had produced so profound an impression upon his mind, that it may readily be believed
that he would be very unwilling to admit that they
were spurious. Nor, perhaps, was it needful that he
should do so. For, however clearly it might be proved
that they were not written by the disciple of St. Paul,
it did not therefore follow that they were merely a
forgery. The Pseudo-Dionysius, whoever he was, must
have been not the less a man of vast moral power and
deep Christian feeling; and possibly he may have had

---

[1] Eras. *Op.* vi. p. 503, F; *Annotationes in loco*, Acts xvii. v. 34. The edition of 1516 does not mention the anecdote at all. Those of 1519 and 1522 mention it as having occurred ' ante complures annos.' Also see ' Declamatio adversus Cen- ' suram Facultatis Theol. Parisien.' Eras. *Op.* ix. p. 917 and Epist. mccv. The former was written in 1530 or 1531, and in it he says :—' Is ante ' annos triginta, Londini in æde

' Divi Pauli,' &c. : which gives the date of Grocyn's lectures as some time before 1500 or 1501. The publication of the Paris edition of Dionysius, in 1498, may have called forth these lectures.

[2] Jewell, however, mentions John Colet as believing that the Areopagite was not the author of these ancient writings. — *Of Private Masse*, ed. 1611, p. 8.

no fraudulent intention in using the pseudonym of the Areopagite, if he did so. The conscience of the age in which he lived, so lax on the point of pious fraud, may possibly have sanctioned his doing so.

It has already been seen that, in accepting the Dionysian speculations, Colet did so because he believed Dionysius himself to have simply committed to writing what he had heard from the Apostles themselves, and because he felt bound to believe that he '*took the greatest pains to appear to know nothing '*according to this world, thinking it unworthy to mix '*up human reason with divine revelations.*' [1]

Supposing that Grocyn's discovery had convinced Colet that the speculations of the Dionysian writings were not of apostolic origin—were, in fact, products of merely ' human reason ' which the Pseudo-Dionysius had ' mixed up ' with Scripture truth, as Augustine and the Schoolmen had mixed up with it their scholastic speculations, it is clear that he would be bound by the principle set forth in the above passage, to reject the Dionysian speculations as he had already rejected those of the Schoolmen.

Colet
driven
more than
ever to the
Bible.
He would be bound to treat the speculations of the Pseudo-Dionysius as of no more authority than those of St. Augustine or Origen, and the practical result would be likely to be, that he would be thrown back more completely than ever upon the Bible itself, and continue all the more earnestly to apply to its interpretation the sound, common-sense, historical methods which he had already applied so successfully to the exposition of the Epistles of St. Paul.

---

[1] Vide supra, p. 82.

In the meantime it may be readily imagined that, to a man of such deep feeling and impulsive nature, as the occasional outbursts of burning zeal in his writings show Colet to have been, such a disappointment would leave a sore place to which he would not care often to recur in conversation with his friends.

Such a shock as Grocyn's discovery must have been to him, may have simply produced in his mind a sense of bewilderment ending in a suspended judgment. He may have returned to his accustomed work feeling more than ever the uncertainty of human speculations, an humbler, a stronger, though perhaps a sadder man, more than ever inclined to cling closely to the Scriptures and his beloved St. Paul, and even ready sometimes to turn with relief, as we are told he did with admiration, from the involved logic [1] of the Apostle to the simple majesty of Christ !

---

[1] 'Apostoli sermo . . (qui in 'hoc loco *artificiosissimus* est) . . .'   MS. on 1 *Corinthians,* Emmanuel Coll. leaf a, 6.

CHAPTER III.

I. ERASMUS COMES TO OXFORD (1498).

In the spring or summer of 1498, the foreign scholar —Erasmus of Rotterdam—arrived at Oxford, brought over to England by Lord Mountjoy from Paris.[1] Erasmus was an entire stranger in England ; he did not know a word of English, but was at once most hospitably received into the College of St. Mary the Virgin, by the prior Richard Charnock. Colet had

---

[1] The date of Erasmus's coming to England may be approximately fixed as follows. Epist. xxix. dated 12th April, and evidently written in 1500, after his visit to England, mentions a fever which nearly killed Erasmus *two years before*. Comparing this with what is said in the 'Life' prefixed to vol. i. of Eras. *Op.*, Epist. vi. vii. and viii., dated 3 Feb., 4 Feb., and 12 Feb., seem to belong to Feb. 1498. Epist. vi. ix. and v. seem to place his studies with Mountjoy, at Paris, in the spring of that year. Epist. xxii. seems to mention the projected visit to England. Epist. xiv. ' Londini tumultuarie,' 5 Dec., is evidently written after he had been to Oxford and seen Colet, Grocyn, and Linacre, and yet, comparatively soon after his arrival in England. It alludes to his coming to England, but gives no hint that he is going to leave England. In the winter of 1499–1500 he was at Oxford, intending to leave, but delayed by political reasons. He really did leave England 27 Jan. 1500. Whilst, therefore, it is just possible that Epist. xiv. may have been written in Dec. 1499, it is more probable that it was written in Dec. 1498, and that the first experience of Erasmus at Oxford had been during the previous summer and autumn. This seems to comport best both with Epist. vi. ix. v. and xxii., and also with the circumstances connected with his stay in England, mentioned in this chapter. See also the next note. The years attached to the early letters of Erasmus are not in the least to be relied on.

indeed, as already mentioned, heard Erasmus spoken
of at Paris as a learned scholar,[1] but as yet no work of
his had risen into note, nor was even his name generally known. He was scarcely turned thirty—just the
age of Colet ; [2] but in his wasted sallow cheeks and
sunken eyes were but few traces left of the physical
vigour of early manhood. In place of the glow of
health and strength, were lines which told that midnight oil, bad lodging, and the harassing life of a poor
student, driven about and ill-served as he had been,
had already broken what must have been at best a
frail constitution. But the worn scabbard told of the
sharpness and temper of the steel within. His was a The cha-
mind restless for mental work, now fighting through racter of
Erasmus.
the obstacles of ill-health and poverty, in pursuit of its
natural bent, as it had once had to fight its way out
of monastic thraldom to secure the freedom of action
which such a mind required.

Though well schooled and stored with learning, yet His object
he had not come to Oxford to teach, or to make a name in coming
to Oxford.
by display of intellectual power, but simply to add new
branches of knowledge to those already acquired.
Greek was now to be learned there—thanks to the
efforts of Grocyn and Linacre—and Erasmus had come
to Oxford bent upon adding a knowledge of Greek to
his Latin lore. To belong to that little knot of men

---

[1] Coletus Erasmo: Eras. Epist. xi.
[2] ' Hic (at Oxford) hominem
' nosse cœpi, nam eodem tum me
' Deus nescio quis adegerat ; natus
' tum erat annos ferme triginta, me
' minor duobus aut tribus mensibus.'
—Eras. *Op.* iii. p. 456, B. Erasmus,
according to his monument at Rotterdam (Eras. *Op.* i. (7)) was born

28 Oct. 1467. Colet would be born,
say, Jan. 1467–8, if three months
younger, and would be ' annos
' ferme triginta, in the spring of
' 1498.' According to Colet's monument he would be 31 at that date,
as he died 16 Sept. 1519, and the
inscription states ' vixit annos 53.'
Knight's *Colet*, p. 261.

north of the Alps who already knew Greek—whose number yet might be counted on his fingers—this had now become his immediate object of ambition. What he meant to do with his tools when he had got them, probably was a question to be decided by circumstances rather than by any very definite plan of his own. To gain his living by taking pupils, and to live the life of a scholar at some continental university, was probably the future floating indistinctly before him.

Erasmus
is intro-
duced to
Colet.
Prior Charnock seems to have at once appreciated Erasmus. He did all in his power to give him a warm welcome to the university.[1] He seems to have taken him at once to hear Colet lecture ; [2] and he very soon informed Colet that his new guest turned out to be no ordinary man.[3] Upon this report Colet wrote to Erasmus a graceful and gentlemanly letter,[4] giving him a hearty welcome to England and to Oxford, and professing his readiness to serve him.

Erasmus replied, warmly accepting Colet's friendship, but at the same time telling him plainly that he would find in him a man of slender or rather of no fortune, with no ambition, but warm and open-hearted, simple, liberal, honest, but timid, and of few words. Beyond this he must expect nothing. But if Colet could love such a man—if he thought such a man worthy of his friendship—he might then count him as his own.[5]

Colet *did* think such a man worthy of his friendship,

---

[1] Epist. xii. Sixtinus Erasmo.
[2] Else how could Erasmus describe Colet's style of speaking so clearly in his first letter to him ?— Epist. xli.

[3] 'Virum optimum et bonitate 'præditum singulari.' — Eras. Epist. xi.
[4] Coletus Erasmo : Epist. xi.
[5] Eras. Epist. xli. *Op.* iii. p. 40, D.

and from that moment Erasmus and he were the best
of friends.   The lord mayor's son, born to wealth and
all that wealth could command, whilst steeling his
heart against the allurements of city and court life,
eagerly received into his bosom-friendship the poor
foreign scholar, whom fortune had used so hardly,
whose orphaned youth had been embittered by the
treachery of dishonest guardians, and who, robbed
of his slender patrimony and cast adrift upon the
world without resources, had hitherto scarcely been
able to keep himself from want by giving lessons to
private pupils.   Whether he was likely to find in
the foreign scholar the fulfilment of his yearnings
after fellowship, it will be for further chapters of
this history to disclose.

II. TABLE-TALK ON THE SACRIFICE OF CAIN AND ABEL
(1498 ?).

It chanced that, after the delivery of a Latin sermon,
the preacher—an accomplished divine—was a guest at
the long table in one of the Oxford halls.   Colet pre-
sided.   The divine took the seat of honour to the left
of Colet ; Charnock, the hospitable prior, sat opposite ;
Erasmus next to the divine ; and a lawyer opposite to
him.   Below them, on either side, a mixed and nameless group filled up the table.   At first the tide of
table-talk ebbed and flowed upon trivial subjects.
The conversation turned at length upon the sacrifices
of Cain and Abel—why the one was accepted and the
other not.

Colet—if we may judge from the earnest way in
which, in his exposition of the Epistle to the Romans,
he had urged the uselessness of outward sacrifices,

unless accompanied by that *living sacrifice* of heart and mind which they were meant to typify—was not likely to advocate any view which should attribute the acceptance of the one offering and the rejection of the other, merely to any difference in the offerings themselves. He would be sure to place the difference in the *character of the men.* Colet seems on this occasion to have done so, and to have fancied he saw in the different occupations chosen by the two brothers evidence of the different spirit under which they acted. The exact course of the conversation we have no means of following. All we know is, that Colet took one side, and Erasmus and the divine the other, and that the chief bone of contention was the suggestion thrown out by Colet, that Cain had in the first instance

The difference between Cain and Abel in the *men,* not in the offerings.

offended the Almighty by his distrust in the Divine beneficence, and too great confidence in his own art and industry, and that this was proved by his having been the first to attempt to till the cursed ground ; while Abel, with greater resignation, and resting content with what nature still spontaneously yielded, had chosen the gentle occupation of a shepherd.[1]

There may have been something fanciful in the view urged by Colet, but it is evident that it covered a truth which he could not give up, however hard and long his opponents might argue.

Erasmus was astonished at Colet's earnestness and power. He seemed to him ' like one inspired. In his

---

[1] ' Dicebat Coletus, Caym ea ' primum culpa Deum offendisse, ' quod tanquam conditoris benignitate diffisus, suæque nimium confisus industriæ, terram primus ' prosciderit, quum Abel, sponte ' nascentibus contentus, oves paverit.'—Eras. Epist. xliv. *Op.* iii. p. 42, F. Compare MS. G. g. 4, 26, fols. 4–6 and 29, 30, and Erasmus's Paraphrases, *in loco*, Hebrews xi. 4.

' voice, his eye, his whole countenance and mien, he
' seemed raised, as it were, out of himself.' [1]

Erasmus and the divine both felt themselves beaten ;
but it is not always easy for the vanquished to yield
gracefully, and the discussion, growing warmer as it
proceeded, might have risen even to intemperate heat,
had not Erasmus dexterously wound it round to a
happy conclusion by pretending to remember that he
had once met with a curious story about Cain in an
old wormeaten manuscript whose title-page time had
destroyed. The disputants were all attention, and
Erasmus, having thus tickled their curiosity, was
induced to tell the story, after extracting a promise
from the listeners that they would not treat it as a
fable. He then drew upon his ready wit, and
improvised the following story :—

' This Cain was a man of art and industry, and
' withal greedy and covetous. He had often heard
' from his parents how, in the garden from which they
' had been driven, the corn grew as tall as alder-bushes
' unchoked by tares, thorns, or thistles. When he
' brooded over these things, and saw how meagre a crop
' the ground produced, after all his pains in tilling it, he
' was tempted to resort to treachery. He went to the
' angel who was the appointed guardian of paradise,
' and, plying him with crafty arts, tempted him with
' promises to give him secretly just a few grains from
' the luxuriant crops of Eden. He argued that so small
' a theft could not be noticed, and that if it were,

---

[1] ' At ille unus vincebat omnes ;
' visus est sacro quodam furore de-
' bacchari, ac nescio quid homine
' sublimius augustiusque præferre.

'Aliud sonabat vox, aliud tuebantur
' oculi, alius vultus, alius adspectus,
' majorque videri, afflatus est nu-
' mine quando.'—Eras. *Op.* iii. 42. F.

' the angel could but fall to the condition men were in.
' Why was his condition better than theirs ? Men were
' driven out of the garden because they had eaten the
' apple. He, being set to guard the gate, could enjoy
' neither paradise nor heaven. He was not even free,
' as they were, to wander where he liked upon earth !
' Many good things were still left to men. With care
' and labour the world might be cultivated, and human
' misery so far lessened by discoveries and arts of all
' kinds, that at length men might not need to be
' envious even of Eden. It was true that they were
' infested by diseases, but human art would find the
' cure for these in time. Perhaps some day something
' might even be found which would make life immortal.
' When man by his industry had made the earth into
' one great garden, the angel would be shut out from
' it, as well as from heaven and Eden. Let him do
' what he could for men without harm to himself, and
' then men would do what they could for him in re-
' turn. The worst man will carry the weakest cause, if
' he be but the best talker. A few grains were obtained
' by stealth, and carefully sown by Cain. These being
' sprung up, produced an increased number. The mul-
' tiplied seed was again sown, and the process repeated
' time after time. Before many harvests had passed
' the produce of the stolen seed covered a wide tract
' of country. When what was taking place on earth
' became too conspicuous to be longer concealed from
' heaven, God was exceedingly wroth. " I see," He
' said, " how this fellow delights in toil and sweat ; I
' " will heap it upon him to his fill." He spoke, and
' sent a dense army of ants and locusts to blight
' Cain's cornfields. He added to these hailstorms and
' hurricanes. He sent another angel to guard the gate

' of paradise, and imprisoned the one who had favoured
' man in a human body. Cain tried to appease God
' by burnt-offerings of fruits, but found that the smoke
' of his sacrifice would not rise towards heaven.
' Understanding from this that the anger of God was
' determined against him, *he despaired*!' [1]

Thus, with this clever impromptu fable did Erasmus
gracefully contrive to throw the weight of his altered
opinion into Colet's scale, and at the same time to
restore the whole party to wonted good-humour.
Meanwhile what he had seen of Colet made a deep
impression upon him. He himself declared that he
never had enjoyed an after-dinner talk so much.
It was, he said, wanting in nothing.[2]

This little glimpse given by Erasmus himself of his
first experience of Oxford life is of value, not only as
revealing his own early impressions of Colet and Oxford,
but also as throwing some little light upon the position
which Colet himself had taken in the University after a
year's labour at his post. That he should be chosen to
preside at the long table on this occasion was a mark
at least of honour and respect ; while the way in which
he evidently gave the tone to the conversation, and
became so thoroughly the central figure in the group,
shows that this respect was true homage paid to
character, and not to mere wealth and station. Then,
again, the fact that Erasmus, a stranger, without purse
or name, should have had assigned to him the second
seat of honour, second only to the special guest of the
day, was in itself a proof of the same hearty appreciation by Charnock and Colet of character, without regard

---

[1] Eras. Epist. xliv.
[2] Erasmus Sixtino, Epist. xliv. *Op.* iii. p. 42, C.

to rank or station.   Would it have been so everywhere ?   Had Erasmus been so treated at Paris ? [1]

Erasmus
delighted
with Colet
and
Charnock.
No wonder that the letters of Erasmus, written
during these his first months spent at Oxford, should
bear witness to the delight with which he found himself received, all stranger as he was, into the midst of
a group of warm-hearted friends, with whom, for the
first time in his life, he found what it was to be at
home. ' I cannot tell you,' he wrote to his friend Lord
Mountjoy, ' how delighted I am with your England.
' With two such friends as Colet and Charnock, I
' would not refuse to live even in Scythia ! ' [2]

III.   CONVERSATION BETWEEN COLET AND ERASMUS ON THE SCHOOLMEN (1498 or 1499).

But although Erasmus had formed the closest friendship with Colet, and was learning more and more to
understand and admire him, it was long before he was
sufficiently one in heart and purpose to induce Colet to
unburden to him his whole mind.

Scholastic
skill of
Erasmus.
He did so only by degrees.   When he thought his
friend really in earnest in any passing argument he
would tell him fully what his own views were.   But
Colet hated the Schoolmen's habit of arguing for
argument's sake, and felt that Erasmus was as yet
not wholly weaned from it.   It was a habit which
had been fostered by the current practice of asserting

---

[1] See his colloquy, *Ichthyophagia*, in which he describes his college experience at Paris, especially his physical hardships.   The latter are probably caricatured, and perhaps too much magnified for the description to be taken literally.

[2] Erasmus to Lord Mountjoy : Epist. xlii. Oxoniæ, 1498.

wiredrawn distinctions and abstruse propositions
for the mere display of logical skill; and Colet's
reverence for truth shrunk from this public vivisec-
tion of it merely to feed the pride of the dissector.
It pained and disgusted him.

Erasmus had been educated at Paris in the
' straitest sect ' of Scholastic theologians. He had
there studied theology in the college of the Scotists,
and been trained in that logical subtlety for which
the school of Duns Scotus was distinguished.[1]

But he found Colet, instead of regarding the Scotists Colet dis-
likes the
Scotists.
as wonderfully clever, declaring that ' they seemed to
' him to be stupid and dull and anything but clever.
' For to cavil about different sentences and words,
' now to gnaw at this and now at that, and to dissect
' everything bit by bit, seemed to him to be the mark
' of a poor and barren mind.' [2]

But Colet had not quarrelled only with the logical
method of the Schoolmen; he owed the scholastic
philosophy itself a still deeper grudge.

The system of the Schoolmen professed to embrace What the
system
of the
School-
men was,
the whole range of universal knowledge. It was not
confined strictly to religion; it included, also, questions
of philosophy and science. And these were settled by
isolated texts from the Bible, or dicta of the earlier
Schoolmen, and not by the investigation of facts. A
theology so dogmatic and capricious could consistently
admit of no progress. Every discovery of science or
philosophy, contrary to the dicta of the Schoolmen,
must be regarded as a crime. It was the logical result
of an inherent vice in the system that Brunos and

---

[1] 'Beatus Rhenanus Cæsari Ca-
' rolo.'—Eras. *Op.* i. leaf * * * 1.

[2] Eras. *Op.* iii. p. 458, D and E.

Galileos, in after ages, were tortured by successors of the Schoolmen into the denial of inconvenient truths.

This might do all very well in stagnant times, but in an age when the new art of printing was reviving ancient learning, and new worlds were turning up in hitherto untracked seas, men who, like Colet, entered into the spirit of the new era, soon found out that the *summæ theologiæ* of the Schoolmen were no sum of theology at all; that their science and philosophy were grossly deficient; and that if Christianity must in truth stand or fall with scholastic dogmas, then the accession of new light would be likely to lead honest enquirers after truth to reject it, and to accept in its place the refined semi-pagan philosophy which had accompanied the revival of learning in Italy. Yet these were the alternatives which the Schoolmen, in common with the champions of dogmatic creeds in all ages, tried to force upon mankind. Their cry was, as that of their scholastic successors has been, and is, '*Our* Christianity or *none.*'

Colet had seen in Italy which of these two alternatives those who came within the influence of the new learning were inclined to take. But he had seen or heard, too, in Italy, of a third alternative. He had found a Christianity, not scholastic, not dogmatic, which did not seem to him to have anything to fear from free enquiry, for it was itself one of those facts which free enquiry had brought once more to light: the reproduction of its ancient records in their original languages was itself one of the results of the new learning. He had found in the New Testament a simple record of the facts of the life of Christ, and a few apostolic letters to the churches. It had brought him, not to an endless

web of propositions to the acceptance of which he
must school his mind, but to a *person* whom to love,
in whom to trust, and for whom to work. He would
not rest even in the teaching of his beloved St. Paul.
He had been taught by the Apostle to look up from on the
him to the 'wonderful majesty of Christ;'[1] and loyalty of Christ
to Christ had become the ruling passion of his life.[2] 'Apostles'
Creed.'

Having rejected the *summœ theologiœ* of the Schoolmen, even before his faith had been shaken, by Grocyn's discovery, in Dionysian speculations, his disappointment also in the latter would seem to have driven
him back upon the Scriptures, upon the writings of St.
Paul, above all upon Christ himself; until at last he
had seemed to find in the simple facts of the Apostles'
Creed the true sum of Christian theology. Having en-
trenched his faith behind its simple bulwarks, he could
look calmly out upon the world of philosophy and
nature, with a mind free to accept truth wherever he
might find it, without anxiety as to what the revival of
ancient learning, or the discoveries of new-born science,
might reveal, anxious chiefly to find out his own life's
work and duty, and right heartily to do it.

And having escaped the trammels of scholastic
theology himself, he could urge others also to do the advice
same. When, therefore, young theological students logical
came to him in despair, on the point of throwing up students
theological study altogether, because of the vexed the Bible
questions in which they found it involved, and dread- and the
ing lest in these days, when everything was called in Apostles'
question, they might be found unorthodox, he was Creed.

---

[1] Eras. *Op.* iii. pt. 1, p. 459, F.

[2] 'Siquidem magnum erat, Cole-
'tum, in ea fortuna, constanter

'sequutum esse, non quo vocabat
'natura, sed quo Christus,' &c.—
Ibid. p. 461, E.

CHAP. III.
———
A.D. 1498.

wont, it seems, to tell them ' to keep firmly to the
' Bible and the Apostles' Creed, and let divines, if they
' like, dispute about the rest.' [1]

But Erasmus as yet had far from attained the
same standpoint.

Erasmus
came to
England
disgusted
with
theology.

He was himself in the very position above described.
His experience in the Scotist college in Paris had not
been lost upon him.   It was not only that its filthy
chambers and diet of rotten eggs [2] had ruined his
constitution for life.   He had contracted within its
walls a disgust of all theological study.   He describes
himself as, previously to his visit to England, ' abhor-
' ring the study of theology ; ' and gives, as his double
reason for it, the fear lest he might run foul of settled
opinions ; and lest, if he did so, he should be branded
with the name of ' heretic.' [3]

Disgusted, however, as he was with theology, all his
theological training had hitherto been scholastic in its

---

[1] See the following extract from
the colloquy of Erasmus, ' *Pietas*
' *puerilis*,' edition Argent. 1522,
leaf e, 4, and Basileæ, 1526, p. 92,
and Eras. *Op.* i. p. 653.

' *Erasmus*. Many abstain from
' divinity because they are afraid
' lest they should waver in the
' catholic faith, when they see there
' is nothing which is not called in
' question.

' *Gaspar*. I believe firmly what
' I read in the Holy Scriptures,
' and the creed called the Apostles',
' and I don't trouble my head any
' further. I leave the rest to be
' disputed and defined by the clergy,
' if they please.

' *Erasmus*. What *Thales* taught
' you that philosophy ?

' *Gaspar*. I was for some time in
' domestic service ' [as More was in
the house of Cardinal Morton before he was sent to Oxford] ' with
' that honestest of men, *John Colet*.
' *He imbued me with these precepts.*'
See Argent. 1522, leaf c, 4.

[2] ' Illic in collegio Montis Acuti
' ex putribus ovis et cubiculo infecto
' concepit morbum, h.e. malam cor-
' poris, antea purissimi, affectio-
nem.' *Vita*, prefixed to Eras. *Op.* i.
written by himself. See the letter
to Conrad Goclenius.

[3] ' A studio theologiæ abhorre-
' bat, quod sentiret animum non pro-
' pensum, ut omnia illorum funda-
' menta subverteret ; deinde futu-
' rum, ut hæretici nomen inurere-
' tur.'—*Vita*, prefixed to Eras. *Op.* i.

character, and, apart from his disgust of theology in
general, he does not seem as yet to have contracted any
special disgust of scholastic theology in particular.
He was still too much enamoured of the logic of the
Schoolmen, and too often was found to take the
Schoolmen's side in his discussions with his friend.

Colet and Erasmus [1] had been conversing one day
upon the character of the Schoolmen. Colet had expressed his sweeping disapprobation of the whole class.
Erasmus, whose knowledge of their works was, as he
afterwards acknowledged, by no means deep, at length
ventured, in renewing the conversation at another time,
to except Thomas Aquinas from the common herd, as
worthy of praise, alleging in his favour that he seemed
to have studied both the Scriptures and ancient literature—which doubtless he had. Colet made no reply.
And when Erasmus pursued the subject still further,
Colet again passed it off, feigning inattention. But
when Erasmus, in the course of further conversation,
again expressed the same opinion in favour of Aquinas,
and spoke more strongly even than before, Colet turned
his full eye upon him in order to learn whether he
really were speaking in earnest ; and concluding that it
was so—' What,' he said passionately, ' do you extol
' to me such a man as Aquinas ? If he had not been
' very arrogant indeed, he would not surely so rashly
' and proudly have taken upon himself to define *all*
' things. And unless his spirit had been somewhat
' worldly, he would not surely have corrupted the
' whole teaching of Christ by mixing with it his
' profane philosophy.' [2]

---

[1] See for this anecdote, Eras.
Op. iii. p. 458, E and F.

[2] ' Tanquam afflatus spiritu quo-
' dam, " Quid tu, inquit, mihi præ-

Erasmus was taken aback, as he had been at the discussion at the public table. He had again been arguing without sufficient knowledge to justify his having any strong opinion at all. Which side he took on the question at issue was a matter almost of indifference to him. But he saw plainly that it was not so with Colet. His first allusion to Aquinas, Colet had resolutely shunned. When compelled to speak his opinion, his soul was moved to its depths, and had burst forth into this passionate reply. There must be something real and earnest at the bottom of Colet's dislike for Aquinas, else he could not have spoken thus.

So Erasmus betakes himself to the more careful study of the great schoolman's writings.

Erasmus
studies
Aquinas.
One may picture him taking down from the shelf the 'Summa Theologiæ,' and, as the first step towards the exploration of its contents, turning to the prologue. He reads :—

The
'Summa.'
' Seeing that the teacher of catholic truth should ' instruct not only those advanced in knowledge, but ' that it is a part of his duty to teach *beginners* (ac-' cording to the words of the Apostle to the Corin-' thians, " even as unto babes in Christ, I have fed you ' " with milk and not with strong meat "), it is our ' purpose in this book to treat of those things which ' pertain to the Christian religion in a manner adapted ' to the instruction of beginners.

' For we have considered that novices in this learn-' ing have been very much hindered in [the study of]

' " dicas istum, qui nisi habuisset
' " multum arrogantiæ, non tanta
' " temeritate tantoque supercilio
' " definisset omnia; et nisi habuis-
' " set aliquid spiritus mundani,

' " non ita totam Christi doctrinam
' " sua profana philosophia conta-
' " minasset."'—Eras. *Op.* iii. p.
458, F.

' works written by others ; partly, indeed, on account
' of the multiplication of useless questions, articles and
' arguments, and partly [for other reasons]. To avoid
' these and other difficulties we shall endeavour,
' relying on Divine assistance, to treat of those things
' which belong to sacred learning, so far as the subject
' will admit, with *brevity* and clearness.'

What could be better or truer than this ? Erasmus
might almost have fancied that Colet himself had
written these words, so fully do they seem to fall in
with his views. But turning from the prologue,
nothing surely could open the eyes of Erasmus more
thoroughly to the real nature of scholastic theology
than a further glance at the body of the treatise. For
what was he to think of a system of theology a ' *brief* '
compendium of which covered no fewer than 1150
folio pages, each containing 2000 words ! And what
was he to think of the wisdom of that Christian doctor
who prescribed this ' Summa ' as ' *milk* ' especially
adapted for the sustenance of theological ' *babes* ' ! To
be told first to digest forty-three propositions concerning the nature of God, each of which embraced several
distinct articles separately discussed and concluded in
the eighty-three folios devoted to this branch of the
subject ; then fifteen similar propositions regarding
the nature of *angels*, embracing articles such as
these :—

Scholastic
' milk for
babes.'

Whether an angel can be in more than one place at
one and the same time ?

Whether more angels than one can be in one and the
same place at the same time ?

Whether angels have local motion ?

And whether, if they have, they pass through inter-
mediate space ? [1]

—then ten propositions regarding *the Creation*, consisting of an elaborate attempt to bring into harmony the
work of the six days recorded in Genesis with mediæval
notions of astronomy ; then forty-five propositions respecting the nature of *man* before and after the Fall,
the physical condition of the human body in Paradise,
the mode by which it was preserved immortal by eating of the tree of life, the place where man was created
before he was placed in Paradise, &c. ; and then, having
mastered the above subtle propositions, stated ' briefly
' and clearly ' in 216 of the aforesaid folio pages, to be
told for his consolation and encouragement that he had
now mastered *not quite one-fifth* part of this ' first book '
for beginners in theological study, and that these propositions, and more than five times as many, were to be
regarded by him as the settled doctrine of the Catholic
Church !—what student could fail either to be crushed
under the dead weight of such a creed, or to rise up,
and, like Samson, bursting its green withes, discard
and disown it altogether ?

Erasmus
goes over
to Colet's
view.

No marvel that Erasmus was obliged to confess
that, in the process of further study of the works of
Aquinas, his former high opinion had been modified.[2]
He could understand now how it was that Colet
could hardly control his indignation at the thought,
how the simple facts of Christianity had been corrupted by the admixture of the subtle philosophy of
this ' best of the Schoolmen.'

[1] *Summa*, i. quest. 52, 53.
[2] ' Omnino decessit aliquid meæ ' de illo existimationi.'—Eras. *Op.*
iii. pt. 1, 458, F.

And yet we may well be free to own that Colet's not
unnatural hatred of the scholastic philosophy had
blinded him in some degree to the personal merits of
the early Schoolmen.   Deeper knowledge of the history of their times, and study of the personal character
at least of some of them, might have enabled him not
only to temper his hatred, but even to recognise that
they occupied in their day a standpoint not widely
different altogether even from his own.

For as earnestly as Colet himself was now seeking   The merit
to bring the Christianity and advanced thought of *his*   of the
early
age into harmony, the early Schoolmen had tried to   School-
do the same thing in *theirs*.   The misfortune of the   men.
Schoolmen was, that they had inherited from St.
Augustine, and the Pseudo-Dionysius, the vicious tendency to fill up blanks in theology by indulging in
hypotheses, capable of receiving the sanction of ecclesiastical authority, and then to be treated as established
although altogether unverified by facts.   They had also
to harmonise the dogmatic theology so manufactured
with a scientific system as dogmatic as itself.   For
while theologians had been indulging in hypotheses
respecting ' original sin,' ' absolute predestination,' and
' irresistible grace,' natural philosophers had been indulging in similar hypotheses respecting the ' crys-
' talline spheres,' ' epicycloids,' and ' *primum mobile.*' [1]

---

[1] See *The Praise of Folly*, Eras.
Op. iv. p. 462, where the dogmatic
science of the age is as severely
satirised by Erasmus as the dogmatic theology of the Schoolmen.
Thus Folly is made to say :—' With
' what ease, truly, do they indulge
' in day-dreams (*delirant*), when
' they invent innumerable worlds,
' and measure the sun, moon, and
' stars, and the earth, as though by
' thumb and thread ; and render
' a reason for thunder, winds,
' eclipses, and other inexplicable
' things, without the least hesita-
' tion, as though they had been
' the secret architects of all the
' works of nature, or as though

And seeing that the method by which the School-men attempted to fuse these *two* dogmatic systems into *one*, itself consisted of a still further indulgence in the same vicious mode of procedure, it was but natural that their attempt as a whole, however well meant, should leave ' confusion worse confounded.'

Still it must not be forgotten that they did succeed by this vicious process in reconciling theology and science to the satisfaction of their own dogmatic age. This praise is, at least, their due.   On the other hand, their successors in the fifteenth and sixteenth centuries could not put forward any such claims for themselves. *They* did not succeed in harmonising the theology and the advanced thought of *their* age.   They strained every nerve to keep them hopelessly apart.   They blindly held on to a worn-out system inherited from their far worthier predecessors, and spent their strength in denouncing, in no measured terms, the scientific spirit and inductive method of the ' new ' learning.'

The de-merits of their suc-cessors.

Hence there can be little doubt that Colet's hatred of what in his day was in truth a huge and bewildering mass of dreary and lifeless subtlety, was a just and righteous hatred.   And though it took some time for Erasmus thoroughly to accept it, he could in after years, when Colet was no more, endorse, from the bottom of his heart, Colet's advice to young theolo-gical students : ' *Keep to the Bible and the Apostles'* ' *Creed ; and let divines, if they like, dispute about* ' *the rest.'*

' they had come down to us from | ' *and whose conjectures nature is*
' the council of the gods.   *At whom* | ' *mightily amused !* '

IV. ERASMUS FALLS IN LOVE WITH THOMAS MORE (1498).

Amongst the broken gleams of light which fall, here and there only, upon the Oxford intercourse of Erasmus with Colet, there are one or two which reveal an already existing friendship with Thomas More, but unfortunately without disclosing how it had begun.

Erasmus, when passing through London on his way to Oxford, had probably been introduced by Lord Mountjoy to his brilliant young friend. It is even possible that there may be a foundation of fact in the story that they had met for the first time, unknown to each other, at the lord mayor's table, or, as is more likely still, at the table of the *ex*-lord mayor, Sir Henry Colet. Erasmus, having perhaps been told Colet's saying, that there was but one genius in England, and that his name was Thomas More, may have been set opposite to him at table without knowing who he was. More in his turn may have been told of the logical subtlety of the great scholar newly arrived from the Scotist college in Paris, without having been personally introduced to him. If this were so, the rest of the story may easily be true. They are said to have got into argument during dinner, Erasmus, in Scotist fashion, 'defending the worser part,' till finding in his young opponent ' a readier wit than ' ever he had before met withal,' he broke forth into the exclamation, ' *Aut tu es Morus aut nullus* ; ' to which the ready tongue of More retorted—so runs the story, ' *Aut tu es Erasmus aut Diabolus.*' [1] Whether at the lord mayor's table, or elsewhere, they *had* become acquainted, and a correspondence had grown up

---

[1] Cresacre More's *Life of Sir Thomas More*, p. 93.

I

between them, one letter of which, like a solitary waif, has been left stranded on the shore of the gulf which has swallowed the rest. It reads thus :—

Erasmus Thomæ Moro suo, S.D.

' I scarcely can get any letters, wherefore I have
' showered down curses on the head of this letter-carrier
' by whose laziness or treachery I fancy it must be
' that I have been disappointed of the most eagerly ex-
' pected letters of my dear More (Mori mei). For that
' you have failed on your part I neither want nor ought
' to suspect. Albeit, I expostulated with you most
' vehemently in my last letter. Nor am I afraid that
' you are at all offended by the liberty I took, for you
' are not ignorant of that Spartan method of fighting
' " usque ad cutem." This joking aside, I do entreat
' you, sweetest Thomas, that you will make amends
' with interest for the suffering occasioned me by the
' too long continued deprivation of yourself and your
' letters. I expect, in short, not a letter, but a huge
' bundle of letters, which would weigh down even an
' Egyptian porter,'

.   .   .   .

' Vale jucundissime More.[1]

' Oxoniæ : Natali Simonis et Judæ. 1499.'

Friend-
ship
between
More and
Erasmus.

Such being the friendship already existing between them, and beginning to show itself in the use of those endearing superlatives without which Erasmus, from the first to the last, never could write a letter to More, it is not surprising that, as winter came on, Erasmus should take the opportunity afforded by the approach-

---

[1] Erasmi aliquot Epistolæ: Paris, 1524, p. 33. Eras. *Op.* iii. Epist. | lxiii. 1521 ed. p. 291. Whether written in 1498 or 1499 is doubtful.

ing vacation for a visit to London. Accordingly we get one chance glimpse of him there, writing a letter to one of his friends, and expressing his delight with everything he had met with in England.

Staying as he most likely was with Mountjoy or with More, enjoying the warmth of their friendship, and feeling himself at home in London as he had done in Oxford, but never had done before anywhere else, it was natural that the foreign scholar should paint, in the warmest colours, this land of friends. Especially of Mountjoy, who had brought him to England, and who found him the means of living at Oxford, he would naturally speak in the highest terms. Such was the politeness, the goodnature, and affectionateness of his noble patron, that he would willingly follow him, he said, *ad inferos*, if need be.

Nor was it only the warm-heartedness of his English friends which filled him with delight. His purpose in coming to Oxford he declared to be fully answered. He had come to England because he could not raise the means for a longer journey to Italy. To prosecute his studies in Italy had been for years an object of anxious yearning ; but now, after a few months' experience of Oxford life, he wrote to his friend, who was himself going to Italy, ' that he had found in ' England so much polish and learning—not showy, ' shallow learning, but profound and exact, both in ' Latin and Greek—that now he would hardly care ' much about going to Italy at all, except for the ' sake of having been there.' ' When,' he added, ' I ' listen to my friend Colet it seems to me like listening ' to Plato himself. In Grocyn, who does not admire ' the wide range of his knowledge ? What could be

I 2

' more searching, deep, and refined than the judgment
' of Linacre ? ' And after this mention of Colet,
Grocyn, and Linacre, he adds : ' Whenever did nature
' mould a character more gentle, endearing, and
' happy than Thomas More's ? ' [1]

Erasmus
falls in
love with
More.

So that while here, as elsewhere, Colet seems to
take his place again as the chief of the little band of
English friends, we learn from this letter that the
picture would not have been complete without the
figure of the fascinating youth with whom Erasmus,
like the rest of them, had fallen in love.

The letter itself was written to Robert Fisher, from
London ' tumultuarie,' 5th December, in 1498 or 1499.

V. DISCUSSION BETWEEN ERASMUS AND COLET ON ' THE
' AGONY IN THE GARDEN,' AND ON THE INSPIRATION
OF THE SCRIPTURES (1499).

Erasmus
attributes
the agony
of Christ
to fear of
death.

The greater part of 1499 was spent by Erasmus
apparently at Oxford. On one occasion Colet and
Erasmus were spending an afternoon together.[2] Their
conversation fell upon the agony of Christ in the
garden. They soon, as usual, found that they did not
agree. Erasmus, following the common explanation
of the Schoolmen, saw only in the agony suffered
by the Saviour that natural fear of a cruel death to
which in his human nature he submitted as one of
the incidents of humanity. It seemed to him that in

---

[1] Erasmus Roberto Piscatori :
Epist. xiv.

[2] The incidents related in this
section are taken from *Disputatiuncula de Tædio, Pavore, Tristitiâ*

*Jesu, instante Supplicio Crucis,
deque Verbis, quibus visus est Mortem deprecari, ' Pater, si fieri potest,
' transeat a me calix iste.'*—Eras.
Op. v. pp. 1265–1294.

His character as truly *man*, left for the moment un-
aided by His divinity, the prospect of the anguish in
store for Him might well wring from Him that cry of
fearful and trembling human nature, ' Father, if it
' be possible, let this cup pass from me ! ' while the
further words, ' not my will but Thine be done,'
proved, he thought, that He had not only felt, but
conquered, this human fear and weakness. Erasmus
further supported this view by adducing the commonly
received scholastic distinction between what Christ
felt as *man* and what He felt as *God*, alleging that it
was only as *man* that He thus suffered.

    Colet dissented altogether from his friend's opinion.
It might be the commonly received interpretation of
recent divines, but in spite of that he declared his own
entire disapproval of it. Nothing could, he thought,
be more inconsistent with the exceeding love of Christ,
than the supposition that, when it came to the point,
He shrank in dread from that very death which He
desired to die in His great love of men. It seemed
utterly absurd, he said, to suppose that while so many
martyrs have gone to torture and death patiently and
even with joy—the sense of pain being lost in the
abundance of their love—Christ, who was love itself,
who came into the world for the very purpose of delivering guilty man by his own innocent death, should
have shrunk either from the ignominy or from the
bitterness of the cross. The sweat of great drops of
blood, the exceeding sorrow even unto death, the
touching entreaty to His Father that the cup might pass
from Him—was all this to be attributed to the mere
fear of death ? Colet had rather set it down to anything but that. For it lies in the essence of love, he

said, that it should cast out fear, turn sorrow into joy, think nothing of itself, sacrifice everything for others. It could not be that He who loved the human race more than anyone else should be inconstant and fearful in the prospect of death. In confirmation of this view he referred to St. Jerome, who alone of all the church fathers had, he thought, shown true insight into the real cause of Christ's agony in the garden. St. Jerome had attributed the Saviour's prayer, that the cup might pass from Him, not to the fear of death but to the sense felt by Him of the awful guilt of the Jews, who, by thus bringing about that death which He desired to die for the salvation of *all mankind*, seemed to be

Christ was
thinking
of the
Jews,
not of
Himself.

bringing down destruction and ruin on themselves— an anxiety and dread bitter enough, in Colet's view, to wring from the Saviour the prayer that the cup might pass from Him, and the drops of bloody sweat in the garden, seeing that it afterwards did wring from Him, whilst perfecting his eternal sacrifice on the cross, that other prayer for the very ministers of his torture, ' Father, forgive them, for they know not what they do ! ' Such was the view expressed by Colet in reply to Erasmus, and in opposition to the view which he was aware was generally received by scholastic divines.

Whilst they were in the heat of the discussion it happened that Prior Charnock entered the room. Colet, with a delicacy of feeling which Erasmus afterwards appreciated, at once broke off the argument, simply remarking, as he took leave, that he did not doubt that were his friend, when alone, to reconsider the matter with care and accuracy, their difference of opinion would not last very long.

When Erasmus found himself alone and at leisure

in his chambers he at once followed Colet's advice.
He reconsidered Colet's argument and his own. He
consulted his books. By far the most of the authorities, both Fathers and Schoolmen, he found beyond
dispute to be on his own side. And his reconsidera-
tion ended in his being the more convinced that he
had himself been right and Colet wrong. Naturally
finding it hard to yield when there was no occasion,
and feeling sure that this time he had the best of the
argument, he eagerly seized his pen, and with some
parade, both of candour and learning, stated at great
length what he thought might be said on both sides.
After having written what, in type, would fill about
fifty of these pages, he confidently wound up his long
letter by saying that, so far as he could see, he had
demonstrated his own opinion to be in accordance
with that of the Schoolmen and most of the early
Fathers, and, whilst not contrary to nature, clearly
consistent with reason. But he knew, he said, to
whom he was writing, and whether he had convinced
Colet he could not tell. For, he wrote in conclusion,
' how rash it is in me, a mere tyro, to dare to encoun-
' ter a commander—for one, *whom you call a rhe-*
' *torician*, to venture upon theological ground, to
' enter an arena which is not mine ! Still I have not
' shrunk from daring everything even with *you*, who
' are so skilled in all elegant and ancient lore, who
' have brought with you from Italy such stores of
' Greek and Latin, and who, on this very account, are
' not as yet appreciated as you ought to be by theo-
' logians. Wherefore, in discussing with you, I have
' chosen to use the old and free way of arguing ; not
' only because I prefer it myself, but also because I

' knew your dislike to the modern and new-fangled
' method of disputation, which, keen and ready as it
' may seem to some, is in your view complicated,
' superstitious, spiritless, and plainly sophistical. And
' perhaps you are right. . . . Yet I would have you
' take care lest you should not be able to stand *alone*
' against so many thousands. Let us not, contented
' with the plain homespun sense of Origen, Ambrose,
' Jerome, Augustine, Chrysostom, and others as
' ancient, grudge to these modern disputants their
' more elaborated doctrines.

   ' And now I await your attack. I await your mighty
' war-trumpet. I await those " Coletian " arrows, surer
' even than the arrows of Hercules.   In the meantime
' I will array the forces of my mind ; I will concen-
' trate my ranks ; I will prepare my reserves of books,
' lest I should not be able to stand your first charge.

   ' As to the rest, the matters which you have pro-
' pounded from the Epistles of St. Paul, since they
' are such as it would be dangerous to dispute of, I
' had rather enter into them by word of mouth when
' we are together than by letter. *Vale !* '

   The reply of Colet was short, and very characteristic
of the man.

Colet
replies.
   ' Your letter, most learned Erasmus, as it is very
' long, so also is it most eloquent and happy. It is
' a proof of a tenacious memory, and gives a faithful
' review of our discussion. . . . . But it contains
' nothing to alter or detract from the opinions which I
' imbibed from St. Jerome. Not that I am perverse
' and obstinate with an uncandid pertinacity, but that
' (though I may be mistaken) I think I hold and
' defend the truth, or what is most like the truth. . . .

' I am unwilling, just now, to grapple with your letter
' as a whole ; for I have neither leisure nor strength
' to do so at once, and without preparation. But I
' will attack the first part of it—your first line of
' battle as it were. . . . In the meantime do you
' patiently hear me, and let us both, if, when striking
' our flints together, any spark should fly out, eagerly
' catch at it. For we seek, not for victory in argu- Colet's
' ment, but for *truth*, which perchance may be elicited love of
' by the clash of argument with argument, as sparks truth.
' are by the clashing of steel against steel ! ' [1]

Erasmus, at the commencement of his long letter, Erasmus
feeling, perhaps, that after all there might be some had fol-
truth in Colet's view not embraced in his own, had theory
fallen back upon the strange theory, already alluded of the
to as held by scholastic divines, that the words of the senses ' of
Scriptures, because of their magic sacredness and Scripture.
absolute inspiration, might properly be interpreted in
several distinct senses. ' Nothing ' (he had said)
' forbids our drawing various meanings out of the
' wonderful riches of the sacred text, so as to render
' the same passage in more than one way. I know
' that, according to Job, " the word of God is mani-
' " fold." I know that the manna did not taste alike
' to all. But if you so embrace *your* opinion that you
' condemn and reject the received opinion, then I
' freely dissent from you.'

This was the first line of battle which Colet, in his
letter, declared that he would at once attack. It was a
notion of Scripture interpretation altogether foreign to
his own. He yielded to none in his admiration of the

---

[1] Eras. *Op.* v. pp. 1291 and 1292.

wonderful fulness and richness of the Scriptures. He had made it the chief matter of his remark to the priest who had called on him during the winter vacation of 1496-7, and had written to the Abbot of Winchcombe an account of the priest's visit in order to press the same point upon him. But from the method adopted in his expositions of St. Paul's Epistles, and the first chapter of Genesis, it appears that he did not hold the theory of uniform verbal inspiration, which ignored the human element in Scripture, round which had grown this still stranger theory of the manifold senses, and upon which alone it could be at all logically held.

Colet's view.

It is true that, in his abstract of the Dionysian writings, he had, upon Dionysian authority, accepted, in a modified form,[1] the doctrine of the ' four senses ' of

---

[1] 'From this order, any one may 'perceive the reason of the *four* '*senses* in the old law which are 'customary in the church. The '*literal* is, when the actions of the 'men of old time are related. When 'you think of the image, even of the 'Christian church which the law 'foreshadows, then you catch the '*allegorical* sense. When you are 'raised aloft, so as from the shadow 'to conceive of the reality which 'both represent, then there dawns 'upon you the *anagogic* sense. And 'when from signs you observe the 'instruction of individual man, then 'all has a *moral* tone for you. . . . 'In the writings of the New Testa-'ment, saving when it pleased the 'Lord Jesus and his Apostles to 'speak in parables, as Christ often 'does in the Gospels, and St. John 'throughout in the Revelation, all 'the rest of the discourse, in which 'either the Saviour teaches his dis-'ciples more plainly, or the disciples 'instruct the churches, has the sense 'that appears on the surface. Nor is 'one thing said and another meant, 'but the very thing is meant which 'is said, and the sense is wholly 'literal. Still, inasmuch as the 'church of God is figurative, con-'ceive always an *anagoge* in what 'you hear in the doctrines of the 'church, the meaning of which will 'not cease till the figure has become 'the truth. From this moreover 'conclude, that where the literal 'sense is, then the allegorical sense 'is *not* always along with it ; but, 'on the other hand, that where 'there is the allegorical sense, the 'literal sense is always underlying 'it.'—Colet's abstract of the *Eccl. Hier.*, Mr. Lupton's translation, pp. 105-107 ; and see Mr. Lupton's note on this passage.

Scripture ; and in his letters to Radulphus, whilst con-
fining himself to the literal sense, he guarded himself
against the denial of the same theory. But he had
never sanctioned the gross abuse of the doctrine to
which Erasmus had appealed, which asserted that even
the *literal* sense of the same passage might be interpreted to mean different things. It was one thing to
hold that some passages must be allegorically understood and not literally, and that other passages have
both a literal and an allegorical meaning (which Colet
seems to have held), or even that *all* passages have
both a literal and an allegorical meaning (which Colet
did not hold). It was quite another thing to hold that
the words of the same passage might, in their *literal*
sense, mean several different things, and be used as
texts in support of statements not within the direct
intention of their human writer.

Thomas Aquinas, in his ' Summa,' had indeed laid Aquinas
down a proposition, which practically amounted to on the
' manifold
this. For in discussing the doctrine of the ' four senses.'
' senses ' of Scripture, he had not only stated that
the spiritual sense of Scripture was threefold, viz.
allegorical, moral, and anagogical, but also that the
literal sense was manifold. He had laid down the
doctrine, that ' Inasmuch as the literal sense is that
' which *the author intends*, and *God* is the author of
' Holy Scripture, who comprehends all things in His
' mind at one and the same time, it is not inconsistent,
' as Augustine says in his twelfth Confession, if even
' according to the literal sense in the one letter of the
' Holy Scriptures there are many senses.' [1]

---

[1] Summa, pt. i. quest. 1, article x. Conclusio.

It may, however, well be doubted whether Aquinas would have sanctioned altogether the absurd length to which this doctrine was carried by scholastic disputants.

Whether Colet, since Grocyn's discovery, had or had not altogether repudiated the doctrine of ' mani-' fold senses,' as one of the notions which he had once held on Dionysian authority, but which the authority of the *Pseudo*-Dionysius was not sufficient to establish, it is clear that in his reply to Erasmus he utterly repudiated the abuse of it to which Erasmus had appealed. ' In the first place ' (he wrote), ' I cannot ' agree with you when you state, along with many ' others, and as I think mistakenly, that the Holy ' Scriptures, at least *uno in aliquo genere*, are so pro-' lific that they give birth to many senses.   Not that ' I would not have them to be as prolific as possible—' their overflowing fecundity and fulness I, more than ' others, admire—but that I consider their fecundity to ' consist in their giving birth not to many [senses], ' but to only one, and that the most true one.'

Colet
on the
' manifold
senses.'

After remarking that whilst the lower forms of life produce the most numerous offspring, the highest forms of life tend towards *unity* of offspring, he argues that the Holy Spirit gives birth in the Scripture, according to its own power, to one and the same simple truth. What if from the simple, divine, and truth-speaking words of the Scriptures of the Spirit of Truth, whether heard or read, many and various persons draw many and varying senses ?   He set that down, he said, not to the fecundity of the Scriptures, but to the sterility of men's minds, and their incapacity of getting at the pure

and simple truth. If they could but reach *that*, they
would as completely agree as now they differ. He
then remarked how mysterious the inspiration of the
Scriptures was; how the Spirit seemed to him, by
reason of its majesty, to have a peculiar method of its
own, singularly absolute and free, blowing where it
lists, making prophets of whom it will, yet so that the
spirit of the prophets is subject to the prophets. He
repeated, in conclusion, that he admired the fulness of
the Scriptures, not because each word may be construed
in several senses—that would be want of fulness—but
because *quot sententiæ totidem sunt verba, et quot verba
tot sententiæ.* Having said this, he was ready to descend
into the arena, and to join battle with Erasmus on the
matter in dispute, but he could not do so now ; he was
called away by other engagements, and must end his
letter for the present.[1]

The letters which followed, in which Colet further
pursued the subject of the Agony in the Garden, have
unfortunately been lost. But enough remains to give,
by a passing glimpse, some idea of the pleasant colloquies and earnest converse, both by mouth and letter,
in which the happy months of college intercourse
glided swiftly by.

---

[1] Eras. *Op.* v. pp. 1291 to 1294. This reply of Colet to the long letter of Erasmus does not seem to have been published in the early editions of the latter. Thus I do not find it in the editions of Schurerius, Argent. 1516, and again 1517. The earliest print of it that I have seen is that appended to the *Enchiridion*, &c. Basle, 1518.

VI. CORRESPONDENCE BETWEEN COLET AND ERASMUS ON THE INTENTION OF ERASMUS TO LEAVE OXFORD (1499—1500).

Erasmus at Court.

The winter vacation of 1499–1500 had apparently dispersed for a while the circle of Oxford students. Erasmus having, it would seem, some friend at Court, had joined the Royal party, probably spending Christmas at Woodstock or some other hunting station. He was at first delighted with Court manners and field sports, and in a letter,[1] written about this time, he jocosely told a Parisian friend, that the Erasmus whom he once had known was now a hunter, and his manners polished up into those of an experienced courtier. He was greatly struck, he added, with the beauty and grace of the English ladies, and urged him to let nothing less than the gout hinder his coming to England.

But soon tires of Court life.

But while Court life might captivate at first, Erasmus had soon found out that its glitter was not gold. As the wolf in the fable lost his relish for the dainties and delicate fare of the house-dog when he saw the mark of the collar on his neck, so when Erasmus had seen how little of freedom and how much of bondage there was in the courtier's life he had left it with disgust ; choosing rather to return to Oxford to share the more congenial society of what students might be found there during these vacation weeks, than to remain longer with ' be-chained courtiers.'[2] He was waiting only for time and tide to return to Paris.

---

[1] Eras. *Op.* iii. Epist. lxv. Erasmus Fausto Andrelino, 1521 ed. p. 260.

[2] 'Torquatis istis aulicis.'— Eras. *Op.* v. p. 126, E.

At present the weather was too rough for so bad a
sailor ; and, owing to political disquiet and danger, it
was difficult to obtain the needful permission to leave
the realm.

The fear that Erasmus was so soon to leave Oxford Erasmus
was one which troubled Colet's vacation thoughts. proposes
to leave
To be left alone at Oxford again to fight his way single- Oxford.
handed was by no means a cheering prospect. But his
saddest feeling was one not merely of sorrow at parting
with his new friend—it was a feeling of disappointment. He had hoped for more than he had found in
Erasmus. That he could have won over Erasmus
all at once to his own views and plans he had never
dreamed. The scholar had his own bent of mind, and
of course his own plans. Such was his love of learning for its own sake, that he was bent on constant and
persevering study ; and his stay at Oxford he looked
upon merely as one step in the ladder, valuable chiefly
because it led to the next. But Colet longed for fellowship. In his friend he had sought, and in some measure
found, fellow-feeling. But feeling and action to him
were too closely linked to make that all he wanted.
Fellow-feeling was to him but a half-hearted thing
unless it ripened into fellow work ; and he had hoped
for this in Erasmus. He had purposely left Erasmus to
find out his views and to discern his spirit by degrees.
He had not tried to force him in anywise. He had
shown his wisdom in this. But now that Erasmus
talked of leaving Oxford, it was Colet's duty to speak
out. He could not let him go without one last appeal. Colet
He therefore wrote to him, telling him plainly of his urges him
to remain
disappointment. He urged him to remain at Oxford. at Oxford.

He urged him, once for all, to come out boldly, as he himself had done, and to do his part in the great work of restoring that old and true theology of Christ, so long obscured by the subtle webs of the Schoolmen, in its pristine brightness and dignity. What could he do more noble than this ? There was plenty of room for both of them. He himself was doing his best to expound the New Testament. Why should not Erasmus take some book of the Old Testament, say Genesis or Isaiah, and expound it, as he had done the Epistles of St. Paul ? If he could not make up his mind to do this at once, Colet urged that, as a temporary alternative, he should lecture on some secular branch of study. Anything was better than that he should leave Oxford altogether.[1]

Erasmus received this letter soon after his return from his short experience of Court life. The tone of disappointment and almost reproof pervading it Erasmus felt was undeserved on his part, yet it evidently made a deep impression upon him. Looking back upon his intercourse with Colet at Oxford, he must have seen how much it had done to change his views, and felt how powerfully Colet's influence had worked upon him. Yet he knew how far his views were from being matured like Colet's, and how foolish it would be to begin publicly to teach before his own mind was fully made up. He knew that Colet had brought him over very much to his way of thinking, and he was ready to confess himself a disciple of Colet's ; but he must digest what he had learned, and make it thoroughly his own, before he could publicly teach it.

---

[1] Colet's letter to Erasmus has been lost, but the above may be gathered from the reply of Erasmus.

Perhaps he might one day be able to join Colet in
his work at Oxford ; but he thought, and probably
wisely, that the time had not yet come. This at
least may be gathered from his reply to Colet's letter.
With some abridgement and unimportant omissions,
it may be translated thus :—

Erasmus to Colet.[1]

. . . ' In what you say of your dislike to the Reply of
' modern race of divines, who spend their lives in mere Erasmus
to Colet's
' logical tricks and sophistical cavils, in very truth entreaties.
' I entirely agree with you.

' Not that, valuing as I do all branches of study, I
' condemn the studies of these men *as such*, but that
' when they are pursued for themselves alone, un-
' seasoned by more ancient and elegant literature, they
' seem to me to be calculated to make men sciolists and
' contentious ; whether they can make men wise I
' leave to others. For they exhaust the mental powers Agrees
' by a dry and biting subtlety, without infusing any with Colet
in dis-
' vigour or spirit into the mind. And, worst of all, liking the
Scholastic
' theology, the queen of all science—so richly adorned System.
' by ancient eloquence—they strip of all her beauty
' by their incongruous, mean, and disgusting style.
' What was once so clear, thanks to the genius of the
' old divines, they clog with some subtlety or other,
' thus involving everything in obscurity while they
' try to explain it. It is thus we see that theology,
' which was once most venerable and full of majesty,
' now almost dumb, poor, and in rags.
' In the meantime we are allured by a never-satiated

---

[1] Eras. *Op.* v. p. 1263.

K

' appetite for strife. One dispute gives rise to another,
' and with wonderful gravity we fight about straws.
' Then, lest we should seem to have added nothing to
' the discoveries of the old divines, we audaciously
' lay down certain positive rules according to which
' God has performed his mysteries, when sometimes
' it might be better for us to believe that a thing *was*
' done, leaving the question of *how* it was done to the
' omnipotence of God. So, too, for the sake of show-
' ing our ingenuity, we sometimes discuss questions
' which pious ears can hardly bear to hear; as, for
' instance, when it is asked whether the Almighty
' could have taken upon Him the nature of the devil
' or of an ass.

' Besides all this, in our times those men in general
' apply themselves to theology, the chief of all studies,
' who by reason of their obtuseness and lack of sense
' are hardly fit for any study at all. I say this not of
' learned and upright professors of theology, whom
' I highly respect and venerate, but of that sordid and
' haughty pack of divines who count all learning as
' worthless except their own.

He
honours
Colet and
his work.

' Wherefore, my dear Colet, in having joined battle
' with this redoubtable race of men for the restoration,
' in its pristine brightness and dignity, of that old and
' true theology which they have obscured by their
' subtleties, you have in very truth engaged in a work
' in many ways of the highest honour—a work of de-
' votion to the cause of theology, and of the greatest
' advantage to all students, and especially the students
' of this flourishing University of Oxford. Still, to
' speak the truth, it is a work of great difficulty, and
' one sure to excite ill-will. Your learning and energy

will, however, conquer every difficulty, and your
' magnanimity will easily overlook ill-will.   There are
' not a few, even among divines themselves, both able
' and willing to second your honest endeavours.   There
' is no one, indeed, who would not give you a hand,
' since there is not even a doctor in this celebrated
' University who has not given attentive audience to
' your public readings on the Epistles of St. Paul, now
' of three years' standing.   And which is the most
' praiseworthy in this, *their* modesty in not being
' ashamed to learn from a young man without doctor's
' degree, or *your* remarkable learning, eloquence, and
' integrity of life, which they have thought worthy of
' such honour ?

  ' I do not wonder that *you* should put your shoulder
' under so great a burden, for you are able to bear it,
' but I do wonder greatly that you should call *me*,
' who am nothing of a man, into the fellowship
' of so glorious a work.   For you exhort—yes, you
' almost reproachfully urge me, that, by expounding
' either the ancient Moses [1] or the eloquent Isaiah, in
' the same way as you have expounded St. Paul, I
' should try, as you say, to kindle up the studies of this
' University, now chilled by these winter months.   But
' I, who have learned to live in solitude, know well
' how imperfectly I am furnished for such a task ; nor
' do I lay claim to sufficient learning to justify my

Erasmus
agrees
with Colet
but is not
ready yet
to join
him in
fellow-
work.

---

[1] It is possible that Colet himself had, at one time, thought of
expounding the book of Genesis,
but the manuscript letters to Radulphus appended to the copy of
the MS. on the ' Romans,' in the
library of Corpus Christi College,
Cambridge, contain no allusion to
any such intention.

'undertaking it.   Nor do I judge that I have strength
'of mind enough to enable me to sustain the ill-will of
'so many men stoutly maintaining their own ground.
'Matters of this kind require not a tyro, but a prac-
'tised general.   Nor can you rightly call me immodest
'in refusing to do what I should be far more immodest
'to attempt.   You act, my dear Colet, in this matter
'as wisely as they who (as Plautus says) " demand
'" water from a rock."   With what face can I teach
'what I myself have not learned ?   How shall I
'kindle the chilled warmth of others while I am
'altogether trembling and shivering myself ? . . .

'But you say you expected this of me, and now you
'complain that you were mistaken.   You should rather
'blame yourself than me for this.   For I have not
'deceived you.   I have neither promised nor held out
'any prospect of any such thing.   But you have
'deceived yourself in not believing me when I told
'you truly what I meant to do.

'Nor indeed did I come here to teach poetry and
'rhetoric, for these ceased to be pleasant to me when
'they ceased to be necessary.   I refuse the one task
'because it does not come up to my purpose, the other
'because it is beyond my strength.   You unjustly
'blame me in the one case, my dear Colet, because I
'never intended to follow the profession of what are
'called secular studies.   As to the other, you exhort
'me in vain, as I know myself to be too unfit for it.

'But even though I were most fit, still it must not
'be.   For soon I must return to Paris.

'In the meantime, whilst I am detained here,
'partly by the winter, and partly because departure
'from England is forbidden, owing to the flight of

'some duke,[1] I have betaken myself to this famous
'University that I might rather spend two or three
'months with men of your class than with those
'be-chained courtiers.

'Be it, indeed, far from me to oppose your glorious
'and sacred labours. On the contrary, I will promise
'(since not fitted as yet to be a coadjutor) sedulously
'to encourage and further them. For the rest,
'whenever I feel that I have the requisite firmness
'and strength I will join you, and, by your side, and
'in theological teaching, I will zealously engage, if
'not in successful at least in earnest labour. In the
'meantime, nothing could be more delightful to me
'than that we should go on as we have begun, whether
'daily by word of mouth, or by letter, discussing the
'meaning of Holy Scripture.

'Vale, mi Colete.
'Oxford : at the College of the Canons of the
'Order of St. Augustine, commonly called
'the College of St. Mary.'[2]

VII. ERASMUS LEAVES OXFORD AND ENGLAND (1500).

Erasmus took leave of Colet, and left Oxford early
in January, 1500.

---

[1] Probably De la Pole. See Mr.
Gairdner's *Letters and Papers, &c. of
Richard III. and Henry VII.* vol. i.
p. 129, and vol. ii. preface, p. xl ;
and appendix, p. 377 ; where Mr.
Gairdner mentions under date,
20th Aug. 14 Henry VII. (1499) a
'Proclamation, against leaving
'the kingdom without license,' and

adds ' N.B. clearly in consequence
'of the flight of Edmund De la
'Pole.' If this prohibition extended
through December, it fixes the date
of this letter as written in the
winter of 1499–1500.

[2] Eras. *Op.* v. p. 1263. This letter
is generally found prefixed to the
various editions of the *Disputati-*

Erasmus
at Lord
Mount-
joy's.

He proceeded to Greenwich, to the country seat of
Lord and Lady Mountjoy; for his patron had, apparently, since his arrival in England, married a wife.[1]

While he was resting under this hospitable roof,-
Thomas More came down to pay him a farewell visit.
He brought with him another young lawyer named
Arnold—the son of Arnold the merchant, a man well
known in London, and living in one of the houses
built upon the arches of London Bridge.[2]

More and
Erasmus
visit the
Royal
Nursery.

More, whose love of fun never slept, persuaded
Erasmus, by way of something to do, to take a walk
with himself and his friend to a neighbouring village.

He took them to call at a house of rather im-
posing appearance. As they entered the hall, Erasmus
was struck with the style of it; it rivalled even that of
the mansion of his noble patron. It was in fact the
Royal Nursery, where all the children of Henry VII.,
except Arthur the Prince of Wales, were living under
the care of their tutor. In the middle of the group
was Prince Henry (afterwards Henry VIII.), then a
boy of nine years old. To his right stood the Princess
Margaret, who afterwards was married to the King of
Scotland. On the left was the Princess Maria, a mere
child at play. The nurse held in her arms the Prince
Edmund, a baby about ten months old.[3]

They see
the Prince
Henry.

More and Arnold at once accosted Prince Henry,
and presented him with some verses, or other literary

---

uncula de Tœdio Christi. And this
is often appended to editions of the
Enchiridion.

[1] Epist. lxiv. Erasmus to Mountjoy, and also see Epist. xlii.

[2] Eras. *Op.* iii. p. 26, E. Epist.
xxix.

[3] The fact that Erasmus saw
Prince *Edmund* fixes the date of
his departure from England to
1500, instead of 1499. He left
England 27th Jan., and it could not
be in 1499, for Prince Edmund was
not born till Feb. 21, 1499.

offering. Erasmus, having brought nothing of the kind with him, felt awkward, and could only promise to prove his courtesy to the Prince in the same way on some future occasion. They were invited to sit down to table, and during the meal the Prince sent a note to Erasmus to remind him of his promise. The result was that More received a merited scolding from Erasmus, for having led him blindfold into the trap; and Erasmus, after parting with More, had to devote three of the few remaining days of his stay in England to the composition of Latin verses in honour of England, Henry VII., and the Royal children.[1] He was in good humour with England. He had been treated with a kindness which he never could forget; and he was leaving England with a purse full of golden crowns, generously provided by his English friends to defray the expenses of his long-wished-for visit to Italy. Under these circumstances it was not surprising if his verses should be laudatory.[2]

By the 27th January,[3] he was off to Dover, to catch the boat for Boulogne.

So the three friends were scattered. Each had evidently a separate path of his own. Their natures and natural gifts were, indeed, singularly different. They had been brought into contact for one short year, as it were by chance, and now again their spheres of life seemed likely to lie wide apart.

CHAP. III.

A.D. 1500.

Erasmus writes verses upon England.

Leaves for Dover.

The three friends are scattered.

---

[1] See the mention of this incident in Erasmus's letter to Botzhem, printed as *Catalogus Omnium Erasmi Roterodami Lucubrationum, ipso Autore*, 1523, Basil, fol. a. 6, and reprinted by Jortin, app. 418, 419.

[2] For the verses see Eras. *Op.* i. p. 1215.

[3] See Ep. xcii. and lxxxi.

How could it be otherwise? Even Colet, who had longed that his friendship for Erasmus might ripen into the fellowship of fellow-work, could not hope against hope. The chances that his dream might yet be realised, seemed slight indeed. ' When- ' ever I feel that I have the requisite firmness and ' strength, I will join you!' So Erasmus had promised. But Colet might well doubtfully ask himself—' When will that be?'

CHAPTER IV.

I. COLET MADE DOCTOR AND DEAN OF ST. PAUL'S (1500–5).

COLET, left alone to pursue the even tenor of his way at Oxford, worked steadily at his post. It mattered little to him that for years he toiled on without any official recognition on the part of the University authorities of the value of his work. What if a Doctor's degree had never during these years been conferred upon him? The want of it had never stopped his teaching. Its possession would have been to him no triumph.

That young theological students were beginning more and more to study the Scriptures instead of the Schoolmen—for this he cared far more. For this he was casting his bread upon the waters, in full faith that, whether he might live to see it or not, it would return after many days. And in truth—known or unknown to Colet—young Tyndale, and such as he, yet in their teens, were already poring over the Scriptures at Oxford.[1] The leaven, silently but surely, was leaven-

---

[1] ' He [Tyndale] was born (about 1484) about the borders of Wales, ' and brought up from a child in ' the University of Oxford, where ' he, by long continuance, grew and ' increased as well in the know- ' ledge of tongues and other liberal ' arts, as specially in the knowledge ' of the Scriptures, whereunto his ' mind was singularly addicted ; ' insomuch that he, lying there in ' Magdalen Hall, read privily to

ing the surrounding mass.   But Colet probably did
not see much of the secret results of his work.   That
it was his duty to do it was reason enough for his doing
it ; that it bore at least some visible fruit was sufficient
encouragement to work on with good heart.

So the years went by ; and as often as each term
came round, Colet was ready with his gratuitous course
of lectures on one or another of St. Paul's Epistles.[1]

Colet
made
Doctor
and
Dean of
St. Paul's.

It happened that, in 1504, Robert Sherborn, Dean of
St. Paul's, was nominated, being then in Rome on an
embassy, to the vacant see of St. David's.   It was probably at the same time [2] that Colet was called to discharge the duties of the vacant deanery, though, as
Sherborn was not formally installed in his bishopric till
April 1505, Colet did not receive the temporalities of
his deanery till May in the same year.[3]

Colet is said to have owed this advancement to the
patronage of King Henry VII.   The title of Doctor
was at length conferred upon him, preparatory to his
acceptance of this preferment, and it would appear as
an honorary mark of distinction.[4]

'certain students and fellows of
'Magdalen College, some parcel of
'divinity, instructing them in the
'knowledge and truth of the Scrip-
'tures.'—Quoted from Foxe in the
biographical notice of William Tyndale, prefixed to his Doctrinal Treatises, p. xiv, Parker Society, 1848.
Magdalen College is supposed to
have been the college in which Colet
resided at Oxford; as, according to
Wood, some of the name of Colet
are mentioned in the records,
though not John Colet himself.

[1] 'How many years did he (Colet)
'following the example of St. Paul,
'teach the people *without reward !* '
Eras. Epist. cccclxxxi. Eras. *Op.*
iii. p. 532, E.

[2] In Colet's epitaph it is stated
'administravit 16 ; ' as he died in
1519, this will bring the commencement of his administration to 1504,
at latest.   See also the note in the
Appendix on Colet's preferments.

[3] Fasti Ecclesiæ Anglicanæ, p.
184.

[4] Eras. *Op.* iii. p. 456, C.

It was to the work, writes Erasmus, and not to the dignity of the deanery, that Colet was called. To restore the relaxed discipline of the College—to preach sermons from Scripture in St. Paul's Cathedral as he had done at Oxford—to secure permanently that such sermons should be regularly preached—this was his first work.[1]

CHAP. IV.

A.D. 1500–5.

Colet's work in London.

By his remove from Oxford to St. Paul's the field of his influence was changed, and in some respects greatly widened. His work now told directly upon the people at large. The chief citizens of London, and even stray courtiers, now and then, heard the plain facts of Christian truth, instead of the subtleties of the Schoolmen, earnestly preached from the pulpit of St. Paul's by the son of an ex-lord mayor of London. The citizens found too, in the new Dean, a man whose manner of life bore out the lessons of his pulpit.

He retained as Dean of St. Paul's the same simplicity of character and earnest devotion to his work for which he had been so conspicuous at Oxford. As he had not sought ecclesiastical preferment, so he was not puffed up by it. Instead of assuming the purple vestments which were customary, he still wore his plain black robe. The same simple woollen garment served him all the year round, save that in winter he had it lined with fur. The revenues of his deanery were sufficient to defray his ordinary household expenses, and left him his private income free. He gave it away, instead of spending it upon himself.[2] The rich living of Stepney, which, in conformity with the custom of the times, he might well have retained

The habits of the new Dean.

---

[1] Eras. *Op.* iii. p. 456, D.   [2] Ibid. E. and F.

along with his other preferment, he resigned at once into other hands on his removal to St. Paul's.[1]

It would seem too that he shone by contrast with his predecessor, whose lavish good cheer had been such as to fill his table with jovial guests, and sometimes to pass the bounds of moderation.[2]

The Dean's table.

There was no chance of this with Colet. His own habits were severely frugal. For years he abstained from suppers, and there were no nightly revels in his house. His table was neatly spread, but neither costly nor excessive. After grace, he would have a chapter read from one of St. Paul's Epistles or the Proverbs of Solomon, and then contrive to engage his guests in serious table-talk, drawing out the unlearned, as well as the learned, and changing the topics of conversation with great tact and skill. Thus, when the citizens dined at his table, they soon found, as his Oxford friends had found at *their* public dinners, that, without being tedious or overbearing, somehow or other he contrived so to exert his influence as to send his guests away better than they came.[3]

Inner circle of intimate friends.

Moreover, Colet soon gathered around him here in London, as he had done at Oxford, an inner circle of personal friends.[4] These were wont often to meet at his table and to talk on late into the night, conversing sometimes upon literary topics, and sometimes speaking together of that invisible Prince whom Colet was as

---

1 Walter Stone, LL.D., was admitted to the vicarage of Stepney, void by the resignation of D. Colet, Sept. 21, 1505.—Kennett's MSS. vol. xliv. f. 234 b (Lansdowne, 978). He seems to have retained

his rectory of Denyngton.
2 Eras. *Op.* iii. p. 465, E.
3 Ibid. E. and F.
4 Grocyn and Linacre had also removed to London. More was already there.

loyally serving now in the midst of honour and preferment as he had done in an humbler sphere.[1] Colet's
loyalty to *Him* seemed indeed to have been deepened
rather than diminished by contact with the outer world.
The place which St. Paul's character and writings had
once occupied in his thoughts and teaching was now
filled by the character and words of St. Paul's Master
and his.[2] He never travelled, says Erasmus, without
reading some book or conversing of Christ.[3] He had
arranged the sayings of Christ in groups, to assist the
memory, and with the intention of writing a book on
them.[4] His sermons, too, in St. Paul's Cathedral bore
witness to the engrossing object of his thoughts. It
was now no longer St. Paul's Epistles but the ' Gospel
' History,' the ' Apostles' Creed,' the ' Lord's Prayer,' [5]
which the Dean was expounding to the people. And
highly as he had held, and still held, in honour the
apostolic writings, yet, as already mentioned, they
seemed to him to shrink, as it were, into nothing, compared with the wonderful majesty of Christ himself.

The same method of teaching which he had applied
at Oxford to the writings of St. Paul he now applied in
his cathedral sermons in treating of these still higher
subjects. For he did not, we are told, take an isolated
text and preach a detached discourse upon it, but went
continuously through whatever he was expounding
from beginning to end in a course of sermons.[6] Thus

CHAP. IV.

A.D. 1505.

Colet's
personal
loyalty to
Christ.

Colet's
sermons at
St. Paul's.

---

[1] ' Impense delectabatur amico-
'rum colloquiis quæ sæpe differebat
' in multam noctem. Sed omnis
' illius sermo, aut de literis erat,
' aut de Christo.'—Eras. *Op.* iii. p.
457, A.

[2] Eras. *Op.* iii. p. 459, F.

[3] *Ibid.* p. 457, A. [4] *Ibid.* p. 459, F.

[5] *Ibid.* p. 456, E.

[6] ' Porro in suo templo non su-
' mebat sibi carptim argumentum
' ex Evangelio aut ex epistolis
' Apostolicis sed unum aliquod
' argumentum proponebat, quod
' diversis concionibus ad finem
' usque prosequebatur : puta

CHAP. IV. these cathedral discourses of Colet's were continuous
─────
A.D. 1505. expositions of the facts of the Saviour's life and teaching, as recorded by the Evangelists, or embodied in
that simple creed which in Colet's view contained the
sum of Christian theology. And thus was he practically illustrating, by his own public example in these
sermons, his advice to theological students, to ' keep to
' the Bible and the Apostles' Creed, letting divines, if
' they like, dispute about the rest.'

II. MORE CALLED TO THE BAR—IN PARLIAMENT—OFFENDS
HENRY VII.—THE CONSEQUENCES (1500–1504).

A.D.
1500–4.

After the departure of Erasmus, More worked on
diligently at his legal studies at Lincoln's Inn. A few
more terms and he received the reward of his industry
in his call to the bar.

More's
legal
studies.

During the years devoted to his legal curriculum,
he had been wholly absorbed in his law books.

Grocyn,
Linacre,
and More
all in
London.

Closely watched by his father, and purposely kept
with a stinted allowance, as at Oxford, so that ' his
' whole mind might be set on his book,' the law student
had found little time or opportunity for other studies.
But being now duly called to the bar, and thus freed
from the restraints of student life, his mind naturally
reverted to old channels of thought. Grocyn and Linacre in the meantime had left Oxford and become near
neighbours of his in London. Thus the old Oxford
circle partially formed itself again, and with the renewal of old intimacies returned, if ever lost, the love
of old studies. For no sooner was More called to the

─────

' Evangelium Matthæi, Symbo- ' nicam.'—Eras. *Op.* iii. p. 456,
' lum Fidei, Precationem Domi- D, E.

bar than he commenced his maiden lectures in the church of St. Lawrence,[1] in the Old Jewry, and chose for a subject the great work of St. Augustine, ' De ' Civitate Dei.'

His object, we are told, in these lectures was not to expound the theological creed of the Bishop of Hippo, but the philosophical and historical [2] arguments contained in those first few books in which Augustine had so forcibly traced the connection between the history of Rome and the character and religion of the Romans, attributing the former glory of the great Roman Commonwealth to the valour and virtue of the old Romans ; tracing the recent ruin of the empire, ending in the sack of Rome by Alaric, to the effeminacy and profligacy of the modern Romans ; defending Christianity from the charge of having undermined the empire, and pointing out that if it had been universally adopted by rulers and people, and carried out into practice in their lives, the old Pagan empire might have become a truly Christian empire and been saved,—those books which, starting from the facts of the recent sack of Rome, landed the reader at last in a discussion of the philosophy of free-will and fate.

Roper tells us that the young lawyer's readings were well received, being attended not only by Grocyn, his old Greek master, but also by ' all the chief learned ' of the city of London.' [3]

More was indeed rising rapidly in public notice and confidence. He was appointed a reader at Furnival's Inn about this time, and when a Parliament was

---

[1] Grocyn was apparently rector of this parish up to 1517, when he vacated it.—Wood, *Ath. Oxon.* p. 32.

[2] Stapleton, p. 160.
[3] Roper, Singer's ed. 1822, p. 5.

CHAP. IV.

A.D.
1500–4.
More in
Parlia-
ment.

called in the spring of 1503-4, though only twenty-five,
he was elected a member of it.

Sent up thus to enter public life in a Parliament of
which the notorious Dudley was the speaker,[1] the last
and probably the most subservient Parliament of a
king who now in his latter days was becoming more
and more avaricious, the mettle of the young member
was soon put to the test, and bore it bravely.

At the last Parliament of 1496-7,[2] the King, in prospect of a war with Scotland, had exacted from the
Commons a subsidy of two-fifteenths, and, finding
they had submitted to this so easily, had, even before
the close of the session, pressed for and obtained the
omission of the customary clauses in the bill, releasing
about 12,000*l.* of the gross amount in relief of decayed
towns and cities.[3] Now all was peace. The war with
Scotland had ended in the marriage of the Princess
Margaret, whom More had seen in the royal nursery a

few years before, to the King of Scots.   But by feudal
right the King, with consent of Parliament,[4] could
claim a ' reasonable aid ' in respect of this marriage of
the Princess Royal, in addition to another for the
knighting of Prince Arthur, who, however, in the
meantime, had died. This Parliament of 1503-4 was
doubtless called chiefly to obtain these ' reasonable
' aids.' But with Dudley as speaker the King meant
to get more than his strictly feudal rights.   Instead of
the two ' aids,' he put in a claim (so Roper was
informed[5]) for three-fifteenths ! i.e. for half as much
again as he had asked for to defray the cost of the

---

[1] Rot. Parl. vi. 521, B.
[2] 12 Henry VII. c. 12, also Rot.
Parl. vi. p. 514.
[3] 12 Henry VII. c. 13.

[4] See 3 Edward I. c. 36, and 25
Edward III. s. 5, c. 11.
[5] Roper, p. 7.

Chap. IV.

A.D. 1504.

More
opposes
the King's
demands;

Scottish war. And Dudley's flock of sheep were going to pass this bill in silence! Already it had passed two readings, when 'at the last debating 'thereof,' More, probably the youngest member of the House, rose from his seat 'and made such 'arguments and reasons there against,' that the King's demands (says Roper) 'were thereby clean 'overthrown.' 'So that' (he continues) 'one of the 'King's Privy Chamber, named Maister Tyler,[1] being 'present thereat, brought word to the King, out of 'the Parliament House, that a beardless boy had 'disappointed all his purpose.'

Instead of three-fifteenths, which would have realised 113,000*l.*[2] or more, the Parliament Rolls bear witness that the King, with royal clemency and grace, had to accept a paltry 30,000*l.*, being less than a third of what he had asked for![3]

---

[1] Possibly, '*our trusty and right 'well-beloved knight and counseller,*' *Sir William Tyler,* who had so often partaken of the royal bounty, being made 'Controller of Works,' 'Mes-'senger of Exchequer,' 'Receiver of 'certain Lordships' &c. &c. (see Rot. Parl. vi. 341, 378 b, 404 b, 497 b), and who was remembered for good in chap. 35 of this very Parliament.

[2] A fifteenth of the three estates was estimated by the Venetian ambassador, in 1500, to produce 37,930*l.*—See *Italian Relation of England,* Camden Soc. p. 52. The amount of a 'fifteenth' was fixed in 1334, by 8 Ed. III. Blackstone (vol. i. p.310) states that the amount was fixed at about 29,000*l.* This was probably the amount, exclusive of the quota derived from the estates

of the clergy, which latter was estimated at 12,000*l.* by the Venetian ambassador in 1500. This being added would raise Blackstone's estimate to 41,000*l.* in all. From this, however, about 4000*l.* was always excused to 'poor towns, cities, &c.,' so that the nett actual amount would be about 37,000*l.* according to Blackstone, which agrees well with the Venetian estimate.

[3] 19 Henry VII. c. 32, Jan. 25, 1503, Rot. Parl. vi. 532–542. In lieu of two reasonable aids, one for making a knight of Prince Arthur deceased, and the other of marriage of Princess Margaret to the King of Scots, and also great expenses in wars, the Commons grant 40,000*l.* less 10,000*l.* remitted, '*of his more 'ample grace and pity, for that the*

L

No wonder that, soon after, the King devised a quarrel with More's father (who, by the way, was one of the commissioners for the collection of the subsidy),[1] threw him into the Tower, and kept him there till he had paid a fine of 100*l*. No wonder that young More himself was compelled at once to retire from public life, and hide himself from royal displeasure in obscurity.[2]

III. THOMAS MORE IN SECLUSION FROM PUBLIC LIFE
(1504–5).

More and
Lilly
think of
becoming
monks or
priests.

Compelled to seek safety in seclusion, More shut himself up in his lodgings near the Charterhouse with William Lilly, another old Oxford student, a contemporary of Colet's, if not of More's, at Oxford, who having spent some years travelling in the East, had recently returned home fresh from Italy. More seems to have shared with him the intention of becoming a monk or a priest.[3]

It was possibly not the first time his thoughts had turned in this direction ; but he had hitherto gone cautiously to work, taking no vow, determined to

---

'*poraill of his comens should not in anywise be contributory or chargeable to any part of the said sum of* ' 40,000*l*.' The 30,000*l*. to be paid by the shires in the sums stated, and to the payment every person to be liable having lands, &c. to the yearly value of 20*s*. of free charter lands, or of 26*s*. 8*d*. of lands held at will, or any person having goods or cattalls to the value of x marks or above, not accounting their cattle for their plough nor stuff or implement of household.

[1] John More was one of the commissioners for Herts.

[2] This story is told in substantially the same form in the manuscript life of More by Harpsfield, written in the time of Queen Mary, and dedicated to William Roper.— *Harleian MSS*. No. 6253, fol. 4.

[3] ' Meditabatur adolescens sacerdotium cum suo Lilio.'—Stapleton, *Tres Thomæ*, ed. 1588, p. 18, ed. 1612, p. 161. See also Roper, pp. 5, 6.

feel his way, and not to rush blindly into what he
might afterwards repent of.

He had now taken to wearing an ' inner sharp shirt
' of hair,' and to sleeping on the bare boards of his
chamber, with a log under his head for a pillow, and
was otherwise schooling, by his powerful will, his
quick and buoyant nature into accordance with the
strict rules of the Carthusian brotherhood.[1]

It was a critical moment in his life. Soon after his
father had been imprisoned and fined, having some
business with Fox, Bishop of Winchester, that great
courtier called him aside, pretending to be his friend,
and promised that if he would be ruled by him, he
would not fail to restore him into the King's favour.
But Fox was only setting a trap for him, from which
he was saved by a friendly hint from Whitford,[2] the
bishop's chaplain. This man told More that his
master would not stick to agree to his own father's
death to serve the King's turn, and advised him to
keep quite aloof from the King. This hint was not
reassuring, but it may have saved More's life.

What would have happened to him had he been
left alone with misadvising friends to give hasty vent
to the disappointment which thus had crushed his
hopes at the very outset of his career—whether the
cloister would have received him as it did his friend
Whitford afterwards, to be another ' *wretch of Sion,*'
none can tell.

---

[1] Stapleton and Roper, *ubi supra.*

[2] Richard Whitford himself, retiring soon after from public life, entered the monastery called 'Sion,' near Brentford in Middlesex, and wrote books, in which he styled himself ' *the* wretch of Sion.' See Roper, p. 8, and Knight's *Life of Erasmus*, p. 64.

CHAP. IV.

A.D. 1504.

When
Colet
comes to
London,
More
chooses
him as his
spiritual
guide.

Happily for him it was at this critical moment that Colet came up to London to assume his new duties at St. Paul's. More was a diligent listener to his sermons, and chose him as his father confessor. Stapleton has preserved a letter from More to Colet,[1] which throws much light upon the relation between them. It was written in October, 1504, whilst Colet, after preaching during the summer, was apparently spending his long vacation in the country. It shows that, under Colet's advice, More was not altogether living the life of a recluse.

Colet had for some time been absent from his pulpit at St. Paul's. As More was one day walking up and down Westminster Hall, waiting while other people's suits were being tried, he chanced to meet Colet's

servant. Learning from him that his master had not yet returned to town, More wrote to Colet this letter, to tell him how much he missed his wonted delightful intercourse with him. He told him how he had ever prized his most wise counsel; how by his most delightful fellowship he had been refreshed; how by his weighty sermons he had been roused, and by his example helped on his way. He reminded him how fully he relied upon his guidance—how he had been wont to hang upon his very beck and nod. Under his protection he had felt himself gaining strength, now without it he was flagging and undone. He acknowledged that, by following Colet's leading, he had escaped almost from the very jaws of hell; but now, amid all the temptations of city life and the noisy wrangling of the law courts, he felt himself

---

[1] Stapleton, ed. 1588, p. 20, ed. 1612, p. 163.

losing ground without his help. No doubt the country
might be much more pleasant to Colet than the city,
but the city, with all its vice, and follies, and temptations, had far more need of his skill than simple
country folk ! ' There sometimes come, indeed,' he
added, ' into the pulpit at St. Paul's, men who
' promise to heal the diseases of the people. But,
' though they seem to have preached plausibly enough,
' their lives so jar with their words that they stir up
' men's wounds, rather than heal them.' But, he said,
his fellow-citizens had confidence in Colet, and all
longed for his return. He urged him, therefore, to
return speedily, for their sake and for his, reminding
Colet again that he had submitted himself in all things
to his guidance. ' Meanwhile,' he concluded, ' I shall
' spend my time with Grocyn, Linacre, and Lilly ; the
' first, as you know, is the director of my life in your
' absence ; the second, the master of my studies ; the
' third, my most dear companion. Farewell, and, as
' you do, ever love me.'

' London : 10 Calend. Novembris ' [1504].[1]

Surrounded as he was by Colet, Grocyn, and Linacre, More soon began to devote his leisure to his old
studies. Lilly, too, had returned home well versed in

---

[1] That this letter was written in 1504 is evident. First, it cannot well have been written before Colet had commenced his labours at St. Paul's ; secondly, it cannot have been written in Oct. 1505, because it speaks of Colet as still holding the living of Stepney, which he resigned Sept. 21, 1505. Also the whole drift of it leads to the conclusion that More was unmarried when he wrote it. And he married in 1505, according to the register on the Burford picture, which, the correct date of More's birth having been found and from it the true date of Holbein's sketch, seems to be amply confirmed by the age there given of More's eldest daughter, Margaret Roper. She is stated to be twenty-two on the sketch made in 1528 and so was probably born in 1506.

CHAP. IV.
———
A.D. 1504.
More
buries
himself in
his studies
with Lilly.

Greek.   He had spent some years in the island of
Rhodes, to perfect his knowledge of it.[1]   Naturally
enough, therefore, the two friends busied themselves
in jointly translating Greek epigrams ; [2] and as, with
increasing zeal, they yielded to the charms of the new
learning, it is not surprising if the fascinations of
monastic life began to lose their hold upon their
minds.   The result was that More was saved from
the false step he once had contemplated.

He had, it would seem, seen enough of the evil side
of the ' religious life ' to know that in reality it did not
offer that calm retreat from the world which in theory
it ought to have done.   He had cautiously abstained
from rushing into vows before he had learned well
what they meant ; and his experience of ascetic
practices had far too ruthlessly destroyed any
pleasant pictures of monastic life in which he may
have indulged at first, to admit of his ever becoming
a Carthusian monk.

Still we may not doubt that, in truth, he had a real
and natural yearning for the pure ideal of cloister
holiness.   Early disappointed love possibly,[3] added to
the rude shipwreck made of his worldly fortunes on
the rock of royal displeasure, had, we may well believe,
effectually taught him the lesson not to trust in those
' gay golden dreams ' of worldly greatness, from which,
he was often wont to say, ' we cannot help awaking
' when we die ; ' and even the penances and scourgings
inflicted by way of preparatory discipline upon his
' wanton flesh,' though soon proved to be of no great

---

[1] *Mori   Epigrammata* :   Basle,
1518, p. 6. See the prefatory letter
by Beatus Rhenanus.

[2] Ibid.

[3] See Epigram entitled ' *Gratu-*

' *latur quod eam repererit Incolu-*
' *mem quam olim ferme Puer ama-*
' *verat.*' — *Epigrammata* : Basle,
1520, p. 108, and *Philomorus*, pp.
37–39.

efficacy, were not the less without some deep root in
his nature ; else why should he wear secretly his
whole life long the ' *sharp shirt of hair* ' which we
hear about at last ? [1]

So much as this must be conceded to More's
Catholic biographers, who naturally incline to make
the most of this ascetic phase of his life.[2]

But that, on the other hand, he did turn in disgust   More
from the impurity of the cloister to the better chances disgusted
which, he thought, the world offered of living a   with the
chaste and useful life, we know from Erasmus ; and   cloister.
this his Catholic biographers have, in their turn,
acknowledged.[3]

IV. MORE STUDIES PICO'S LIFE AND WORKS.
HIS MARRIAGE (1505).

More appears to have been influenced in the course
he had taken mainly by two things :—first, a sort of
hero-worship for the great Italian, Pico della Mirandola ; and, secondly, his continued reverence for Colet.

The ' Life of Pico,' with divers Epistles and other
' Works ' of his, had come into More's hands. Very
probably Lilly may have brought them home with him
amongst his Italian spoils. More had taken the pains
to translate them into English. He had doubtless

---

[1] 'From whence [the Tower], the
' day before he suffered, he sent his
' shirt of hair, not willing to have it
' seen, to my wife, his dearly beloved
' daughter.'—Roper, p. 91.

[2] Walter's *Life of More*, London,
1840, pp. 7, 8. Cresacre More's
Life of More, pp. 24–26.

[3] 'Maluit igitur maritus esse
' castus quam sacerdos impurus.'—
Erasmus to Hutten : Eras. *Op.* iii.

p. 75, c. Stapleton, 1612 ed. pp.
161, 162. Cresacre More's *Life of
More*, pp. 25, 26. Even Walter
allows that his 'finding that at that
' time religious orders in England
' had somewhat degenerated from
' their ancient strictness and fervour
' of spirit,' was the cause of his
' altering his mind.'—Walter's *Life
of More*, p. 8.

More
translates
the life
and works
of Pico.

Pico's
warm
piety and
zeal.

A layman
to the end.

heard all about Pico's outward life from those of his friends who had known him personally when in Italy. But here was the record of Pico's inner history, for the most part in his own words ; and reading this in More's translation, it is not hard to see how strong an influence it may have exercised upon him. It told how, suddenly checked, as More himself had been, in a career of worldly honour and ambition, the proud vaunter of universal knowledge had been transformed into the humble student of the Bible ; how he had learned to abhor scholastic disputations, of which he had been so great a master, and to search for truth instead of fame. It told how, ' giving no great force ' to outward observances,' ' he cleaved to God in very ' fervent love,' so that, ' on a time as he walked with ' his nephew in an orchard at Ferrara, in talking of the ' love of Christ, he told him of his secret purpose to give ' away his goods to the poor, and fencing himself with ' the crucifix, barefoot, walking about the world, in ' every town and castle to preach of Christ.' It told how he, too, ' scourged his own flesh in remembrance ' of the passion and death that Christ suffered for our ' sake ; ' and urged others also ever to bear in mind two things, ' that the Son of God died for thee, and ' that thou thyself shalt die shortly; ' and how, finally, in spite of the urgent warnings of the great Savonarola, he remained a layman to the end, and in the midst of indefatigable study of the Oriental languages, and, above all, the Scriptures, through their means, died at the early age of thirty-five, leaving the world to wonder at his genius, and Savonarola to preach a sermon on his death.[1]

---

[1] Sir Thomas More's *Works*, pp. 1–34 ; and see the note on Pico's religious history, and his connection with Savonarala, above, p. 19.

And turning from the ' *Life* of Pico ' to his *'Works,'* and reading these in More's translation, they present to the mind a type of Christianity, so opposite to the ceremonial and external religion of the monks, that one may well cease to wonder that More, having caught the spirit of Pico's religion, could no longer entertain any notion of becoming a Carthusian brother.

It will be worth while to examine carefully what these works of Pico's were.

The first is a letter from Pico to his nephew—a letter of advice to a young man somewhat in More's position, longing to live to some ' virtuous purpose,' but finding it hard to stem the tide of evil around him. To encourage his nephew, he speaks of the ' great ' peace and felicity it is to the mind when a man hath ' nothing that grudgeth his conscience, nor is appalled ' with the secret touch of any privy crime.' . . . . ' Doubtest thou, my son, whether the minds of wicked ' men be vexed or not with continual thought and ' torment ? . . . . . The wicked man's heart is like ' the stormy sea, that may not rest. There is to him ' nothing sure, nothing peaceable, but all things fear- ' ful, all things sorrowful, all things deadly. Shall ' we, then, envy these men ? Shall we follow them, ' forgetting our own country—heaven, and our own ' heavenly Father—where we were free-born ? Shall ' we wilfully make ourselves bondmen, and with them, ' wretched living, more wretchedly die, and at the last ' most wretchedly in everlasting fire be punished ? '

Having warned his nephew against wicked com- panions, Pico proceeds to make evident allusion to the sceptical tendencies of Italian society. ' It is verily ' a great madness ' (he says) ' not to believe the Gospel, ' whose *truth* the blood of martyrs crieth, the voice of

' Apostles soundeth, miracles prove, *reason confirmeth,*
' the world testifieth, the elements speak, devils con-
' fess ! ' [1] ' But,' he continues, ' a far greater madness
' is it, if thou doubt not but that the Gospel is true,
' to live then as though thou doubtest not but that
' it were false.'

Its reason-
ableness
and har-
mony with
the laws
of nature.

And it is worth notice, that the perception of the
reasonableness of Christianity, and its harmony with
the laws of nature, breaks out again a little further on.
Pico writes to his nephew : ' Take no heed what thing
' *many* men do, but [take heed] *what thing the very law*
' *of nature,* what thing *very reason,* what thing *our Lord*
' *himself showeth thee to be done.'*

A little further on Pico points out two remedies,
or aids, whereby his nephew may be strengthened in
his course. First, charity ; and secondly, prayer.
With regard to the first he wrote :—' Certainly He
' shall not hear thee when thou callest on *Him,* if thou
' hear not first the poor man when he calleth upon *thee.'*

With regard to prayer, he wrote thus :—' When I stir
' thee to prayer, I stir thee not to the prayer that
' standeth in many words, but to that prayer which, in
' the secret chamber of the mind, in the privy-closet of
' the soul, with very affect speaketh unto God, and in
' the most lightsome darkness of contemplation, not
' only presenteth the mind to the Father, but also
' uniteth it with Him by unspeakable ways, which only
' *they* know that have assayed. Nor I care not how
' long or how short thy prayer be, but how effectual, how
' ardent. . . . Let no day pass, then, but thou once at
' the leastwise present thyself to God by prayer, and
' falling down before Him flat to the ground, with an

---

[1] Compare this with the line of argument pursued by Marsilio Ficino
in his *De Religione Christianâ.* Vide supra, p. 11.

' humble affect of devout mind, not from the extremity
' of thy lips, but out of the inwardness of thine heart,
' cry these words of the prophet : " The offences of
' " my youth, and mine ignorances, remember not,
' " good Lord, but after thy goodness remember me."
' What thou shalt in thy prayer ask of God, both the
' Holy Spirit, which prayeth for us and eke thine own
' necessity, shall every hour put into thy mind, and
' also what thou shalt pray for thou shalt find matter
' enough *in the reading of Holy Scripture*, which that
' thou wouldst now (setting poets, fables, and trifles
' aside) take ever in thine hand I heartily pray thee ;
' . . . . there lieth in *them* a certain heavenly strength
' quick· and effectual, which with marvellous power
' transformeth and changeth the readers' mind into the
' love of God, if they be clean and lowly entreated.'
Lastly, he said he would ' make an end with this one
' thing. I warn thee (of which when we were last
' together I often talked with thee) that thou never
' forget these two things : that both the Son of God
' died for thee, and that thou thyself shalt die
' shortly ! ' [1]

Pico on the Scriptures.

This, then, was the doctrine which Pico, ' fencing
' himself with a crucifix, barefoot, walking about the
' world, in every town and castle,' purposed to preach !

The next letter is a reply to a friend of his who had
urged him to leave his contemplative and studious
life, and to mix in political affairs, in which, as an
Italian prince, lay his natural sphere. He replied,
that his desire was ' not *so to embrace Martha as utterly
' to forsake Mary* '—to ' love them and use them both,

---

[1] This remarkable letter was written, ' Ferrariæ, 15 May, 1492 '
(Pici *Op.* p. 233), scarcely six weeks after Pico's visit to the deathbed
of Lorenzo de Medici.

CHAP. IV.
———
A.D. 1505.

' as well study as worldly occupation.' ' I set more '
(he continued) ' by my little house, my study, the
' pleasure of my books, the rest and peace of my mind,
' than by all your king's palaces, all your business, all
' your glory, all the advantage that ye hawke after,
' and all the favour of the court ! '

Pico's
study of
Eastern
languages.

Then he tells his friend that what he looks to do is,
' *to give out some books of mine to the common profit,*'
and that he is mastering the Hebrew, Chaldee, and
Arabic languages.[1]

Another
letter
to his
nephew.

Then follows another letter to his nephew, who, in
trying to follow the advice given in his first letter,
finds himself slandered and called a hypocrite by his
companions at court. It is a letter of noble encouragement to stand his ground, and to heed not the
scoffs and sneers of his fellows.

These letters are followed by an exposition of
Psalm xvi., in which Pico incidentally uses his knowledge of the Hebrew text and of Eastern customs.[2]

Pico's
verses.

All the foregoing are in prose ; after them come
More's translations of some of Pico's verses.

The first is entitled, ' Twelve rules, partly exciting
' and partly directing a man in spiritual battle,' and
reminds one of the ' Enchiridion ' of Erasmus. The
second is named, ' The twelve weapons of spiritual
' battle.' The striking feature in both these metrical
works is the holding up of Christ's example as an
incentive to duty and to love. Thus :—

---

[1] This letter is dated in More's
translation M.cccclxxxii. from
Paris, in mistake for M.cccclxxxvi.

from *Perugia*. See Pici *Op.* p. 257.
[2] See More's *Works*, p. 19, *in
loco*, v. 4 and v. 6.

'Consider, when thou art movèd to be *wroth*,
  He who that was God and of all men the best,
Seeing himself scornèd and scourgèd both,
  And as a thief between two thievès threst,
  With all rebuke and shame ; yet from his breast
Came never sign of wrath or of disdain,
But patiently endurèd all the pain ! '

And again, after speaking of the shortness of life—

  'How fast it runneth on, and passen shall
  As doth a dream or shadow on a wall.'

he continues :—

  'Think on the very lamentable pain,
  Think on the piteous cross of woeful Christ,
    Think on his blood, beat out at every vein,
    Think on his precious heart carvèd in twain :
  Think how for thy redemption all was wrought.
  Let him not lose, what he so dear hath bought.'

There is another poem in which the feelings of a lover towards his love are made to show what the Christian's feelings ought to be to Christ ; and lastly, there is a solemn and beautiful ' Prayer of ' Picus Mirandola to God,' glowing with the same adoration of

  . . . . 'that mighty love
  Which able was thy dreadful majesty
  To draw down into earth from heaven above
  And crucify God, that we poor wretches, *we*
  Should from our filthy sin yclensèd be ! '

and the same earnest longing

  'That when the journey of this deadly life
  My silly ghost hath finished, and thence
  Departen must,' . . . .
  ' He may Thee find . . . .
  In thy lordship, not as a lord, but rather
  As a very tender, loving father ! '

Pico's en-
lightened
piety.

I have made these quotations, and thus endeavoured
to put the reader in possession of the contents of this
little volume, which More in his seclusion was translating, because I think they throw some light upon the
current in which his thoughts were moving, and because, whilst the name of Pico is known to fame as that
of a great linguist and most precocious genius, his enlightened piety and the extent of the influence of his
heroic example have scarcely been appreciated.

This little book, indeed, has a special significance
in relation to the history of the Oxford Reformers.
Whatever doubt may rest upon the direct connection
between *their* views and those of Savonarola, there is
here in More's translation of these writings of a disciple
of Savonarola, another *in*direct connection between
them and that little knot of earnest Christian men in
Italy of which Savonarola was the most conspicuous.

Position
of the
Neo-
Platonic
philoso-
phers of
Florence.

The extracts made and translated by More from
Pico's writings may also help us to recognise in the
Neo-Platonic philosophers of Florence, by whose writings Colet had been so profoundly influenced, a vein of
earnest Christian feeling of which it may be that we
know too little.   Like their predecessors of a thousand
years before, they stood between the old world and the
new.   They were the men who, when the learning of the
old Pagan world was restored to light, and backed
against the dogmatic creed of priest-ridden degraded
Christendom, built a bridge, as it were, between
Christian and Pagan thought.   That their bridge was
frail and insecure it may be, but, to a great extent, it
served its end.   A passage was effected by it from the
Pagan to the Christian shore.   Ficino, the representative Neo-Platonist, who, as has been seen, had
aided in its building, had himself passed over it.

Savonarola too had crossed it. Pico had crossed it.
It is true that these men may, to some extent, have
Platonised Christianity in becoming Christian ; but
it will be recognised at once that the earnest Christian
feeling found by More in Pico, so to speak, rose far
above his Platonism.

That the life and writings of such a man should have
awakened in his breast something of hero-worship [1]
is, therefore, not surprising. That he should have
singled out these passages, and taken the trouble to
translate them, is some proof that he admired Pico's
practical piety more than his Neo-Platonic speculations ; that he shared with Colet those yearnings
for practical Christian reform with which Colet had
returned from Italy ten years before. That a few
years after this translation should be published and
issued in English in More's name was further proof of
it. For here was a book not only in its drift and spirit
boldly taking Colet's side against the Schoolmen, and
in favour of the study of Scripture and the Oriental
languages, but as boldly holding up Savonarola as ' a
' preacher, as well in cunning as in holiness of living,
' most famous,'—' a holy man '—' a man of God ' [2]— More calls
in the teeth of the fact that he had been denounced Savonarola a
by the Pope as a ' son of blasphemy and perdition,' ' man of
excommunicated, tortured, and, refusing to abjure, God.'
hung and burned as a heretic ! [3]

And if the fire of hero-worship for Pico had lit Colet's
up something of heroism in More's heart—something influence
on More.

---

[1] Stapleton, ed. 1612, p. 162.
Cresacre More's *Life of Sir T.
More*, p. 27.

[2] Sir T. More's *Works*, p. 9.

[3] There is a copy of this translation of More's in the British

Museum Library. ' 276, c. 27, *Pico,
' &c.*, 4°, *London*, 1510.' This is
probably the original edition. More
may have waited till Henry VIII.'s
accession before daring to publish
it.

which yearned for the battle of life, and not for the rest of the cloister—so the living example of Colet was ready to feed the flame into strength and steadiness.

The result was that, in 1505,[1] in spite of early disappointments, and, it is said, under Colet's ' advice ' and direction,' [2] More married Jane Colt, of New Hall in Essex, took a house in Bucklersbury, and gave up for ever all longings for monastic life.

V. HOW IT HAD FARED WITH ERASMUS (1500–5).

Soon after Colet's elevation to the dignities of Doctor and Dean, a letter of congratulation arrived from Erasmus.

Colet had written no letter to him, and had almost lost sight of him during these years. It would seem that, after his departure from Oxford, Colet had given up all hopes of his aid. Nor had any other kindred soul risen up to take that place in fellow-work beside him, which at one time he had hoped the great scholar might have filled.

But Erasmus on his side had not forgotten Colet. His intercourse with Colet at Oxford had changed the current of his thoughts, and the course of his life. Colet little knew by what slow and painful steps he had been preparing to redeem the promise he had made on leaving Oxford.

We left him making the best of his way to Dover,

---

[1] This date of More's marriage is the date given in the register contained on the Burford family picture ; and as it is in no way dependent on the other dates, probably it rested upon some family tradition or record. It is confirmed by the age of Margaret Roper on the Basle sketch—22 in 1528. Vide supra, p. 149, n. 1.

[2] Cresacre More's *Life of Sir T. More*, p. 39.

with his purse full of golden crowns, kindly bestowed
by his English friends in order that he might now
carry out his long-cherished intention of going to Italy.
But the Fates had decreed against him. King Henry
VII. had already reached the avaricious period of his
life and reign. Under cover of an old obsolete statute,
he had given orders to the Custom House officers to
stop the exportation of all precious metals, and the
Custom House officers in their turn, construing their
instructions strictly to the letter, had seized upon
Erasmus's purseful of golden crowns, and relieved him
of the burden, for the benefit of the King's exchequer.[1]
The poor scholar proceeded without them to cross to
Boulogne.

He was a bad sailor, and the hardships of travel
soon told upon his health. He was heart-sick also ;
as well he might be, for this unlucky loss of his purse
had utterly disconcerted once more his long-cherished
plans. On his arrival at Paris, after a wretched and
dangerous journey,[2] he was taken ill, and recovered
only to bear his bitter disappointment as best he could.
Before he had yet recovered from his illness he wrote
this touching letter to Arnold, the young legal friend
of More, with whom a few weeks before he and More
had visited the Royal nursery.

Erasmus to Arnold.[3]

' Salve, mi Arnolde. Now for six weeks I have
' been suffering much from a nocturnal ague, of a

---

[1] Erasmus Botzhemo : *Catalogus Omnium Erasmi Lucubrationum* : Basle, 1523.

[2] Epist. lxxxi. He arrived at Paris ' postridie Calend. Februarias' (p. 73, E.), i.e. Feb. 2, 1500.

[3] Epist. iii. This letter is dated in the Leyden edition, 1490, and

Erasmus
gives up
all hope
of going
to Italy.

' lingering kind but of daily recurrence, and it has
' nearly killed me.   I am not yet free from the disease,
' but still somewhat better.   I don't yet *live* again, but
' some hope of life dawns upon me.   You ask me to
' tell you my plans.   Take this only, to begin with :
' To mortify myself to the world, I dash my hopes.   I
' long for nothing more than to give myself rest, in
' which I might live wholly to God alone, weep away
' the sins of a careless life, devote myself to the study
' of the Holy Scriptures, either read somewhat or
' write.   This I cannot do in a monastery or college.
' One could not be more delicate than I am ;   my
' health will bear neither vigils, nor fasts, nor any
' disturbance, even when at its best.   Here, where I
' live in such luxury, I often fall ill ;   what should I do
' amid the labours of college life ?

' I had determined to go to Italy this year, and to
' work at theology some months at Bologna ;   also
' there to take the degree of Doctor ;   then in the year
' of Jubilee to visit Rome ;   which done, to return to
' my friends and then to settle down.   But I am afraid
' that these things that I *would*, I shall *not be able* to
' accomplish.   I fear, in the first place, that my health
' would not stand such a journey and the heat of the
' climate.   Lastly, I reckon that I could not go to

Cost of
going to
Italy.

' Italy, nor live there without great expense.   It costs
' a great deal also to prepare for a degree.   And the
' Bishop of Cambray gives very sparingly.   He al-
' together loves more liberally than he gives, and
' promises everything much more largely than he

---

in the edition of 1521, p. 264,
M.LXXXIX. (*sic*), but it evidently
was written shortly after the illness
of Erasmus at Paris in the spring
of 1500.   See also the mention of

' Arnold ' in Epist. xxix. (Paris, 12
April) and a repetition in it of much
that is said in this letter respecting
Erasmus's illness and intention of
visiting Italy. See also Ep. dii. App.

' performs. It is partly my own fault for not pressing
' him. There are so many who are even *extorting.*
' In the meantime I shall do what seems for the best.
' Farewell.'

What was he to do? It was clear that he did not
know what to do. The worst of it was that the unfortunate loss of the price of many months leisure [1] not
only obliged him to postpone *sine die* his project of
visiting Italy, but also to spend a large portion of his
time and strength for the next few years in a struggle
almost for subsistence. For the wolf must in some
way or other be kept from the door; and Erasmus
was *poor !*

For a few months he struggled on at Paris, living in
lodgings with an old fellow student ' sparingly,' [2] hard
at work at a collection of Greek and Latin proverbs—
his *Adagia*—partly in order to raise the wind, partly to
improve himself in Greek. Sometimes borrowing and
sometimes begging, whatever money came to his hands
went forthwith first in buying Greek books and then in
clothes.[3] Later in the year, the prevalence of the
Plague in Paris drove him to Orleans. He would have
gone to Italy, but he had not the means.[4] In December
he returned to Paris to continue his struggling life.[5]

Poverty of
Erasmus.

His Greek
studies.

---

[1] 'In Britannico littore pecuniola
' mea, studiorum meorum alimonia,
' naufragium fecit.'—Epist. xcii.
p. 84 C.

[2] ' *Tenuiter.*'—Eras. *Op.* iii. p.73
F. Epist. lxxxi. and see also lxxx.

[3] Erasmus to Battus : Epist.xxix.
Paris, 12 April, probably in 1500.
See also Epist. lxxx. ' Græcæ literæ
' animum meum propemodum ene-

' cant: verum neque precium datur,
' neque suppetit, quo libros, aut
' præceptoris operam redimam. Et
' dum hæc omnia tumultuor, vix
' est unde vitam sustineam.'

[4] Epist. xciv.

[5] Epistolæ xxxvi. lxxvi. lxxi. (20
Nov.), lxxii. (9 Dec.), xciv. xcix.
(11 Dec.), lxxiii. (11 Dec.), and
lxxiv. seem to belong to this period

In a letter written in January, 1501, on the anniversary of his misfortune at Dover, he described himself ' as having now for a whole year been sailing under ' a stormy sky against the waves and against the ' winds.' [1] To add to his troubles, the Plague again broke out in Paris ; and, terrified by the number of funerals passing his door, the poor scholar fled from the city to spend a few weeks in his native country. [2] During his stay in Holland he visited the monastery at Stein, [3] where in early years he had tasted the bitters of the monastic life. Neither there nor elsewhere in Holland did he find a resting-place.

Fortunately for him, one true friend at least turned up, willing and able to enter into sympathy with him. This was Battus, tutor to the Marchioness of Vere. Erasmus had already corresponded with him from Paris, pouring out his troubles to him, and declaring that he had no other hope but in him alone. [4] Kept away from Paris by the Plague, and finding not even a temporary home in Holland, he at last found a refuge for a while from his fears and cares in a visit to the castle of Tornahens, [5] the residence of the Marchioness of Vere and of Battus. It had the additional attrac-

---

of flight to Orleans. Epist. xv. and lxxvii.(14 Dec.), lxxviii. (18 Dec.), and xci. (14 Jan.), seem to mark the date of his return to Paris.

[1] Epist. xcii. Paris, 27 Jan. 1500 (should be 1501).

[2] Epist. xxxix.

[3] Epist. ccccvii. App.

[4] ' Nec est in ullo mortalium aliquid solidæ spei nisi in uno Batto' Eras. *Op.* iii. p. 48, C. Epist. liii.

[5] Epist. xxx. 2 July [1501] seems to be the first letter written from

St. Omer, where Erasmus was then staying with the Abbot. See also Ep. xxxix., where he speaks of having been terrified at Paris with the numbers of funerals. On 12 July and 18 July he writes Epist. liv.– lviii. (' Tornaco ' evidently meaning the castle of Tornahens). Ep. lix. also was written about the same time. Epist. xcviii. 30 July, if written by Erasmus, shows he was still at St. Omer. All these letters seem to belong to the year 1501.

tion of being near to St. Omer, where lived a former
patron of Erasmus, the Abbot of St. Bertin.

Whilst staying with Battus he wrote to a friend, that he sometimes thought of returning to England to spend a month or two more with Colet, in order to confer further with him on some theological questions. He knew well, he said, how much good he should gain from doing so, but he could not get over the unlucky experience of his last voyage. As to his journey to Italy, that, too, was knocked on the head. He told his friend that he longed to visit Italy as ardently as ever, but it was out of the question ; for, according to the adage of Plautus, ' Sine pennis volare haud facile ' est.' [1]

Battus also wrote to Lord Mountjoy to tell him with what pleasure he had embraced Erasmus, but, ' alas, ' how ill-treated and spoiled ! ' He told him how he had been commiserating Erasmus on his ill-fortune in England, and how the philosopher had smiled and bade him put a good face on it. He did not regret having visited England ; he cared more for the friends he had found in England than for all the gold of Crœsus. Battus concluded by telling Lord Mountjoy how Erasmus had described to him the courtesy of the Prior Charnock, the learning of Colet, the good nature of More, the virtues of his noble patron.[2] It was during this visit to St. Omer, in the summer of 1501, that Erasmus wrote his ' Enchiridion.'

There happened to be staying in the castle a lady, a friend of Battus, who had a bad husband. The latter, whilst holding other divines at arm's length, took to Erasmus. The wife, thinking that he possibly might have some influence over her husband, begged

---

[1] Eras. *Op.* iii. p. 52, E. Epist. lix.   [2] Epist. lxii.

him, without betraying that it was at her instigation, to write something which might produce in him some religious impressions.[1] The 'Enchiridion' was the result, of which more will be said by and by.

John Vitrarius.

It was at St. Omer also that Erasmus became acquainted with John Vitrarius—a second John Colet in the earnestness of his Christian zeal against the corruptions of the church and vices of the clergy, in his love for St. Paul, in his outspoken preaching, and even in his manner of preaching, in his dislike of the Scholastic subtlety of Scotus, and even in his preference for Ambrose, Cyprian, Jerome, and Origen over Augustine. Erasmus ever afterwards linked the names of Colet and Vitrarius together, and admitted them both deservedly into his calendar of uncanonised saints.[2] The 'Enchiridion' was submitted to the judgment of Vitrarius, and obtained his approval.[3]

Return of Erasmus to Paris.

After many refreshing days passed at St. Omer, Erasmus returned to Paris to pursue his literary labours. These, notwithstanding all the hindrances of ill-health and poverty, never seem to have flagged.[4] He had already made up his mind to devote himself to the Herculean task of correcting the text of St. Jerome's voluminous works, with a view to their publication.[5] The first edition of his 'Adagia' had

---

[1] Erasmus to Botzhem: *Catalogus Omnium Erasmi Lucubrationum*: Basle, 1523, leaf b, 4.

[2] Erasmus to Justus Jonas: Epist. ccccxxxv.

[3] 'Ea quum placerent etiam eru-'ditis, præsertim Ioanni Viterio 'Franciscano cujus erat in illis 'regionibus autoritas summa.'—

Letter to Botzhem, leaf b, 4. There can be no doubt that the John Viterius mentioned in this letter is the same person as the Vitrarius of the letter to Justus Jonas. See also Mr. Lupton's introduction to his translation of Colet on Dionysius.

[4] Eras. Epist. clxxiii.

[5] Ibid. xciv.

been printed in 1501 ; and during a visit to Louvain
and Antwerp, in 1503, he was able to publish some
other works—his afterwards famous ' Enchiridion '
amongst the rest.[1] But notwithstanding all his
indomitable energy, and the often repeated kindness
of Battus and the Marchioness, it would be difficult to
imagine a longer catalogue of troubles and disappointments—and these too of that harassing and vexatious
kind which are most trying to the temper—than is
contained in the letters of Erasmus during these
dreary years.[2]

He might well have been excused if, lost sight of as
it would seem by his English friends, he had himself
forgotten his promise to Colet on leaving Oxford,
amidst the cares of his continental life.

But whilst these necessities not a little interrupted, Erasmus
as was likely, those studies to which Colet's example remem-
and precept had urged him, and lengthened out the promise
preliminary labours which Erasmus had made up his to Colet.
mind must precede his active participation in Colet's
work, they did not, it seems, damp his energy, or
induce him to look back after putting his hand to the
plough.   This and more lies touchingly hinted in the
following letter written by Erasmus to Colet on receipt
of the news of the elevation of his friend to the dignity
of Doctor and Dean.

---

[1] *Lucubratiunculæ aliquot Erasmi* : Antwerp, 1503. *Biogr. de
Thierry Martins* : par A. F. Van
Iseghem : Alost, 1852, 8vo. See
also Letter to Botzhem (*Catalogus,
&c.*), fol. b, 4.

[2] It is very difficult to fix the true

dates of these letters, and to ascertain to what year they belong.
Ep. ccccxlvi. App., from Louvain,
mentions the death of Battus, and
that the Marchioness of Vere had
married below her. He speaks of
himself as buried in Greek studies.

Erasmus to Colet.[1]

' If our friendship, most learned Colet, had been of
' a common-place kind, or your habits those of the
' common run of men, I should indeed have been some-
' what fearful lest it might have been extinguished, or
' at least cooled, by our long and wide separation. . .
' But I prefer to believe that the cause of my having
' received no letter from you now for *several years*,
' lies rather in your press of business, or ignorance of
' my whereabouts, or even in myself, than in your
' forgetfulness of an old friend. . . . .

   ' I am much surprised that you have not yet given
' to the world any of your commentaries on St. Paul
' and the Gospels. I know your modesty, but surely
' you ought to conquer that, and print them for the
' *public good.*

Erasmus
congratu-
lates Colet
on his pre-
ferment.

   ' As to the title of Doctor and Dean, I do not so
' much congratulate *you* about these—for I know well
' they will bring you nothing but labour—as those for
' whose good you are to bear them.

Wants to
devote
himself to
Scripture
studies.

   ' I cannot tell you, dearest Colet, how, by hook and
' by crook, I struggle to devote myself to the study
' of sacred literature—how I regret everything which
' either delays me or detains me from it. But
' constant ill-fortune has prevented me from extricat-
' ing myself from these hindrances. When in France,
' I determined that if I could not conquer these
' difficulties I would cast them aside, and that once
' freed from them, with my whole mind I would set to
' work at these sacred studies, and devote the rest of

---

[1] Eras. *Op.* iii. p. 94. Epist. cii. Dated 1504, but should be probably 1505.

' my life to them. Although three years before I had
' attempted something on St. Paul's Epistle to the
' Romans,[1] and had completed four volumes at one
' pull, I was nevertheless prevented from going on with
' it, owing chiefly to the want of a better knowledge of
' Greek. Consequently, for nearly these three years
' past, I have buried myself in Greek literature ; nor
' do I think the labour has been thrown away. I
' began also to dip into Hebrew, but, deterred by the
' strangeness of the words, I desisted, knowing that one
' man's life and genius are not enough for too many
' things at a time. I have read through a good part
' of the works of Origen, under whose guidance I
' seemed really to get on, for he opened to me, as it
' were, the springs and the method of theological
' science.

' I send you [herewith], as a little literary present,
' some lucubrations of mine. Among them is our dis-
' cussion, when in England, on the Agony of Christ,
' but so altered that you will hardly know it again.
' Besides, your reply and my rejoinder to it could not
' be found. The " Enchiridion " I wrote to display
' neither genius nor eloquence, but simply for this—to
' counteract the vulgar error of those who think that
' religion consists in ceremonies, and in more than
' *Jewish* observances, while they neglect what really
' pertains to piety. I have tried to teach, as it were,
' the *art* of piety in the same way as others have laid
' down the rules of [military] discipline. . . . The rest
' were written against the grain, especially the
' " Pæan " and " Obsecratio," which I wrote to please
' Battus and Anna, the Princess of Vere. As to the

---

1 See Erasmus Edmundo : Epist. xcvi. ' ex arce Courtemburnensi.'

Chap. IV.

A.D.
1500–5.

The
'Adagia.'

Eras mus
wants help
from his
friends.

'"Panegyric," [1] it was so contrary to my taste, that
'I do not remember ever having written anything
'more reluctantly; for I saw that such a thing
'could not be done without adulation. . . . .
'   I wrote, if you recollect, some time past, about the
'100 copies of the "Adagia" which I sent at my own
'expense into England, now three years ago.   Grocyn
'wrote me word that he would arrange with the
'greatest fidelity and diligence that they should be
'sold according to my wish, and I do not doubt but
'that he has performed his promise, for he is the best
'and most honourable man that ever lived in England.
'Will you be so good as to aid me in this matter, so far
'as to advise and spur on those by whom you think
'the business ought to be settled ?   For one cannot
'doubt but that, in so long a time, the books must be
'sold ; and the money must of necessity have come to
'somebody's hand ; and it is likely to be of more use
'to me now than ever before.   For, by some means or
'other, I must contrive to have a few months entirely
'to myself, that I may extricate myself somehow
'from my labours in secular literature.   This I trusted
'I could have done this winter, had not so many hopes
'proved illusive.   Nor, indeed, "with a great sum can
'"I obtain this freedom," even for a few months.   I
'entreat you, therefore, to do what you can to aid me,
'panting as I do eagerly after sacred studies, in disen-
'gaging myself from those [secular] studies which have
'now ceased to be pleasant to me.   It would not do
'for me to beg of my friend, Lord Mountjoy, although
'it would not seem unreasonable or impertinent if, of

---

[1] The Panegyric upon Philip, King of Spain, on his return to the
Netherlands.   See Epist. ccccxlv. App. Erasmus Gulielmo Goudano.

'his own good will, he had chosen to aid me, both on
'the ground of his habitual patronage of my studies,
'and also because the " Adagia " were undertaken at
'his suggestion, and inscribed with his name. I am
'ashamed of the first edition [of the " Adagia "]
'both on account of the blundering mistakes of the
'printers, which seem made almost on purpose, and
'because, urged on by others, I hurried over the
'work which had now begun to seem to me dry and
'poor after my study of the Greek authors. Conse-
'quently, another edition is resolved upon, in which
'the errors of both author and printer are to be cor-
'rected, and the work made as useful as possible to
'students.

'Although, however, I may for a while be engaged
'upon an humble task, yet whilst thus working in the
'Garden of the Greeks, I am gathering much fruit by
'the way for the time to come, which may hereafter be
'of use to me in sacred studies. For I have learned
'this by experience, that without Greek one can do
'nothing in any branch of study; for it is one thing
'to conjecture, and quite another thing to judge—one
'thing to see with other people's eyes, and quite an-
'other thing to believe what you see with your own.

'But to what a length this letter has grown ! Love,
'however, will excuse loquacity. Farewell, most
'learned and excellent Colet.

'Pray let me know what has happened to our friend
'Sixtinus ; also what your friend the Prior Richard
'Charnock is doing.

'In order that whatever you may write or send to
'me may duly come to hand, be so good as to have
'them addressed to Christopher Fisher (a most loving

' friend and patron of all learned men, and you
' amongst the rest), in whose family I am now a guest.'
Paris, 1504 [in error for 1505].

Thus had the poor scholar worked on, for the most
part in silence, during these years, struggling alone,
yet manfully, in the midst of the manifold hindrances
cast in his way by ill-health and straitened means,
neither free-born (as his friend Colet was), and thus able
to tread unencumbered the path of duty, nor finding
himself able even ' with a great sum to obtain freedom '
for a while. Yet through all had Erasmus kept
courageously to the collar, steadily toiling on through
five years of preliminary labours, with earnest purpose
to redeem his promise to Colet—first, fully to equip
himself with the proper tools and then, but not till
then, to join him in fellow work.

Why
Colet
had not
written.

Colet surely had forgotten the promise of Erasmus
on leaving Oxford, or perchance the hope it held out
was too slender for him to rest on, else he would
hardly have left him during these years without
letters of brotherly encouragement.

It is true that Erasmus still confessed himself to be
occupied in merely preliminary labours. His great
work, no less than it had been five years before, was
still in the future. Yet the fire caught from his contact with Colet at Oxford was at least flickering on
the hearth, and with fresh stirring and fuel might
perhaps after all be kindled into active flame.

Colet's reply to this letter has not come down to us,
but from the result we may be sure that it contained
a pressing invitation to revisit England, and the
promise of a warm reception.

VI. THE 'ENCHIRIDION,' ETC. OF ERASMUS (1501–5).

In the meantime, closer inspection of the literary present sent by Erasmus, must have proved to Colet to how large an extent, after so long a process of study and digestion, his friend had really adopted the views which he himself had held and consistently preached for the last ten years.

The ' Enchiridion ' was, in truth, a re-echo of the very key-note of Colet's faith. It openly taught, as Colet now for so many years had been teaching, that the true Christian's religion, instead of consisting in the acceptance of scholastic dogmas, or the performance of outward rites and ceremonies, really consists in a true, self-sacrificing loyalty to Christ, his ever-living Prince ; that life is a warfare, and that the Christian must sacrifice his evil lusts and passions, and spend his strength, not in the pursuit of his own pleasure, but in active service of his Prince ;—such was the drift and spirit of this ' Handybook of the ' Christian Soldier.' [1]

It must not be assumed, however, that Erasmus had adopted all the views which Colet had expressed in their many conversations at Oxford. On the contrary, I think there may be traced in the ' Enchi-'ridion ' [2] a tendency to interpret the text of Scripture *allegorically*, rather than to seek out its *literal* meaning—a tendency which must have been somewhat

---

[1] More literally ' The *Pocket Dag-* ' *ger* of the Christian Soldier.' But Erasmus himself regarded it as a ' Handybook.' See *Enchiridion*, ch. viii. English ed. 1522. ' We must ' haste to that which remaineth lest ' it should not be an " Enchiri-' dion," that is to say " a lytell ' " treatyse hansome to be caryed ' " in a man's hande," but rather ' a great volume.'

[2] See especially chap. ii. *Allegoria de Manna*, Eras. *Op.* v. fol. 6–10, &c.

opposed to the strong convictions of Colet, and even to those of Erasmus, in after years. But he had just then been studying Origen, and it is not strange that he should for a while be fascinated, as so many others have been, by the allegorical method of interpretation adopted by that father. He had learned so much from his writings, that he yielded the more readily perhaps in this particular to the force of Origen's rich imagination.[1]

But if Colet did not find his own views reflected in all points in this early production of Erasmus, he would not the less rejoice to find its general tone so spiritual, so anti-ceremonial, and so free from superstitious adherence to ecclesiastical authority. That it was so, no stronger proof could be given than the fact that, whilst for years after it was written it was known only in select circles, and was far from being a popular book; yet no sooner had the Protestant movement commenced than, with a fresh preface, it passed through almost innumerable editions with astonishing rapidity. Nor was it read only by the learned. It was translated into English by Tyndale, and again in an abridged form reissued in English by Coverdale. And whilst in this country it was thus treated almost as a Protestant book, so in Spain also it had a remarkably wide circulation. 'The work,' wrote the Archdeacon of Alcor, in 1527—twenty years after its first silent publication—' has gained such applause ' and credit to your name, and has proved so useful to ' the Christian faith, that there is no other book of our ' time which can be compared with the " Enchiridion " ' for the extent of its circulation, since it is found in

---

1 It is evident that Erasmus had not yet appreciated as fully as he did afterwards the *historical* method which Colet had applied to St. Paul's Epistles to get at their real meaning and 'spirit.'

' everybody's hands. There is scarcely anyone in the
' court of the Emperor, any citizen of our cities, or
' member of our churches and convents, no not even
' a hotel or country inn, that has not a copy of the
' " Enchiridion " of Erasmus in Spanish. The Latin
' version was read previously by the few who under-
' stood Latin, but its full merit was not perfectly
' perceived even by these. Now in the Spanish it is
' read by all without distinction ; and this short work
' has made the name of Erasmus a household word in
' circles where it was previously unknown and had not
' been heard of.' [1]

Strong as must have been the Protestant tendencies
of this little book to have made it so great a favourite
with Protestant Reformers, it is worthy of note that
its tone was as moderate and anti-Augustinian upon
the great questions of free will and grace, and in this
respect as decidedly opposed to the extreme Augustinian views adopted by the Protestant Reformers, as
anything that Erasmus ever afterwards wrote during
the heat of the controversy.

Anti-Augustinian on free will and grace.

To abridge what is said in the ' Enchiridion ' on this
subject into a few sentences, but retaining, as nearly
as may be, the words of Erasmus, it is this :—

' The good man is he whose body is a temple of the
' Holy Spirit ; the bad man is like a whited sepulchre
' full of dead men's bones. If the soul loathes its
' proper food, if it cannot see what is truth, if it cannot
' discern the Divine voice speaking in the inner ear ;
' if, in fact, it has become *senseless*, it is *dead*. And
' wherefore dead ? Because God, who is its life, has

---

[1] Alfonso Fernandez, Archdeacon of Alcor, to Erasmus : Palencia, Nov. 27, 1527. *Life and Writings* of *Juan de Valdès*, by Benjamin Wiffen : London, Quaritch, 1865, p. 41.

' forsaken it. Now if the soul be dead it cannot be
' raised into life again but by the gracious power of
' God only. But we have God on our side. Our
' enemy has been conquered by Christ. In ourselves
' we are weak ; in Him we are strong. The victory
' lies in his hands, but he has put it also in ours. No
' one need fail to conquer, unless he does not choose to
' conquer. Aid is withheld from none who desire it.
' If we accept it, he will fight for us, and impute his
' love as merit to us. The victory is to be ascribed to
' him who, alone being sinless, overcame the tyranny
' of sin ; but we are not on that account to expect it
' without our own exertions. We must steer our
' course between Scylla and Charybdis. We must
' neither sit down in idle security, relying on Divine
' grace ; nor, in view of the hardness of the struggle,
' lay down our arms in despair.' [1]

Thus early had Erasmus, following the lead of Colet,
taken up the position as regards this question to which
he adhered through life.

Other
works of
Erasmus.

But the ' Enchiridion ' was not the only work published by Erasmus during this interval. Probably an-
nexed to it, and under the same cover, he had published his long report of the conversation between him-

Conversa-
tion at
Oxford
on the
' Agony of
Christ.'

self and Colet at Oxford on the causes of the Agony of
Christ in the Garden. This showed at least that he
had not forgotten what had passed between them on
that occasion. As, however, he did not append to it
Colet's reply, it cannot be concluded that he had given
up his own opinion, either on the question directly in

---

[1] The above is an abridged translation from the *Enchiridion*, ed.
Argent. June, 1516, pp. 7, 8, which,
being published before the Lutheran
controversy commenced, is probably a reprint of the earlier
editions. The editions of 1515 are
the earliest that I have seen.

dispute, or on the still more important one, which
came out of it, on the inspiration of the Scriptures
and the theory of ' manifold senses.'

Very clearly, however, did the letter which accompanied these works show that Erasmus had already resolved to dedicate his life to the great work of bringing
out the Scriptures into their proper prominence, and
thereby throwing into the background all that mass of
scholastic subtlety which had for so long formed the
food of theologians. If now for years he had been
wading through Greek literature, it was not merely
for its own sake, but with this great object in view.
If, on account of his learning and eloquence, his friends
at the court of the Netherlands had pressed him into
their service, and induced him to compose a flattering
oration on the occasion of the return of Philip from
Spain, he had counted the labour as lost, except so far
as it probably helped to keep the wolf from the door
for a week or two. Even the two editions of the
' Adagia' were evidently regarded only as stepping-
stones to that knowledge without which he felt that
it would be useless for him to attempt to master
the Greek New Testament. Of this he gave further
practical proof before his arrival again in England.
For whilst still under the hospitable roof of his friend
Fisher, the Papal protonotary at Paris, he brought out
his edition of Laurentius Valla's ' Annotations upon
' the New Testament;' a copy of which he had
chanced to light upon in an old library during the
previous summer. And to this edition was prefixed
a prefatory letter to his kind host, remarkable for the
boldness of its tone and the freedom of its thought.

The
' Adagia.'

Preface to
an edition
of Valla's
' Annota-
tions on
the New
Testa-
ment.'

He knew well, he wrote, that some readers would
cry out, ' Oh, Heavens ! ' before they had got to the

end of the titlepage ; but such as these he reminded of the advice of Aristophanes : ' First listen, my friends, ' and then you may shriek and bluster ! ' He knew, he went on to say, that theologians, who ought to get more good out of the book than any one else, would raise the greatest tumult against it ; that they would resent as a sacrilegious infringement of their own sacred province, any interference of Valla, the grammarian, with the sacred text of the Scriptures. But he boldly vindicated the right and the necessity of a fair criticism, as in many passages the Vulgate was manifestly at fault, was a bad rendering of the original Greek, or had itself been corrupted. If any one should reply that the theologian is above the laws of grammar, and that the work of interpretation depends solely upon inspiration, this were, he said, indeed to claim a new dignity for divines. Were they alone to be allowed to indulge in bad grammar ? He quoted from Jerome to show that he claimed no inspiration for the translator ; and asked what would have been the use of Jerome's giving directions for the translation of Holy Scripture if the power of translating depended upon inspiration. Again, how was it that Paul was evidently so much more at home in Hebrew than in Greek ? Finally he urged, if there be errors in the Vulgate, is it not lawful to correct them ? Many indeed he knew would object to change any word in the Bible, because they fancy that in every letter is hid some mystic meaning. Suppose that it were so, would it not be all the more needful that the exact original text should be restored ? [1]

Correction of the text of Scripture.

---

[1] This letter was republished in the edition of some letters of Erasmus printed at Basle, 1521, p. 221, and see also Eras. *Op.* iii. Epist. ciii.

This was a bold public beginning of that work of Biblical criticism to which Colet's example so powerfully urged Erasmus.

The edition of Valla's 'Annotations,' with this letter prefixed to it, was published at Paris in 1505, while he was busily engaged in bringing out the second edition of the 'Adagia.' And it would seem that he only waited for the completion of these works before again crossing the Straits to pay another visit to his English friends.

CHAPTER V.

I. SECOND VISIT OF ERASMUS TO ENGLAND (1505–6).

Towards the close of 1505, Erasmus arrived in England, to renew his intimacy with his English friends.[1] He had not this time to visit Oxford in order to meet them. Colet, Grocyn, Linacre, More, and his friend Lilly, all were ready to receive him with open arms in London. He seems, for a time at least, to have been More's guest.[2]

Erasmus again is More's guest.

Since Erasmus had last seen him, the youth had matured into the man. He had passed through much discipline and mental struggle. But his grey eye sparkled still with native wit, and a hasty glance round his rooms was enough to assure his old friend that his tastes were what they used to be—that in heart and mind, in spite of all that had befallen him, he was the same high-toned and happy-hearted soul he always had been.

More's wife.

More's young and gentle wife, fresh from the retirement of her father's country home, was too uncultured to attract much notice from the learned foreigner; but he tells us More had purposely chosen

---

[1] Letter to Fox, Bishop of Winchester. London, Cal. Jan. 1506. Eras. *Op.* i. p. 214.

[2] Erasmus's letter to Botzhem, *Catalogus, &c.* Basle, 1523, leaf b, 3.

a wife whom he could mould to his own liking for Снар. v.
a life companion. Both were young, and she was apt A.D. 1505.
to learn. Whilst, therefore, he himself found time
to devote to his favourite Greek books and his lyre,
he was imparting by degrees to her his own fondness
for literature and music.[1]

Erasmus found him writing Latin epigrams and More's
verses, in which the pent-up bitter thoughts of the past epigrams.
year or two were making their escape. Some were on
priests and monks—sharp biting satires on their evil
side, and by no means showing abject faith in monk-
hood.[2]

Nor was he courting back again the favour of
offended royalty by melodious and repentant whinings.
Rather his pen gave vent to the chafed and untamed
spirit of the man who knew he had done his duty, and

---

[1] Eras. *Op.* iii. p. 475, D.

[2] The epigrams have no dates, and it is impossible, therefore, to say positively which of them were written during this period. The following translation of one of them from Cayley's *Life of Sir Thomas More*, vol. i. p. 270 (with this reservation as to its date), may be taken as a sample :—

A squall arose ; the vessel's tossed ;
The sailors fear their lives are lost.
' Our sins, our sins,' dismayed they cry,
' Have wrought this fatal destiny ! '

A monk it chanced was of the crew,
And round him to confess they drew.
Yet still the restless ship is tossed,
And still they fear their lives are lost.

One sailor, keener than the rest,
Cries, ' With our sins she's still oppress'd ;
Heave out that monk, who bears them all,
And then full well she 'll ride the squall.'

So said, so done ; with one accord
They threw the caitiff overboard.
And now the bark before the gale
Scuds with light hull and easy sail.

Learn hence the weight of sin to know,
With which a ship could scarcely go.

[For the Latin, see *Epigrammata Thomæ Mori*, Basil. 1520, pp. 72, 73.]

was unjustly suffering for it.   His unrelenting hatred of the king's avarice and tyranny may be read in the very headings of his epigrams.[1]

Translations from Lucian.

Erasmus joined More in his studies.[2]   He was translating into Latin some of Lucian's Dialogues and his ' Declamatio pro Tyrannicidâ.'   At More's suggestion they both wrote a full answer to Lucian's arguments in favour of tyrannicide, imitating Lucian's style as nearly as possible ; and Erasmus, in sending a copy of these essays to a friend, spoke of More in terms which show how fully he had again yielded to the fascination and endearing charms of his character.   As he had once spoken of the youth, so now he spoke of the man.

Fascination of Erasmus for More.

Never, he thought, had nature united so fully in one mind so many of the qualities of genius—the keenest insight, the readiest wit, the most convincing eloquence, the most engaging manners—he possessed, he said, every quality required to make a perfect advocate.[3]

Such a man, with fair play and opportunity, was sure to rise into distinction.   But as yet he must bide his time, waiting for the day when he could pursue his proper calling at the bar without risk of incurring royal displeasure.

---

[1] E. g. :—
' T. Mori in Avarum.'
' Dives Avarus Pauper est.'
' Sola Mors Tyrannicida est.'
' Quid inter Tyrannum et Prin-
    ' cipem.'
' Sollicitam esse Tyranni Vitam.'
' Bonum Principem esse Patrem
    ' non Dominum.'
' De bono Rege et Populo.'
' De Principe bono et malo.'

' Regem non satellitium sed virtus
    ' reddit tutum.'
' Populus consentiens regnum dat
    ' et aufert.'
' Quis optimus reipub. status.'
[2] Alluding to this time, Erasmus spoke of More as ' Tum studiorum 'sodali.'—Letter to Botzhem, 1523, leaf b, 3.
[3] See letter of Erasmus to Richard Whitford, Eras. *Op.* i. p. 265, dated May, ex rure (1506).

II. ERASMUS AGAIN LEAVES ENGLAND FOR ITALY (1506).

Erasmus seems to have spent some months during the spring of 1506 with his English friends, busying himself, as already mentioned, in translating in More's company portions of Lucian's works, and, so far as his letters show at first sight, not very eagerly pursuing those sacred studies at which he had told Colet that he longed to labour.

Nor was there really anything inconsistent in this. The truth was that, in order to complete his knowledge of Greek, without which he had declared he could do nothing thoroughly, he had yet to undertake that journey to Italy which had been the dream of his early manhood, and the realisation of which six years ago had only been prevented by his unlucky accident at Dover. This journey to Italy lay between him and the great work of his life, and still the adage of Plautus remained inexorable, ' Sine pennis volare haud facile ' est.'

Erasmus longs to visit Italy, but wants funds.

It was therefore that he was translating Lucian. It was therefore that he dedicated one dialogue to one friend, another to another.[1] It was therefore that he paid court to this patron of learning and that. It was not that he was importunate and servilely fond of begging, but that, by hook or by crook, the necessary means must be found to carry out his project.

It was thus that we find Grocyn rowing with him to

---

[1] Lucian's dialogue called *Somnium* he sent to Dr. Christopher Urswick, a well-known statesman (Eras. *Op.* i. p. 243); *Toxaris, sive de Amicitiâ*, to Fox, Bishop of Winchester (*Ibid.* p. 214); *Timon* to Dr. Ruthall, afterwards Bishop of Durham (*Ibid.* p. 255); *De Tyrannicidâ*, to Dr. Whitford, chaplain to Fox (*Ibid.* p. 267).

Lambeth to introduce him to Archbishop Warham, and the two joking together as they rowed back to town, upon the small pecuniary result of their visit.[1]

Funds, it appeared, did not come in as quickly as might have been wished, but at length the matter was arranged. Erasmus was to proceed to Italy, taking under his wing two English youths, sons of Dr. Baptista, chief physician to Henry VII. A young Scotch nobleman, the Archbishop of St. Andrews, was also to be placed under the scholar's care.[2] By this arrangement Erasmus was, as it were, to work his passage ; which he thankfully agreed to do, and set out accordingly. With what feelings he left England, and with what longings to return, may be best gathered from the few lines he wrote to Colet from Paris, after having recovered from the effects of the journey, including a rough toss of four days across the Straits :—

Erasmus to Colet.

'Paris: June 19, 1506.

' When, after leaving England, I arrived once more
' in France, it is hard to say how mingled were
' my feelings. I cannot easily tell you which pre-
' ponderated, my joy in visiting again the friends
' I had before left in France, or my sadness in
' leaving those whom I had recently found in Eng-
' land. For this I can say truly, that there is no whole
' country which has found me friends so numerous,
' so sincere, learned, obliging, so noble and accom-
' plished in every way, as the one City of London has

Margin note: Erasmus leaves for Italy, with two pupils.

Margin note: Letter to Colet from Paris.

---

[1] See an amusing account of this visit to Lambeth Palace in the letter to Botzhem (*Catalogus*, leaf a, 5); also Knight's *Life of Erasmus*, p. 83.

[2] See Knight's *Life of Erasmus*, pp. 96–101. *Adagia. Op.* ii. 554. Epist. dccclxxiv. and dccccliii.

' done. Each has so vied with others in affection and
' good offices, that I cannot tell whom to prefer. I am
' obliged to love all of them alike. The absence of
' these must needs be painful ; but I take heart again
' in the recollection of the past, keeping them as
' continually in mind as if they were present, and
' hoping that it may so turn out that I may shortly
' return to them, never again to leave them till
' death shall part us. I trust to you, with my other
' friends, to do your best for the sake of your love
' and interest for me to bring this about as soon and
' as propitiously as you can.

 ' I cannot tell you how pleased I am with the dis-
' position of the sons of Baptista : nothing could be
' more modest or tractable ; nor could they be more
' diligent in their studies. I trust that this arrange-
' ment for them may answer their father's hopes and
' my desires, and that they may hereafter confer great
' honour upon England.   Farewell.' [1]

To Linacre, too, Erasmus wrote in similar terms.
He alluded to the unpleasant consequences to his
health of his four days' experience of the winds and
waves, and wished, he said, that Linacre's medical
skill were at hand to still his throbbing temples.
He expressed, as he had done to Colet, the hope that
he soon might be able to return to England, and that
the task he had undertaken with regard to his two
pupils might turn out well; and he ended his letter by
urging his friend to write to him often.   Let it be in
few words, if he liked, but he must write.[2]

---

[1] Eras. *Op.* iii. Epist. civ.   [2] Epist. cv.

III. ERASMUS VISITS ITALY AND RETURNS TO ENGLAND
(1507–10).

At length Erasmus really was on his way to Italy,
trudging along on horseback, day after day, through
the dirt of continental roads, accompanied by the two
sons of Dr. Baptista, their tutor, and a royal courier,
commissioned to escort them as far as Bologna.

Erasmus
on his
way to
Italy.

It is not easy to realise the toil of such a journey to
a jaded delicate scholar, already complaining of the
infirmities of age, though as yet not forty. Strange
places, too, for a fastidious student were the roadside

German
inns.

inns of Germany, of which Erasmus has left so vivid a
picture, and into which he turned his weary head each
successive night, after grooming his own horse in the
stable. One room serves for all comers, and in this
one room, heated like a stove, some eighty or ninety
guests have already stowed themselves—boots, baggage, dirt and all. Their wet clothes hang on the
stove iron to dry, while they wait for their supper.
There are footmen and horsemen, merchants, sailors,
waggoners, husbandmen, children, and women—sound
and sick—combing their heads, wiping their brows,
cleaning their boots, stinking of garlic, and making as
great a confusion of tongues as there was at the building of Babel! At length, in the midst of the din and
stifling closeness of this heated room, supper is spread
—a coarse and ill-cooked meal—which our scholar
scarcely dares to touch, and yet is obliged to sit out to
the end for courtesy's sake. And when past midnight
Erasmus is shown to his bedchamber, he finds it to be
rightly named—there is nothing in it but a *bed* ; and

the last and hardest task of the day is now to find
between its rough unwashed sheets some chance hours
of repose.

So, almost in his own words,[1] did Erasmus fare on
his way to Italy. Nor did comforts increase as Germany was left behind. For as the party crossed the
Alps, the courier quarrelled with the tutor, and they
even came to blows. After this, Erasmus was too
angry with both to enjoy the company of either, and so
rode apart, composing verses on those infirmities of
age which he felt so rapidly encroaching upon his own
frail constitution.[2] At length the Italian frontier was
reached, and Erasmus, as Luther did three or four
years after,[3] began the painful task of realising what
that Italy was about which he had so long and so
ardently dreamed.

It is not needful here to trace Erasmus through all
his Italian experience. It presents a catalogue of disappointments and discomforts upon which we need
not dwell. How his arrangement with the sons of
Baptista, having lasted a year, came to an end, and
with it the most unpleasant year of his life ;[4] how he
took his doctor's degree at Turin; how he removed to
Bologna to find the city besieged by Roman armies,[5]
headed by Pope Julius himself; how he visited
Florence[6] and Rome ;[7] how he went to Venice to su-
perintend a new edition of the 'Adagia ;' how he was
flattered, and how many honours he was promised, and

---

[1] See his colloquy, *Diversoria.*
[2] Eras. *Op.* iv. p. 755. Erasmus
to Botzhem, leaf a, 4.
[3] Luther visited Rome in 1510,
or a year or two later. Luther's
Briefe, De Wette, l. xxi.

[4] ' Nullum enim annum vixi in-
' suavius ! '—Erasmus to Botzhem,
leaf a, 4.
[5] Eras. Ep. cccclxxxvi. App.
[6] Epist. cccclxxxvii. App.
[7] Eras. to Botzhem, leaf b, 8.

how many of these promises he found to be, as injuries ought to be, written on sand;—these and other particulars of his Italian experience may be left to the biographer of Erasmus. In 1509, on the accession of Henry VIII. to the English throne, the friends of Erasmus sent him a pressing invitation to return to England,[1] which he gladly accepted. For our present purpose it were better, therefore, to see him safely on his horse again, toiling back on the same packhorse roads, lodging at the same roadside inns, and meeting the same kind of people as before, but his face now, after three or four years' absence, set towards England, where there are hearts he can trust, whether he can or cannot those in Rome, and where once again, safely housed with More, he can write and talk to Colet as he pleases, and forget in the pleasures of the present the toils and disappointments of the past.[2]

Erasmus returns to England.

For what most concerns the history of the Oxford Reformers is this—that it was to beguile these journeys that Erasmus conceived the idea of his ' Praise of

---

[1] Mountjoy to Erasmus, Epist. x., dated May 27, 1497, but should be 1509.

[2] It is difficult to fix the date of the arrival of Erasmus in England. He was at Venice in the autumn of 1508. (See the Aldine edition of his *Adagia*, dated Sept. 1508.) After this he wintered at Padua (see *Vita Erasmi*, prefixed to Eras. *Op.* i.); and after this went to Rome (ibid.). This brings the chronology to the spring of 1509. In April, 1509, Henry VIII. ascended the English throne. On May 27, 1509, Lord Mountjoy wrote to Erasmus,

who seems to have been then at Rome, pressing him to come back to England (Eras. Epist. x., the date of which is fixed by its contents).

The letter prefixed to the *Praise of Folly* is dated *ex rure*, ' *quinto* ' *Idas Junias*,' and states that the book is the result of his meditations during his long journeys on horseback on his way from Italy to England. This letter must have been dated June 9, 1510, at earliest, or 1511, at latest. 1510 is the probable date (see *infra*, note at p. 204). The later editions of the *Praise o Folly* put the year 1508 to this

' Folly,' a satire upon the follies of the times which had grown up within him at these wayside inns, as he met in them men of all classes and modes of life, and the keen edge of which was whetted by his recent visit to Italy and Rome.[1]   What most concerns the subject of these pages is the mental result of the Italian journey, and it was not long before it was known in almost every wayside inn in Europe.

CHAP. V.

A.D. 1509.

' *Praise of Folly.*'

IV. MORE RETURNS TO PUBLIC LIFE ON THE ACCESSION OF HENRY VIII. (1509–10).

But little can be known of what happened to Colet and More during the absence of Erasmus in Italy.

That Colet was devoted to the work of his Deanery may well be imagined.

As to More ; during the remaining years of Henry VII.'s reign, he was living in continual fear—thinking of flying the realm [2]—going so far as to pay a visit to the universities of Louvain and Paris,[3] as though to make up his mind where to flee to, if flight became needful.[4]

More thinks of fleeing from England.

Nor were these fears imaginary. More was not alone in his dread of the King. Daily the royal avarice was growing more unbounded. Cardinal Morton's

letter ; but the edition of August, 1511 (Argent.) gives no year, nor does the Basle edition of 1519, to which the notes of Lystrius were appended. So that the printed date is of no authority, and it is entirely inconsistent with the history of the book as given by Erasmus. The first edition, printed by *Gourmont*, at Paris, I have not seen, but, according to Brunet, it has *no date*.

In the absence of direct proof, it is probable on the whole that Erasmus returned to England between the autumn of 1509 and June, 1510.

[1] See the letter to More prefixed to the *Praise of Folly*.

[2] Roper, p. 9.

[3] See More's letter to Dorpius, in which he mentions this visit.

[4] Roper, p. 6.

celebrated fork—the two-pronged dilemma with which benevolences were extracted from the rich by the clever prelate—had been bad enough.   The legal plunder of Empson and Dudley was worse.   It filled every one with terror.   'These two ravening wolves,' writes Hall, who lived near enough to the time to feel some of the exasperation he described, ' had such a guard of false ' perjured persons appertaining to them, which were ' by their commandment empannelled on every quest, ' that the King was sure to win whoever lost.   Learned ' men in the law, when they were required of their ' advice, would say, " to agree is the best counsel I can ' " give you."   By this undue means, these covetous ' persons filled the King's coffers and enriched them- ' selves.   At this unreasonable and extortionate doing ' noblemen grudged, mean men kicked, poor men ' lamented, preachers openly at Paul's Cross and other ' places exclaimed, rebuked, and detested, but yet they ' would never amend.' [1]   Then came the general pardon, the result, it was said, of the remorse of the dying King, and soon after the news of his death.

Henry VIII. was proclaimed King, 23rd April, 1509. The same day Empson and Dudley were sent to the Tower, and on the 17th of August, in the following year, they were both beheaded.

More was personally known to the new King, and presented to him on his accession a richly illuminated vellum book, containing verses of congratulation.[2] These verses have been disparaged as too adulatory in their tone.   And no doubt they were so ; but More had written them evidently with a far more honest loyalty than Erasmus was able to command when he

<hr/>

[1] Hall, ed. 1548, fol. lix.   [2] *Epigrammata Mori* : Basil. 1520, p. 17.

Marginal notes:
CHAP. V.

A.D. 1509.

Empson and Dudley.

Henry VII.'s exactions.

Henry VII. dies.

Accession of Henry VIII.

wrote a welcome to Philip of Spain on his return to
the Netherlands.   More honestly did rejoice, and with
good reason, on the accession of Henry VIII. to the
throne.   It not only assured him of his own personal
safety ; it was in measure like the rise of his own little
party into power.

Not that More and Colet and Linacre were suddenly
transformed into courtiers, but that Henry himself,
having been educated to some extent in the new learning, would be likely at least to keep its enemies in
check and give it fair play.   There had been some
sort of connection and sympathy between Prince
Henry in his youth and More and his friends ; witness
More's freedom in visiting the royal nursery.   Linacre
had been the tutor of Henry's elder brother, and was
made royal physician on Henry's accession.[1]   From
the tone of More's congratulatory verses it may be
inferred that he and his friends had not concealed
from the Prince their love of freedom and their hatred
of his father's tyranny.   For these verses, however
flattering in their tone, were plain and outspoken
upon this point as words well could be.   With the
suaviter in modo was united, in no small proportion,
the *fortiter in re*.   It would be the King's own fault if,
knowing, as he must have done, More's recent history,
he should fancy that these words were idle words, or
that he could make the man, whose first public act
was one of resistance to the unjust exactions of his
father, into a pliant tool of his own !   If he should
ever try to make More into a courtier, he would do
so at least with his royal eyes open.

How fully Henry VIII. on his part sided with the

---

[1] Johnson's *Life of Linacre*, pp. 179 *et seq.*

CHAP. V.

A.D. 1509.

More
made
under-
.sheriff of
London.

people against the counsellors of his father was not
only shown by the execution of Dudley, but also by
the appointment, almost immediately after, of Thomas
More to the office of under-sheriff in the City, the very
office which Dudley himself had held at the time when,
as Speaker of the House of Commons, he had been
a witness of More's bold conduct—an office which he
and his successor had very possibly used more to the
King's profit than to the ends of impartial justice.

The young lawyer who had dared to incur royal displeasure by speaking out in Parliament in defence of
the pockets of his fellow-citizens, had naturally become
a popular man in the City.   And his appointment to
this judicial office was, therefore, a popular appointment.

The spirit in which More entered upon its responsible
duties still more endeared him to the people.   Some
years after, by refusing a pension offered him by Henry

VIII., he proved himself more anxious to retain the
just confidence of his fellow-citizens, in the impartiality of his decisions in matters between them and
the King, than to secure his own emolument or his
Sovereign's patronage.[1]   The spirit too in which he *re-*
entered upon his own private practice as a lawyer was
illustrated both by his constant habit of doing all he
could to get his clients to come to a friendly agreement
before going to law, and also by his absolute refusal to
undertake any cause which he did not conscientiously
consider to be a rightful one.[2]   It is not surprising
that a man of this tested high principle should rapidly
rise upon the tide of merited prosperity.   Under the
circumstances in which More was now placed, his

---

[1] *Vide infra,* p. 380.   [2] Stapleton, 1588 ed. pp. 26, 27.

practice at the bar became rapidly extensive.[1] Everything went well with him. Once more he was drinking the wine of life.

There was probably no brighter home—brighter in present enjoyment, or more brilliant in future prospects—than that home in Bucklersbury, into which Erasmus, jaded by the journey, entered on his arrival from Italy. He must have found More and his gentle wife rejoicing in their infant son, and the merry voices of three little daughters echoing the joy of the house.[2]

More's domestic happiness.

V. ERASMUS WRITES THE ' PRAISE OF FOLLY' WHILE RESTING AT MORE'S HOUSE (1510 OR 1511).

For some days Erasmus was chained indoors by an attack of a painful disease to which he had for long been subject. His books had not yet arrived, and he was too ill to admit of close application of any kind.

To beguile his time, he took pen and paper, and began to write down at his leisure the satirical reflections on men and things which, as already mentioned, had grown up within him during his recent travels, and served to beguile the tedium of his journey from Italy to England. It was not done with any grave design, or any view of publication ; but he knew his friend More was fond of a joke, and he wanted something to do, to take his attention from the weariness of the pain which he was suffering. So he worked away at his manuscript. One day when More came home from business, bringing a friend or two with him, Erasmus

The ' Praise of Folly,' written in More's house.

---

[1] Roper, p. 9.
[2] More's son John—nineteen in 1528, according to Holbein's sketch —was probably born in 1509. More's three daughters, Margaret, Elizabeth and Cicely, were all older.

O

brought it out for their amusement. The fun would be so much the greater, he thought, when shared by several together. He had fancied Folly putting on her cap and bells, mounting her rostrum, and delivering an address to her votaries on the affairs of mankind. These few select friends, having heard what he had already written, were so delighted with it that they insisted on its being completed. In about a week the whole was finished.[1] This is the simple history of the ' Praise of Folly.'

It was a satire upon follies of all kinds. The book-worm was smiled at for his lantern jaws and sickly look; the sportsman for his love of butchery; the superstitious were sneered at for attributing strange virtues to images and shrines, for worshipping another Hercules under the name of St. George, for going on pilgrimage when their proper duty was at home. The wickedness of fictitious pardons and the sale of indul-gences,[2] the folly of prayers to the Virgin in shipwreck or distress, received each a passing censure.

Gram-marians and schools.

Grammarians were singled out of the regiment of fools as the most servile votaries of folly. They were described as ' A race of men the most miserable, who ' grow old in penury and filth in their schools—*schools*, ' did I say? *prisons! dungeons!* I should have said— ' among their boys, deafened with din, poisoned by a ' fœtid atmosphere, but, thanks to their folly, perfectly ' self-satisfied, so long as they can bawl and shout to ' their terrified boys, and box, and beat, and flog them,

---

[1] See the letter of Erasmus to Botzhem, ed. Basle, 1523, leaf b, 3, and Jortin, App. 428. Also *Erasmi ad Dorpium Apologia*, Louvain,

1515, leaf F, iv.

[2] Argent. 1511, leaf D, iii., where occurs the marginal reading, ' In-' dulgentias taxat.'

‘ and so indulge in all kinds of ways their cruel dis-
‘ position.’ [1]

After criticising with less severity poets and authors,
rhetoricians and lawyers, Folly proceeded to re-echo
the censure of Colet upon the dogmatic system of the
Schoolmen.

She ridiculed the logical subtlety which spent itself
on splitting hairs and disputing about nothing, and to
which the modern followers of the Schoolmen were
so painfully addicted. She ridiculed, too, the prevalent dogmatic philosophy and science, which having
been embraced by the Schoolmen, and sanctioned by
ecclesiastical authority, had become a part of the
scholastic system. ‘ With what ease do they dream
‘ and prate of the creation of innumerable worlds,
‘ measuring sun, moon, stars, and earth as though by
‘ a thumb and thread ; rendering a reason for thunder,
‘ wind, eclipses, and other inexplicable things ; never
‘ hesitating in the least, just as though they had been
‘ admitted into the secrets of creation, or as though
‘ they had come down to us from the council of the
‘ Gods—*with whom, and whose conjectures, Nature is
‘ mightily amused !* ’ [2]

Scholastic
science.

From dogmatic science Folly turned at once to
dogmatic theology, and proceeded to comment in
her severest fashion on a class whom, she observes, it
might have been safest to pass over in silence—
divines.[3] ‘ Their pride and irritability are such (she
‘ said) that they will come down upon me with their
‘ six hundred conclusions, and compel me to recant ;

Scholastic
theology.

---

[1] Argent. 1511, E, 8, and Eras.
Op. iv. p. 457.
[2] Argent. 1511, leaf E, viii., and

Eras. *Op.* iv. p. 462.
[3] Argent. 1511, leaf F, and Eras.
Op. iv. p. 465.

' and, if I refuse, declare me a heretic forthwith. . . .
' They explain to their own satisfaction the most
' hidden mysteries : how the universe was constructed
' and arranged—through what channels the stain of
' original sin descends to posterity—how the mira-
' culous birth of Christ was effected—how in the
' Eucharistic wafer the accidents can exist without a
' substance, and so forth.   And they think themselves
' equal to the solution of such questions as these :—
' Whether . . . God could have taken upon himself

Foolish
questions.

' the nature of a woman, a devil, an ass, a gourd, or a
' stone ?   And how in that case a gourd could have
' preached, worked miracles, and been nailed to the
' cross ?   *What* Peter would have consecrated if he
' had consecrated the Eucharist at the moment that
' the body of Christ was hanging on the Cross ?
' Whether at that moment Christ could have been
' called a man ?   Whether we shall eat and drink after
' the resurrection ? ' [1]   In a later edition [2] Folly is
' made to say further: ' These Schoolmen possess such
' learning and subtlety that I fancy even the Apostles
' themselves would need another Spirit, if they had to
' engage with this new race of divines about questions
' of this kind.   Paul was able " to keep the faith," but
' when he said " Faith is the substance of things hoped
' " for," he defined it very loosely.   He was full of
' *charity*, but he treated of it and defined it very illogi-
' cally in the thirteenth chapter of the first epistle to the
' Corinthians. . . . .   The Apostles knew the mother of
' Jesus, but which of them demonstrated so philosophi-
' cally as our divines do in what way she was preserved
' from the taint of original sin ?   Peter received the

---

[1] Argent. 1511, leaf F, and Eras. *Op.* iv. p. 465.

[2] Basle, 1519, p. 178 *et seq.*, and Eras. *Op.* ix. pp. 466 *et seq.*

' keys, and received them from Him who would not
' have committed them to one unworthy to receive
' them, but I know not whether *he* understood (cer-
' tainly he never touched upon the subtlety !) in what
' way the *key of knowledge* can be held by a man who
' *has no knowledge.* They often baptized people, but
' they never taught what is the formal, what the
' material, what the efficient, and what the ultimate
' cause of baptism ; they say nothing of its delible
' and indelible character. They worshipped indeed,
' but *in spirit*, following no other authority than the
' gospel saying, " God is a Spirit, and they that
' " worship Him must worship Him in spirit and in
' " truth." But it hardly seems to have been revealed
' to them, that in one and the same act of worship the
' picture of Christ drawn with charcoal on a wall was
' to be adored, as well as Christ *himself.* . . . Again,
' the Apostles spoke of " grace," but they never distin-
' guished between " gratiam gratis datam," and " gra-
' " tiam gratificantem." They preached charity, but
' did not distinguish between charity " infused " and
' " acquired," nor did they explain whether it was an
' accident or a substance, created or *un*created. They
' abhorred " *sin*," but I am a fool if they could define
' scientifically *what we call sin*, unless indeed they were
' inspired by the spirit of the Scotists ! ' [1]

After pursuing the subject further, Folly suggests
that an army of them should be sent against the
Turks, not in the hope that the Turks might be
converted by them so much as that Christendom
would be relieved by their absence, and then she

---

[1] Basle, 1519, p. 181.

is made quietly to say : [1]—' You may think all this
' is said in joke, but seriously, there are some,
' even amongst divines themselves, versed in better
' learning, who are disgusted at these (as they think)
' frivolous subtleties of divines.   There are some who
' execrate, as a kind of sacrilege, and consider as the
' greatest impiety, these attempts to dispute with un-
' hallowed lips and profane arguments about things
' so holy that they should rather be adored than ex-
' plained, to define them with so much presumption,
' and to pollute the majesty of Divine theology with
' cold, yea and sordid, words and thoughts.   But, in
' spite of these, with the greatest self-complacency
' divines go on spending night and day over their
' foolish studies, so that they never have any leisure
' left for the perusal of the gospels, or the epistles
' of St. Paul.' [2]

*There are
some who
hate the
scholastic
method.*

Finally, Folly exclaims, ' Are they not the most
' happy of men whilst they are treating of these
' things ? whilst describing everything in the infernal
' regions as exactly as though they had lived there for
' years ? whilst creating new spheres at pleasure, one,
' the largest and most beautiful, being finally added,
' that, forsooth, happy spirits might have room enough
' to take a walk, to spread their feasts, or to play at
' ball ? ' [3]

With this allusion to the ' empyrean ' heavens of the
Schoolmen, the satire of Folly upon their dogmatic
theology reaches its climax.   And in the notes added
by Lystrius to a later edition, it was thus further

---

[1] Basle, 1519, p. 183, and Eras.
Op. iv. p. 468.

[2] Basle, 1519, p.183, and Argent.
1511, leaf F ; which contains, however, only part of this paragraph.

[3] Basle, 1519, p. 185.   Argent.
1511, leaf F, ii., and Eras. *Op.* iv.
p. 469.

explained in terms which aptly illustrate the relation
of theology and science in the scholastic system :—

' The ancients believed . . . . in seven spheres
' —one to each planet—and to these they added the
' one sphere of the fixed stars.   Next, seeing that these
' eight spheres had two motions, and learning from
' Aristotle that only one of these motions affected all
' the spheres, they were compelled to regard the other
' motion as *violent*.   A superior sphere could not, how-
' ever, be moved in its violent motion by an inferior
' one.   So outside all they were obliged to place a
' ninth sphere, which they called " primum mobile."
' To these, in the next place, *divines added a tenth*,
' which they called the " empyrean sphere," as though
' the saints could not be happy unless they had a
' heaven of their own ! ' [1]

And that the ridicule and satire of Erasmus were
aimed at the dogmatism of both science and theology
is further pointed out in a previous note, where the presumption of ' neoteric divines ' in attempting to account
for everything, however mysterious, is compared to
the way in which ' astronomers, not being able to find
' out the cause of the various motions of the heavens,
' constructed eccentrics and epicycles on the spheres.' [2]

Thus were the scholastic divines censured for just
those faults to which the eyes of Erasmus had been
opened ten years before by his conversation with Colet
at Oxford, and words of more bitter satire could hardly
have been used than those now chosen.

Monks came in for at least as rough a handling.
There is perhaps no more severe and powerful passage

---

[1] Basle, 1519, pp. 185 and 186.   [2] Ibid. p. 180.

anywhere in the whole book than that in which Folly is made to draw a picture of their appearance on the Judgment Day, finding themselves with the goats on the left hand of the Judge, pleading hard their rigorous observance of the rules and ceremonies of their respective orders, but interrupted by the solemn question from the Judge, ' Whence this race of new ' Jews ? I know only of one law which is really mine ; ' but of that I hear nothing at all. When on earth, ' without mystery or parable, I openly promised my ' Father's inheritance, not to cowls, matins, or ' fastings, but to the practice of faith and charity. I ' know you not, ye who know nothing but your own ' works. Let those who wish to be thought more holy ' than I am inhabit their newly-discovered heavens ; ' and let those who prefer their own traditions to my ' precepts, order new ones to be built for them.' When they shall hear this (continues Folly), ' and see ' sailors and waggoners preferred to themselves, how ' do you think they will look upon each other ? '[1]

On kings, &c.

Kings, princes, and courtiers next pass under review, and here again may be traced that firm attitude of resistance to royal tyranny which has already been marked in the conduct of More. If More in his congratulatory verses took the opportunity of publicly asserting his love of freedom and hatred of tyranny in the ears of the new King, his own personal friend, as he mounted the throne, so Erasmus also, although come back to England full of hope that in Henry VIII. he might find a patron, not only of learning in general but of himself in particular, took this opportunity of putting into the mouth of Folly a similar assertion of

---

[1] This paragraph is not inserted in the edition Argent. 1511, but appears in the Basle edition, 1519, p. 192, and Eras. *Op.* iv. pp. 473, 474.

the sacred rights of the people and the duties of a king :—

'It is the duty (she suggests) of a true prince to seek 'the public and not his own private advantage. 'From the laws, of which he is both the author and 'executive magistrate, he must not himself deviate 'by a finger's breadth. He is responsible for the 'integrity of his officials and magistrates. . . . But '(continues Folly) by my aid princes cast such cares 'as these to the winds, and care only for their own 'pleasure. . . . They think they fill their position well 'if they hunt with diligence, if they keep good horses, 'if they can make gain to themselves by the sale of 'offices and places, if they can daily devise new means 'of undermining the wealth of citizens, and raking it 'into their own exchequer, disguising the iniquity of 'such proceedings by some specious pretence and 'show of legality.' [1]

If the memory of Henry VII. was fresh in the minds of More and Erasmus, so also his courtiers and tools, of whom Empson and Dudley were the recognised types, were not forgotten. The cringing, servile, abject, and luxurious habits of courtiers were fair game for Folly.

From this cutting review of kings, princes, and courtiers, the satire, taking a still bolder flight, at length swooped down to fix its talons in the very flesh of the Pope himself.

The Oxford friends had some personal knowledge of Rome and her pontiffs. When Colet was in Italy, the notoriously wicked Alexander VI. was Pope, and what Colet thought of him has been mentioned.

CHAP. V.

A.D. 1510.

Duties of princes.

Their practice.

On the Pope.

---

[1] Argent. 1511, leaf F, viii. and Eras. *Op.* iv. p. 479.

While Erasmus was in Italy Julius II. was Pope.   He
had succeeded to the Papal chair in 1503.

Julius II., in the words of Ranke, ' devoted himself
' to the gratification of that innate love of war and
' conquest which was indeed the ruling passion of his
' life. . . . It was the ambition of Julius II. to extend
' the dominions of the Church.   He must therefore
' be regarded as the founder of the Papal States.' [1]
Erasmus, during his recent visit, had himself been
driven from Bologna when it was besieged by the
Roman army, led by Julius in person.   He had
written from Italy that ' literature was giving place to
' war, that Pope Julius was warring, conquering,
' triumphing, and openly acting the Cæsar.' [2]   Mark
how aptly and boldly he now hit off his character in
strict accordance with the verdict of history, when in
the course of his satire he came to speak of popes.
Folly drily observes that—

' Although in the gospel Peter is said to have
' declared, " *Lo, we have left all, and followed thee,*"
' yet these Popes speak of " *St. Peter's patrimony* " as
' consisting of lands, towns, tributes, customs, lord-
' ships ; for which, when their zeal for Christ is stirred,
' they fight with fire and sword at the expense of much
' Christian blood, thinking that in so doing they are
' Apostolical defenders of Christ's spouse, the Church,
' from her enemies.   As though indeed there were any
' enemies of the Church more pernicious than impious
' Popes ! . . . . Further, as the Christian Church was
' founded in blood, and confirmed by blood, and
' advanced by blood, now in like manner, as though

---

[1] Ranke, *Hist. of the Popes,*
chap. ii. s. 1.

[2] Erasmus Buslidiano : Bononiæ,
15 Cal. Dec. 1506, Eras. *Op.* i. p. 311.

' Christ were *dead* and could no longer defend his
' own, they take to the sword.   And although war be
' a thing so savage that it becomes wild beasts rather
' than men, so frantic that the poets feigned it to be
' the work of the Furies, so pestilent that it blights at
' once all morality, so unjust that it can be best waged
' by the worst of ruffians, so impious that it has
' nothing in common with Christ, yet to the neglect
' of everything else they devote themselves to war
' alone.' [1]

And this bold satire upon the warlike passions of
the Pope was made still more direct and personal by
what followed.   To quote Ranke once more :—' *Old as*

' *Julius now was*, worn by the many vicissitudes of
' good and evil fortune, and most of all by the conse-
' quences of intemperance and licentious excess, in the
' extremity of age he still retained an indomitable
' spirit.   It was from the tumults of a general war that
' he hoped to gain his objects.   He desired to be the
' lord and master of the game of the world.   In
' furtherance of his grand aim he engaged in the
' boldest operations, risking all to obtain all.' [2]   Compare with this picture of the old age of the warlike
Pope the following words put by Erasmus into the
mouth of Folly, and printed and read all over Europe
in the lifetime of Julius himself !

' Thus you may see even decrepit old men display
' all the vigour of youth, sparing no cost, shrinking
' from no toil, stopped by nothing, if only they can
' turn law, religion, peace, and all human affairs
' upside down.' [3]

---

[1] Argent. 1511, leaf G, iii. Eras.
Op. iv. p. 484.

[2] Ranke, *Hist. of the Popes,*

chap. ii. s. 1, (abridged quotation).
[3] *Moriæ Encomium*: Argent.
M.DXI. leaf G, iii. This edition

In conclusion, Folly, after pushing her satire in other directions, was made to apologise for the bold flight she had taken. If anything she had said seemed to be spoken with too much loquacity or petulance, she begged that it might be remembered that it was spoken by *Folly*. But let it be remembered, also, she added, that

A fool oft speaks a seasonable truth.

She then made her bow, and descended the steps of her rostrum, bidding her most illustrious votaries farewell—*valete, plaudite, vivite, bibite!*

Such was the ' Praise of Folly,' the manuscript of which was snatched from Erasmus by More or one of his friends, and ultimately sent over to Paris to be printed there, probably in the summer of 1511, and to pass within a few months through no less than seven editions.[1]

---

contains all the above passages on Popes, and was published during the lifetime of Julius II., as he did not die till the spring of 1513.

[1] Erasmus writes : ' It was sent ' over into France by the arrange- ' ment of those at whose instigation ' it was written, and there printed ' from a copy not only full of mis- ' takes, but even incomplete. Upon ' this within a few months it was ' reprinted more than seven times ' in different places.'—*Erasmi ad Dorpium Apologia*, Louvain, 1515.

See also Erasmus to Botzhem, where Erasmus says ' Aderam Lu- ' tetiæ quum per Ricardum Crocum ' pessimis formulis depravatissime ' excuderetur.' (First edition of this letter : Basle, 1523 ; leaf b, 4.) In the copy fixed to Eras. *Op.* i. ' *nescio quos* ' is substituted for

' *Ricardum Crocum,*' *who was not the printer, but the friend of More who got it published.* (See Erasmus to Colet, Epist. cxlix. Sept. 13, 1511 (wrongly dated 1513), where Eras- mus says of Crocus, ' qui nunc ' Parisiis dat operam bonis literis.' Erasmus was at Paris in April 1511. (See Epistolæ clxix., cx., and clxxv. taken in connection with each other.)) In a catalogue of the works of Erasmus (a copy of which is in the British Museum Library), entitled *Lucubrationum Erasmi Roterodami Index,* and printed by Froben, at Basle, in 1519, it is stated that the *Moriæ Encomium* was ' sæpius excusum, *primum* ' *Lutetiæ per Gormontium, deinde* ' *Argentorati per Schurerium,*' &c. The latter edition is the earliest which I have been able to procure,

Meanwhile, after recruiting his shattered health under More's roof, spending a few months with Lord Mountjoy[1] and Warham,[2] and paying a flying visit to Paris, it would seem that Erasmus, aided and encouraged by his friends, betook himself to Cambridge to pursue his studies, hoping to be able to eke out his income by giving lessons in the Greek language to such pupils as might be found amongst the University students willing to learn,—the chance fees of students being supplemented by the promise of a small stipend from the University.[3]

It seems to have been taken for granted that the ' new learning' was now to make rapid progress, having Henry VIII. for its royal patron, and Erasmus for its professor of Greek at Cambridge.

---

and it is dated ' mense Augusti ' M.DXI.' But the date of the first edition printed at Paris by Gourmont I have not been able to fix certainly. According to Brunet, it had no date attached.

After staying at More's house, and there writing the book itself, he may have added the prefatory letter ' Quinto Idus Junias,' 1510, ' ex ' rure,' whilst spending a few months with Lord Mountjoy, as we learn he did from a letter to Servatius from ' London from the 'Bishop's house' (Brewer, No. 1418, Epist. cccclxxxv., under date 1510); it is most probable that in 1511 Erasmus paid a visit to Paris, being at Dover 10 April, 1511; at Paris 27 April (see *Epistolæ* clxix., cx. and clxxv); and thus was there when the first edition was printed. His letters from Cambridge do not seem to begin till Aug. 1511. See Brewer, Nos. 1842, Epist. cxvi. ; and 1849, Epist. cxviii. No. 1652 belongs, I think, to 1513. Possibly No. 1842, Epist. cxvi., belongs to a later date ; and, if so, No. 1849, Epist. cxviii., may be the first of his Cambridge letters, and with this its contents would well agree.

[1] Brewer, No. 1418. Eras. Epist. App. cccclxxxv. and see cccclxxxiv. dated 1 April, London.

[2] Brewer, No. 1478. Eras. Epist. cix. 6, Id. Feb., and it seems, in March 1511, Warham gave him a pension out of the rectory of Aldington. Knight, p. 155.

[3] Brewer, No. 4427.

CHAPTER VI.

I. COLET FOUNDS ST. PAUL'S SCHOOL (1510).

FULLY as Colet joined his friends in rejoicing at the accession to the throne of a king known to be favourable to himself and his party, he had drunk by far too deeply of the spirit of self-sacrifice to admit of his rejoicing with a mere courtier's joy.

Fortune had indeed been lavish to him. His elevation unasked to the dignity of Doctor and Dean ; the popular success of his preaching ; the accession of a friendly king, from whom probably further promotion was to be had for the asking ; and, lastly, the sudden acquisition on his father's death of a large independent fortune in addition to the revenues of the deanery ;— here was a concurrence of circumstances far more likely to foster habits of selfish ease and indulgence than to draw Colet into paths of self-denial and self-sacrificing labour. Had he enlisted in the ranks of a great cause in the hasty zeal of enthusiasm, it had had time now to cool, and here was the triumphal arch through which the abjured hero might gracefully retire from work amidst the world's applause.

But Colet, in his lectures at Oxford, had laid great stress upon the necessity of that living sacrifice of men's hearts and lives without which all other sacri-

fices were empty things, and it seems that after he
was called to the deanery he gave forth ' A right fruit-
' full Admonition concerning the Order of a good
' Christian Man's Life,' [1] which passed through many
editions during the sixteenth century, and in which
he made use of the following language :—

  ' Thou must know that thou hast nothing that good
' is of thyself, but of God.   For the gift of nature and
' all other temporal gifts of this world . . . . well con-
' sidered have come to thee by the infinite goodness
' and grace of God, and not of thyself. . . . . But in
' especial is it necessary for thee to know that God of
' his great grace has made thee his image, having re-
' gard to thy memory, understanding, and free will,
' and that God is thy maker, and thou his wretched
' creature, and that thou art redeemed of God by the
' passion of Jesus Christ, and that God is thy helper,
' thy refuge, and thy deliverance from all evil. . . . .
' And therefore, think, and thank God, and utterly
' despise thyself, ... in that God hath done so
' much for thee, and thou hast so often offended his
' highness, and also done Him so little service.   And
' therefore, by his infinite mercy and grace, call unto
' thy remembrance the degree of dignity which
' Almighty God hath called thee unto, and according
' thereunto yield thy debt, and do thy duty.'

Colet was not the man to preach one thing and
practise another.   No sooner had he been appointed

CHAP. VI.

A.D. 1510.

Colet on
the duty
of self-
sacrifice.

---

[1] ' A right fruitfull Admonition
' concerning the Order of a good
' Christian Man's Life, very profit-
' able for all manner of Estates,
' &c., made by the famous Doctour
' Colete sometime Deane of Paules.
' Imprinted at London for Gabriell
' Cawood, 1577.'—Brit. Museum
Library.

to the deanery of St. Paul's, than he had at once resigned the rich living of Stepney,[1] the residence of his father, and now of his widowed mother. And no sooner had his father's fortune come into his hands, than he earnestly considered how most effectually to devote it to the cause in which he had laboured so unceasingly at Oxford and St. Paul's.

Colet
founds
St. Paul's
School.
After mature deliberation he resolved, whilst living and in health, to devote his patrimony [2] to the foundation of a school in St. Paul's Churchyard, wherein 153 children,[3] without any restriction as to nation or country, who could already read and write, and were of ' good parts and capacities,' should receive a sound Christian education. The ' Latin adulterate, which ' ignorant blind fools brought into this world,' poisoning thereby ' the old Latin speech, and the very ' Roman tongue used in the time of Tully and Sallust, ' and Virgil and Terence, and learned by St. Jerome, ' St. Ambrose, and St. Augustine,'—all that ' abusion ' which the later blind world brought in, and which ' may rather be called Blotterature than Literature,'— should be ' utterly abanished and excluded ' out of

Colet's
object in
founding
it.
this school. The children should be taught good literature, both Latin and Greek, ' such authors that ' have with wisdom joined pure chaste eloquence '— ' specially Christian authors who wrote their wisdom ' in clean and chaste Latin, whether in prose or verse ; ' for,' said Colet, ' *my intent is by this school specially to* ' *increase knowledge, and worshipping of God and Our*

---

[1] In Sept. 1505. Knight's *Life of Colet*, p. 265, and n. a.

[2] ' Insumpto patrimonio universo ' vivus etiam ac superstes solidam ' hæreditatem cessi,' &c. Letter of Colet to Lilly, dated 1513, prefixed to the several editions of *De Octo Orationis Partibus, &c.*

[3] The number of the 'miraculous ' draught of fishes.'

' *Lord Jesus Christ, and good Christian life and*
' *manners in the children.*' [1]

And, as if to keep this end always prominently in
view, he placed an image of the ' Child Jesus,' to whom
the school was dedicated, standing over the master's
chair in the attitude of teaching, with the motto, ' Hear
' ye him ; ' [2] and upon the front of the building, next
to the cathedral, the following inscription :—' Schola
' catechizationis puerorum in Christi Opt. Max. fide
' et bonis Literis. Anno Christi MDX.' [3]

The building consisted of one large room, divided
into an upper and lower school by a curtain, which
could be drawn at pleasure ; and the charge of the two
schools devolved upon a high-master and a sub-master
respectively.

The forms were arranged so as each to seat sixteen
boys, and were provided each with a raised desk, at
which the head boy sat as president. The building
also embraced an entrance-porch and a little chapel
for divine service. Dwelling-houses were erected, adjoining the school, for the residence of the two masters ;
and for their support Colet obtained, in the spring of
1510, a royal license to transfer to the Wardens and
Guild of Mercers in London, real property to the value
of 53*l.* per annum [4] (equivalent to at least 530*l.* of present money). Of this the headmaster was to receive
as his salary 35*l.* (say 350*l.*) and the under-master 18*l.*
(say 180*l.*) per annum. Three or four years after, Colet

---

[1] Statutes of St. Paul's School.
Knight's *Life of Colet*, p. 364. See
also the letter from Colet to Lilly,
prefixed to the *Rudiments of Grammar*, 1510. Knight's *Life of Colet*,
p. 124, n. r.

[2] Eras. *Op.* iii. p. 457, c.
[3] Knight's *Life of Colet*, p. 109.
[4] Brewer's *Calendar of State
Papers*, Henry VIII., vol. i. No.
1076, under date June 6, 1510.

made provision for a chaplain to conduct divine service in the chapel, and to instruct the children in the Catechism, the Articles of the faith, and the Ten Commandments—in *English*; and ultimately, before his death, he appears to have increased the amount of the whole endowment to 122*l*. (say 1200*l*.) per annum.

Cost of Colet's school.

So that it may be considered, roughly, that the whole endowment, including the buildings, cannot have represented a less sum than 30,000*l*. or 40,000*l*. of present money.[1]

And if Colet thus sacrificed so much of his private fortune to secure a liberal (and it must be conceded his was a liberal) provision for the remuneration of the masters who should educate his 153 boys, he must surely have had deeply at heart the welfare of the boys themselves. And, in truth, it was so. Colet was like a father to his schoolboys. It has indeed been assumed that a story related by Erasmus, to exhibit the low state of education and the cruel severity exercised in the common run of schools, was intended by him to describe the severe discipline maintained by Colet and his masters; but I submit that this is a pure assumption, without the least shadow of proof, and contrary to every kind of probability. The story itself is dark enough truly, and, in order that Colet's name may be cleared once for all from its odium, may as well be given to the reader as it is found in Erasmus's work ' On the Liberal Education of Boys.'

It occurs, let it be remembered, in a work written by Erasmus to expose and hold up to public scorn the private schools, including those of monasteries and

---

[1] Compare licenses mentioned in Brewer's *Calendar of State Papers* of Henry VIII. (vol. i. Nos. 1076, 3900, and 4659), with documents given in Knight's *Life of Colet*, *Miscellanies*, No. v. and No. iii.

colleges, in which honest parents were blindly induced to place their children—at the mercy, it might
be, of drunken dames, or of men too often without
knowledge, chastity, or judgment. It was a work in
which he described these schools as he had described
them in his ' Praise of Folly,' and in which he detailed
scandals and cruelty too foul to be translated, with the
express object of enforcing his opinion, that if there
were to be any schools at all, they ought to be *public*
schools—in fact, precisely such schools as that which
Colet was establishing. The story is introduced as
an example of the scandals which were sometimes
perpetrated by incompetent masters, in schools of the
class which he had thus harshly, but not *too* harshly,
condemned.

After saying that no masters were more cruel to
their boys than those who, from ignorance, can teach
them least (a remark which certainly could not be
intended to refer to Colet's headmaster), he thus
proceeded :—

'What can such masters do in their schools but get
' through the day by flogging and scolding ? I once
' knew a divine, and intimately too—a man of reputa-
' tion—who seemed to think that no cruelty to scholars
' could be enough, since he would not have any but
' flogging masters. He thought this was the only way
' to crush the boys' unruly spirits, and to subdue the
' wantonness of their age. Never did he take a meal
' with his flock without making the comedy end in a
' tragedy. So at the end of the meal one or another
' boy was dragged out to be flogged. . . . I myself
' was once by when, after dinner, as usual, he called out
' a boy, I should think, about ten years old. He had

' only just come fresh from his mother to school. His
' mother, it should be said, was a pious woman, and
' had especially commended the boy to him. But he
' at once began to charge the boy with unruliness,
' since he could think of nothing else, and must
' find something to flog him for, and made signs to
' the proper official to flog him. Whereupon the
' poor boy was forthwith floored then and there, and
' flogged as though he had committed sacrilege. The
' divine again and again interposed, " That will do—
' " that will do ; " but the inexorable executioner con-
' tinued his cruelty till the boy almost fainted. By-
' and-by the divine turned round to me and said,
' " He did nothing to deserve it, but the boys'
' " spirits must be subdued." ' [1]

*Story of
cruelty,
wrongly
attributed
to Colet.*

This is the story which we are told it would be difficult to apply to anyone but Colet,[2] as though Colet
were the only ' divine of reputation ' ever intimately
known to Erasmus ! or as though Erasmus would thus
hold up his friend Colet to the scorn of the world !

*Colet's
gentleness
and love
of
children.*

The fact is that no one could peruse the ' precepts
' of living ' laid down by Colet for his school without
seeing not only how practical and sound were his views
on the education of the heart, mind, and body of his
boys, but also how at the root of them lay a strong
undercurrent of warm and gentle feelings, a real love
of youth.[3]

---

[1] ' De pueris statim ac liberaliter
' instituendis.'—*Eras. Op.* i. p. 505.

[2] Knight's *Life of Colet*, p. 175,
and copied from him by Jortin,
vol. i. pp. 169, 170.

[3] Take the following examples :
' Revere thy elders. Obey thy

' superiors. Be a fellow to thine
' equals. Be benign and loving to
' thy inferiors. Be always well
' occupied. Lose no time. Wash
' clean. Be no sluggard. Learn
' diligently.

In truth, Colet was fond of children, even to tenderness. Erasmus relates that he would often remind his
guests and his friends how that Christ had made children the examples for men, and that he was wont to
compare them to the angels above.[1] And if any further
proof were wanted that Colet showed even a touching
tenderness for children, it must surely be found in the
following ' lytell proheme ' to the Latin Grammar
which he wrote for his school, and of which we shall
hear more by-and-by :—

  ' Albeit many have written, and have made certain   Colet's
' introductions into Latin speech, called *Donates* and preface
  to his
' *Accidens*, in Latin tongue and in English ; in such grammar.
' plenty that it should seem to suffice, yet nevertheless,
' for the love and zeal that I have to the new school
' of Paul's, and to the children of the same, I have also
' . . . . of the eight parts of grammar made this little
' book. . . . In which, if any new things be of me, it
' is alonely that I have put these "parts" in a more
' clear order, and I have made them a little more easy
' to young wits, than (methinketh) they were before :
' judging that nothing may be too soft, nor too
' familiar for little children, specially learning a tongue
' unto them all strange. In which little book I have
' left many things out of purpose, considering the
' tenderness and small capacity of little minds. . . .[1]
' I pray God all may be to his honour, and to the
' erudition and profit of children, my countrymen
' *Londoners* specially, whom, digesting this little work,
' I had always before mine eyes, considering more what

' Teach what thou hast learned lov- *Life of Colet. Miscellanies*, No.
' ingly.'—Colet's *Precepts of Living* xi.
for the Use of his School. Knight's   [1] Eras. *Op.* iii. p. 458, D.

' was for *them* than to show any great cunning ; willing
' to speak the things often before spoken, in such man-
' ner as gladly young beginners and tender wits might
' take and conceive.   Wherefore I pray you, all little
' babes, all little children, learn gladly this little trea-
' tise, and commend it diligently unto your memories,
' trusting of this beginning that ye shall proceed and
' grow to perfect literature, and come at the last to
' be *great clerks*.   *And lift up your little white hands for*
' *me*, which prayeth for you to God, to whom be all
' honour and imperial majesty and glory.   Amen.'

Colet's
tender-
ness
towards
little
children.

The man who, having spent his patrimony in the
foundation of a school, could write such a preface as
this to one of his schoolbooks, was not likely to insist
' upon having none but flogging masters.'

Moreover, this preface was followed by a short note,
addressed to his ' well-beloved masters and teachers of
' grammar,' in which, by way of apology for its brevity,
and the absence of the endless rules and exceptions
found in most grammars, he tells them : ' In the begin-
' ning men spake not Latin because such rules were
' made, but, contrariwise, because men spake such
' Latin the rules were made.   That is to say, Latin
' speech was before the rules, and not the rules before
' the Latin speech.'   And therefore the best way to
learn ' to speak and write clean Latin is busily to
' learn and read good Latin authors, and note how they
' wrote and spoke.'   ' Wherefore,' he concludes, ' after
' " the parts of speech " sufficiently known in your
' schools, read and expound plainly unto your scholars
' good authors, and show to them every word, and in
' every sentence what they shall note and observe ;
' warning them busily to follow and to do like, both in

Colet
will not
trouble
them with
many
rules.

' writing and in speaking, and be to them your own
' self also, speaking with them the pure Latin, very pre-
' sent, and *leave the rules.* For reading of good books,
' diligent information of taught masters, studious
' advertence and taking heed of learners, hearing
' eloquent men speak, and finally busy imitation with
' tongue and pen, more availeth shortly to get the
' true eloquent speech, than all the traditions, rules,
' and precepts of masters.'

Nor would it seem that Colet's first headmaster, at
all events, failed to appreciate the practical common
sense and gentle regard for the ' tenderness of little
' minds,' which breathes through these prefaces ; for at
the end of them he himself added this epigram :—

> Pocula si linguæ cupias gustare Latinæ,
> Quale tibi monstret, ecce *Coletus* iter !
> Non per Caucaseos montes, aut summa Pyrene ;
> Te ista per Hybleos sed via ducit agros.[1]

II. HIS CHOICE OF SCHOOLBOOKS AND SCHOOLMASTERS
(1511).

The mention of Colet's ' Latin Grammar ' suggests
one of the difficulties in the way of carrying out of his
projected school, his mode of surmounting which was
characteristic of the spirit in which he worked. It was
not to be expected that he should find the schoolbooks
of the old grammarians in any way adapted to his
purpose. So at once he set his learned friends to work
to provide him with new ones. The first thing wanted

---

[1] This epigram and the above-mentioned prefaces are inserted by Knight in his *Life of Colet* (*Miscellanies,* No. xiii.), and were taken by him from what he calls *Grammatices Rudimenta,* London, M.DXXXIIII. in ' *Bibl. publ. Cantabr. inter MS. ' Reg.*' But see note 1 on the next page. They were in the preface to Colet's *Accidence.*

was a Latin Grammar for beginners. Linacre under-took to provide this want, and wrote with great pains and labour a work in six books, which afterwards came into general use. But when Colet saw it, at the risk of displeasing his friend, he put it altogether aside. It was too long and too learned for his ' little beginners.' So he condensed within the compass of a few pages two little treatises, an ' Accidence' and a ' Syntax,' in the preface to the first of which occur the gentle words quoted above.[1] These little books, 'after receiving additions from the hands of Erasmus, Lilly, and others, finally became generally adopted and known as *Lilly's Grammar*.[2]

' Lilly's Grammar.'

This rejection of his Grammar seems to have been a sore point with Linacre, but Erasmus told Colet not to be too much concerned about it : he would, he said, get over it in time,[3] which probably he did much sooner than Colet's school would have got over the loss which would have been inflicted by the adoption of a schoolbook beyond the capacity of the boys.

' De Copiâ Verborum.'

Erasmus, in the same letter in which he spoke of Linacre's rejected grammar, told Colet that he was working at his ' De Copiâ Verborum,' which he was writing expressly for Colet's school. He told him, too, that he had sometimes to take up the cudgels for him against the ' Thomists and Scotists of Cambridge ; '

---

[1] See also the characteristic letter from Colet to Lilly, prefixed to the *Syntax*. The editions of 1513, 1517, and 1524 are entitled, *Absolutissimus de Octo Orationis Partium Constructione Libellus.* The *Accidence* was entitled *Coleti Editio unà cum quibusdam*, &c.

[2] Knight's *Life of Colet*, p. 126.

[3] Eras. Epist. cxlix. Erasmus to Colet, Sept. 13, 1513 (Brewer, i. 4447), but should be 1511. See 4528 (Eras. Epist. cl.), which mentions the *De Copiâ* being in hand, which was printed in May 1512 (?).

that he was looking out for an under-schoolmaster, but
had not yet succeeded in finding one. Meanwhile he
enclosed a letter, in which he had put on paper his
notions of what a schoolmaster ought to be, and the
best method of teaching boys, which he fancied Colet
might not altogether approve, as he was wont somewhat more to despise rhetoric than Erasmus did.
He stated his opinion that—

' In order that the teacher might be thoroughly up
' to his work, he should not merely be a master of one
' particular branch of study. He should himself have
' travelled through the whole circle of knowledge. In
' philosophy he should have studied Plato and Aristotle,
' Theophrastus and Plotinus; in Theology the Sacred
' Scriptures, and after them Origen, Chrysostom, and
' Basil among the Greek fathers, and Ambrose and
' Jerome among the Latin fathers; among the poets,
' Homer and Ovid; in geography, which is very im-
' portant in the study of history, Pomponius Mela,
' Ptolemy, Pliny, Strabo. He should know what
' ancient names of rivers, mountains, countries, cities,
' answer to the modern ones; and the same of trees,
' animals, instruments, clothes, and gems, with regard
' to which it is incredible how ignorant even educated
' men are. He should take note of little facts about
' agriculture, architecture, military and culinary arts,
' mentioned by different authors. He should be able
' to trace the origin of words, their gradual corruption
' in the languages of Constantinople, Italy, Spain, and
' France. Nothing should be beneath his observation
' which can illustrate history or the meaning of the
' poets. But you will say what a load you are putting
' on the back of the poor teacher! It is so; but I

' burden the one to relieve the many.　I want the
' teacher to have traversed the whole range of know-
' ledge, that it may spare each of his scholars doing it.
' A diligent and thoroughly competent master might
' give boys a fair proficiency in both Latin and Greek,
' in a shorter time and with less labour than the com-
' mon run of pedagogues take to teach their babble.' [1]

On receipt of this letter and its enclosure, Colet
wrote to Erasmus :—

Colet to Erasmus.

' London, 1511.[2]

' " What !　I shall not approve ! "　So you say !
' What is there of Erasmus's that I do not approve ?　I
' have read your letter " De Studiis " hastily, for as yet
' I have been too busy to read it carefully.　Glancing
' through it, not only do I approve everything, but
' also greatly admire your genius, skill, learning, ful-
' ness, and eloquence.　I have often longed that the
' boys of my school should be taught in the way in
' which you say they should be.　And often also have
' I longed that I could get such teachers as you have
' so well described.　When I came to that point at the
' end of the letter where you say that you could edu-
' cate boys up to a fair proficiency in both tongues in
' fewer years than it takes those pedogagues to teach
' their babble, O Erasmus, how I longed that I could
' make you the master of my school !　I have indeed

---

[1] *De Ratione Studii Commen-
tariolus :* Argent. 1512, mense Julio, and printed again with additions, Argent. 1514, mense Augusto.

The above translation is greatly
abridged.
[2] Eras. Epist. App. iv.

' some hope that you will give us a helping hand
' in teaching our teachers when you leave those
' " Cantabrigians."

' With respect to our friend Linacre, I will follow
' your advice, so kindly and prudently given.

' Do not give up looking for an undermaster, if
' there should be anyone at Cambridge who would not
' think it beneath his dignity to be under the head-
' master.

' As to what you say about your occasional skir-
' mishes with the ranks of the Scotists on my behalf, I
' am glad to have such a champion to defend me. But
' it is an unequal and inglorious contest for you ; for
' what glory is it to you to put to rout a cloud of flies ?
' What thanks do you deserve from me for cutting
' down reeds ? It is a contest more necessary than
' glorious or difficult ! '

While Colet acquiesced in the view expressed by
Erasmus as to the high qualities required in a schoolmaster, he gave practical proof of his sense of the
dignity of the calling by the liberal remuneration he
offered to secure one.

At a time when the Lord Chancellor of England
received as his salary 100 marks, with a similar sum
for the commons of himself and his clerk, making in
all 133*l.* per annum,[1] Colet offered to the high-master
of his school 35*l.* per annum, and a house to live in
besides. This was practical proof that Colet meant
to secure the services of more than a mere common

---

[1] In 4 Henry VIII. (1513) Lord
Chancellor Warham received 100
marks salary, and 100 marks for
commons of himself and clerk—200
marks, or 133*l.* Brewer, i. Introduction, cviii. note (3).

CHAP. VI.

A.D. 1511.

Lilly head-
master of
Colet's
school.
grammarian. He had in view for his headmaster, Lilly, the friend and fellow-student of More, who had mastered the Latin language in Italy, and even travelled farther East to perfect his knowledge of Greek. He was well versed not only in the Greek authors, but in the manners and customs of the people, having lived some years in the island of Rhodes.[1] He had returned home, it is said, by way of Jerusalem, and had recently opened a private school in London.[2] He was, moreover, the godson of Grocyn, and himself an Oxford student. He had at one time, as already mentioned, shared with More some ascetic tendencies, but, like his friend, had wisely stopped short of Carthusian vows. He was, in truth, thoroughly imbued with the spirit of Colet and his friends, and, in the opinion of Erasmus, ' a thorough master in the art of ' educating youth.'[3] Thus Colet had found a high-master ready to be fully installed in his office, as soon
as the building was completed. But an under-master was not so easy to find. Colet had written to Erasmus, in September 1511, wishing him to look one out for him,[4] and in the letter last quoted had again repeated his request. Erasmus wrote again in October, and informed him that he had mentioned his want to some of the college dons. One of them had replied by sneeringly asking, ' Who would put up with the life of ' a schoolmaster who could get a living in any other

---

[1] Prefatory Letter of Beatus Rhenanus, prefixed to the edition of More's *Epigrammata*, printed at Basle, 1518 and 1520.

[2] Knight's *Life of Colet*, p. 370. *Miscellanies*, No. vi.

[3] ' Recte instituendæ pubis arti-

' fex.' Preface of Erasmus to *De Octo Orationis Partium Construc-tione*, &c. Basle, 1517.

[4] Colet to Erasmus, Sept. 1511, not 1513 (Brewer, No. 4448), for the same reason as Nos. 4447 and 4528.

' way ? ' Whereupon Erasmus modestly urged that he thought the education of youth was the most honourable of all callings, and that there could be no labour more pleasing to God than the Christian training of boys. At which the Cambridge doctor turned up his nose in contempt, and scornfully replied, ' If ' anyone wants to give himself up entirely to the ' service of Christ, let him enter a monastery ! ' Erasmus ventured to question whether St. Paul did not place true religion rather in works of charity—in doing as much good as possible to our neighbours ? The other rejected altogether so crude a notion. ' Behold,' said he, ' we must leave all ; in that is perfection.' ' *He* scarcely can be said to leave all,' promptly returned Erasmus, ' who, when he has a chance of doing ' good to others, refuses the task because it is too ' humble in the eyes of the world.' ' And then,' wrote Erasmus, ' lest I should get into a quarrel, I bade the ' man good-bye.' [1]

This, he said, was an example of ' Scotistical ' wisdom,' and he told Colet that he did not care often to meddle with these self-satisfied Scotists, well knowing that no good would come of it.

It would seem that, after all, a worthy under-master did turn up at Cambridge, willing to work under Lilly, and thereafter to become his son-in-law ;[2] so that with schoolmasters already secured, and schoolbooks in course of preparation, Colet's enterprise seemed likely fairly to get under way so soon as the building should be completed in St. Paul's Churchyard.

---

[1] Eras. Epist.cl. Brewer, p. 4528. Dated October 29, 1513, but, as it mentions the *De Copiâ* being in hand, it must have been written in 1511.

[2] John Ritwyse, or Rightwyse.

CHAPTER VII.

I. CONVOCATION FOR THE EXTIRPATION OF HERESY
(1512).

COLET's labours in connection with his school did not interfere with his ordinary duties. He was still, Sunday after Sunday, preaching those courses of sermons on ' the Gospels, the Apostles' Creed, and ' the Lord's Prayer,' which attracted by their novelty and unwonted earnestness so many listeners. The Dean was no Lollard himself, yet those whose leanings were toward Lollard views naturally found, in Colet's simple Scripture teaching from his pulpit at St. Paul's, what they felt to be the food for which they were in search, and which they did not get elsewhere. They were wont, it seems, to advise one another to go and hear Dr. Colet ; and it was not strange if, in the future examination of heretics, a connection should be traced between Colet's sermons and the increase of heresy.[1] That heresy was on the increase could not be doubted. Foxe has recorded that several Lollards suffered in 1511 under Archbishop Warham, and, strange to say, Colet's name appears on the list of judges.[2] Foxe

[1] ' Moreover, that Thomas ' Geffrey caused this John Butler ' divers Sundays to go to London to ' hear Dr. Colet.'—Foxe, ed. 1597, p. 756.

[2] Ibid. p. 1162.

also mentions no fewer than twenty-three heretics who were compelled by Fitzjames, Bishop of London, to abjure during 1510 and 1511. And so zealous was the Bishop in his old age against them that he burned at least two of them in Smithfield during the autumn of 1511.[1] So common, indeed, were these martyr-fires, that Ammonius, Latin secretary to Henry VIII., writing from London, a few weeks after, to Erasmus at Cambridge, could jestingly say, that ' he does not ' wonder that wood is so scarce and dear, the heretics ' cause so many holocausts ; and yet (he said) their ' numbers grow—nay, even the brother of Thomas, ' my servant, dolt as he is, has himself founded a sect, ' and has his disciples ! ' [2]

It was under these circumstances that a royal mandate was issued, in November 1511, to the Archbishop of Canterbury, to summon a convocation of his province to meet in St. Paul's Cathedral, February 6, 1512.[3]

The King—under the instigation, it was thought, of Wolsey [4]—was just then entering into a treaty with the Pope and other princes with a view to warlike proceedings against France ; and the King's object in calling this convocation was doubtless to procure from the clergy their share of the taxation necessary to meet the expenses of equipping an army, which it was convenient to represent as required ' for the defence of ' the *Church* as well as the kingdom of England ; ' but there was another object for which a convocation was required besides this of taxation—one more palatable

Marginal notes:

CHAP. VII.

A.D. 1512.

Two heretics burned at Smithfield.

Convocation summoned.

---

[1] William Sweeting and John Brewster, on October 18, 1511.— Foxe, ed. 1597, p. 756.

[2] Eras. Epist. cxxvii. Brewer, i.

No. 1948.

[3] Brewer, i. p. 2004.

[4] Ibid. i. Introduction.

to Bishop Fitzjames and his party—that of the ' *extirpation of heresy.*' [1]

On Friday, February 6, 1512, members of both Houses of Convocation assembled, it would seem, in St. Paul's Cathedral, to listen to the sermon by which it was customary that their proceedings should be opened.

Colet appointed to preach the opening sermon.

Dean Colet was charged by the Archbishop with the duty of preaching this opening address.

It was a task by no means to be envied, but Colet was not the man to shirk a duty because it was unpleasant. He had accepted the deanery of St. Paul's not simply to wear its dignities and enjoy its revenues, but to do its duties ; and one of those duties, perhaps *the* one to which he had felt himself most clearly called, had been the duty of *preaching.* Probably, there was not a pulpit in England which offered so wide a sphere of influence to the preacher as that of St. Paul's.

St. Paul's Cathedral.

The noble cathedral itself was *then,* in a sense which can hardly be realised *now,* the centre of the metropolis of England. In architectural merits, in vastness, and in the beauty of its proportions, it was rivalled by few in the world ; but it was not from these alone that it derived its importance. Under the shadow of its gracefully-tapering spire, 534 feet in height, its nave and choir and presbytery extended 700 feet in one long line of Gothic arches, broken only by the low screen between the nave and choir. And pacing up and down this nave might be seen men of every class in

---

[1] Brewer, i. p. 4312. Warham to Henry VIII.—a document referring to this convocation as held at St. Paul's from Feb. 6, 1511 (i.e. 1512) to Dec. 17 following. This document is in many places wholly illegible, but these words are visible: ' concessimus . . . [pro defen-' sione ecclesiæ] Anglicanæ et hujus ' inclyti regni vestri Angliæ ; nec-' non ad sedandum et extirpandum ' hereses et schismata in universali ' ecclesia quæ his diebus plus solito ' pullulant.'

life, from the merchant and the courtier down to the mendicant and the beggar. *St. Paul's Walk* was like a 'change, thronged by men of business and men of the world, congregated there to hear the news, or to drive their bargains ; while in the long aisles kneeled the devotees of saints or Virgin, paying their devotions at shrines and altars loaded with costly offerings and burning tapers ; and in the chantries, priests in monotonous tones sang masses for departed souls.

In *this* cathedral had Colet preached now for seven successive years. He had preached to the humblest classes in their own English tongue,[1] and, in order to bring down his teaching to their level, had given them an English translation of the Paternoster [2] for their use. He had seen them kneeling before the shrines, and had faithfully warned them against the worship of images.[3] He had preached to the merchants and citizens of London, and they had recognised in him a preacher who practised what he preached, whose life did not give the lie to what he taught ; and he had done all this in spite of any talk his plain-speaking might create amongst the orthodox, and notwithstanding the open opposition of his bishop. If poor Lollards found in him an earnestness and simple faith they did not find elsewhere, he knew that it was not *his* fault.

---

[1] That Colet preached in English, see the remark of Erasmus that he had studied *English* authors in order to polish his style and to prepare himself for preaching the gospel.—Eras. *Op.* iii. p. 456, B. It may also be inferred from the Lollards going to hear his sermons. In his rules for his school he directed that the chaplain should instruct the children in the Catechism and the Articles of the faith and the Ten Commandments in *English*.—Knight's *Life of Colet. Miscellanies*, Num. v. p. 361.

[2] Tyndale, p. 168 (Parker Society).

[3] Eras. *Op.* iii. p. 460, D.

Q

It was not *he* who was making heretics so fast, but the priests and bishops themselves, who were driving honest souls into heretical ways by the scandal of their worldly living, and the pride and dryness of their orthodox profession. And now, when he was called upon to preach to these very priests and bishops, was he to shrink from the task?

Colet had already, in his lectures at Oxford, given expression to the pain which ecclesiastical scandals had given him; and in his abstracts of the Dionysian treatises he had recorded, with grief and tears, his longings for ecclesiastical reform. These, however, had never been printed. They lay in manuscript in his own hands, and could easily be suppressed. It remained to be seen whether seven years' enjoyment of his own preferment had closed his lips to the utterance of unpopular truths.

Condition of the clergy.
If it were possible so far to look behind the screen of the past as to see the bishops of the province of Canterbury with the sight and knowledge of Colet, as he saw them assembled at St. Paul's on that Friday morning, then, and then only, would it be possible to appreciate fairly what it must have cost him to preach the sermon he did on this occasion.

The bishops and their benefices.
The Archbishop and some of the bishops were friends of his and of the new learning; but even some of these were so far carried away by the habits of the times, as to fall inevitably under the censure of any honest preacher who should dare to apply the Christian standard to their episcopal conduct. There might be honourable exceptions to the rule, but, *as a rule*, the bishops looked upon their sees as *property* conferred upon them often for political services, or as the natural result of family position or influence.

The pastoral duties which properly belonged to their
position were too often lost sight of. A bishopric
was a thing to be sued for or purchased by money
or influence. It mattered little whether the aspirant
were a boy or a greyheaded old man, whether he lived
abroad or in England, whether he were illiterate or
educated. There was one bishop, for instance, whom
Erasmus speaks of as a ' youth,' and who was so
illiterate that he had offered Erasmus a benefice and a
large sum of money if he would undertake his tuition
for a year—a bribe which Erasmus, albeit at the time
anxiously seeking remunerative work of a kind which
would not interfere with his studies, refused with contempt.[1] Then there was James Stanley, an old man,
whose only title to preferment was his connection
with the Royal Family and a noble house, who, in spite
of his absolute unfitness, had been made Bishop of
Ely in 1506, and was now living, it is said, a life of open
profligacy, to the great scandal of the English Church,
and of the noble house to which he belonged.[2]

There was a bishop, too, whom More satirised
repeatedly in his epigrams, under the name of ' Post-
' humus ; ' at whose promotion he expresses his delight
inasmuch as, whilst bishops were ' generally selected at
' *random,* this bishop had evidently been chosen with
' *exceptional care.* If an error had been made in this
' case, it could not certainly have arisen from *haste* in
' selection ; for had the choice been made out of a thou-
' sand, a *worse or more stupid* bishop could not possibly

---

[1] Erasmus to Werner : Eras. Ep.
Lond. ed. lib. xxxi. Ep. 23. The
person alluded to in this letter was
clearly not James Stanley, as has
sometimes been assumed.

[2] Cooper's *Athenæ Cantab.* p. 16.
Also *Philomorus,* Lond. Pickering,
1842, pp. 55–57, and *Fasti Ecclesiæ
Anglicanæ,* p. 70.

' have been found ! ' [1]   From another epigram, it may be inferred that this ' Posthumus ' was one of the ignorant Scotists whose opposition the Oxford Reformers had so often to combat ; for More represents him as fond of quoting the text, ' *The letter killeth, but* ' *the spirit giveth life*,'—the text which is mentioned by Tyndale as quoted by the Scotists against the literal interpretation of Scripture ;—and then he drily remarks, that this bishop was too illiterate for any ' *letters* to have killed him, and that, if they had, ' he had no *spirit* to bring him to life again ! ' [2]

The
bishops
and their
benefices. These may, indeed, have been exceptional or, at all events, extreme cases ; but, however the bishops of the province of Canterbury had come by their bishoprics, their general practice seems to have been to use their benefices only as stepping-stones to higher ones.   No sooner were they promoted to one see than they aspired to another, of higher rank and greater revenue.   This, at least, was no exceptional thing.   The Bishop of Bath and Wells had been Bishop of Hereford ; the Bishop of Chichester had been translated from the see of St. David's.   The Bishop of Lincoln had been Bishop of Lichfield and Coventry.   Audley had filled the sees of Rochester and Hereford in succession, and was now Bishop of Salisbury.   Fitzjames had been first

---

[1] Epigram ' In Posthumum Epi-' scopum.'

[2] Epigram ' In Episcopum illite-' ratum, de quo ante Epigramma ' est sub nomine Posthumi.' There is no reason, I think, to conclude that More's satire was directed in these epigrams against the Bishop of Ely. There may have been plenty of Scotists whom the cap might fit as well, or better. In the same year that Stanley was made Bishop of Ely, Fitzjames was made Bishop of London. The late Dean Milman (*Annals of St. Paul's*, p. 120) shows, however, that Fitzjames was not unlearned, as he had been Warden of Merton and Vice-chancellor of Oxford.

promoted to the see of Rochester, after that to the see of Chichester, and from thence, in his old age, to the most lucrative of all—the see of London. Fox had commenced his episcopal career as Bishop of Exeter ; he had from thence been translated, in succession, to the sees of Bath and Wells, and Durham, and was now Bishop of Winchester. And be it remembered that these numerous promotions were not in reward for the successful discharge of pastoral duties : those who had earned the most numerous and rapid promotions were the men who were the most deeply engaged in *political* affairs, sent on embassies, and so forth, whose benefices were thus the reward of purely secular services, and who, consequently, had hardly had a chance of discharging with diligence their spiritual duties. The Bishop of Bath and Wells was a foreigner, and lived abroad ; and so also the Bishop of Worcester owed his bishopric to Papal provision, and lived and died at Rome. His predecessor and his successor also both were foreigners.[1]

There was also, amongst the clergy of the province of Canterbury, a man who was to surpass all others in these particulars ; who was to be handed down to posterity as the very type of an ambitious churchman ; Wolsey. who was already high in royal favour, always engaged in political affairs, and considered to be the instigator of the approaching war ; who had the whole charge of equipping the army committed to his care ; who had lately been promoted to the deanery of Lincoln, and was waiting for the bishopric as soon as it should be vacant ; who had already had conferred upon him, in

---

[1] *Fasti Ecclesiæ Anglicanæ*, p. 298 ; and Knight's *Life of Erasmus*, p. 229.

CHAP. VII.

A.D. 1512.

addition to the deanery, two rectories, a prebend, and a canonry ; who, before another year was out, without giving up any of these preferments, was to be made Dean of York ; and who was destined to aspire from bishopric to archbishopric, to hold abbeys and bishoprics *in commendam,* sue for and obtain from the Pope a cardinal's hat and legatine authority, and to rule England in Church and State—England's king

Wolsey's
ambition.

amongst the rest—failing only in his attempt to get himself elected to the Papal chair. This Dean of Lincoln, so aspiring, ambitious, fond of magnificence and state, was sure to be found at his place in a convocation called that the clergy might tax themselves in support of his warlike policy, and in aid of his ambitious dreams. Wolsey, we may be sure, would be there to watch anxiously the concessions of his ' dismes,' as Bishop Fitzjames would be there also, to await the measures to be taken for the ' extirpation ' of heresy.'

It was before an assembly composed of such bishops and churchmen as these, that Colet rose to deliver the following address :—

Colet's
sermon.

' You are come together to-day, fathers and right ' wise men, to hold a council. In which what ye will ' do, and what matters ye will handle, I do not yet ' know ; but I wish that, at length, mindful of your ' name and profession, ye would consider of the ' reformation of ecclesiastical affairs : for never was it ' more necessary, and never did the state of the Church ' more need your endeavours. For the Church—the

Need of
reforma-
tion in the
church.

' spouse of Christ—which He wished to be without ' spot or wrinkle, is become foul and deformed. As ' saith Esaias, " The faithful city is become a harlot ; "

' and as Jeremias speaks, " She hath committed
' " fornication with many lovers," whereby she hath
' conceived many seeds of iniquity, and daily bringeth
' forth the foulest offspring. Wherefore I have come
' here to-day, fathers, to admonish you with all your
' minds to deliberate, in this your Council, concerning
' the reformation of the Church.

' But, in sooth, I came not of my own will and plea-
' sure, for I was conscious of my unworthiness, and
' I saw too how hard it would be to satisfy the most
' critical judgment of such great men. I judged it
' would be altogether unworthy, unfit, and almost
' arrogant in me, a servant, to admonish you, my
' masters!—in me, a son, to teach you, my fathers! It
' would have come better from some one of the fathers,
' —that is, from one of you prelates, who might have
' done it with weightier authority and greater wisdom.
' But I could not but obey the command of the most
' reverend Father and Lord Archbishop, the President
' of this Council, who imposed this duty, a truly heavy
' one, upon me; for we read that it was said by Samuel
' the prophet, " Obedience is better than sacrifice."
' Wherefore, fathers and most worthy sirs, I pray and
' beseech you this day that you will bear with my
' weakness by your forbearance and patience; next,
' in the beginning, help me with your pious prayers.
' And, before all things, let us pour out our prayers to
' God the Father Almighty; and first, let us pray for
' his Holiness the Pope, for all spiritual pastors, with
' all Christian people; next, let us pray for our most
' reverend Father the Lord Archbishop, President of
' this Council, and all the lords bishops, the whole
' clergy, and the whole people of England; let us pray,

Colet's
modesty.

' lastly, for this assembly and convocation, praying
' God that He may inspire your minds so unanimously
' to conclude upon what is for the good and benefit
' of the Church, that when this Council is concluded
' we may not seem to have been called together in
' vain and without cause. Let us all say " the *Pater*
' " *noster,* &c." '

The Paternoster concluded, Colet proceeded :—

' As I am about to exhort you, reverend fathers, to
' endeavour to reform the condition of the Church ;
' because nothing has so disfigured the face of the
' Church as the secular and worldly way of living on
' the part of the clergy, I know not how I can com-
' mence my discourse more fitly than with the Apostle
' Paul, in whose cathedral ye are now assembled :

' (Romans xii. 2)—" Be ye not conformed to this
' " world, but be ye reformed in the newness of your
' " minds, that ye may prove what is the good, and
' " well-pleasing, and perfect will of God." This the
' Apostle wrote to all Christian men, but emphatically
' to priests and bishops : for priests and bishops are
' the lights of the world, as the Saviour said to them,
' " Ye are the light of the world ; " and again He said,
' " If the light that is in you be darkness, how great
' " will be that darkness ! " That is, if priests and
' bishops, the very lights, run in the dark way of the
' world, how dark must the lay-people be ! Where-
' fore, emphatically to priests and bishops did St. Paul
' say, " Be ye not conformed to this world, but be ye
' " reformed in the newness of your minds."

' By these words the Apostle points out two things :
' First, he prohibits our being *conformed* to the
' world and becoming *carnal* ; and then he commands

'that we be *reformed* in the Spirit of God, in order CHAP. VII.
'that we may be *spiritual.* I therefore, following A.D. 1512.
'this order, shall speak first of *Conformation,* and
'after that of *Reformation.*

'"Be not," he says, "conformed to this world." Of
'By the *world* the Apostle means the worldly way and 'confor-
'manner of living, which consists chiefly in these four mation.'
'evils—viz. in *devilish pride,* in *carnal concupiscence,*
'in *worldly covetousness,* and in *worldly occupations.*
'These things are in the world, as St. John testifies in
'his canonical epistle ; for he says, "All things that
'"are in the world are either the lust of the flesh, or
'"the lust of the eye, or the pride of life." These
'things in like manner exist and reign in the Church,
'and amongst ecclesiastical persons, so that we seem
'able truly to say, "All things that are in the *Church*
'"are either the lust of the flesh, the lust of the eye,
'"or the pride of life ! "

'In the *first* place, to speak of *pride of life*—what Pride
'eagerness and hunger after honour and dignity are of life.
'found in these days amongst ecclesiastical persons !
'What a breathless race from benefice to benefice,
'from a less to a greater one, from a lower to a higher !
'Who is there who does not see this ? Who that sees
'it does not grieve over it ? Moreover, those who
'hold these dignities, most of them carry themselves
'with such lofty mien and high looks, that their place
'does not seem to be in the humble priesthood of
'Christ, but in proud worldly dominion !—not acknow-
'ledging or perceiving what the master of humility,
'Christ, said to his disciples whom he called to the
'priesthood. "The princes of the nations " (said
'He) "have lordship over them, and those who are

' " amongst the great have power.　But it shall not be
' " so with you : but he who is great among you, let
' " him be your minister ;　he who is chief, let him be
' " the servant of all.　For the Son of Man came not
' " to be ministered unto, but to minister."　By which
' words the Saviour plainly teaches, that magistracy
' in the Church is nothing else than humble service.

Lust of
the flesh.

'As to the second worldly evil, which is the *lust of the*
' *flesh*—has not this vice, I ask, inundated the Church
' as with the flood of its lust, so that nothing is more
' carefully sought after, in these most troublous times,
' by the most part of priests, than that which ministers
' to sensual pleasure ?　They give themselves up to
' feasting and banqueting ; spend themselves in vain
' babbling, take part in sports and plays, devote them-
' selves to hunting and hawking ;　are drowned in the
' delights of this world ; patronise those who cater for
' their pleasure.　It was against this kind of people
' that Jude the Apostle exclaimed :　" Woe unto
' " them !　for they have gone in the way of Cain, and
' " ran greedily after the error of Balaam for reward,
' " and perished in the gainsaying of Core.　These are
' " spots in your feasts of charity, when they feast with
' " you, feeding themselves without fear ; clouds they
' " are without water, carried about of winds ; trees
' " whose fruit withereth, without fruit, twice dead,
' " plucked up by the roots ; raging waves of the sea,
' " foaming out their own shame ; wandering stars,
' " to whom is reserved the blackness of darkness for
' " ever."

Covetous-
ness.

' *Covetousness* also, which is the *third* worldly evil,
' which the Apostle John calls *the lust of the eye*, and
' Paul *idolatry*—this most horrible plague—has so
' taken possession of the hearts of nearly all priests,

'and has so darkened the eyes of their minds, that
'nowadays we are blind to everything, but that
'alone which seems to be able to bring us gain. For
'in these days, what else do we seek for in the Church
'than rich benefices and promotions ? In these same
'promotions, what else do we count upon but their
'fruits and revenues ? We rush after them with such
'eagerness, that we care not how many and what
'duties, or how great benefices we take, if only they
'have great revenues.

' O Covetousness ! Paul rightly called thee " the
'" root of all evil ! " For from *thee* comes all this
'piling-up of benefices one on the top of the other ;
'from *thee* come the great pensions, assigned out of
'many benefices resigned ; from *thee* quarrels about
'tithes, about offerings, about mortuaries, about
'dilapidations, about ecclesiastical right and title,
'for which we fight as though for our very lives !
'O Covetousness ! from *thee* come burdensome visi-
'tations of bishops ; from *thee* corruptions of Law
'Courts, and those daily fresh inventions by which the
'poor people are harassed ; from *thee* the sauciness
'and insolence of officials ! O Covetousness ! mother
'of all iniquity ! from *thee* comes that eager desire on
'the part of ordinaries to enlarge their jurisdiction ;
'from *thee* their foolish and mad contention to get hold
'of the probate of wills ; from *thee* undue seques-
'trations of fruits ; from *thee* that superstitious
'observance of all those laws which are lucrative, and
'disregard and neglect of those which point at the
'correction of morals ! Why should I mention the
'rest ?—To sum up all in one word : every corrup-
'tion, all the ruin of the Church, all the scandals of
'the world, come from the covetousness of priests,

' according to the saying of Paul, which I repeat
' again, and beat into your ears, " Covetousness is
' " the root of all evil ! "

Worldly
occupa-
tion.

' The *fourth* worldly evil which mars and spots the
' face of the Church is the incessant *worldly occupation*
' in which many priests and bishops in these days en-
' tangle themselves—servants of men rather than of
' God, soldiers of this world rather than of Christ.   For
' the Apostle Paul writes to Timothy, " No man that
' " warreth for God entangleth himself in the affairs
' " of this life."   But priests are " soldiers of God."
' Their warfare truly is not carnal, but spiritual : for
' our warfare is to pray, to read, and to meditate upon
' the Scriptures ; to minister the word of God, to ad-
' minister the sacraments of salvation, to make sacri-
' fice for the people, and to offer masses for their souls.
' For we are mediators between men and God, as Paul
' testifies, writing to the Hebrews : " Every priest "
' (he says) " taken from amongst men is ordained for
' " men in things pertaining to God, to offer gifts and

Apostolic
priests.

' " sacrifices for sins."   Wherefore the Apostles, the
' first priests and bishops, so shrank from every taint
' of worldly things that they did not even wish to
' minister to the necessities of the poor, although this
' was a great work of piety : for they said, " It is not
' " right that we should leave the word of God and
' " serve tables ; we will give ourselves continually to
' " prayer, and the ministry of the word of God."   And
' Paul exclaims to the Corinthians, " If you have any
' " secular matters, make those of you judges who are
' " of least estimation in the Church."   Indeed from
' this worldliness, and because the clergy and priests,
' neglecting spiritual things, involve themselves in
' earthly occupation, many evils follow.   First, the

' priestly dignity is dishonoured, which is greater than
' either royal or imperial dignity, for it is equal to that
' of angels. And the splendour of this high dignity
' is obscured by darkness when priests, whose con-
' versation ought to be in heaven, are occupied with
' the things of earth. Secondly, the dignity of priests
' is despised when there is no difference between such
' priests and laymen ; but (according to Hosea the
' prophet) " as the people are, so are the priests."
' Thirdly, the beautiful order of the hierarchy in the
' Church is confused when the magnates of the Church
' are busied in vile and earthly things, and in their
' stead vile and abject persons meddle with high and
' spiritual things. Fourthly, the laity themselves are
' scandalised and driven to ruin, when those whose
' duty it is to draw men *from* this world, teach men to
' love this world by their own devotion to worldly
' things, and by their love of this world are [them-
' selves] carried down headlong into hell. Besides,
' when priests themselves are thus entangled, it must
' end in *hypocrisy* ; for, mixed up and confused with
' the laity, they lead, under a priestly exterior, the
' mere life of a layman. Also their spiritual weakness
' and servile fear, when enervated by the waters of
' this world, makes them dare neither to do nor say
' anything but what they know will be grateful and
' pleasing to their princes. Lastly, such is their
' ignorance and blindness, when blinded by the
' darkness of this world, that they can discern nothing
' but earthly things. Wherefore not without cause
' our Saviour Christ admonished the prelates of his
' Church, " Take heed lest your hearts be burdened
' " by surfeiting or banqueting, and the cares of this
' " world." " By the cares (He says) of this world ! "

' The hearts of priests weighed down by riches cannot
' lift themselves on high, nor raise themselves to
' heavenly things.

' Many other evils there be, which are the result of
' the worldliness of priests, which it would take long
' to mention ; but I have done.   These are those four
' evils, O fathers ! O priests ! by which, as I have said,
' we are conformed to this world, by which the face
' of the Church is marred, by which her influence is
' destroyed, plainly, far more than it was marred and
' destroyed, either at the beginning by the persecution

*Invasion
of
heretics.*
' of tyrants, or after that by the invasion of heresies
' which followed.   For by the persecution of tyrants
' the persecuted Church was made stronger and more
' glorious ; by the invasion of heretics, the Church
' being shaken, was made wiser and more skilled in
' Holy Scriptures.   But after the introduction of this
' most sinful worldliness, when worldliness had crept
' in amongst the clergy, the root of all spiritual life—
' charity itself—was extinguished.   And without this
' the Church can neither be wise nor strong in God.

' In these times also we experience much opposition
' from the laity, but they are not so opposed to us as
' we are to ourselves.   Nor does *their* opposition do us

*Wicked
life of
priests the
worst kind
of heresy.*
' so much hurt as the opposition of our own wicked
' lives, which are opposed to God and to Christ ; for
' He said, " He that is not with me is against me."
' We are troubled in these days also by heretics—men
' mad with strange folly ;—but this heresy of theirs is
' not so pestilential and pernicious to us and the people
' as the vicious and depraved lives of the clergy, which,
' if we may believe St. Bernard, is a species of heresy,
' and the greatest and most pernicious of all ; for that
' holy father, preaching in a certain convocation to the

' priests of his time, in his sermon spake in these
' words :—" There are many who are catholic in their
' " speaking and preaching who are very heretics in
' " their actions, for what heretics do by their false
' " doctrines these men do by their evil examples—
' " they seduce the people and lead them into error of
' " life—and they are by so much worse than heretics
' " as actions are stronger than words." These things
' said Bernard, that holy father of so great and ardent
' spirit, against the faction of wicked priests of his
' time ; by which words he plainly shows that there
' be two kinds of heretical pravity—one of perverse
' doctrine, the other of perverse living—of which the
' latter is the greater and more pernicious ; and this
' reigns in the Church, to the miserable destruction of
' the Church, her priests living after a worldly and not
' after a priestly fashion. Wherefore do you fathers,
' you priests, and all of you of the clergy, awake at
' length, and rise up from this your sleep in this for-
' getful world : and being awake, at length listen to
' Paul calling unto you, " Be ye not conformed to this
' " world."

' This concerning the *first* part.

' Now let us come to the *second* — concerning
' *Reformation.*

Reforma-
tion

' " But be ye reformed in the newness of your
' " minds." What Paul commands us secondly is,
' that we should " be *re*formed into a new mind ; " that
' we should savour the things which are of God ; that
' we should be reformed to those things which are
' contrary to what I have been speaking of—*i.e.* to
' humility, sobriety, charity, spiritual occupations ;
' just as Paul wrote to Titus, " Denying ungodliness

must
begin
with the
bishops.

' " and worldly lusts, we should live soberly, right-
' " eously, and godly in this present world."

' But this reformation and restoration in ecclesi-
' astical affairs must needs begin with *you*, our fathers,
' and then afterwards descend upon us your priests
' and the whole clergy. For you are our chiefs—
' you are our examples of life. To you we look as way-
' marks for our direction. In you and in your lives
' we desire to read, as in living books, how we ourselves
' should live. Wherefore, if you wish to see our motes,
' first take the beams out of your own eyes ; for it is
' an old proverb, " Physician, heal thyself." Do you,
' spiritual doctors, first assay that medicine for the
' purgation of morals, and then you may offer it to us
' to taste of it also.

' The way, moreover, by which the Church is to be
' reformed and restored to a better condition is not to
' enact any new laws (for there are laws enough and to
' spare). As Solomon says, " There is no new thing
' " under the sun." The diseases which are now in the
' Church were the same in former ages, and there is
' no evil for which the holy fathers did not provide
' excellent remedies ; there are no crimes in pro-
' hibition of which there are not laws in the body of

Existing
laws
must be
enforced.

' the Canon Law. The need, therefore, is not for the
' enactment of new laws and constitutions, but for the
' observance of those already enacted. Wherefore, in
' this your congregation, let the existing laws be pro-
' duced and recited which prohibit what is evil, and
' which enjoin what is right.

' First, let those laws be recited which admonish
' you, fathers, not to lay your hands on any, nor to
' admit them to holy orders, rashly. For here is the
' source from whence other evils flow, because if the
' entrance to Holy Orders be thrown open, all who

'offer themselves are forthwith admitted without
'hindrance. Hence proceed and emanate those hosts
'of both unlearned and wicked priests which are in the
'Church. For it is not, in my judgment, enough that
'a priest can construe a collect, propound a propo-
'sition, or reply to a sophism; but much more needful
'are a good and pure and holy life, approved morals,
'moderate knowledge of the Scriptures, some know-
'ledge of the Sacraments, above all fear of God and
'love of heavenly life.

'Let the laws be recited which direct that eccle-
'siastical benefices should be conferred on the worthy,
'and promotions in the Church made with just regard
'to merit; not by carnal affection, nor the acceptation
'of persons, whereby it comes to pass in these days,
'that boys instead of old men, fools instead of wise
'men, wicked instead of good men, reign and rule!

'Let the laws be recited against the guilt of
'simony; which plague, which contagion, which dire
'pestilence, now creeps like a cancer through the
'minds of priests, so that most are not ashamed in
'these days to get for themselves great dignities by
'petitions and suits at court, rewards and promises.

'Let the laws be recited which command the per-
'sonal residence of curates at their churches: for
'many evils spring from the custom, in these days, of
'performing all clerical duties by help of vicars and
'substitutes; men too without judgment, unfit, and
'often wicked, who will seek nothing from the people
'but sordid gain—whence spring scandals, heresies,
'and bad Christianity amongst the people.

'Let the laws be rehearsed, and the holy rules
'handed down from our ancestors concerning the life

CHAP. VII.

A.D. 1512.

Wicked
and un-
learned
men ad-
mitted
to holy
orders.

R

'and character of the clergy, which prohibit any
'churchman from being a merchant, usurer, or
'hunter, or common player, or from bearing arms—
'the laws which prohibit the clergy from frequenting
'taverns, from having unlawful intercourse with
'women—the laws which command sobriety and
'modesty in vestment, and temperance in dress.

'Let also the laws be recited concerning monks
'and religious men, which command that, leaving the
'broad way of the world, they enter the narrow way
'which leads to life; which command them not to
'meddle in business, whether secular or ecclesiastical;
'which command that they should not engage in
'suits in civil courts for earthly things. For in the
'Council of *Chalcedon* it was decreed that monks
'should give themselves up entirely to prayer and
'fasting, the chastisement of their flesh, and ob-
'servance of their monastic rule.

Worldly
bishops.
'Above all, let those laws be recited which concern
'and pertain to *you*, reverend fathers and lords bishops
'—laws concerning your just and canonical election,
'in the chapters of your churches, with the invocation
'of the Holy Spirit: for because this is not done in
'these days, and prelates are often chosen more by
'the favour of men than the grace of God, so, in con-
'sequence, we sometimes certainly have bishops too
'little spiritual—men more worldly than heavenly,
'wiser in the spirit of this world than in the spirit of
'Christ!

'Let the laws be rehearsed concerning the residence
'of bishops in their dioceses, which command that
'they watch over the salvation of souls, that they
'disseminate the word of God, that they personally

‘ appear in their churches at least on great festivals,
‘ that they sacrifice for their people, that they hear
‘ the causes of the poor, that they sustain the father-
‘ less, and widows, that they exercise themselves
‘ always in works of piety.

  ‘ Let the laws be rehearsed concerning the due dis-
‘ tribution of the patrimony of Christ—laws which
‘ command that the goods of the Church be spent not
‘ in sumptuous buildings, not in magnificence and
‘ pomp, not in feasts and banquets, not in luxury and
‘ lust, not in enriching kinsfolk nor in keeping hounds,
‘ but in things useful and needful to the Church.
‘ For when he was asked by Augustine, the English
‘ bishop, in what way English bishops and prelates
‘ should dispose of those goods which were the offer-
‘ ings of the faithful, Pope Gregory replied (and his
‘ reply is placed in the *Decretals*, ch. xii. q. 2), that
‘ the goods of bishops should be divided into four
‘ parts, of which one part should go to the bishop and
‘ his family, another to his clergy, a third for repair-
‘ ing buildings, a fourth to the poor.

  ‘ Let the laws be recited, and let them be recited Reform of
‘ again and again, which abolish the scandals and Ecclesiastical
‘ vices of courts, which take away those daily newly Courts.
‘ invented arts for getting money, which were designed
‘ to extirpate and eradicate that horrible covetous-
‘ ness which is the root and cause of all evils, which
‘ is the fountain of all iniquity.

  ‘ Lastly, let those laws and constitutions be renewed Councils
‘ concerning the holding of Councils, which com- should be
held
‘ mand that Provincial Councils should be held more oftener.
‘ frequently for the reformation of the Church. For
‘ nothing ever happens more detrimental to the

' Church of Christ than the omission of Councils, both
' general and provincial.

' Having rehearsed these laws and others, like
' them, which pertain to this matter, and have for
' their object the correction of morals, it remains that
' with all authority and power their *execution* should
' be commanded, so that having a law we should at
' length live according to it.

The
bishops
must
first be
reformed,

' In which matter, with all due reverence, I appeal
' most strongly to *you*, fathers !   For this execution of
' laws and observance of constitutions ought to begin
' with *you*, so that by your living example you may
' teach us priests to imitate you.   Else it will surely
' be said of you, " They lay heavy burdens on other
' " men's shoulders, but they themselves will not move
' " them even with one of their fingers."   But you, if
' you keep the laws, and first reform your own lives
' to the law and rules of the Canons, will thereby

then the
clergy,

' provide us with a light, in which we shall see what
' we ought to do—the light, *i.e.* of your good example.
' And we, seeing our fathers keep the laws, will gladly
' follow in the footsteps of our fathers.

' The clerical and priestly part of the Church being
' thus reformed, we can then with better grace proceed
' to the reformation of the lay part, which indeed it
' will be very easy to do, if we ourselves have been re-
' formed first.   For the body follows the soul, and as

then the
lay part
of the
Church.

' are the rulers in a State such will the people be.
' Wherefore, if priests themselves, the rulers of souls,
' were good, the people in their turn would become
' good also ; for our own goodness would teach others
' how they may be good more clearly than all other
' kinds of teaching and preaching.   Our goodness
' would urge them on in the right way far more

' efficaciously than all your suspensions and excom-
' munications. Wherefore, if you wish the lay-people
' to live according to your will and pleasure, you
' must first live according to the will of God, and
' thus (believe me) you will easily attain what you
' wish in them.

' You want obedience from them. And it is right ;
' for in the Epistle to the Hebrews are these words of
' Paul to the laity : " Be obedient " (he says) " to
' " your rulers, and be subject to them." But if you
' desire this obedience, first give reason and cause of
' obedience on your part, as the same Paul teaches in
' the following text—" Watch as those that give an
' " account of their souls," and then they will obey
' you.

' You desire to be honoured by the people. It is
' right ; for Paul writes to Timotheus, " Priests who
' " rule well are worthy of double honour, chiefly
' " those who labour in word and doctrine." There-
' fore, desiring honour, first rule well, and labour in
' word and doctrine, and then the people will hold
' you in all honour.

' You desire to reap their carnal things, and to
' collect tithes and offerings without any reluctance
' on their part. It is right ; for Paul, writing to the
' Romans, says : " They are your debtors, and ought
' " to minister to you in carnal things." But if you
' wish to reap their carnal things, you must first sow
' your spiritual things, and then ye shall reap abun-
' dantly of their carnal things. For that man is hard
' and unjust who desires " to reap where he has not
' " sown, and to gather where he has not scattered."

' You desire ecclesiastical liberty, and not to be
' drawn before civil courts. And this too is right ;

'for in the Psalms it is said, "Touch not mine
'"anointed." But if ye desire this liberty, loose
'yourselves first from worldly bondage, and from the
'cringing service of men, and claim for yourselves
'that true liberty of Christ, that spiritual liberty
'through grace from sin, and serve God and reign in
'Him, and then (believe me) the people will not
'touch the anointed of the Lord their God!

'You desire security, quiet, and peace. And this is
'fitting. But, desiring peace, return to the God of
'love and peace; return to Christ, in whom is the true
'peace of the Spirit which passeth all understanding;
'return to the true priestly life. · And lastly, as Paul
'commands, "Be ye reformed in the newness of your
'"minds, that ye may know those things which are of
'"God; and the peace of God shall be with you!"

Con-
clusion.

'These, reverend fathers and most distinguished
'men, are the things that I thought should be spoken
'concerning the reformation of the clergy. I trust
'that, in your clemency, you will take them in good
'part. If, by chance, I should seem to have gone too
'far in this sermon—if I have said anything with too
'much warmth—forgive it me, and pardon a man
'speaking out of zeal, a man sorrowing for the ruin of
'the Church; and, passing by any foolishness of mine,
'consider the thing itself. Consider the miserable
'state and condition of the Church, and bend your
'whole minds to its reformation. Suffer not, fathers,
'suffer not this so illustrious an assembly to break up
'without result. Suffer not this your congregation
'to slip by for nothing. Ye have indeed often been
'assembled. But (if by your leave I may speak the

'truth) I see not what fruit has as yet resulted,
'especially to the Church, from assemblies of this
'kind! Go now, in the Spirit whom you have in-
'voked, that ye may be able, with his assistance, to
'devise, to ordain, and to decree those things which
'may be useful to the Church, and redound to your
'praise and the honour of God: to whom be all
'honour and glory, for ever and ever, Amen!'

Comparing this noble sermon with the passages
quoted in an earlier chapter from Colet's lectures at
Oxford and his Abstracts of the Dionysian writings,
it must be admitted that what, fourteen years before,
he had uttered as it were in secret, he had now, as
occasion required, proclaimed upon the housetops.
What effect it had upon the assembled clergy no
record remains to tell.

The object which Wolsey had in view in the Con- Wolsey
vocation was, it may be presumed, attained to his obtains
satisfaction. The clergy granted the King 'four dismes.
'dismes,' to be paid in yearly instalments.[1] And this
was the full amount of taxation usually demanded
by English sovereigns from the clergy in time of war,
except in cases of extreme urgency.[2]

Whether Bishop Fitzjames succeeded equally well
in securing the inhuman object which was nearest to
his heart, is not equally clear.

---

[1] Brewer, i. 4312.

[2] A 'tenth,' of the clergy, produced in 1500 about 12,000*l.* See
Italian Relation of England, C. S.
p. 52. Four-tenths would be equal
to about half a million sterling in
present money.

'If the King should go to war,
'he .... immediately compels
'the clergy to pay him one, two, or
'three fifteenths or tenths ... and
'more if the urgency of the war
'should require it.'—Ibid. p. 52.

But one authentic picture of a scene which there can be little doubt occurred in *this* Convocation has been preserved, to give a passing glimpse into the nature of the discussion which followed upon the subject of the ' extirpation of heresy.' In the course of the debate, the advocates of increased severity against poor Lollards were asked, it seems, to point out, if they could, a single passage in the Canonical Scriptures which commands the capital punishment of heretics. Whereupon an old divine [1] rose from his seat, and with some severity and temper quoted the command of St. Paul to Titus : ' A man that is an ' heretic, after the first and second admonition, reject.' The old man quoted the words as they stand in the Vulgate version : ' Hæreticum hominem post unam ' et alteram correptionem *devita !* '—' *De-vita !* ' he repeated with emphasis ; and again, louder still, he thundered ' DE-VITA ! ' till everyone wondered what had happened to the man. At length he proceeded to explain that the meaning of the Latin verb ' devitare ' being ' de vita tollere ' (!), the passage in question was clearly a direct command to punish heretics by death ! [2]

---

[1] ' Senex quidam theologus et ' imprimis severus.'—*Erasmi Annotationes*, edit. 1519, p. 489 ; and edit. 1522, p. 558. ' Senex quidam ' severus et vel supercilio teste ' theologus, magno stomacho, re- ' spondit.'—*Erasmi Moriæ Encomium*, Basle, 1519, p. 225.

[2] See note of Erasmus in his ' Annotationes,' *in loco* Titus iii. 10 ; also the *Praise of Folly*, where the story is told in connection with further particulars. The exact coincidence between the two ac- counts of the old divine's construction of Titus iii. 10 leads to the conclusion that the rest of the story, as given in the *Praise of Folly*, may also very probably be literally true. Knight, in his *Life of Colet*, concludes that as the story is told in the *Praise of Folly*, the incident must have occurred in a *previous convocation*, as this satire was written *before* 1512.—Knight, pp. 199, 200. But the story is not inserted in the editions of 1511 and of 1515, whilst it is inserted in the Basle

A smile passed round among those members of Convocation who were learned enough to detect the gross
ignorance of the old divine ; but to the rest his logic
appeared perfectly conclusive, and he was allowed
to proceed triumphantly to support his position by
quoting, again from the Vulgate, the text translated
in the English version, ' Suffer not a witch to live.'
For the word ' witch ' the Vulgate version has ' male-
' ficus.' A heretic, he declared, was clearly ' maleficus,'
and therefore ought not to be suffered to live. By
which conclusive logic the learned members of the
Convocation of 1512 were, it is said, for the most part
completely carried away.[1]

This story, resting wholly or in part upon Colet's
own relation to Erasmus, is the only glimpse which
can be gathered of the proceedings of this Convocation ' for the extirpation of heresy.'

II. COLET IS CHARGED WITH HERESY (1512).

Before the spring of 1512 was passed, Colet's
Sermon to Convocation was printed and distributed

---

edition of the *Encomium Moriæ,*
November 12, 1519, published just
after Colet's death (p. 226). Nor is
the first part of the story relating
to Titus iii. 10 to be found in the
first edition of the *Annotationes*
(1516). The story is first told by
Erasmus in the second edition
(1519), published just before Colet's
death, and then without any mention of Colet's name ; the latter
being possibly omitted lest, as
Bishop Fitzjames was still living,
its mention should be dangerous
to Colet. It was not till the third
edition was published (in 1522),
when both Colet and Colet's persecutor were dead, that Erasmus
added the words, ' Id, ne quis
' suspicetur meum esse commen-
' tum, accepi *ex Johanne Coleto,*
' viro spectatæ integritatis, quo
' præsidente res acta est.'—*Annotationes,* 3rd ed. 1522, p. 558.
[1] *Praise of Folly,* 1519, p. 226.

in Latin, and probably in English [1] also ; and as there was an immediate lull in the storm of persecution, he may possibly have come off rather as victor than as vanquished, in spite of the seeming triumph of the persecuting party in Convocation.

The bold position he had taken had rallied round him not a few honest-hearted men, and had made him, perhaps unconsciously on his part, the man to whom earnest truth-seekers looked up as to a leader, and upon whom the blind leaders of the blindly orthodox party vented all their jealousy and hatred.

Comple-
tion of
Colet's
school.

He was henceforth a marked man. That school of his in St. Paul's Churchyard, to the erection of which he had devoted his fortune, which he had the previous autumn made his will to endow, had now arisen into a conspicuous building, and the motives of the Dean in building it were of course everywhere canvassed. The school was now fairly at work. Lilly, the godson of Grocyn, the late Professor of Greek at Oxford, was already appointed headmaster ; and as he was known to have himself travelled in Greece to perfect his classical knowledge, it could no longer be doubted by any that here, under the shadow of the great cathedral, was to be taught to the boys that ' heretical Greek ' which

Jealousy
against
Colet's
school.

was regarded with so much suspicion. Here was, in fact, a school of the ' new learning,' sowing in the minds of English youth the seeds of that free thought and

---

[1] There is an old English translation given by Knight in his *Life of Colet* (pp. 289–308), printed by ' Thomas Berthelet, regius impres-' sor,' and without date. *Pynson* was the King's printer in 1512 (Brewer, i. p. 1030), and accord-ingly he printed the Latin edition of 1511, *i.e.* 1512.—Knight, p. 271. Knight speaks of the old English version as ' written probably by the ' Dean himself,' but he gives no evidence in support of his conjecture. See Knight's *Life of Colet*, p. 199.

heresy which Colet had so long been teaching to the people from his pulpit at St. Paul's. More had already facetiously told Colet that he could not wonder if his school should raise a storm of malice ; for people cannot help seeing that, as in the Trojan horse were concealed armed Greeks for the destruction of barbarian Troy, so from this school would come forth those who would expose and upset their ignorance.[1]

No wonder, indeed, if the wrath of Bishop Fitzjames should be kindled against Colet ; no wonder if, having failed in his attempt effectually to stir up the spirit of persecution in the recent Convocation, he should now vent his spleen upon the newly founded school.

But how fully, amid all, Colet preserved his temper and persevered in his work, may be gathered from the following letter to Erasmus, who, in intervals of leisure from graver labours, was devoting his literary talents to the service of Colet's school, and whose little book, ' De Copiâ Verborum,' was part of it already in the printer's hands :—

Colet to Erasmus.[2]

' Indeed, dearest Erasmus, since you left London ' I have heard nothing of you. . . .

' I have been spending a few days in the country ' with my mother, consoling her in her grief on the

---

[1] ' Neque valde miror si clarissi-
' mæ scholæ tuæ rumpantur in-
' vidia. Vident enim uti ex equo
' Trojano prodierunt Græci, qui
' barbaram diruere Trojam, sic è
' tuâ prodire *scholâ* qui ipsorum
' arguunt atque subvertunt insci-

' tiam.'—Stapleton's *Tres Thomæ*,
p. 166, ed. 1612 ; p. 23, ed. 1588.

[2] Brewer, vol. ii. No. 3190. The
true date, 1512, is clearly fixed by
the allusion to the ' De Copia,'
&c.—Eras. Epist. App. ccccvi.

'death of my servant, who died at her house, whom
'she loved as a son, and for whose death she wept as
'though he had been more than a son. The night on
'which I returned to town I received your letter.

A bishop
blasphemes
Colet's
school.

'Now listen to a joke! A certain bishop, who is
'held, too, to be one of the wiser ones, has been
'blaspheming our school before a large concourse
'of people, declaring that I have erected what is a
'useless thing, yea a bad thing—yea more (to give
'his own words), a temple of idolatry. Which,
'indeed, I fancy he called it, because the poets are to
'be taught there! At this, Erasmus, I am not angry,
'but laugh heartily. . . .

'I send you a little book containing the sermon '
[to the Convocation ?]. 'The printers said they had
'sent some to Cambridge.

'Farewell! Do not forget the verses for our boys,
'which I want you to finish with all good nature and
'courtesy. Take care to let us have the second part
'of your " Copia." '

'De
Copiâ,'
preface of
Erasmus.

The second part of the 'Copia' was accordingly
completed, and the whole sent to the press in May,
with a prefatory letter to Colet,[1] in which Erasmus
paid a loving tribute to his friend's character and
work. He dwelt upon Colet's noble self-sacrificing
devotion to the good of others, and the judgment he
had shown in singling out two main objects at which
to labour, as the most powerful means of furthering
the great cause so dear to his heart.

Colet's
preaching.

To implant Christ in the hearts of the common
people, by constant preaching, year after year, from

---

[1] Dated 'M.DXII. iii. Kal. Maias : Londini.'

his pulpit at St. Paul's—this, wrote Erasmus, had Chap. VII.
been Colet's first great work; and surely it had A.D. 1512.
borne much fruit !

To found a school, wherein the sons of the people Colet's
should drink in Christ along with a sound education school.
—that thereby, as it were in the cradle of coming
generations, the foundation might be laid of the
future welfare of his country—this had been the
second great work to which Colet had devoted time,
talents, and a princely fortune.

' What is this, I ask, but to act as a father to all your Erasmus
' children and fellow-citizens ? You rob yourself to in praise
of Colet's
' make them rich ; you strip yourself to clothe them. work.
' You wear yourself out with toil, that they may be
' quickened into life in Christ. In a word, you spend
' yourself away that you may gain them for Christ !

' He must be envious, indeed, who does not back
' with all his might the man who engages in a work
' like this. He must be wicked, indeed, who can
' gainsay or interrupt him. That man is an enemy
' to England who does not care to give a helping
' hand where he can.'

Which words in praise of Colet's self-sacrificing
work were not merely uttered within hearing of those
who might hang upon the lips of the aged Fitzjames
or the bishop who had ' blasphemed ' the school ; they
passed, with edition after edition of the ' Copia ' of
Erasmus, into the hands of every scholar in Europe,
until they were known and read of all men ! [1]

But Bishop Fitzjames, whose unabating zeal against

---

[1] The first edition was printed
at Paris by Badius. Another was
printed by Schurerius (Argentorat.), January 1513. And, in
Oct. 1514, Erasmus sent to Schurerius a *revised* copy for publication.

heretics had become the ruling passion of his old age, no longer able to control his hatred of the Dean, associated with himself two other bishops of like opinion and spirit in the ignoble work of making trouble for Colet. They resorted to their usual weapon—*persecution.* They exhibited to the Archbishop of Canterbury articles against Colet extracted from his sermons. Their first charge was that he had preached that images ought not to be worshipped. The second charge was that he had denied that Christ, when He commanded Peter the third time to ' feed ' his lambs,' made any allusion to the application of episcopal revenues in hospitality or anything else, seeing that Peter was a poor man, and had no episcopal revenues at all. The third charge was, that in speaking once from his pulpit of those who were accustomed to *read* their sermons, he meant to give a side-hit at the Bishop of London, who, on account of his old age, was in the habit of reading his sermons.[1]

Colet
charged
with
heresy
by his
bishop.

But the Archbishop, thoroughly appreciating as he did the high qualities of the Dean, became his protector and advocate, instead of his judge. Colet himself, says Erasmus, did not deign to make any reply to these foolish charges, and others ' more ' foolish still.'[2] And the Archbishop, therefore, without hearing any reply, indignantly rejected them.

Proceed-
ings
quashed
by
Warham.

What the charges ' *more foolish still* ' may have been Erasmus does not record. But Tyndale mentions, as a well-known fact, that ' the Bishop of ' London would have made Dean Colet of Paules a ' heretic for *translating the Paternoster in English,*

---

[1] Eras. *Op.* iii. p. 460, D and E. [2] Ibid. p. 460, E.

'had not the [Arch]bishop of Canterbury helped the Chap. VII.
'Dean.'[1] Colet's English translation or paraphrase A.D. 1512.
of the Paternoster still remains to show that he was
open to the charge.[2] But for once, at least, the
persecutor was robbed of his prey!

For a while, indeed, Colet's voice had been silenced;
but now Erasmus was able to congratulate his friend
on his return to his post of duty at St. Paul's.

' I was delighted to hear from you ' [he wrote from Erasmus
Cambridge], ' and have to congratulate you that you to Colet.
' have returned to your most sacred and useful work
' of preaching. I fancy even this little interruption
' will be overruled for good, for your people will
' listen to your voice all the more eagerly for having
' been deprived of it for a while, May Jesus, *Optimus*
' *Maximus*, keep you in safety! '[3]

III. MORE IN TROUBLE AGAIN (1512).

In closing this chapter, it may perhaps be remarked
that little has been heard of More during these the
first years of his return to public life.

The fact is, that he had been too busy to write More en-
many letters even to Erasmus. He had been rapidly grossed in
business.
drawn into the vortex of public business. His judicial
office of undersheriff of London had required his close
attention every Thursday. His private practice at the

---

[1] 3 Tyndale, p. 168 (Parker
Society).

[2] ' The Seven Peticyons of the
' Paternoster, by Joan Colet, Deane
' of Paules,' inserted in the collection of Prayer entitled ' *Horæ beate*

' *Marie Virginis secundum usum*
' *Sarum totaliter ad longum.*'—
Knight's *Life of Colet*, App. *Mis-
cellanies*, No. xii. p. 450.

[3] Eras. Epist. cvii. Brewer, No.
3495, under date 1st Nov. 1512.

More
writes his
history of
Richard
III.

Death of
his wife.

His four
children.

bar had also in the meantime rapidly increased, and drawn largely on his time. When Erasmus wrote to know what he was doing, and why he did not write, the answer was that More was constantly closeted with the Lord Chancellor, engaged in ' grave business,' [1] and would write if he could. What leisure he could snatch from these public duties he would seem to have been devoting to his ' History of Richard III.' [2] the materials for which he probably obtained through his former connection with Cardinal Morton.

And were we to lift the veil from his domestic life, we should find the dark shadow of sorrow cast upon his bright home in Bucklersbury. But a few short months ago, such was the air of happiness about that household, that Ammonius, writing as he often did to Erasmus, to tell him all the news, whilst betraying, by the endearing epithets he used, his fascination for the loveliness of More's own gentle nature, had spoken also of his ' most good-natured wife,' and of the ' children ' and whole family ' as ' charmingly well.' [3]

Now four motherless children nestle round their widowed father's knee.[4] Margaret, the eldest daughter

---

[1] Eras. Epist. cxxviii. and cxvi.

[2] ' Written by Master Thomas ' More, then one of the under-' sheriffs of London, about the year 1513.' — *More's English Works*, p. 35.

[3] ' Morus noster melitissimus, ' cum sua facillima conjuge . . . ' et liberis ac universa familia pul-' cherrime valet.'—Ammonius to Erasmus: Epist. clxxv. This letter, dated May 19, 1515, evidently belongs to an earlier date. It is

apparently in reply to Epist. cx. dated April 27, from Paris, and written by Erasmus during his stay there in 1511.

[4] The date of the death of More's first wife it is not easy exactly to fix. Cresacre More says, ' His wife ' Jane, as long as she lived, which ' was but some six years, brought ' unto him almost every year a ' child.'—*Life of Sir T. More*, p. 40. This would bring her death to 1511, or 1512.

—the child of six years old—henceforth it will be *her*
lot to fill her lost mother's place in her father's heart,
and to be a mother to the little ones.   And she too
is not unknown to fame.   It was she

> . . . . 'who clasped in her last trance
> 'Her murdered father's head.' . . . .

CHAPTER VIII.

I. COLET PREACHES AGAINST THE CONTINENTAL WARS— THE FIRST CAMPAIGN (1512–13).

IF Colet returned to his pulpit after a narrow escape of being burned for heresy, it was to continue to do his duty, and not to preach in future only such sermons as might escape the censure of his bishop. His honesty and boldness were soon again put to the test.

It was in the summer of 1512 that Henry VIII. for the first time mingled the blood of English soldiers in those Continental wars which now for some years became the absorbing object of attention.

European rulers had not yet accepted the modern notion of territorial sovereignty. Instead of looking upon themselves as the rulers of nations, living within the settled boundaries of their respective countries, they still thirsted for war and conquest, and dreamed of universal dominion. To how great an extent this was so, a glance at the ambitious schemes of the chief rulers of Europe at this period will show.

How Pope Julius II. was striving to add temporal to spiritual sovereignty, and desired to be the 'lord 'and master of the game of the world,' has been already noticed in mentioning how it called forth the satire of Erasmus, in his 'Praise of Folly.' This warlike Pope was still fighting in his old age. Side by side with Pope Julius was Cæsar Maximilian, Archduke of Austria, King of the Romans, Emperor of Germany, &c.—fit representative of the ambitious House of Hapsburg! Not contented with all these titles and dominions, Maximilian was intriguing to secure by marriages the restoration of Hungary and Bohemia, and the annexation of the Netherlands, Franche-Comté, and Artois, as well as of Castile and Arragon, to the titles and possessions of his royal house. And what he could not secure by marriages he was trying to secure by arms. Had his success equalled his lust of dominion, east and west would have been united in the one 'Holy Empire' of which he dreamed, independent even of Papal interference, and hereditary for ever in the House of Hapsburg. Then there was Louis XII., the 'Most Christian' King of France, laying claim to a great part of Italy, pushing his influence and power so far as to strike terror into the minds of other princes; assuming to himself the rank of the first prince in Christendom; his chief minister aspiring to succeed Julius II. in the Papal chair; his son Francis ready to become a candidate for the Empire on the death of Maximilian. And, lastly, there was Henry VIII. of England, eager to win his spurs, and to achieve military renown at the first opportunity; reviving old obsolete claims on the crown of France; ready to offer himself as a candidate for the Empire when it became vacant, and to plot to secure the election of Wolsey to the Papal chair! Throw all these rival claims and objects of ambition into a wild medley, consider to what plots and counterplots, leagues and breaches of them, all this vast entanglement of interests and ambitions must give rise, and some faint idea may be gained of the state of European politics.

Already in December 1511, a Holy Alliance had been formed between Pope Julius, Maximilian, Ferdinand, and Henry VIII., to arrest the conquests and humble the ambition of Louis XII. How the clergy had been induced to tax themselves in support of this holy enterprise has already been seen. Parliament also had granted a subsidy of two fifteenths and tenths, and had made some needful provision for the approaching war. Everything was ready, and in the summer of 1512 the first English expedition sailed.

Ferdinand persuaded Henry VIII. to aid him in attacking Guienne, and, all unused to the stratagems of war, he fell into the snare. While his father-in-law was playing his selfish game, and reducing the kingdom of Navarre, Henry's fleet and soldiers were left to play their part alone. The whole expedition, owing to delays and gross mismanagement, wofully miscarried. There were symptoms of mutiny and desertion ; and at length the English army returned home utterly demoralised, and in the teeth of their commands. The English flag was disgraced in the eyes of Europe. French wits wrote biting satires ' De Anglorum e Gal- ' liis Fuga,' [1] and in bitter disappointment Henry VIII., to avoid further disgrace, was obliged to hush up the affair, allowing the disbanded soldiers to return to their homes without further inquiry. [2] It was in vain that More replied to the French wits with epigram for epigram, correcting their exaggerated satire, and turning the tables upon their own nation. [3] He laid the

---

[1] *Philomorus*, p. 71.
[2] See Brewer, i. preface p. xl et seq., and authorities there cited.

[3] ' *In Brixium Germanum falsa* ' *scribentem de Chordigera.*' ' *In* ' *eundem : Versus excerpti e Chordi-*

foundation of a controversy by which he was annoyed in after-years,[1] and did little at the time to remove the general feeling of national disgrace which resulted from this first trial of Henry VIII. at the game of war.

Meanwhile Colet, ever prone to speak out plainly what he thought, had publicly from his pulpit expressed his strong condemnation of the war. And the old Bishop of London, ever lying in wait, like the persecuting Pharisees of old, to find an occasion of evil against him, eagerly made use of this pretext to renew the attempt to get him into trouble. He had failed to bring down upon the Dean the terrors of ecclesiastical authority, but it would answer his purpose as well if he could provoke against him royal displeasure. He therefore informed the King, now eagerly bent upon his Continental wars, that Colet had condemned them; that he had publicly preached, in a sermon, that an unjust peace was ' to be preferred before the justest ' war.' While the Bishop was thus whispering evil against him in the royal ear, others of his party were zealously preaching up the war, and launching out invectives against Colet and ' *the poets,*' as they designated those who were suspected of preferring classical Latin and Greek to the ' *blotterature,*' as Colet called it, of the monks. By these means they appear to have hoped to bring Colet into disgrace, and themselves into favour, with the King.

But it would seem that they watched and waited

CHAP.
VIII.
____
A.D. 1512.

Colet
preaches
against
the war.

' *gera Brixii ;* ' ' *Postea de eadem* ' *Chordigera ;* ' ' *Epigramma Mori* ' *alludens ad versus superiores :* ' *Aliud de eodem,*' &c.—*Mori Epigrammata.*

[1] See the several epigrams relating to Brixius in *Mori Epigram-* mata. For the wearisome correspondence which resulted from the publication of these epigrams and the ' *Antimorus* ' of Brixius in reply, see Eras. *Op.* iii., index under the head ' Brixius (Germanus).' See also *Philomorus,* p. 71.

Chap.
VIII.

A.D. 1512.

The King
supports
Colet
against
his
enemies.

in vain for any visible sign of success. The King
appeared strangely indifferent alike to the treasonable
preaching of the Dean and to their own effervescent
loyalty.

Unknown to them, the King sent for Colet, and
privately encouraged him to go on boldly reforming
by his teaching the corrupt morals of the age, and by
no means to hide his light in times so dark. He knew
full well, he said, what these bishops were plotting
against him, and also what good service he had done
to the British nation both by example and teaching.
And he ended by saying, that he would put such a
check upon the attempts of these men, as would make
it clear to others that if any one chose to meddle with
Colet it would not be with impunity !

Upon this Colet thanked the King for his kind inten-
tions, but, as to what he proposed further, beseeched
him to forbear. ' He had no wish,' he said, ' that any
' one should be the worse on his account ; he had
' rather resign his preferment than it should come to
' that.' [1]

II. COLET'S SERMON TO HENRY VIII. (1513).

The spring of 1513 was spent by Henry VIII. in
energetic preparations for another campaign, in which
he hoped to retrieve the lost credit of his arms. The
young King, in spite of his regard for better counsellors,
was intent upon warlike achievements. His first
failure had made him the more eager to rush into the
combat again. Wolsey, the only man amongst the
war party whose energy and tact were equal to the

[1] Eras. *Op.* iii. pp. 460, 461. See
also ' *Richardi Pacei . . . de Fructu
qui ex doctrina percipitur, liber.*' Basle, 1517, Oct. And Cresacre
More's *Life of More,* App.

emergency, found in this turn of affairs the stepping-
stone to his own ambitious fortune. The preparations
for the next campaign were entrusted to his hands.

Rumours were heard that the French would be
likely to invade England if Henry VIII. long delayed
his invasion of France. To meet this contingency, the
sheriffs of Somerset and Dorset had been already ordered to issue proclamations, that every man between
sixty and sixteen should be ready in arms [1] to defend
his country. Ever and anon came tidings that the
French navy was moving restlessly about on the
opposite shore,[2] in readiness for some unknown enterprise. Diplomatists were meanwhile weaving their
wily webs of diplomacy, deceiving and being deceived.
Even between the parties to the League there were
constant breaches of confidence and double-dealing.
The entangled meshes of international policy were
thrown into still greater confusion, in February, by
the death of Julius II., the head of the Holy Alliance.
The new Pope might be a Frenchman, instead of the
leader of the league against France, for anything men
knew. The moment was auspicious for the attempt
to bring about a peace. But Henry VIII. was bent
upon war. He urged on the equipment of the fleet,
and was impatient of delay. On March 17 he conferred upon Sir Edward Howard the high-sounding
title of ' Admiral of England, Wales, Ireland, Nor-
' mandy, Gascony, and Aquitaine.' [3] On Saturday,
the 21st, he went down to Plymouth to inspect the
fleet in person, and left orders to the Admiral to put
to sea. He had set his heart upon his fleet, and in
parting from Howard commanded him to send him

---

[1] Brewer, i. 3723.   [2] Ibid. 3752, 3821.   [3] Ibid. 3809.

word ' how every ship did sail.' [1]   With his royal head thus full of his ships and sailors, and eagerly waiting for tidings of the result of their first trial-trip in the Channel, Henry VIII. entered upon the solemnities of Holy Passion Week.

On Good Friday, the 27th, the King attended Divine service in the Chapel Royal.   Dean Colet was the preacher for the day.   It must have been especially difficult and even painful for Colet, after the kindness shown to him so recently by the King, again to express in the royal presence his strong condemnation of the warlike policy upon which Henry VIII. had entered in the previous year, and in the pursuit of which he was now so eagerly preparing for a second campaign.   The King too, coming directly from his fleet full of expectation, was not likely to be in a mood to be thwarted by a preacher.   But Colet was firm in his purpose, and as, when called to preach before Convocation, he had chosen his text expressly for the bishops, so now in the royal presence he preached his sermon to the King.

' He preached wonderfully ' (says Erasmus) ' on the ' *victory of Christ*, exhorting all Christians to fight and ' conquer under the banner of their King.   He showed ' that when wicked men, out of hatred and ambition, ' fought with and destroyed one another, they fought ' under the banner, not of Christ, but of the devil. ' He showed, further, how hard a thing it is to die a ' Christian death [on the field of battle]; how few ' undertake a war except from hatred or ambition; ' how hardly possible it is for those who really have ' that brotherly love without which " no one can see

---

[1] Brewer, i. xlvii, and No. 3820.   Edward Lord Howard to Henry VIII.

' " the Lord " to thrust their sword into their brother's
' blood ; and he urged, in conclusion, that instead of
' imitating the example of Cæsars and Alexanders,
' the Christian ought rather to follow the example of
' Christ his Prince.' [1]

So earnestly had Colet preached, and with such
telling and pointed allusion to the events of the day,
that the King was not a little afraid that the sermon
might damp the zeal of his newly enlisted soldiers.
Thereupon, like birds of evil omen, the enemies of
Colet hovered round him as though he were an owl,
hoping that at length the royal anger might be stirred
against him. The King sent for Colet. He came at
the royal command. He dined at the Franciscan
monastery adjoining the Palace at Greenwich. When
the King knew he was there, he went out into the
monastery garden to meet him, dismissing all his
attendants. And when the two were quite alone, he
bade Colet to cover his head and be at ease with him.
' I did not call you here, Dean,' he said to him, ' to
' interrupt your holy labours, for of these I altogether
' approve, but to unburden my conscience of some
' scruples, that by your advice I may be able more
' fully to do my duty.' They talked together nearly
an hour and a half; Colet's enemies, meanwhile, im-
patiently waiting in the court, scarcely able to contain
their fury, chuckling over the jeopardy in which they
thought Colet at last stood with the King. As it was,
the King approved and agreed with Colet in everything
he said. But he was glad to find that Colet had not
intended to declare absolutely that there could be no

---

[1] Eras. *Op.* iii. p. 461. Compare *Enchiridion*, ' Canon VI.'

just war, no doubt persuading himself that his own was one of the very few just ones. The conversation ended in his expressing a wish that Colet would some time or other explain himself more clearly, lest the raw soldiers should go away with a mistaken notion, and think that he had really said that *no* war is lawful to Christians.[1] ' And thus ' (continues Erasmus) ' Colet, ' by his singular discretion and moderation, not only ' satisfied the mind of the King, but even rose in his ' favour.' When he returned to the palace at parting,

the King graciously drank to his health, embracing him most warmly, and, promising all the favours which it was in the power of a most loving prince to grant, dismissed him. Colet was no sooner gone than the courtiers flocked again round the King, to know the result of his conference in the convent garden. Whereupon the King replied, in the hearing of all : ' Let ' every one have his own doctor, and let every one ' favour his own ; this man is the doctor for me.' Upon this the hungry wolves departed without their bone, and thereafter no one ever dared to meddle with Colet. This is Erasmus's version [2] of an incident which, especially when placed in its proper historical setting, may be looked upon as a jewel in the crown both of the young King and of his upright subject. It has been reported that Colet complied with the King's wish, and preached another sermon in favour of the war against France, of the necessity and justice of which, as strictly *defensive*, the King had convinced

---

[1] Colet, and Erasmus, and More, notwithstanding their very severe condemnation of the wars of the period, and wars in general, never went so far as to lay down the doctrine, that ' *All* War is unlawful ' to the Christian.'

[2] Eras. *Op.* iii. p. 461. A, E.

him. But with reference to this second sermon, if ever it was preached, Erasmus is silent.[1]

III. THE SECOND CAMPAIGN OF HENRY VIII. (1513).

While the King was trying to pacify his conscience, and allay the scruples raised in his mind by Colet's preaching, his ambassador (West) was listening to a Good Friday sermon at the Chapel Royal of Scotland, and using the occasion to urge upon the Queen to use her influence with the Scotch king in favour of peace with England. There were rumours that the Scotch king was playing into the hands of the King of France —that he was going to send a 'great ship' to aid him in his wars. A legacy happened to be due from England to the Queen of Scotland, and West was instructed to threaten to withhold payment unless James would promise to keep the peace with England. James gave shuffling and unsatisfactory replies. There were troubles ahead in that quarter![2]

The news sent by West from Scotland must have raised some forebodings in Henry's mind. The chance of finding one enemy behind him, if he attempted to invade France, in itself was not encouraging. As to any scruples raised by Colet's preaching, his head was probably far too full of the approaching campaign, and his heart too earnestly set upon the success of his fleet, to admit of his impartially considering the right and the wrong of the war in which he was already involved, or the evils it would bring upon his country.

---

[1] Knight's *Life of Colet*, p. 207, note quoted from *Antiq. Britann.*, Sub. Wil. Warham, ed. Han. p. 306.

Brewer, Nic. West to Henry VIII. 3838.

Meanwhile, probably only a few days after Colet's sermon was preached, the anxiously expected news reached England of the election to the Papal chair of Cardinal de' Medici, an acquaintance of Erasmus, and the fellow-student of his friend Linacre, under the title of Leo X. The letter which conveyed the news to Henry VIII. spoke of the ' gentleness, innocence, ' and virtue ' of the new Pope, and his anxiety for a ' *universal peace.*' He had declared that he would· abide by the League, but the writer expressed his opinion that ' he would not be fond of war like Julius ' —that he would favour literature and the arts, and ' employ himself in building [St. Peter's], but not ' enter upon any war except from compulsion, unless ' it might be against the infidels.' [1]

Leo X. in
favour of
peace.

Henry—just then receiving reports from his fleet, dating to April 5,[2] full of eager expectation and confidence on the part of the Admiral, ' that an engagement ' with the French might be looked for in five or six ' days, and that by the aid of God and of St. George ' they hoped to have a fair day with them '—was not at all in a humour to hear of a general peace. So on April 12, all good advice of Colet's forgotten, he wrote to his minister at Rome,[3] instructing him to express his joy that Leo X. had adhered to the Holy League, and to state that he (Henry) could not think of entertaining any propositions for peace, considering the magnitude and vast expense of his preparations, at all events without the consent of all parties. A fleet of 12,000 soldiers, the minister was to say, was already at sea, and Henry was preparing to invade France

Henry
VIII. will
not listen
to it.

_____

[1] Brewer, i. 3780.
[2] Ibid. 3857. Sir E. Howard to Wolsey.
[3] Henry VIII. to Cardinal Bainbridge. Brewer, i. 3876.

himself with 40,000 more, and powerful artillery. It would be most expedient to cripple the power of the King of France *now*, and prevent his ambition for the future.[1]

This letter was written on April 12. On the 17th Sir Arthur Plantagenet came with letters from the fleet, under leave of absence. He could ill be spared, wrote the Admiral; but his ship had struck upon a rock, and in great peril he had made a vow that, if it pleased God to deliver him, he would not eat flesh or fish till he had made a pilgrimage to the shrine of Our Lady of Walsingham;[2] and accordingly thither he was bound.

This was only the beginning of troubles. On April 25, Admiral Howard, with a personal bravery and daring which immortalised his name, boarded the ship of the French admiral with sixteen companions, but, in the struggle which ensued, was thrust overboard with ' morris pykes ' and lost. The English fleet, disheartened by the loss of its brave admiral, returned to Plymouth without proper orders, and without having inflicted any considerable blow upon the French fleet.[3]

The King, just then preparing to cross over to Calais with his main army, to invade France in person, hastily appointed Thomas Lord Howard admiral in the place of his brother ; and in letters to the captains, gave vent to his royal displeasure at their return to Plymouth without his orders—letters which disheartened still more an army which the new Admiral found

---

[1] Brewer, i. 3876.
[2] Ibid. 3903, Sir E. Howard to Henry VIII.
[3] Ibid. 4005, Echyngham to Wolsey.

'very badly ordered, more than half on land, and 'a great number stolen away.'[1]

But still Henry was determined to press on with his enterprise. He wrote to his ambassadors to urge the King of Spain at once to invade Guienne or Gascony, as the English navy, though amounting to 10,000 men, was not sufficient to meet the combined forces of the enemy without Ferdinand's aid. Yet for all this, they were to say, 'he would not forbear the invasion of 'France.'[2] He was not even deterred by receipt of intelligence, before he set sail, that his treacherous father-in-law had already forsaken him, and made a year's truce with France.[3] On June 30 the watchers on the walls of Calais beheld the King, with 'such 'a fleet as Neptune never saw before,' approaching amid 'great firing of guns from the ships and towers,' to commence in good earnest his invasion of France.

Little as did the 'Oxford Reformers' sympathise with the war, they were no indifferent spectators. Even Erasmus for the time could not but share the feelings of an Englishman, though he had many friends in France, and hated the war. From the list of the ships of the navy, in the handwriting of Wolsey, it appears that one or more of them had been christened '*Erasmus.*'[4] Some of his intimate friends followed the army in the King's retinue. Ammonius, the King's Latin secretary, was one of them; and Erasmus was kept informed by his letters of what was going on, and amused by his quaint sketches of camp-life.[5]

---

[1] Brewer, i. 4019, Thomas Lord Howard to Wolsey; 4020, Thomas Lord Howard to Henry VIII.

[2] Ibid. 4055, Henry VIII. to his ambassadors in Arragon.

[3] Ibid. 4075, Fox to Wolsey.

[4] Ibid. 3977, 5761.

[5] Eras. Epist. cxix. Brewer, i. 4427, Erasmus to Ammonius.

He was even ready himself with an epigram upon the
flight of the French after the Battle (or rather the no-
battle) of Spurs. He could not resist the temptation
to turn the tables upon the French poets, who had
indulged their vein of satire at the expense of the
English during the last year's campaign, and had thereby so nettled the spirit of More and his friends. To
the ' De Anglorum e Galliis fuga ' of the French poet,
Erasmus was now ready with a still more biting satire,
' In fugam Gallorum insequentibus Anglis.' [1] More
also wrote an epigram, in which he contrasted the
bloody resistance of the Nervii to Cæsar with the feeble
opposition offered by their modern French successors
to Henry VIII.[2]

It would be out of place here to follow the details
of the campaign. Suffice it to say that, like the first
game of a child, it was carelessly and blunderingly
played,—not, however, without buoyant spirit, and
that air of exaggerated grandeur which betokens the
inexperienced hand. The towns of Terouenne and
Tournay were indeed taken, and that without much
bloodshed; but they were taken under the selfish
advice of Maximilian, who throughout never lost sight
of his own interest, and was pleased enough to use the
lavish purse and the ardent ambition of his young ally
to his own advantage. The power of France was not
crippled by the taking of these unimportant towns.
The whole enterprise was confined within the narrow
limits of so remote a corner of France that her soil
could hardly be regarded as really invaded. So small
a portion of the French army was engaged in opposing

Success
of the
campaign.

---

[1] Erasmi *Epigrammata*: Basle,
1518, p. 353; and Eras. *Op.* i.
p. 1224, F.

[2] *De Deditione Nervæi, Mori
Epigrammata*: Basle, 1518, p. 263,
and ed. 1522, p. 98.

it, that it was scarcely a war with Louis XII. Henry VIII. himself spent more time in tournaments and brilliant pageants than in actual fighting. He was emphatically playing at the game of war.

But while Henry was thus engaged in France, King James of Scotland, in spite of treaties and promises, treacherously took opportunity to cross the borders, and recklessly to invade England with a large but ill-trained army. Queen Katherine, whom Henry had appointed Regent during his absence, sharing his love of chivalrous enterprise, zealously mustered what forces were left in England ; and thus it came about, that just as Henry was entering Tournay, the news arrived of the Battle of Flodden. From 500 to 1000 English and about 10,000 Scotch, it was reported, lay dead upon that bloody field. The King of Scots fell near his banner, and at his side Scotch bishops, lords, and noblemen, amongst whom was the friend and pupil of Erasmus—the young Archbishop of St. Andrew's. Queen Katherine wrote, with a thankful heart, to her royal husband, giving an account of the great victory, and informing him that she was about to go on pilgrimage to Our Lady of Walsingham, in performance of past promises, and to pray for his return.

Before the end of October the King, finding nothing better to do, amid great show of triumph returned to England. Thus ended this second campaign, with just sufficient success to induce the King and Wolsey to prepare for a third.[1]

---

[1] For the particulars mentioned in this section, it will be seen how much I am indebted to Mr. Brewer. See vol. i. of his Calendar, preface pp. l–lv, in addition to the particular authorities cited.

IV. ERASMUS VISITS THE SHRINE OF OUR LADY OF
WALSINGHAM (1513).

While Sir Arthur Plantagenet and Queen Katherine
were going on pilgrimage to the shrine of Our Lady of
Walsingham, to give thanks, the one for the defeat of
the Scots, and the other for deliverance from shipwreck, Erasmus took it into his head to go on pilgrimage also. He had told his friend Ammonius, in May,
that he meant to visit the far-famed shrine to pray for
the success of the Holy League, and to hang up a *Greek
Ode* as a votive offering.[1] He appears to have made
the pilgrimage from Cambridge in the autumn of 1513,
accompanied by his young friend Robert Aldridge,[2]
afterwards Bishop of Carlisle. It was probably this
visit which Erasmus so graphically described many
years afterwards in his Colloquy of the ' *Religious
' Pilgrimage.* '

The College of Canons, under their Sub-prior, maintained chiefly by the offerings left by pilgrims upon the
Virgin's altar ; the Priory Church, a relic of which still
stands to attest its architectural beauty ; the small
unfinished chapel of the Virgin herself, the sea-winds
whistling through its unglazed windows ; the inner
windowless wooden chapel, with its two doors for
pilgrims' ingress and egress ; the Virgin's shrine, rich
in jewels, gold and silver ornaments, lit up by burning
tapers ; the dim religious light and scented air ; the
Canon at the altar, with jealous eye watching each pilgrim and his gift, and keeping guard against sacrilegious theft ; the little wicket in the gateway through

Erasmus
visits the
shrine of
Our Lady
of Wal-
singham.

---

[1] Eras. Epist. cxiv. Brewer, i.
1652.

[2] See mention of Aldridge in
Eras. Epist. dcclxxxii.

T

the outer wall, so small that a man must stoop low to pass through it, and yet through which, by the Virgin's aid, an armed knight on horseback once escaped from his pursuer ; the plate of copper, on which the knight's figure was engraved in ancient costume with a beard like a goat, and his clothes fitting close to his body, with scarcely so much as a wrinkle in them ; the little chapel towards the east, containing the middle joint of St. Peter's finger, so large, the pilgrims thought, that Peter must needs have been a very lusty man ; the house hard by, which it was said was ages ago brought suddenly, one winter time, when all things were covered with snow, from a place a great way off (though to the eyes of Erasmus its thatch, timber, walls, and everything about it, seemed of modern date) ; the concreted milk of the Holy Virgin, which looked like beaten chalk tempered with the white of an egg; the bold request of Erasmus, to be informed what evidence there was of its really being the milk of the Virgin ; the contracted brows of the verger, as he referred them to the ' authentic record ' of its pedigree, hung up high against the wall,—all this is described with so much of the graphic detail of an eyewitness, that one feels, in reading the ' Colloquy,' that it must record the writer's vivid recollections of his own experience.

The concluding incident of the ' Colloquy,' whether referring to a future visit, or only an imaginary one, evidently alludes to the Greek Ode mentioned in the letter to Ammonius. It tells how that, before they left the place, the Sub-prior, with some hesitation, modestly ventured to ask whether his present visitor was the same man who, about two years before, had

hung up a votive tablet inscribed in *Hebrew* letters :
for Erasmus remarks, they call everything Hebrew
which they cannot understand.   The Sub-prior is then
made to relate what great pains had been taken to
read the Greek verses ; what wiping of glasses ; how
one wise man thought they were written in Arabic
letters, and another in altogether fictitious ones ; how
at length one had been able to make out the title,
which was Latin written in Roman capitals—the
verses themselves being in Greek, and written in
Greek capitals.   In reward for the explanation and
translation of the Ode, the ' Colloquy ' goes on to
relate that the Sub-prior pulled out of his bag, and
presented to his visitors a piece of wood cut from a
beam on which the Virgin mother had been seen to
rest.

Whether this concluding incident related in the
' Colloquy ' was a real occurrence or not, it, at all
events, confirms the testimony of the ' Colloquy ' itself
to the fact that Erasmus made this pilgrimage in a
satirical and unbelieving mood, and that his votive ode
was rather a joke played upon the ignorant canons,
than any proof that he himself was a worshipper of
the Virgin, or a believer in the efficacy of pilgrimages
to her shrine.

CHAPTER IX.

I. ERASMUS LEAVES CAMBRIDGE, AND MEDITATES LEAVING ENGLAND (1513–14).

DURING the autumn of 1513 Erasmus made up his mind to leave Cambridge. He had come to England on the accession of Henry VIII. with full purpose to make it his permanent home.[1] That his friends would try to bring this about had been his last entreaty on leaving England for his visit to Italy. They had done their best for him. They had found all who cared for the advance of learning anxious to secure the residence of so great a scholar in their own country. The promises were indeed vague, but there were plenty of them, and altogether the chances of a fair maintenance for Erasmus had appeared to be good. He had settled at Cambridge intending to earn his living by teaching Greek to the students; expecting, from them and from the University, fees and a stipend sufficient to enable him to pay his way. But the drudgery of teaching Greek was by no means the work upon which Erasmus had set his heart. It was rather, like St. Paul's tent-making, the price he had to pay for that leisure which he was bent upon devoting to his

---

[1] *Compendium Vitæ Erasmi*: Eras. *Op.* i. preface.

real work. This work was his fellow-work with Colet.
Apart from the aid he was able to give to his friend, by
taking up the cudgels for him at the University, and
finding him teachers and schoolbooks for his school—
for all this was done by-the-bye—he was labouring to
make his own proper contribution towards the object
to which both were devoting their all. He was labouring hard to produce an edition of the New Testament
in the original Greek, with a new and free translation
of his own, and simultaneously with this a corrected
edition of the works of St. Jerome—the latter in itself
an undertaking of enormous labour.

In letters written from Cambridge during the years
1511–1513, we catch stray glimpses of the progress
of these great works. He writes to Colet, in August
1511, that ' he is about attacking St. Paul,' [1] and in
July 1512, that he has finished collating the New
Testament, and is attacking St. Jerome.[2]

To Ammonius, in the camp, during the French campaign of 1513, he writes that he is working with almost
superhuman zeal at the correction of the text of St.
Jerome ; and shortly after the close of the campaign
against France, he tells his friend that ' he himself has
' been waging no less fierce a warfare with the blunders
' of Jerome.' [3] And now, with his editions of the New
Testament and Jerome nearly ready for the press,
why should he waste any further time at Cambridge ?
He had complained from the first that he could get

---

[1] Eras. Epist. cxvii. Brewer, i.
1847.

[2] Eras. Epist. cxv. Brewer, i.
4336. The allusion to the ' De
' Copiâ ' (printed in May 1512)
fixes the date.

[3] Eras. Epist. cxxix. Brewer,
i. 4576. See also Brewer, i. 2013,
which belongs to the same autumn.
Epist. cxli.

nothing out of the students.[1]　All these years he had been, in spite of all his efforts, and notwithstanding an annual stipend secured upon a living in Kent, through the kindness of Warham, to a great extent dependent on his friends, obliged most unwillingly to beg, till he had become thoroughly ashamed of begging.[2] And now this autumn of 1513 had brought matters to a crisis.　At Michaelmas the University had agreed to pay him thirty nobles,[3] and, on September 1, they had begged the assistance of Lord Mountjoy in the payment of this ' enormous stipend ' for their Greek professor, adding, by way of pressing the urgency of their claim, that they must otherwise soon lose him.[4]

On November 28, Erasmus wrote to Ammonius that he had for some months lived like a cockle shut up in his shell, humming over his books.　Cambridge, he said, was deserted because of the plague ; and even when all the men were there, there was no large company.　The expense was intolerable, the profits not a brass farthing.　The last five months had, he said, cost him sixty nobles, but he had never received more than one from his audience.　He was going to throw out his sheet-anchor this winter.　If successful he would make his nest, if not he would flit.[5]

---

[1] From the letters referred to by Brewer, i. p. 963, Nos. 5731 (Eras. Epist. clxv.), 5732, 5733, and 5734, it would seem that he had undertaken the education of a boy to whom he had been ' *more* ' *than a father.*' This does not prove that he was in the habit at Cambridge of taking private pupils, as possibly this boy was placed under his care somewhat in the same way as More had been placed with

Cardinal Morton.

[2] See Eras. Epist. cl.　Brewer, i. 4528.

[3] Eras. Epist. cxix. Brewer, i. 4427.

[4] Brewer, i. 4428.

[5] Eras. Epist. cxxxi. Brewer, i. 2001, under the date 1511.　The allusion to the King of Scots, as well as the passage quoted, fix the date 1513. See also Eras. Epist. cxxix. Brewer, i. 4576.

The result was that in the winter of 1513–14
Erasmus finally left Cambridge. The disbanding of
disaffected and demoralised soldiers had so increased
the number of robbers on the public roads,[1] that
travelling in the winter months was considered
dangerous; but Erasmus was anxious to proceed
with the publication of his two great works. He was
in London by February 1514.

He found Parliament sitting, and the war party
having all their own way. He found the compliant
Commons supporting by lavish grants of subsidies
Henry VIII.'s ambition ' to recover the realm of
' France, his very true patrimony and inheritance,
' and to reduce the same to his obedience,' [2] and
carried away by the fulsome speeches of courtiers who
drew a triumphant contrast between the setting
fortunes and growing infirmities of the French king and
the prospects of Henry, who, ' like the rising sun, was
' growing brighter and stronger every day.' [3]   While
tax-collectors were pressing for the arrears of half a
dozen previous subsidies, and Parliament was granting
new ones, the liberality of English patrons was likely
to decline. Their heads were too full of the war, and
their purses too empty, to admit of their caring much
at the moment about Erasmus and his literary projects.

No wonder, therefore, that when his friends at the
Court of the Netherlands urged his acceptance of an
honorary place in the Privy Council of Prince Charles,
which would not interfere with his literary labours,
together with a pension which would furnish him with

---

[1] Eras. Epist. cxxxi. Brewer, i. 2001.

[2] 5 Henry VIII. c. i.

[3] Brewer, i. 4819. Notes of a speech in this parliament.

the means to carry them on—no wonder that under these circumstances Erasmus accepted the invitation and concluded to leave England.

In reply to the Abbot of St. Bertin, he wrote an elegant letter,[1] gracefully acknowledging his great kindness in wishing to restore him to his fatherland. Not that he disliked England, or was wanting in patrons there. The Archbishop of Canterbury, if he had been a brother or a father, could not have been kinder to him, and by his gift he still held the pension out of the living in Kent. But the war had suddenly diverted the genius of England from its ordinary channels. The price of everything was becoming dearer and dearer. The liberality of patrons was becoming less and less. How could they do other than give sparingly with so many war-taxes to pay? He then proceeded :—

Letter to the Abbot of St. Bertin.

'Oh that God would deign to still the tempest of 'war! What madness is it! The wars of Christian 'princes begin for the most part either out of ambition 'or hatred or lust, or like diseases of the mind. Con-'sider also by whom they are carried on : by homi-'cides, by outcasts, by gamblers, by ravishers, by the 'most sordid mercenary troops, who care more for a 'little pay than for their lives. These offscourings of 'mankind are to be received into your territory and 'your cities that you may carry on war. Think, too, 'of the crimes which are committed under pretext of 'war, for amid the din of arms good laws are silent ; 'what rapine, what sacrilege, what other crimes of 'which decency forbids the mention ! The demoralisa-'tion which it causes will linger in your country for 'years after the war is over. . . . .

---

[1] Eras. Epist. cxliv.

'It is much more glorious to found cities than to
'destroy them.   In our times it is the *people* who build
'and improve cities, while the madness of princes
'destroys them.   But, you may say, princes must
'vindicate their rights.   Without speaking rashly of
'the deeds of princes, one thing is clear, that there
'are some princes at least who first do what they like,
'and then try to find some pretext for their deeds.
'And in this hurlyburly of human affairs, in the con-
'fusion of so many leagues and treaties, who cannot
'make out a title to what he wants ?   Meanwhile these
'wars are not waged for the good of the *people*, but to
'settle the question, who shall call himself their prince.

'We ought to remember that *men*, and especially
'Christian men, are *free*-men.   And if for a long time
'they have flourished under a prince, and now
'acknowledge him, what need is there that the world
'should be turned upside down to make a change ?
'If even among the heathen, long-continued consent
'[of the people] makes a *prince*, much more should
'it be so among Christians, with whom royalty is an
'*administration*, not a *dominion*.[1] . . . .'

He concluded by urging the abbot to call to mind
all that Christ and his apostles said about peace, and
the tolerance of evil.   If he did so, surely he would
bring all his influence to bear upon Prince Charles
and the Emperor in favour of a 'Christian peace
'among Christian princes.'[2]

---

[1] Compare More's *Epigrams*,
headed :   'Populus consentiens
'Regnum dat et aufert,' and
'Bonum Principem esse patrem
'non dominum.'
[2] Eras. Epist. cxliv. and published among 'Auctarium Selecta-
'rum aliquot Epistolarum Erasmi,'
&c. Basil. 1518, p. 62.   The above
extracts are abridged in the translation.

In writing to the Prince de Vere on the same subject Erasmus had expressed his grief that their common country had become mixed up with the wars, and his wish that he could safely put in writing what he thought upon the subject.[1] Whether safely or not, he had certainly now dared to speak his mind pretty fully in the letter to the Abbot of St. Bertin.

II. ERASMUS AND THE PAPAL AMBASSADOR (1514).

Erasmus had other opportunities of speaking out his mind about the war.

Erasmus dines with Ammonius and the Papal Ambassador in disguise.

There was a rumour afloat that a Papal ambassador had arrived in England—a Cardinal in disguise. It happened that Erasmus was invited to dine with his friend Ammonius. He went as a man goes to the house of an intimate friend, without ceremony, and expecting to dine with him alone. He found, however, another guest at his friend's table—a man in a long robe, his hair bound up in a net, and with a single servant attending him. Erasmus, after saluting his friend, eyed the stranger with some curiosity. Struck by the military sternness of the man's look, he asked of Ammonius in Greek, ' Who is he ? ' He replied, also in Greek, ' A great merchant.' ' I thought so,' said Erasmus ; and caring to take no further notice of him, they sat down to table, the stranger taking precedence. Erasmus chatted with Ammonius as though they had been alone, and, amongst other things, happened to ask him whether the rumour was true that an ambassador had come from Leo X. to negotiate a peace between England and France. ' The Pope,' he continued, ' did not take me into his councils ; but if he had

---

[1] Eras. Epist. cxliii.

' I should not have advised him to propose a peace.'
' Why ? ' asked Ammonius.   ' Because it would not be
' wise to talk about peace,' replied Erasmus.   ' Why ? '
' Because a peace cannot be negotiated all at once ; and
' in the meantime, while the monarchs are treating
' about the conditions, the soldiers, at the very thought
' of peace, will be incited to far worse projects than in
' war itself ;   whereas by a *truce* the hands of the
' soldiery may be tied at once.   I should propose a
' truce of three years, in order that the terms might
' be arranged of a *really permanent treaty of peace.*'
Ammonius assented, and said that he thought this
was what the ambassador was trying to do.   ' Is
' he a Cardinal ? ' asked Erasmus.   ' What made you
' think he was ? ' said the other.   ' The Italians say
' so.'   ' And how do they know ? ' asked Ammonius,
again fencing with Erasmus's question.   ' Is it true
' that he is a Cardinal ? ' repeated Erasmus by-and-bye,
as though he meant to have a straightforward answer.
' His spirit is the spirit of a Cardinal,' evasively
replied Ammonius, brought to bay by the direct
question.   ' It is something,' observed Erasmus,
smiling, ' to have a Cardinal's spirit ! '

The stranger all this time had remained silent,
drinking in this conversation between the two friends.

At last he made an observation or two in Italian,
mixing in a Latin word now and then, as an intelligent
merchant might be expected to do.   Seeing that Erasmus took no notice of what he said, he turned round,
and in Latin observed, ' I wonder you should care
' to live in this barbarous nation, unless you choose
' rather to be all *alone* here than *first* at Rome.'

Erasmus astonished and somewhat nettled to hear

a merchant talk in this way, with disdainful dryness replied that he was living in a country in which there was a very great number of men distinguished for their learning. He had rather hold the last place among these than be nowhere at Rome.

Ammonius, seeing the awkward turn that things were taking, and that Erasmus in his present humour might probably, as he sometimes did, speak his mind rather more plainly than might be desirable, interposed, and, to prevent further perplexity, suggested that they should adjourn to the garden.[1]

Erasmus found out afterwards that the merchant stranger with whom he had had this singular brush was the Pope's ambassador himself—*Cardinal Canossa!*

III. PARTING INTERCOURSE BETWEEN ERASMUS AND COLET (1514).

Meanwhile, in spite of Papal Nuncios, the preparations for the continuance of the war proceeded as before. There were no signs of peace. The King had had a dangerous illness, but had risen from his couch ' fierce as ever against France.'[2]

With heavy hearts Colet and Erasmus held on their way. The war lay like a dark cloud on their horizon. It was throwing back their work. How it had changed the plans of Erasmus has been shown. It had also made Colet's position one of greater difficulty. It is true that hitherto royal favour had protected him from the hatred of his persecutors, but the Bishop of London and his party were more exasperated against him than ever, and who could tell how soon the King's

---

[1] Eras. Germano Brixio : Eras. Epist. mccxxxix.

[2] Brewer, i. 4845, 5173, and 4727.

fickle humour might change ? His love of war was
growing wilder and wilder. He was becoming intoxi-
cated by it. And who could tell what the young King
might do if his passions ever should rise into mastery
over better feelings ? Even the King's present favour,
though it had preserved Colet as yet unharmed in
person, did not prevent his being cramped and
hindered in his work. Whatever he might do was
sure to be misconstrued, and to become the subject
of the ' idle talk of the malevolent.' [1]

It would seem also that other clouds than that of
the war cast their shadow at this time over Colet's
life. By the erection and foundation of his school, he
had reduced his income almost more than he could
well afford,[2] and accustomed, as he was, to abundant
means, it was natural that he should be harassed and
annoyed by anything likely still further to narrow his
resources. He seems to have been troubled with
vexed questions of property and family dispute—
most irksome of all others to a man who was giving
life and wealth away in a great work.

Erasmus, six months previously, in July 1513, had
written to Colet thus :—

' The end of your letter grieved me, for you write
' that you are more harassed than usual by the troubles
' of business. I desire indeed for you to be removed
' as far as possible from worldly business ; not because
' I am afraid lest this world, entangled though it be,
' should get hold of you and claim you for its own, but

---

[1] Eras. Epist. cxv. Eras. *Op.*
iii. p. 107, D. Brewer, i. 4336.

[2] Eras. Epist. cxv. Eras. *Op.*
iii. p. 106, E and F.

'because I had rather such genius, such eloquence,
'such learning should be devoted wholly to Christ.
'What if you should be unable to extricate yourself
'from it! Take care lest little by little you become
'more and more deeply immersed in it. Perhaps it
'might be better to *give in*, rather than to purchase
'victory at so great a cost. For peace of mind is worth
'a great deal. And these things are the thorns which
'accompany riches. In the meantime, oppose a good
'honest conscience to the idle talk of the malevolent.
'Wrap yourself up in Christ and in him alone, and
'this entangled world will disturb you less. But why
'should I, like the sow, preach to Minerva; or, like
'the sick man, prescribe for the doctor? Farewell,
'my best beloved teacher!'— *From Cambridge,
July* 11 [1513].[1]

Erasmus
advises
Colet to
give in.

Six months had passed since Erasmus had thus
advised his friend to *give in* rather than to conquer
at the cost of his peace of mind, but Colet had not
yet succeeded in getting rid of his perplexities. It
would almost seem that the same old quarrel was still
lingering on unhealed; for there was now a dispute
between Colet and an aged uncle of his, and the bone
of contention was a large amount of property.[2]

One day Colet took Erasmus with him by boat to
dine with Archbishop Warham at Lambeth Palace.
As they rowed up the Thames, Colet sat pensively
reading in his book. At dinner, being set opposite his
uncle at table, Erasmus noticed that he was ill at ease,
caring neither to talk nor to eat. And the uncle would
doubtless have remained as silent as the nephew, had
not the Archbishop drawn out the garrulousness of

---

[1] Eras. Epist. cxv.   [2] Eras. *Op.* iii. p. 785, A.

his old age by cheerful conversation. After dinner
the three were closeted together. Erasmus knew not
what all this meant. But, as they were rowing back
to town in the boat, Colet said, ' Erasmus, you're a
' happy man, and have done me a great service ; ' and
then he went on to tell his friend how angry he had
been with his uncle, and how he had even thought of
going to law with him, but in this state of mind,
having taken a copy of the ' Enchiridion ' with him,
he had read the ' rule ' there given ' against anger and
' revenge,' and it had done him so much good that
he had held his tongue at dinner, and with the Colet does
Archbishop's kind assistance after dinner, made up give in at
matters with his uncle.[1] last.

Apart from these cares and troubles, Colet's heart
was naturally saddened with the thought of so soon
parting with his dearest friend, and, as he now could
feel, his ablest fellow-worker. The two were often
together. Colet sometimes would send for Erasmus to
be his companion when he dined out, or when he had
to make a journey.[2] At these times Erasmus testifies
that no one could be more cheerful than Colet was.
It was his habit always to take a book with him. His
conversation often turned upon religious subjects ;
and though in public he was prudently reserved and
cautious in what he said, at these times to his bosom
friend he most freely spoke out his real sentiments.

On one occasion Colet and Erasmus paid a visit Pilgrim-
together to the shrine of St. Thomas-à-Becket. Going age to
on pilgrimage was now the fashionable thing. How bury.

---

[1] Eras. *Op.* iii. p. 785, A. C.
[2] *Ibid.* p. 457, A. See also Eras. Epist. viii. App.

admirals and soldiers who had narrowly escaped in the war went to the shrine of Our Lady at Walsingham to fulfil the vows they had made whilst their lives were in peril; how even Queen Katherine had been to invoke the Virgin's aid upon her husband's French campaign, and to return thanks for the victory over the Scots, has already been seen. It has also been mentioned that Erasmus had paid a visit to Walsingham from Cambridge in a satirical and sceptical mood, and had returned convinced of the absurdity of the whole thing, doubting the genuineness of the relics, and ridiculing the credulity of pilgrims. It seems that before leaving England he had a desire to pay a similar visit to the rival shrine of St. Thomas-à-Becket.

The same 'Colloquy' in which Erasmus describes his visit to Walsingham enables us to picture the two friends on this occasion threading the narrow rustic lanes of Kent on horseback, making the best of their way to Canterbury.[1]

---

[1] The companion of Erasmus was, according to the 'Colloquy,' '*Gratianus Pullus*, an Englishman, 'learned and pious, but with less 'liking for this part of religion than 'I could wish.' 'A *Wickliffite*, 'I fancy!' suggested the other spokesman in the 'Colloquy.' 'I 'do not think so' (was the reply), '*although he had read his books*, 'somewhere or other.'—*Colloquia :* Basle, 1526, p. 597. In his letter to Justus Jonas, Erasmus mentions that Colet was in the habit of reading heretical books.—Eras. *Op.* iii. p. 460, A. It has been suggested also (*Pilgrimages to Walsingham*, &c. by J. G. Nichols, F.S.A.

Westminster, 1849, p. 127), that as in the same letter he describes Colet as wearing *black* vestments (*pullis* vestibus), instead of the usual purple (Eras. *Op.* iii. p. 457, B.), hence the name '*Pullus*' may in itself point to Colet. There is also an allusion by Erasmus in his treatise, '*Modus Orandi*,' to his visit to the shrine of St. Thomas-à-Becket, in which he says, 'Vidi ipse quum 'ostentarent linteola lacera quibus 'ille dicitur abstersisse muccum 'narium, abbatem ac cæteros, qui 'adstabant, aperto scriniolo venera-'bundos procidere ad genua, ac ma-'nibus etiam sublatis adorationem 'gestu repræsentare. Ista *Joanni*

As they approach the city the outline of the cathedral church rises imposingly above all surrounding objects. Its two towers seem to stand, as it were, bidding welcome to approaching pilgrims. The sound of its bells rolls through the country far and wide in melodious peals. At length they reach the city, and armed with a letter of introduction from Archbishop Warham, enter the spacious nave of the cathedral. This is open to the public, and beyond its own vastness and solemn grandeur, presents little of mark, save that they notice the gospel of Nicodemus among other books affixed to the columns, and here and there sepulchral monuments of the nameless dead. A vaulted passage under the steps ascending to the iron grating of the choir, brings them into the north side of the church. Here they are shown a plain ancient wooden altar of the Virgin, whereupon is exhibited the point of the dagger with which St. Thomas's brain was pierced at the time of his murder, and whose sacred rust pilgrims are expected most devoutly to kiss. In the vault below they are next shown the martyr's skull, covered with silver, save that the place where the dagger pierced it is left bare for inspection : also

---

' *Coleto, nam is mecum aderat,* vide-
' bantur indigna, mihi ferenda vide-
'bantur donec se daret opportunitas
' ea citra tumultum corrigendi.'—
Eras. *Op.* v. p. 1119, F, and p. 1120,
A. This allusion to Colet so accurately comports with what is said in the Colloquy of ' Gratianus Pullus,' that the one seems most probably suggested only as a *nom de plume* for the other. I am further indebted to Mr. Lupton for the suggestion that when Ammonius, writing to

Erasmus (Epist. clxxv.), says ' tuus
' *Leucophœus* salvere te jubet,' he alludes to Colet : ' Leucophæus ' being a Greek form of the same nickname as 'Pullus' might be in a Latin form. Mr. Lupton has also shown that ' *Gratian* ' is a rendering of ' *John.*' See his introduction to his edition of *Colet on the Sacraments of the Church,* pp. 6, 7. So that the identification of Colet with the *Gratianus Pullus* of the Colloquy is now complete.

the hair shirt and girdle with which the saint was wont to mortify his flesh. Thence they are taken into the choir to behold its treasures—bones without end ; skulls, jaw-bones, teeth, hands, fingers, arms—to all which the pilgrim's kiss is duly expected.

But Colet having had about enough of this, begins to show evident tokens of dislike to kiss any more. Whereupon the verger piously shuts up the rest of his treasures from the gaze of the careless and profane. The high altar and its load of costly ornaments next claim attention ; after which they pass into the vestry, where is preserved the staff of St. Thomas, surrounded by a wonderful display of silk vestments and golden candlesticks. Thence they are conducted up a flight of steps into a chapel behind the high altar, and shown the face of the saint set in gold and jewels. Here, again, Colet breaks in upon the dumb show with awkward bluntness. He asks the guide whether St. Thomas-à-Becket when he lived was not very kind to the poor ? The verger assents. ' Nor can he have ' changed his mind on this point, I should think,' continues Colet, ' unless it be for the better ? ' The verger nods a sign of approbation. Whereupon Colet submits the query whether the saint, having been so liberal to the poor when a poor man himself, would not now rather permit them to help themselves to some of his vast riches, in relief of their many necessities, than let them so often be tempted into sin by their need ? And the guide still listening in silence, Colet in his earnest way proceeds boldly to assert his own firm conviction that this most holy man would be even delighted that, now that he is dead, these riches of his should go to lighten the poor man's load of poverty, rather than be hoarded up here. At

which sacrilegious remark of Colet's the verger, contracting his brow and pouting his lips, looks upon his
visitors with a wondering stare out of his gorgon eyes,
and doubtless would have made short work with them
were it not that they have come with letters of introduction from the archbishop. Erasmus throws in a
few pacifying words and pieces of coin, and the two
friends pass on to inspect, under the escort now of the
prior himself, the rest of the riches and relics of the
place. All again proceeds smoothly till a chest is
opened containing the rags on which the saint, when
in the flesh, was accustomed to wipe his nose and
the sweat from his brow. The prior, knowing the
position and dignity of Colet, and wishing to do him
becoming honour, graciously offers him as a present
of untold value one of these rags! Colet, breaking   Colet's
through all rules of politeness, takes up the rag be-   disgust at
                                                         the relics
tween the tips of his fingers with a somewhat fastidious of St.
air and a disdainful chuckle, and then lays it down   Thomas-
                                                         à-Becket.
again in evident disgust. The prior, not choosing to
take notice of Colet's profanity, abruptly shuts up the
chest and politely invites them to partake of some
refreshment. After which the two friends again
mount their horses, and make the best of their way
back to London.

Their way lies through a narrow lane, worn deep by
traffic and weather, and with a high bank on either
side. Colet rides to the left of the road. Presently an
old mendicant monk comes out of a house [1] on Colet's
side of the way, and proceeds to sprinkle him with
holy water. Though not in the best of tempers,

---

[1] The lazar-house of Harbledown. See Dean Stanley's *Historical Memorials of Canterbury*, ed. 1868, p. 243.

Colet submits to this annoyance without quite losing it. But when the old mendicant next presents to him the upper leather of an old shoe for his kiss, Colet abruptly demands what he wants with him. The old man replies that the relic is a piece of St. Thomas's shoe! This is more than Colet knows how to put up with. 'What!' he says passionately, turning to Erasmus, 'do these fools want us to kiss the shoes of 'every good man? They pick out the filthiest things 'they can find, and ask us to kiss them.' Erasmus to counteract the effect of such a remark upon the mind of the astonished mendicant, gives him a trifle, and the pilgrims pass on their journey, discussing the difficult question how abuses such as they have witnessed this day are to be remedied. Colet cannot restrain his indignant feeling, but Erasmus urges that a rough or sudden remedy might be worse than the disease. These superstitions must, he thinks, be tolerated until an opportunity arises of correcting them without creating disorder.

There can be little doubt that the graphic picture of which the above is only a rapid sketch was drawn from actual recollections, and described the real feelings of Erasmus and his bolder friend.

Little did the two friends dream, as they rode back to town debating these questions, how soon they would find a final solution. Men's faith was then so strong and implicit in 'Our Lady of Walsingham' that kings and queens were making pilgrimage to her shrine, and the common people, as they gazed at night upon the 'milky way,' believed that it was the starry pathway marked out by heaven to direct pilgrims to the place where the milk of the Holy Virgin

was preserved, and called it the ' *Walsingham way.*'
Little did they dream that in another five and twenty
years the canons would be convicted of forging relics
and feigning miracles, and the far-famed image of the
Virgin dragged to Chelsea by royal order to be there
publicly burned. Then pilgrims were flocking to
Canterbury in crowds to adore the relics and to
admire the riches of St. Thomas's shrine. Little did
they dream that in five and twenty years St. Thomas's
bones would share the fiery fate of the image of the
Virgin, and the gold and jewellery of St. Thomas's
shrine be carried off in chests upon the shoulders of
eight stout men, and cast without remorse into the
royal exchequer ! [1]

---

[1] The colloquy from which the particulars given in this section have been obtained is entitled *Peregrinatio Religionis ergo.* It was not contained in the edition of 1522 (Argent.), but it was inserted probably in that of 1524 (which, however, I have not seen). It was contained in the Basle edition of 1526, which is probably a reprint of that of 1524, the prefatory letter at the beginning being dated Calen. Aug. 1524.

CHAPTER X.

I. ERASMUS GOES TO BASLE TO PRINT HIS NEW TESTAMENT (1514).

CHAP. X.

A.D. 1514.

Erasmus
crosses
the
Channel.

IT was on a July morning in the year 1514 that Erasmus again crossed the Channel. The wind was fair, the sea calm, the sky bright and sunny ; but during the easy passage Erasmus had a heavy heart. He had once more left his English friends behind him, bent upon a solitary pilgrimage to Basle, in order that his edition of the letters of St. Jerome and his Greek New Testament might be printed at the press of Froben the printer. But, always unlucky on leaving British shores, he missed his baggage from the boat when, after the bustle of embarkation, he looked to see that all was right. To have lost his manuscripts—his Jerome, his New Testament, the labours of so many years—to be on his way to Basle without the books for the printing of which he was taking the long journey—this was enough to weigh down his heart with a grief which he might well compare to that of a parent who has lost his children. It turned out, after all, to be a trick of the knavish sailors, who threw the traveller's luggage into another boat in order to extort a few coins for its recovery. Erasmus, in the end, got his luggage back again ; but he might well say that, though the passage was a good one, it was an anxious one to him.[1]

Chap. X.

A.D. 1514.

On his arrival at the castle of *Hammes*, near Calais, where he had agreed to spend a few days with his old pupil and friend Lord Mountjoy, he found waiting for him a letter from Servatius, prior of the monastery of Stein, in Holland—*the* monastery into which he had been ensnared when a youth against his judgment by treachery and foul play.

Letter from Servatius.

It was a letter doubtless written with kindly feeling, for the prior had once been his companion; but still he evidently took it as a letter from the prior of the convent from which he was a kind of runaway, not only inviting, but in measure *claiming* him back again, reproachfully reminding him of his vows, censuring his wandering life, his throwing off the habit of his order, and ending with a bribe—the offer of a post of great advantage if he would return.

Erasmus return! No, truly; that he would not! But the very naming of it brought back to mind not only the wrongs he had suffered in his youth; the cruelty and baseness of his guardians; his miserable experience of monastic life; how hardly he had escaped out of it; his trials during a chequered wandering life since; but also his entry upon fellow-work with Colet; the noble-hearted friends with whom he had been privileged to come in contact; the noble work in which they were now engaged together. What! give up these to put his neck again under a yoke which had so galled him in dark times gone by! And for what? To become perchance the father-

---

[1] Eras. Ammonio: Eras. Epist. clix.

confessor of a nunnery ! It was as though Pharaoh had sent an embassy to Moses offering to make him a taskmaster if he would but return into Egypt.

No wonder that Erasmus, finding this letter from Servatius waiting for him on his arrival at the castle of his friend, took up his pen to reply somewhat warmly before proceeding on his journey. His letter lies as a kind of waymark by the roadside of his wandering life, and with some abridgment and omissions may be thus translated :—

Erasmus to Servatius.

' . . . . Being on a journey, I must reply in but ' few words, and confine myself to matters of the ' most importance.

' Men hold opinions so diverse that it is impossible ' to please everybody. That *my* desire is in very deed ' to follow that which is really the best, God is my ' witness ! It was never my intention to change my ' mode of life or my habit ; not because I approved ' of either, but lest I should give rise to scandal. *You* ' know well that it was by the pertinacity of my guar- ' dians and the persuasion of wicked men that I was ' forced rather than induced to enter the monastic life. ' Afterwards, when I found out how entirely unsuited ' it was for me, I was restrained by the taunts of Cor- ' nelius Wertem and the bashfulness of youth. . . . . . ' But it may be objected that I had a year of what is ' called " probation," and was of mature age. Ridicu- ' lous ! As though anyone could require that a boy ' of seventeen, brought up in literary studies, should ' have attained to a self-knowledge rare even in an ' old man—should be able to learn in one year what

Erasmus alludes to his youth.

' many men grow grey without learning ! Be this as
' it may, I never liked the monastic life ; and I liked
' it less than ever after I had tried it ; but I was en-
' snared in the way I have mentioned. For all this,
' I am free to confess that a man who is really a good
' man may live well in any kind of life.

CHAP. X.

A.D. 1514.
Erasmus
hates the
monastic
life.

' I have in the meantime tried to find that mode of
' living in which I should be least prone to evil. And
' I think assuredly that I have found it ; I have lived
' with sober men, I have lived a life of literary study,
' and these have drawn me away from many vices. It
' has been my lot to live on terms of intimacy with
' men of true Christian wisdom, and I have been
' bettered by their conversation. . . . . Whenever
' the thought has occurred to me of returning into
' your fraternity it has always called back to my re-
' membrance the jealousy of many, the contempt of
' all ; converse how cold, how trifling ! how lacking in
' Christian wisdom ! feastings more fit for the laity !
' the mode of life, as a whole, one which, if you sub-
' tract its ceremonies from it, has nothing left that
' seems to me worth having. Lastly, I have called to
' mind my bodily infirmities, now increased upon me
' by age and toil, by reason of which I should have
' both failed in coming up to your mark and also sacri-
' ficed my own life. For some years now I have been
' afflicted with the stone, and its frequent recurrence
' obliges me to observe great regularity in my habits.

' I have had some experience both of the climate of
' Holland and of your particular diet and habits, and
' I feel sure that, had I returned, nothing else could
' have come of it but trouble to you and death to me.

' But it may be that you deem it a blessed thing to

'die at a good age in the midst of your brotherhood.
'This is a notion which deceives and deludes not you
'alone, but almost everybody. We think that Christ
'and religion consist in certain places, and garments
'and modes of life, and ceremonial observances. It is
'all up, we think, with a man who changes his white
'habit for a black one, who substitutes a hat for a
'hood, and who frequently changes his residence. I
'will be bold to say that, on the other hand, great
'injury has arisen to Christian piety from what we call
'the " religious orders," although it may be that they
'were introduced with a pious motive. . . . . Pick
'out the most lauded and laudable of all of them, and
'you may look in vain, so far as I can see, for any
'likeness to Christ, unless it be in cold and Judaical
'ceremonies. It is on account of these that they think
'so much of themselves ; it is on account of these that
'they judge and condemn others. How much more
'accordant to the teaching of Christ would it be to
'look upon all Christendom as one home ; as it were,
'one monastery ; to regard all men as canons and
'brothers ; to count the sacrament of baptism the
'chief religious vow ; not to care where you live, if
'only you live well ! . . . . . . And now to say a

His works. 'word about my works. The " Enchiridion " I fancy
'you have read. . . . . The book of " Adagia,"
'printed by Aldus, I don't know whether you have
'seen. . . . . I have also written a book, " De
'" Rerum et Verborum Copiâ," which I inscribed to
'my friend Colet. . . . . For these two years past,
'amongst other things, I have been correcting the
'text of the " Letters of Jerome.". . . . By the col-
'lation of Greek and ancient codices, I have also

' corrected the text of the whole New Testament, and
' made annotations not without theological value on
' more than one thousand places. I have commenced
' Commentaries on St. Paul's Epistles, which I shall
' finish when the others are published ; for I have
' made up my mind to work at sacred literature to
' the day of my death. Great men say that in these
' things I am successful where others are not. In
' your mode of life I should entirely fail. Although I
' have had intercourse with so many men of learning,
' both here and in Italy and in France, I have never
' yet found one who advised me to betake myself
' back again to you. . . . . I beg that you will not
' forget to commend me in your prayers to the keeping
' of Christ. If ever I should come really to know
' that it would be doing my duty to *Him* to return
' to your brotherhood, on that very day I will start
' on the journey. Farewell, my once pleasant com-
' panion, but now reverend father.

' From Hammes Castle, near Calais, 9th July,
1514.' [1]

This bold letter written, Erasmus took leave of his
host, and hastened to repay by a short embrace the
kindness of another friend, the Abbot of St. Bertin.[2]
After a two days' halt to accomplish this object, he
again mounted his horse, and, followed by his servant
and baggage, set his face resolutely towards Basle :
cheered in spirit by the marks of friendship received

Visits the
Abbot of
St. Bertin.

On his
way to
Basle.

---

[1] Eras. Epist. App. viii. There
is a reference in the letter to Wolsey
as ' Episcopus Lincolniensis,' and
this confirms the correctness of the
date, as Wolsey was translated to
the Archbishopric of York Aug.
1514.—*Fasti Eccl. Anglicanæ*, p.
310.

[2] Eras. *Op.* iii. p. 160, A.

during the past few days, and anxious to reach his journey's end that he might set about his work.

But all haste is not good speed. As he approached the city of Ghent, while he chanced to be turning *one* way to speak to his servant, his horse took fright at something lying on the road, and turned round the *other* way, severely straining thereby Erasmus's back.

It was with the greatest difficulty and torture that he reached Ghent. There he lay for some days motionless on his back at the inn, unable to stand upright, and fearing the worst. By degrees, however, he again became able to move, and to write an amusing account of his adventure to Lord Mountjoy ; [1] telling him that he had vowed to St. Paul that, if restored to health, he would complete the Commentaries he was writing on the Epistle to the Romans ; and adding that he was already so much better that he hoped ere long to proceed another stage to Antwerp. Antwerp was accordingly reached in due course, and from thence he was able to pursue his journey.

At Louvain he prepared for publication a collection of stray pieces, including amongst them the ' *Institutes* ' *of a Christian Man,*' written by Colet for his school in English prose, and turned into Latin verse by Erasmus. In the letter prefixed to the collection [2] he spoke of Colet as a man ' *than whom, in my opinion, the* ' *kingdom of England has not another more pious, or who* ' *more truly knows Christ.*' [3] Two editions of this

---

[1] Eras. Epist. clxxxii. Partly written at Antwerp, but finished at Basle, Aug. 29, 1514.

[2] The letter is dated ' Lovanii, A.D. mdxiiii. Kal. Aug.'

[3] ' Quo viro non alium habet ' mea quidem sententia Anglorum ' Imperium vel magis pium, vel qui ' Christum verius sapiat.'

volume were published at Cologne in the course of a Chap. X.
few months by different typographers.[1] A.D. 1514.

At Maintz he appears to have halted a while, and he At Maintz.
afterwards informed Colet [2] that 'much was made of
'him there.' That it was so may be readily conjec-
tured, for it was at Maintz that the Court of Inqui-
sition had sat in the autumn of the previous year,
which, had it not been for the timely interference of
the Archbishop of Maintz, would have condemned the
aged Reuchlin as a heretic. In this city Erasmus Reuchlin
would probably fall in with many of Reuchlin's and his
friends.
friends, and as the matter was now pending the decision of the authorities of Rome, they may well have
tried to secure his influence with the Pope, to whom he
was personally known. Be this as it may, from the
date of his visit to Maintz, Erasmus seems not only
never to have lost an opportunity of supporting the
cause of Reuchlin at Rome or elsewhere, but also to
have himself secured the friendship and regard of
Reuchlin's protector, the archbishop.[3]

Leaving Maintz, he proceeded to Strasburg, where Erasmus
he was surrounded and entertained by a galaxy of at Stras-
burg.
learned men. Another stage brought him to Schele-
stadt.[4] The chief men of this ancient town, having

---

[1] *Cato Erasmi. Opuscula aliquot
Erasmo Roterodamo Castigatore et
Interprete, &c.* ' Colonie in edibus
'Quentell. A.D. mcccccxv; 'and Ibid.
' Colonie in edibus Martini Wer-
' denensis xii. Kal. Dec. (1514 ?) '

[2] Coletus Erasmo : Epist. lxxxv.
App.

[3] Ranke's *History of the Reformation,* bk. ii. c. 1. See Erasmus's
mention of Reuchlin in the letter

written this autumn to Wimphelingus, appended to the 2nd edition
of *De Copiâ.* Schelestadt, 1514 ;
and Eras. Epist. clxvii. and clxviii.
As to his friendship with the
Archbishop of Maintz, *vide* Epist.
cccxxxiv.

[4] See letter to Wimphelingus,
Basle, xi. Kal. Oct. 1514, *ubi supra,*
for these and the following particulars.

heard of his approach, sent him a present of wines, requested his company to dinner on the following day, and offered him the escort of one of their number for the remainder of his journey. Erasmus declined to be further detained, but gladly accepted the escort of *John Sapidus.*

After having been thus lionised at each stage of the journey, and to prevent a similar annoyance, on his arrival at Basle, Erasmus requested his new companion to conceal his name, and if possible to introduce him to a few choice friends before his arrival was known. Sapidus complied with this request. He had no difficulty in making his choice.

Arrives at Basle incognito.

Circle of learned men at Basle.

Round the printing establishment of Froben, the printer had gathered a little group of learned and devoted men, whose names had made Basle famous as one of the centres of reviving learning. There was a university at Basle, but it was not this which had attracted the little knot of students to the city. The patriarch of the group was *Johann Amerbach.* He was now an old man. More than thirty years had passed since he had first set up his printing-press at Basle, and during these years he had devoted his ample wealth and active intellect to the reproduction in type of the works of the early Church Fathers. The works of St. Ambrose and St. Augustine had already issued from his press at vast cost of labour, time, and wealth. To publish St. Jerome's works before he died, or at least to see the work in hand, was now the aged patriarch's ambition. Many years ago he had imported Froben, that he might secure an able successor in the printing department. His own three sons, also, he had educated in Latin, Greek, and Hebrew, so as to

Amer-
bach.

His three
sons.

qualify them thoroughly for the work he wished them
to continue after he was gone. And the three
brothers Amerbach did not belie their father's hopes.
They had inherited a double portion of his spirit.[1]
Froben, too, had caught the old printer's mantle, and
worked like him, for love, and not for gain.[2] Others
had gathered round so bright a nucleus. There was
Beatus Rhenanus, a young scholar of great ability and
wealth, whose gentle loving nature endeared him to
his intimate companions. He, too, had caught the
spirit of reviving learning, and thought it not beneath
his dignity to undertake the duties of corrector of the
press in Froben's printing-office.[3] Gerard Lystrius, a
youth brought up to the medical profession, with no
mean knowledge both of Greek and Hebrew, had also
thrown in his lot with them.[4]

Such was the little circle of choice friends into which
Sapidus, without betraying who he was, introduced
the stranger who had just arrived in Basle, who addressing himself at once to Froben, presented letters
from Erasmus, with whom he said that he was most
closely intimate, and from whom he had the fullest
commission to treat with reference to the printing of
his works, so that Froben might regard whatever
arrangement he might make with him as though it

Margin notes:
CHAP. X.
A.D. 1514.
Froben.
Beatus Rhenanus.
Lystrius.
Erasmus introduced incognito to Froben and his friends.

---

[1] Eras. *Op.* iii. p. 1249 ; and see Epist. clxxiv. Erasmus to Leo X. p. 154, C and D.

[2] Epist. dccccxxii. Eras. *Op.* iii. pp. 1054, 1055.

[3] See the *Life of Beatus Rhenanus,* by John Sturmius, ' Vita clarissi- ' morum Historicorum.' Buderi, 1740, pp. 53–62 ; and Eras. *Op.* iii. pp. 154, C, &c. (see Index under his

name); and especially the prefatory letter from Erasmus to Beatus Rhenanus, prefixed to ' Enarratio ' in Primum Psalmum, Beatus vir,' &c. Louvain, 1515. There is also a mention of him worth consulting in Du Pin's *Ecclesiastical Writers,* iii. p. 399.

[4] Eras. *Op.* iii. p. 222, E; and the letter to Wimphelingus.

had been made with Erasmus himself. Finding still that he was undiscovered, and wishing to slide easily from under his *incognito*, he soon added drily that Erasmus and he were ' so alike that to see one was ' to have seen the other ! ' Froben then, to his great amusement, discovered who the stranger was. He was received with open arms. His bills at the inn were forthwith paid, and himself, servant, horses, and baggage transferred to the home of Froben's father-in-law, there to enjoy the luxuries of private hospitality.

When it was known in the city that Erasmus had arrived he was besieged by doctors and deans, rectors of the University, poets-laureate, invitations to dine, and every kind of attention which the men of Basle could give to so illustrious a stranger.

But Erasmus had come back to Basle not to be lionised, but to push on with his work. He was gratified ; and, indeed, he told his friends, almost put to the blush by the honours with which he had been received ; but, finding their constant attentions to interfere greatly with his daily labours at Froben's office, he was obliged to request that he might be left to himself.[1]

Erasmus at work in Froben's printing office.

At Froben's office he found everything prepared to his hand. The train was already laid for the publication of St. Jerome. Beatus Rhenanus and the three brothers Amerbach were ready to throw themselves heart and soul into the work. The latter undertook to share the labour of collating and transcribing portions which Erasmus had not yet completed, and so the ponderous craft got fairly under way. By the

---

[1] Erasmus to Mountjoy, Epist. clxxxii., and the letter above mentioned to Wimphelingus.

end of August, he was thoroughly immersed in types
and proof-sheets, and, to use his own expression, no
less busy in superintending his little enterprise than
the Emperor in his war with Venice.[1]

Thus he could report well of his journey and his
present home to his English friends. He felt that he
had done right in coming to Basle, but, none the less
on that account, that his true home was in the hearts
of these same English friends. In his letters to them *Writes*
he expressed his longing to return.[2] His late ill- *to his*
English
fortune in England he had always set down to the war, *friends.*
which had turned the thoughts of the nation and the
liberality of patrons into other channels, and he hoped
that now, perhaps, the war being over, a better state
of things might reign in England, and better fortunes
be in store for the poor scholar.

What Colet thought of this and things in general,
how clouds and storms seemed gathering round him,
may be learned from his reply to his friend's letter,
brief as was his wont, but touchingly graphic in its
little details about himself and his own life during
these passing months. He was already preparing to
resign his preferments, and building a house within
the secluded precincts of the Charterhouse at Sheene
near Richmond, wherein, with a few bosom friends,
he hoped to spend the rest of his days in peace, un-
molested by his evil genius, the Bishop of London.

Colet to Erasmus.[3]

'Dearest Erasmus—I have received your letter

---

[1] Epist. clxxxii.
[2] Epist. Erasmi clix. and Epist. lxxxv. App.
[3] Epist. lxxxv. App.

' written from Basle, 3 Cal. Sept. I am glad to know
' where you are, and in what clime you are living. I
' am glad, too, that you are well. See that you per-
' form the vow which you say you made to St. Paul.
' That so much was made of you at Maintz, as you tell
' me, I can easily believe. I am glad you intend to re-
' turn to us some day. But I am not very hopeful
' about it. As to any better fortune for you, I don't
' know what to say. I don't know, because those who
' have the means have not the will, and those who have
' the will have not the means. All your friends here
' are well. The Archbishop of Canterbury keeps as
' kindly disposed as ever. The Bishop of Lincoln
' [Wolsey] now reigns " Archbishop of York ! " The

Colet still
harassed
by Bishop
Fitzjames. ' Bishop of London never ceases to harass me. Every
' day I look forward to my retirement and retreat with
' the Carthusians. My nest is nearly finished. When
' you come back to us, so far as I can conjecture, you
' will find me there, " *mortuus mundo.*" Take care of
' your health and let me know where you go to.
' Farewell.—*From London, Oct.* 20 (1514).'

II. ERASMUS RETURNS TO ENGLAND—HIS SATIRE UPON KINGS (1515).

Erasmus had at first intended to remain at Basle
till the Ides of March (1515), and then, in compliance
with the invitation of his Italian friends, to spend a
few weeks in Italy.[1] But after working six or eight
months at Froben's office, he was no longer inclined to
carry out the project ; and so, a new edition of the
' Adagia ' being well nigh completed, and the pon-

---

[1] Epist. ad Wimphelingum.

derous folios of Jerome proceeding to satisfaction,
under the good auspices of the brothers Amerbach,
when spring came round Erasmus took sudden flight
from Basle, and turned up, not in Italy, but in England. Safely arrived in London, he was obliged to do
his best, by the discreet use of his pen, to excuse to
his friends at Rome this slight upon their favours.

He wrote, therefore, elegant and flattering letters to
the Cardinal Grimanus, the Cardinal St. George, and
Pope Leo,[1] describing the labours in which he was engaged, the noble assistance which the little fraternity
at Basle were giving, and which could not have been
got in Italy nor anywhere else ; alluding in flattering
terms to the advantages offered at Rome, and the
kindness he had there received on his former visit ;
but describing in still more glowing terms the love and
generosity of his friends in England, and declaring
' with that frankness which it becomes a German to
' use,' that ' England was his adopted country, and
' the chosen home of his old age.' [2] He also took the
opportunity of strongly urging the two cardinals to
use their utmost influence in aid of the cause of
Reuchlin. He told them how grieved he was, in
common with all the learned men of Germany, that
these frivolous and vexatious proceedings should have
been taken against a man venerable both on account
of age and service, who ought now in his declining
years to be peacefully wearing his well-earned laurels.
And lastly, in his letter to the Pope, Erasmus took
occasion to express his hatred of the wars in which

---

[1] Epist. clxvii. clxviii. and clxxiv.   [2] Eras. *Op.* iii. p. 141, C and D.

CHAP. X.

A.D. 1515.

Peace
between
England
and
France.

Europe had been recently involved, and his thank-
fulness that the efforts of his Holiness to bring about
a peace had at last been crowned with success.

Peace had indeed been proclaimed between France
and England, while Erasmus had been working at
Basle, but under circumstances not likely to *lessen*
those feelings of indignation with which the three
friends regarded the selfish and reckless policy of
European rulers. For peace had been made with
France merely to shuffle the cards. Henry's sister,
the Princess Mary (whose marriage with Henry's ally,
Prince Charles, ought long ago to have been solemnised
according to contract), had been married to their
common enemy, Louis XII. of France, with whom
they had just been together at war. In November,
Henry and his late enemy, Louis, were plotting to combine against Henry's late ally, King Ferdinand ; and
England's blood and treasure, after having been
wasted in helping to wrest Navarre from France for
Ferdinand, were now to be wasted anew to recover the
same province back to France from Ferdinand.[1] On
the first of January this unholy alliance of the two

courts was severed by the death of Louis XII. The
Princess Mary was a widow. The young and ambitious Francis I. succeeded to the French throne, and
he, anxious like Henry VIII. to achieve military glory,
declared his intention, on succeeding to the crown,
that ' the monarchy of Christendom should rest under
' the banner of France as it was wont to do.' [2]   Before
the end of July he had already started on that Italian
campaign in which he was soon to defeat the Swiss in
the great battle of Marignano—a battle at the news of

---

[1] Brewer, i. lxix, and ii. i, *et seq.*   [2] Ibid. ii. xxxviii.

which Ferdinand and Henry were once more to be made secret friends by their common hatred of so dangerous a rival ! [1]

These international scandals, for such they must be called, wrung from Erasmus other and far more bitter censure than that contained in his letter to the Pope. He was laboriously occupied with great works passing through the printing-press at Basle, but still he stole the time to give public vent to his pent-up feelings. It little mattered that the actors of these scandals were patrons of his own—kings and ministers on whose aid he was to some extent dependent, even for the means wherewith to print his Greek New Testament. His indignation burst forth in pamphlets printed in large type, and bearing his name, or was thrust into the new edition of the ' Adagia,' or bound up with other new editions which happened now to be passing through Froben's press.[2] And be it remembered that these works and pamphlets found their way as well into royal courts as into the studies of the learned.

What could exceed the sternness and bitterness of the reproof contained in the following passages ?—

' Aristotle was wont to distinguish between a *king*
' and a *tyrant* by the most obvious marks : the tyrant
' regarding only his own interest ; the king the interest
' of his people. But the title of " king," which the
' first and greatest Roman rulers thought to be
' immodest and impolitic, as likely to stir up jealousy,
' is not enough for some, unless it be gilded with the
' most splendid lies. Kings who are scarcely men are

---

[1] Brewer, ii. liv.
[2] See Eras. Epist. App. xxvii. xxi. and xxiii. These letters are dated 1515 ; and, from the men- tion of the New Testament as not yet placed in Froben's hand, this date would seem to be correct.

' called " divine ; " they are " invincible," though they
' never have left a battlefield without being con-
' quered ; " serene," though they have turned the
' world upside down in a tumult of war ; " illustrious,"
' though they grovel in profoundest ignorance of
' everything noble ; " Catholic," though they follow
' anything rather than Christ.

' And these divine, illustrious, triumphant kings . . .
' have no other desire than that laws, edicts, wars,
' peaces, leagues, councils, judgments, sacred or pro-
' fane, should bring the wealth of others into their
' exchequer—*i.e.* they gather everything into their
' leaking reservoir, and, like the eagles, fatten their
' eaglets on the flesh of innocent birds.

' Let any physiognomist worth anything at all con-
' sider the look and the features of an eagle—those
' rapacious and wicked eyes, that threatening curve of
' the beak, those cruel jaws, that stern front . . .
' will he not recognise at once the image of a king ?—
' a magnificent and majestic king ? Add to this a
' dark ill-omened colour, an unpleasing, dreadful,
' appalling voice, and that threatening scream at
' which every kind of animal trembles. Every one
' will acknowledge this type who has learned how
' terrible are the threats of princes, even uttered in
' jest. . . . . At this scream of the eagle the people
' tremble, the senate yields, the nobility cringes, the
' judges concur, the divines are dumb, the lawyers
' assent, the laws and constitutions give way, neither
' right nor religion, neither justice nor humanity, avail.
' And thus while there are so many birds of sweet and
' melodious song, the unpleasant and unmusical scream
' of the eagle alone has more power than all the

' rest. . . . . Of all birds the eagle alone has seemed
' to wise men the type of royalty—not beautiful, not
' musical, not fit for food ; but carnivorous, greedy,
' hateful to all, the curse of all, and, with its great
' powers of doing harm, surpassing them in its desire
' of doing it.' [1]

Again :—

' The office of a prince is called a " dominion,"
' when in truth a prince has nothing else to do but
' to administer the affairs of the commonwealth.

' The intermarriages between royal families, and
' the new leagues arising from them, are called " the
' " bonds of Christian peace," though almost all wars
' and all tumults of human affairs seem to rise out of
' them. When princes conspire together to oppress
' and exhaust a commonwealth, they call it a " just
' " war." When they themselves *unite* in this object,
' they call it " *peace.*"

' They call it the extension of the empire when
' this or that little town is added to the titles of the
' prince at the cost of the plunder, the blood, the
' widowhood, the bereavement of so many citizens.' [2]

These passages may serve to indicate what feelings
were stirred up in the heart of Erasmus by the condition of international affairs, and in what temper
he returned to England. The works in which they
appeared he had left under the charge of Beatus

---

[1] Eras. *Op.* ii. pp. 870–2 ; and in
part translated in Hallam's *Literature of the Middle Ages*, part 1, c. iv.
These passages are quoted from the
explanation given in the *Adagia* of
the proverb, ' *Scarabeus Aquilam*
' *quærit.*' They occur in the edition
separately printed by Froben in
large type and in an octavo form,
entitled ' Scarabeus:' Basle, mense
Maio, 1517, ff. 21–23.

[2] Eras. *Op.* ii. p. 775. From the
Adagia, ' Sileni Alcibiadis.'

CHAP. X.

A.D. 1515.

Rhenanus, to be printed at Basle in his absence. And some notion of the extent to which whatever proceeded from the pen of Erasmus was now devoured by the public, may be gained from the fact that Rhenanus, in April of this very year, wrote to Erasmus, to tell him that out of an edition of 1800 of the 'Praise of Folly' just printed by Froben, with notes by Lystrius, only sixty remained in hand.[1]

Rapid sale of the 'Praise of 'Folly.'

III. RETURNS TO BASLE TO FINISH HIS WORKS.— FEARS OF THE ORTHODOX PARTY (1515).

It will be necessary to recur to the position of international affairs ere long ; meanwhile, the quotations we have given will be enough to show that, buried as Erasmus was in literary labour, he was alive also to what was passing around him—no mere bookworm, to whom his books and his learning were the sole end of life. As we proceed to examine more closely the object and spirit of the works in which he was now engaged, it will become more and more evident that their interest to him was of quite another kind than that of the mere bookworm.

Erasmus returns to Basle.

Before the summer of 1515 was over he was again on his way to Basle, where his editions of Jerome and of the New Testament were now really approaching completion. Their appearance was anxiously expected by learned men all over Europe. The bold intention of Erasmus to publish the Greek text of the New Testament with a new Latin translation of his own,

---

[1] Eras. Epist. App. xxi. That this edition was printed in 1515, see mention of it in Erasmus's letter to Dorpius, dated Antwerp, 1515, and published at Louvain, Oct. 1515,

a rival of the sacred Vulgate, had got wind. Divines of the traditional school had already taken alarm. It was whispered about amongst them that something ought to be done. The new edition of the ' Praise of ' Folly,' with notes by Lystrius, had been bought and read with avidity. Men now shook their heads, who had smiled at its first appearance. They discovered heresies in it unnoticed before. Besides, the name of Erasmus was now known all over Europe. It mattered little what he wrote a few years ago, when he was little known ; but it mattered much what he might write now that he was a man of mark.

While Erasmus was passing through Belgium on his way to Basle, these whispered signs of discontent found public utterance in a letter from Martin Dorpius,[1] of the Louvain University, addressed to Erasmus, but printed, and, it would seem, in the hands of the public, before it was forwarded to him. He met with it by accident at Antwerp.[2] It was written at the instigation of others. Men who had not the wit to make a public protest of this nature for themselves, had urged Martin Dorpius to employ his talents in their cause, and to become their mouthpiece.[3]

Thus this letter from Dorpius was of far more importance than would at first sight appear. It had a representative importance which it did not possess in itself. It was the public protest of a large and

---

[1] Martinus Dorpius Erasmo : *D. Erasmi, &c. Enarratio in Primum Psalmum, &c. &c.* Louvain, Oct. 1515.

[2] See the commencement of the reply of Erasmus.

[3] ' Martinus Dorpius instiganti-

' bus quibusdam primus omnium ' cœpit in me velitari. . . . Scirem ' illum non odio mei huc venisse, ' sed juvenem tum, ac natura ' facilem, aliorum impulsu pro- ' trudi.'—*Erasmus Botzemo, Catalogus,* &c. Basle, 1523 ; leaf b, 5,

powerful party. As such it required more than a mere private reply from Erasmus, and deserves more than a passing mention here, for it affords an insight into the plan and defences of a theological citadel against which its defenders considered that Erasmus was meditating a bold attack.

Letter
from
Dorpius.

' I hear ' (wrote Dorpius, after criticising severely the ' Praise of Folly ')—' I hear that you have been ' expurgating the epistles of Saint Jerome from the ' errors with which they abound . . . . and this is a ' work in all respects worthy of your labour, and by ' which you will confer a great benefit on divines. . . . ' But I hear, also, that you have been correcting the ' text of the New Testament, and that " you have ' " made annotations not without theological value on ' " more than one thousand places." '

Here Dorpius evidently quotes the words of the letter of Erasmus to *Servatius*, so that *he* too is silently behind the scenes, handing Erasmus's letter about amongst his theological friends, perhaps himself inciting Dorpius to write as he does.

Dorpius
asserts
that there
are no
errors
in the
Vulgate.

' . . . . If I can show you that the Latin transla- ' tion has in it no errors or mistakes ' (continued Dorpius), ' then you must confess that the labour of ' those who try to correct it is altogether null and ' void. . . . I am arguing now with respect to the ' truthfulness and integrity of the translation, and I ' assert this of our Vulgate version. For it cannot be ' that the unanimous universal Church now for so ' many centuries has been mistaken, which always has ' used, and still both sanctions and uses, this version. ' Nor in the same way is it possible that so many holy ' fathers, so many men of most consummate authority,

' could be mistaken, who, relying on the same version,
' have defined the most difficult points even in *General*
' *Councils* ; have defended and elucidated the faith,
' and enacted canons to which even kings have bowed
' their sceptres. That councils rightly convened never
' can err in matters of faith is generally admitted by
' both divines and lawyers. . . . . What matters it
' whether you believe or not that the Greek books are
' more accurate than the Latin ones ; whether or not
' *greater* care was taken to preserve the sacred books
' in all their integrity by the Greeks than by the
' Latins ;—by the Greeks, forsooth, amongst whom the
' Christian religion was very often almost overthrown,
' and who affirmed that none of the gospels were free
' from errors, excepting the one gospel of John ? What
' matters all this when, to say nothing of anything
' else, amongst the Latins the Church has continued
' throughout the inviolate spouse of Christ ? . . . .
' What if it be contended that the sense, as rendered
' by the Latin version, differs in truth from the Greek
' text ? Then, indeed, adieu to the Greek. I adhere
' to the Latin because I cannot bring my mind to
' believe that the Greek are more correct than the
' Latin codices.

  ' But it may be said, Augustine ordered the Latin
' rivulets to be supplied from the Greek fountain-
' head. He did so ; and wisely in his age, in which
' neither had any one Latin version been received by
' the Church as now, nor had the Greek fountain-head
' become so corrupt as it now seems to be.

  ' You may say in reply, " I do not want you to
' " change anything in your codices, nor that you should
' " believe that the Latin version is a false one. I only

A single
error
would
destroy
the au-
thority of
the Bible.

' " point out what discrepancies I discover between the
' " Greek and Latin copies, and what harm is there in
' " that ? " In very deed, my dear Erasmus, there is
' great harm in it. Because, about this matter of the
' integrity of the Holy Scriptures many will dispute,
' many will doubt, if they learn that even one jot or
' tittle in them is false, ... and then will come to
' pass what Augustine described to Jerome : " If any
' " error should be admitted to have crept into the
' " Holy Scriptures, what authority would be left to
' " them ? " All these considerations, my dear Eras-
' mus, have induced me to pray and beseech you, by
' our mutual friendship, by your wonted courtesy and
' candour, either to limit your corrections to those pas-
' sages only of the New Testament in which you are
' able, without altering the sense, to substitute more
' expressive words ; or if you should point out that
' the sense requires any alteration at all, that you will
' reply to the foregoing arguments in your preface.'

Erasmus
replies to
Dorpius.

Erasmus replied to this letter of Dorpius with
singular tact, and reprinted the letter itself with his
reply.

He acknowledged the friendship of Dorpius, and
the kind and friendly tone of his letter. He received,
he said, many flattering letters, but he had rather
receive such a letter as this, of honest advice and
criticism, by far. He was knocked up by sea-sickness,
wearied by long travel on horseback, busy unpacking
his luggage ; but still he thought it was better, he said,
to send some reply, rather than allow his friend to
remain under such erroneous impressions, whether the
result of his own consideration, or instilled into him by
others, who had over-persuaded him into writing this

letter, and thus made a cat's-paw of him, in order to
fight their battles without exposure of their own
persons.

He told him freely how and when the ' Praise of
' Folly ' was written, and what were his reasons for
writing it, frankly and courteously replying to his
criticisms.

He described the labour and difficulty of the correction of the text of St. Jerome—a work of which
Dorpius had expressed his approval. But he said,
with reference to what Dorpius had written upon the
New Testament, he could not help wondering what
had happened to him—what could have thrown all
this dust into his eyes !

' You are unwilling that I should alter anything,
' except when the Greek text expresses the sense of
' the Vulgate more clearly, and you deny that in the
' Vulgate edition there are any mistakes. And you
' think it wrong that what has been approved by the
' sanction of so many ages and so many synods should
' be unsettled by any means. I beseech you to con-
' sider, most learned Dorpius, whether what you have
' written be *true* !   How is it that Jerome, Augustine,
' and Ambrose all cite a text which differs from the
' Vulgate ?   How is it that Jerome finds fault with
' and corrects many readings which we find in the
' Vulgate ?   What can you make of all this concurrent
' evidence—when the Greek versions differ from the
' Vulgate, when Jerome cites the text according to the
' Greek version, when the oldest Latin versions do the
' same, when this reading suits the sense much better
' than that of the Vulgate,—will you, treating all this
' with contempt, follow a version perhaps corrupted by

CHAP. X.
—————
A.D. 1515.

' some copyist ? . . . . In doing so you follow in the
' steps of those vulgar divines who are accustomed to
' attribute ecclesiastical authority to whatever in any
' way creeps into general use. . . . . I had rather be
' a common mechanic than the best of their number.'

With regard to some other points, it was, he said,
more prudent to be silent ; but he told Dorpius that
he had submitted the rough draft of his Annotations
to divines and bishops of the greatest integrity and
learning, and these had confessed that they threw
much light on Scripture study.   He concluded with
the expression of a hope that even Dorpius himself,
although now protesting against the attempt, would
welcome the publication of the book when it came
into his hands.

This letter [1] written and despatched to the printer,
Erasmus proceeded with his journey.   The Rhine,
swollen by the rains and the rapid melting of Alpine
snows, had overflowed its banks ; so that the journey,
always disagreeable and fatiguing, was this time more
than usually so.   It was more like swimming, Erasmus

Erasmus
at Basle.

said, than riding.   But by the end of August [2] he was
again hard at work in Froben's printing-office putting
the finishing strokes to his two great works.[3]   By the

---

[1] Erasmus to Dorpius : *D.
Erasmi, &c. Enarratio in Primum
Psalmum, &c. &c.* Louvain, Oct.
1515.

[2] Erasmus to Wolsey: *Eras.
Op.* iii. p. 1565; App. Epist. lxxiv.
wrongly dated 1516 instead of
1515.

[3] In a letter prefixed to the
Erasmi Epigrammata, Basle, 1518,

Froben pays a just tribute to the
good humour and high courtesy of
Erasmus while at work in his printing-office, interrupted as he often
was, in the midst of his laborious
duties, by frequent requests from
all kinds of people for an epigram
or a letter from the great scholar.
Pp. 275, 276.

7th of March 1516 he was able to announce that Chap. X.
the New Testament was out of the printer's hands, A.D. 1515.
and the final colophon put to St. Jerome.[1]

It is time therefore that we should attempt to
realise what these two great works were, and
what the peculiar significance of their concurrent
publication.

---

[1] Erasmus Urbano Regio : Eras. *Op.* iii. p. 1554, App. Epist. liii.

CHAPTER XI.

THE 'NOVUM INSTRUMENTUM' COMPLETED.—
WHAT IT REALLY WAS (1516).

Main
object
of the
' Novum
Instru-
mentum.'

THE New Testament of Erasmus ought not to be regarded by any means as a mere reproduction of the Greek text, or criticised even *chiefly* as such. The labour which falls to the lot of a pioneer in such a work, the multiplied chances of error in the collation by a single hand, and that of a novice in the art of deciphering difficult manuscripts, the want of experience on the part of the printers in the use of Greek type, the inadequate pecuniary means at the disposal of Erasmus, and the haste with which it was prepared considering the nature of the work,—all tended to make his version of the Greek text exceedingly imperfect, viewed in the light of modern criticism. He may even have been careless, and here and there uncandid and capricious in his choice of readings,—all this, of which I am incapable of forming a conclusive judgment, I am willing to grant by-the-bye. The

merit of the New Testament of Erasmus does not mainly rest upon the accuracy of his Greek text,[1] although this had cost him a great deal of labour, and was a necessary part of his plan.

---

[1] In one place he even supplied a portion of the Greek text which was missing by translating the Latin back into Greek !

I suppose the object of an author may be most
fairly gathered from his own express declarations,
and that the prefaces of Erasmus to his first edition—
the ' Novum Instrumentum,' as he called it—are the
best evidence that can possibly be quoted of the
purpose of Erasmus in its publication. To these,
therefore, I must beg the reader's attention.

Now a careful examination of these prefaces cannot
fail to establish the identity of the purpose of Erasmus
in publishing the ' Novum Instrumentum ' with that
which had induced Colet, nearly twenty years before,
to commence his lectures at Oxford.

During those twenty years the divergence between
the two great rival schools of thought had become
wider and wider.

The intellectual tendencies of the philosophic
school in Italy had become more and more decidedly
sceptical. The meteor lights of Savonarola, Pico,
and Ficino had blazed across the sky and vanished.
The star of semi-pagan philosophy was in the ascendant, and shed its cold light upon the intellect of Italy.

Leo X. was indeed a great improvement upon
Alexander VI. and Julius II.—of this there could be no
doubt. Instead of the gross sensuality of the former
and the warlike passions of the latter, what Ranke has
well designated ' *a sort of intellectual sensualism* ' now
reigned in the Papal Court. Erasmus had indeed entertained bright hopes of Leo X. He had declared himself in favour of a peaceful policy ; he was, too, an
enemy to the blind bigotry of the Schoolmen. Nor
does he seem to have been openly irreligious. His
choice of Sadolet as one of his secretaries was not
like the act of a man who himself would scoff at the

CHAP. XI.

A.D. 1516.

Christian faith ; though, on the other hand, this enlightened Christian was unequally yoked in the office with the philosophical and worldly Bembo. Under former Popes the fear of Erasmus had been ' *lest Rome should degenerate into Babylon.*' He hoped now that, under Leo X., ' the tempest of war being ' hushed, both letters and religion might be seen ' flourishing at Rome.' [1]

Its sceptical tendencies.

At the same time he was not blind to the sceptical tendencies of the Italian schools. Thus whilst in a letter written not long after this period, expressing his faith in the ' revival of letters,' and his belief that the ' authority of the Scriptures will not in the long run be ' lessened by their being read and understood correctly ' instead of incorrectly '—whilst thus, in fact, taking a hopeful view of the future—we yet find him confessing to a fear, ' lest, under the pretext of the revival of ' ancient literature, Paganism should again endeavour ' to rear its head.' [2] The atmosphere of the Papal Court was indeed far more semi-pagan than Christian. With the revival of classical literature it was natural that there should be a revival of classical taste. And just as the mediæval church of St. Peter was demolished to make room for a classical temple, so it was the fashion in high society at Rome to profess belief in the philosophy of Plato and Aristotle and to scoff at the Christian faith.[3]

---

[1] *Epist. ad Car. Grymanum,* prefixed to the Paraphrase on the Epistle to the Romans. Edition Louvain, 1517.

[2] Erasmus Gwolfgango Fabricio Capitoni : Epist. ccvii. *Op.* iii. p. 189, 89, A, C, Feb. 22, 1516, from Antwerp, but probably the year should be 1518. See also his reference to the same pagan tendencies of Italian philosophy in his treatise entitled ' *Ciceronianus,*' and the letter prefixed to it.

[3] Ranke's *History of the Popes,* i. ch. ii. sec. 3.

The extent to which anti-Christian and sceptical tendencies were carried in the direction of speculative philosophy was shown by the publication in this very year, 1516, by *Pomponatius*, whom Ranke speaks of as ' the most distinguished philosopher of the day,' [1] of a work in which he denied the immortality of the soul. [2] This philosopher was, in the words of Hallam, ' the ' most renowned professor of the school of Padua, ' which for more than a century was the focus of ' atheism in Italy.' [3]

That the same anti-Christian and sceptical tendencies were equally prevalent in the sphere of practical morality and politics as in that of speculative philosophy, was also painfully obvious. That popes themselves had discarded Christianity as the standard of their own morality both in social and political action, had for generations been trumpeted forth to the world by their own sensual lives, and their faithless and immoral political conduct. When in the ' Praise ' of Folly ' Erasmus had satirised the policy of popes, he had put a sting to his description of their unchristian conduct by adding that they acted ' *as though Christ* ' *were dead.*' [4] The greatest political philosopher of the age had already written his great work ' *The Prince,*' in which he had *codified*, so to speak, the maxims of the dominant anti-Christian school of politics, and framed a system of political philosophy based upon keen and godless self-interest, and defying, if not in terms denying, both the obligation and policy of the

---

[1] *Ubi supra.*
[2] See the authorities mentioned by Ranke, and also Hallam's *Literature of Europe*, chap. iv. ed.

1837, p. 435.
[3] Hallam, p. 436.
[4] Moria, ed. 1511, Argent. fol. G. iii.

CHAP. XI.

A.D. 1516.

golden rule—a system which may be best described, in a word, by reference to the name of its author, as *Machiavellian.*[1]

The dogmatic school equally anti-Christian in its practice,

On the other hand, opposed to the new 'learning,' and its anti-Christian tendencies, was the dogmatic system of the Schoolmen, defended with blind bigotry by monks and divines of the old school. These had done nothing during the past twenty years to reconcile their system with the intellectual tendencies of their age. They were still straining every nerve to keep Christianity and reviving science hopelessly apart. Their own rigidly defined scholastic creed, with all its unverified hypotheses, rested as securely as ever, in their view, on the absolute inspiration of the Vulgate version of the Bible : witness the letter of Dorpius. No new light had disturbed the entire satisfaction with which they regarded their system, or the assurance with which they denounced Greek and Hebrew as 'heretical tongues,' derided all attempts at free inquiry, and scornfully pointed to the sceptical tendencies of the Italian school as the result to which the 'new learning' must inevitably lead.

and in its politics.

And yet the practical results of this proudly orthodox philosophy were as notoriously anti-Christian, both as regards social and political morality, as was the Machiavellian philosophy, at which these professed Christians pointed with the finger of scorn. Again and again had Erasmus occasion bitterly to satirise the gross sensuality in which as a class they grovelled. Again and again had he to condemn their *political* influence, and the part they played in prompting the

---

[1] Hallam's *Literature of the Middle Ages,* ed. 1837, p. 555, *et seq.*

warlike and treacherous policy of princes whose courts Chap. XI. they infested.[1]

And passages have already been quoted from the ' Praise of Folly ' in which Erasmus pointed out how completely they had lost sight of the one rule of Christian morals—the golden rule of Christ—how they had substituted a new notion of virtue for the Christian one, and how the very meaning of the word ' *sin* ' had undergone a corresponding change in their theological vocabulary.

Such were the two opposing parties, which, in this age of intellectual re-awakening and progress, were struggling in hopeless antagonism ; both of them for the sake of ecclesiastical emoluments still professing allegiance to the Church, and keeping as firm a foothold as possible within her pale, but both of them practically betraying at the same time their real want of faith in Christianity by tacitly setting it aside as a thing which would not work as the rule of social and political life.

Neither party had practical faith in Christianity.

Erasmus, in writing the preface to his ' Novum ' Instrumentum,' had his eye on both these dominant parties. He, like Colet, believed both of them to be leading men astray. He believed, with Colet, that there *was* a Christianity which rested on facts and not upon speculation, and which therefore had nothing to do with the dogmatic theology of the Schoolmen on the one hand, and nothing to fear from free inquiry

---

[1] Compare the satire on Monks in ' *Scarabeus*,' and the colloquy called ' *Charon*,' with the following passage, in which Erasmus alludes to the continental wars of Henry VIII. : ' Id enim temporis adorna- ' batur bellum in Gallos, et hujus ' fabulæ non minimam partem Mi- ' noritæ duo agebant, quorum alter, ' fax belli, mitram meruit, alter ' bonis lateribus vociferabatur in ' concionibus in *Poetas*. Sic enim ' designabat Coletum,' &c. Eras. *Op.* iii. p. 460, F.

on the other. To 'call men as with the sound of a 'trumpet' to this, was the object of the earnest ' Paraclesis ' which he prefixed to his Testament.

He first appealed to the free-thinking philosophic school :—

· · · · · · · · · ·

The
' Para-
clesis.'

' In times like these, when men are pursuing with ' such zest all branches of knowledge, how is it that ' the philosophy of Christ should alone be derided by ' some, neglected by many, treated by the few who ' do devote themselves to it with coldness, not to say ' insincerity ? Whilst in all other branches of learning ' the human mind is straining its genius to master all ' subtleties, and toiling to overcome all difficulties, why ' is it that this one philosophy alone is not pursued ' with equal earnestness, at least by those who profess ' to be Christians ? Platonists, Pythagoreans, and ' the disciples of all other philosophers, are well ' instructed and ready to fight for their sect. Why do ' not Christians with yet more abundant zeal espouse ' the cause of *their* Master and Prince ? Shall Christ ' be put in comparison with Zeno and Aristotle— ' his doctrines with their insignificant precepts ? ' Whatever other philosophers may have been, he ' alone is a teacher from heaven ; he alone was able ' to teach certain and eternal wisdom ; he alone ' taught things pertaining to our salvation, because he ' alone is its author ; he alone absolutely practised ' what he preached, and is able to make good what he ' promised. . . . The philosophy of Christ, moreover, ' is to be learned from its few books with far less labour ' than the Aristotelian philosophy is to be extracted ' from its multitude of ponderous and conflicting

'commentaries. Nor is anxious preparatory learning
'needful to the Christian. Its viaticum is simple, and
'at hand to all. Only bring a pious and open heart,
'imbued above all things with a pure and simple faith.
'Only be teachable, and you have already made much
'way in this philosophy. It supplies a spirit for a
'teacher, imparted to none more readily than to the
'simple-minded. Other philosophies, by the very
'difficulty of their precepts, are removed out of the
'range of most minds. No age, no sex, no condition
'of life is excluded from this. The sun itself is not
'more common and open to all than the teaching of
'Christ. For I utterly dissent from those who are
'unwilling that the sacred Scriptures should be read
'by the unlearned translated into their vulgar tongue,
'as though Christ had taught such subtleties that they
'can scarcely be understood even by a few theologians,
'or as though the strength of the Christian religion
'consisted in men's ignorance of it. The mysteries of
'kings it may be safer to conceal, but Christ wished
'his mysteries to be published as openly as possible.
'I wish that even the weakest woman should read the
'Gospel—should read the epistles of Paul. And I
'wish these were translated into all languages, so that
'they might be read and understood, not only by Scots
'and Irishmen, but also by Turks and Saracens. To
'make them understood is surely the first step. It
'may be that they might be ridiculed by many, but
'some would take them to heart. I long that the
'husbandman should sing portions of them to himself
'as he follows the plough, that the weaver should hum
'them to the tune of his shuttle, that the traveller
'should beguile with their stories the tedium of his
'journey.'

All men
should
read the
Gospels,
&c., in
their
vulgar
tongue.

Then turning more directly to the Schoolmen, Erasmus continued :—

Why is a greater portion of our lives given to the study of the Schoolmen than of the Gospels ? The rules of St. Francis and St. Benedict may be considered sacred by their respective followers ; but just as St. Paul wrote that the law of Moses was not glorious in comparison with the glory of the Gospel, so Erasmus said he wished that these might not be considered as sacred in comparison with the Gospels and letters of the Apostles. What are Albertus, Alexander, Thomas, Ægidius, Ricardus, Occam, in comparison with Christ, of whom it was said by the Father in heaven, ' This is my beloved Son ' ? (Oh, how sure and, as they say, ' irrefragable ' his authority !) What, in comparison with Peter, who received the command to feed the sheep ; or Paul, in whom, as a chosen vessel, Christ seemed to be reborn ; or John, who wrote in his epistles what he learned as he leaned on his bosom ? ' If the footprints of Christ be ' anywhere shown to us, we kneel down and adore. ' Why do we not rather venerate the living and ' breathing picture of Him in these books ? If the ' vesture of Christ be exhibited, where will we not go ' to kiss it ? Yet were his whole wardrobe exhibited ' nothing could represent Christ more vividly and ' truly than these evangelical writings. Statues of ' wood and stone we decorate with gold and gems for ' the love of Christ. They only profess to give us the ' form of his body ; these books present us with a ' living image of his most holy mind.[1] Were we to

The Gospels give a living image of the mind of Christ.

---

[1] Compare the similar views expressed in the *Enchiridion* (Canon V.) fifteen years before.

' have seen Him with our own eyes, we should not have
' had so intimate a knowledge as they give of Christ,
' speaking, healing, dying, rising again, as it were, in
' our own actual presence.'

Such was the earnest ' Paraclesis ' [1] with which
Erasmus introduced his Greek and Latin version of
the books of the New Testament.

To this he added a few pages to explain what he
considered the right ' method ' to be adopted by the
Scripture student.[2]

First, as to the spirit in which he should work :—

' Let him approach the New Testament, not with an
' unholy curiosity, but with *reverence* ; bearing in mind
' that his first and only aim and object should be that
' he may catch and be changed into the spirit of what
' he there learns. It is the food of the soul ; and to
' be of use, must not rest only in the memory or lodge
' in the stomach, but must permeate the very depths of
' the heart and mind.'

Then, as to what special acquirements are most
useful in the prosecution of these studies :—

' A fair knowledge of the three languages, Latin,
' Greek, and Hebrew, of course, are the first things.
' Nor let the student turn away in despair at the diffi-
' culty of this. If you have a teacher and the will to
' learn, these three languages can be learned almost
' with less labour than every day is spent over the
' miserable babble of one mongrel language under
' ignorant teachers. It would be well, too, were
' the student tolerably versed in other branches of

---

[1] Both the above passages are
slightly abridged in the translation.
Novum Instrumentum, leaf aaa,
3 to bbb.

[2] *Id.* leaf bbb to bbb 5. The quotations in this case also are abridged.

' learning—dialectics, rhetoric, arithmetic, music,
' astrology, and especially in knowledge of the natural
' objects—animals, trees, precious stones—of the
' countries mentioned in the Scriptures ; for if we are
' familiar with the country, we can in thought follow
' the history and picture it to our minds, so that we
' seem not only to read it, but to see it ; and if we do
' this, we shall not easily forget it.   Besides, if we know
' from study of history not only the position of those
' nations to whom these things happened, or to whom
' the Apostles wrote, but also their origin, manners,
' institutions, religion, and character, it is wonderful
' how much light and, if I may so speak, *life* is thrown
' into the reading of what before seemed dry and life-
' less.   Other branches of learning—classical, rhetori-
' cal, or philosophical—may all be turned to account ;
' and especially should the student learn to quote
' Scripture, not second-hand, but from the fountain-
' head, and take care not to distort its meaning as
' some do, interpreting the " Church " as the clergy,
' the laity as the " world," and the like.   To get at the
' real meaning, it is not enough to take four or five
' isolated words ;   you must look where they came
' from, what was said, by whom it was said, to whom
' it was said, at what time, on what occasion, in what
' words, what preceded, what followed.   And if you
' refer to commentaries, choose out the best, such
' as Origen (who is far above all others), Basil, &c.,
' Jerome, Ambrose, &c. ;   and even these read with
' discrimination and judgment, for they were men
' ignorant of some things, and mistaken in others.

' As to the Schoolmen, I had rather be a pious
' divine with Jerome than invincible with Scotus.
' Was ever a heretic converted by their subtleties ?

' Let those who like follow the disputations of the
' schools ; but let him who desires to be instructed
' rather in piety than in the art of disputation, first and
' above all apply himself to the fountain-head—to those
' writings which flowed immediately from the fountain-
' head. The divine is " invincible " enough who never
' yields to vice or gives way to evil passions, even
' though he may be beaten in argument. That doctor
' is abundantly " great " who purely preaches Christ.'

I have quoted these passages very much at length,
that there may be no doubt whatever how fully
Erasmus had in these prefaces adopted and made himself the spokesman of Colet's views. An examination
of the ' Novum Instrumentum ' itself, and of the
' Annotations ' which formed the second part of the
volume, reveals an equally close resemblance between
the *critical method of exposition* used by Colet and that
here adopted by Erasmus. There was the same
rejection of the theory of verbal inspiration which was
noticed in Colet as the result of an honest attempt to
look at the facts of the case exactly as they were,
instead of attempting to explain them away by
reference to preconceived theories.

The ' An
notations.

Theory of
verbal in-
spiration
rejected.

Thus the discrepancy between St. Stephen's speech
and the narrative in Genesis, with regard to a portion
of the history of the Patriarch Abraham, was freely
pointed out, without any attempt at reconcilement.[1]
St. Jerome's suggestion was quoted, that Mark, in the

---

[1] *Novum Instrumentum*: Annotationes in loco Acts vii. p. 382:—' Et
' hunc locum annotavit Hieronymus
' in Libro ad Pammachium de Opti-
' mo Genere Interpretandi, qui se-
' cus habeatur in Genesi, ubi legitur
' quod Abraham emerit ab Ephron

' Etheo filio Saor juxta Hebron
' quadringentis drachmis speluncam
' duplicem, et agrum circa eam,
' sepelieritque in ea Saram uxorem
' suam; atque in eodem legimus libro
' postea revertentem de Mesopota-
' mia Jacob cum uxoribus et filiis

second chapter of his Gospel, had, by a lapse of
memory, written ' Abiathar ' in mistake for ' Ahime-
lech,' [1] and that Matthew, in the twenty-seventh
chapter, instead of quoting from Jeremiah, as stated
in the text, was really quoting from the Prophet
Zachariah.[2]

The fact that in a great number of cases the quotations from the Old Testament are by no means exact,
either as compared with the Hebrew or Septuagint

' suis posuisse tabernaculum ante
' Salem, urbem Sichymorum, quæ
' est in terra Chanaan, et habitasse
' ibi et emisse partem agri, in quo
' habebat tentoria, ab Emor patre
' Sychem, centum agnis, et sta-
' tuisse ibi altare et invocasse
' deum Israel. Proinde Abraham
' non emit specum ab Emor patre
' Sychem, sed ab Ephron filio Saor,
' nec sepultus est in Sychem sed
' in Hebron, quæ corrupte dicitur
' Arboch.   Porro duodecim pa-
' triarchæ non sunt sepulti in
' Arboch sed in Sychem, qui ager
' non est emptus ab Abraham sed
' a Jacob. Hunc nodum illic nectit
' Hieronymus nec eum dissolvit.'

[1] In loco Mark ii. p. 299, where
Erasmus writes:—'Divus Hierony-
' mus in libello de Optimo Genere
' Interpretandi indicat nomen Abia-
' thar pro Achimelech esse positum,
' propterea quod libro Regum
' primo, capite 22, ubi refertur
' hujusce rei historia, nulla mentio
' fiat Abiathar sed duntaxat Ach-
' imelech.   Sive id acciderit lapsu
' memoriæ, sive vitio scriptorum,
' sive quod ejusdem hominis
' vocabulum sit Abiathar et Abi-
' melech ; nam Lyra putat Abia-
' thar fuisse filium Achimelech

' qui sub patre functus sit officio
' paterno, et eo cæso jussu Saulis
' comes fuerit fugæ Davidicæ.'

[2] In loco Matt. xxvii. p. 290 :—
' Annotavit hunc quoque locum
' divus Hieronymus in libro cui ti-
' tulus de Optimo Genere Interpre-
' tandi, negans quod hic citat ex
' Hieremia Matthæus, prorsus ex-
' stare apud Hieremiam, verum
' apud Zachariam prophetam, sed
' ita ut quæ retulit evangelista,
' parum respondeant ad Hebraicam
' veritatem, ac multo minus ad vul-
' gatam editionem Septuaginta.
' Etenim ut idem sit sensus
' tamen inversa esse verba, imo
' pene diversa.   Cæterum locus
' est apud Zachariam, cap. ii., si
' quis velit excutere. Nam res
' perplexior est quam ut hic paucis
' explicari possit, et prope πάρεργον
' est. Refert Hieronymus Hiere-
' maiam apocryphum sibi exhibi-
' tum a quodam Judæo factionis
' Nazarenæ in quo hæc ad verbum
' ut ab evangelista citantur habe-
' rentur. Verumnon probat ut apo-
' stolus ex apocryphis adduxerit
' testimonium, præsertim cum his
' mos sit evangelistis et apostolis ut,
' neglectis verbis, sensum utcumque
' reddant in citandis testimoniis.'

text, was freely alluded to, and the suggestion as freely thrown out that the Apostles habitually quoted from memory, without giving the exact words of the original.[1]

All these were little indications that Erasmus had closely followed in the steps of Colet in rejecting the theory of the verbal inspiration of the Scriptures ; and they bear abundant evidence to prove that he did so, as Colet had done, not because he wished to undermine men's reverence for the Bible, but that they might learn to love and to value its pages infinitely more than they had done before—not because he wished to explain away its facts, but that men might discover how truly real and actual and heart-stirring were its histories—not to undermine the authority of its moral teaching, but to add just so much to it as the authority of the Apostle who had written, or of the Saviour who had spoken, its Divine truths, exceeds the authority of the Fathers who had established the canon, or of the Schoolmen who had buried the Bible altogether under the rubbish of the thousand and one propositions which they professed to have extracted from it.

Let it never be forgotten that the Church party which had staked their faith upon the plenary inspiration of the Bible was the Church party who had succeeded in putting it into the background. They were the party whom Tyndale accused of ' knowing no more ' Scripture than they found in their Duns.' They were the party who throughout the sixteenth century resisted every attempt to give the Bible to the people and to make it the people's book. And they were perfectly logical in doing so. Their whole system was

[1] See especially *Novum Instrumentum*, pp. 295, 290, 377, 382, 270.

based upon the absolute inspiration of the Holy Scriptures, and even to a great extent of the Vulgate version. If the Vulgate version was not verbally inspired, it was impossible to apply to it the theory of ' manifold ' senses.' And if a text could not be interpreted according to that theory, if it could not properly be strained into meanings which it was never intended by the writer to convey, the scholastic theology became a castle of cards. Its defenders adopted, and in perfect good faith applied to the Vulgate, the words quoted from Augustine : ' If any error should be ' admitted to have crept into the Holy Scriptures, ' what authority would be left to them ? ' If Colet and Erasmus should undermine men's faith in the absolute inspiration of the Scriptures, it would result, in their view, as a logical necessity, in the destruction of the Christian religion. For the Christian religion, in their view, consisted in blind devotion to the Church, and in gulping whole the dogmatic creed which had been settled by her ' invincible ' and ' irrefragable ' doctors.

The Christian religion loyalty to Christ.
But this was not the faith of Colet and Erasmus. With them the Christian religion consisted not in gulping a creed upon any authority whatever, but in loving and loyal devotion to the *person* of Christ. They sought in the books which they found bound up into a Bible not so much an infallible standard of doctrinal truth as an authentic record of *his* life and teaching. Where should they go for a knowledge of Christ, if not to the writings of those who were nearest in their relations to Him ? They valued these writings because they sought and found in them a ' living and breathing ' picture of Him ; ' because ' nothing could represent ' Christ more vividly and truly ' than they did ;

because 'they present a living image of his most holy 'mind,' so that ' even had we seen Him with our own ' eyes we should not have had so intimate a knowledge ' as they give of Christ speaking, healing, dying, rising ' again as it were in our own actual presence.' It was because these books brought them, as it were, so close to Christ and the facts of his actual life, that they wished to get as close to *them* as they could do. They would not be content with knowing something of them secondhand from the best Church authorities. The best of the Fathers were ' men ignorant of some things, ' and mistaken in others.' They would go to the books themselves, and read them in their original languages, and, if possible, in the earliest copies, so that no mistakes of copyists or blunders of translators might blind their eyes to the facts as they were. They would study the geography and the natural history of Palestine that they might the more correctly and vividly realise in their mind's eye the events as they happened. And they would do all this not that they might make themselves ' irrefragable ' doctors—rivals of Scotus and Aquinas—but that they might catch the Spirit of Him whom they were striving to know for themselves, and that they might place the same knowledge within reach of all—Turks and Saracens, learned and unlearned, rich and poor—by the translation of these books into the vulgar tongue of each.

The 'Novum Instrumentum' of Erasmus was at once the result and the embodiment of these views.

Hence it is easy to see the significance of the concurrent publication of the works of St. Jerome. St. Jerome belonged to that school of theology and criticism which now, after the lapse of a thousand

Works of St. Jerome.

years, Colet and Erasmus were reviving in Western Europe. St. Jerome was the father who in his day strove to give to the people the Bible in their vulgar tongue. St. Jerome was the father against whom St. Augustine so earnestly strove to vindicate the verbal inspiration of the Bible. It was the words of St. Augustine used against St. Jerome that, now after the lapse of ten centuries, Martin Dorpius had quoted against Erasmus. We have seen in an earlier chapter how Colet clung to St. Jerome's opinion, against that of nearly all other authorities, in the discussion which led to his first avowal to Erasmus of his views on the inspiration of the Scriptures. Finally, the Annotations to the ' Novum Instrumentum ' teem with citations from St. Jerome.

The concurrent publication of the works of this father was therefore a practical vindication of the ' Novum Instrumentum ' from the charge of presumption and novelty. It proved that Colet and Erasmus were teaching no new doctrines—that their work was correctly defined by Colet himself to be ' to restore ' that old and true theology which had been so long ' obscured by the subtleties of the Schoolmen.'

Under this patristic shield, dedicated by permission to Pope Leo, and its copyright secured for four years by the decree of the Emperor Maximilian, the ' Novum ' Instrumentum ' went forth into the world.

CHAPTER XII.

I. MORE IMMERSED IN PUBLIC BUSINESS (1515).

WHILE the work of Erasmus had for some years past lain chiefly in the direction of laborious literary study, it had been far otherwise with More. His lines had fallen among the busy scenes and cares of practical life. His capacity for public business, and the diligence and impartiality with which he had now for some years discharged his judicial duties as under-sheriff, had given him a position of great popularity and influence in the city. He had been appointed by the Parliament of 1515 a Commissioner of Sewers—a recognition at least of his practical ability. In his private practice at the Bar he had risen to such eminence, that Roper tells us ' there was at that time ' in none of the prince's courts of the laws of this realm ' any matter of importance in controversy wherein he ' was not with the one party of counsel.' [1] Roper further reports that ' by his office and his learning ' (as I have heard him say) he gained without grief not ' so little as 400*l*. by the year ' (equal to 4000*l*. a year in present money). He had in the meantime married a second wife, Alice Middleton, and taken her daughter also into his household ; and thus tried, for the sake of his little orphans, to roll away the cloud of domestic sorrow from his home.

More's practice at the Bar.

His second marriage.

---

[1] Roper, 9.

Becoming himself more and more of a public man, he had anxiously watched the course of political events.

The long continuance of war is almost sure to bring up to the surface social evils which in happier times smoulder on unobserved. It was especially so with these wars of Henry VIII. Each successive Parliament, called for the purpose of supplying the King with the necessary ways and means, found itself obliged reluctantly to deal with domestic questions of increasing difficulty. In previous years it had been easy for the flattering courtiers of a popular king, by talking of victories, to charm the ear of the Commons so wisely, that subsidies and poll-taxes had been voted without much, if any, opposition. But the Parliament which had met in February 1515 had no victories to talk about. Whether right or wrong in regarding ' the ' realm of France his very true patrimony and inheri- ' tance,' Henry VIII. had not yet been able ' to reduce ' the same to his obedience.' Meanwhile the long continuance of war expenditure had drained the national exchequer. It is perfectly true that under Wolsey's able management the expenditure had already been cut down to an enormous extent, but during the three years of active warfare—1512, 1513, and 1514—the revenues of more than twelve ordinary years [1] had been spent, the immense hoards of wealth inherited by the young king from Henry VII. had

---

[1] 1512	£286,269	1515	£74,007
1513	699,714	1516	130,779
1514	155,757	1517	78,887
	£1,141,740		£283,673

See Brewer, ii. preface, cxciv.

been squandered away, and even the genius of Wolsey
was unable to devise means to collect the taxes which
former Parliaments had already voted. The temper
of the Commons was in the meantime beginning to
change. They now, in 1515, for the first time entered
their complaint upon the rolls of Parliament, that
whereas the King's noble progenitors had maintained
their estate and the defences of the realm out of the
ordinary revenues of the kingdom, he now, by reason
of the improvident grants made by him since he came
to the throne, had not sufficient revenues left to meet
his increasing expenses. The result was that all
unusual grants of annuities, &c., were declared to be
void.[1] The Commons then proceeded to deal with the
large deficiency which previous subsidies had done
little to remove. Of the 160,000*l.* granted by the
previous Parliament only 50,000*l.* had been gathered,
and all they now attempted to achieve was the collection, under new arrangements, of the remaining
110,000*l.*[2]

It was evident that the temper of the people would
not bear further trial ; and no wonder, for the tax
which in the previous year had raised a total of 50,000*l.*
was practically an income-tax of sixpence in the pound,
descending even to the wages of the farm-labourer. In
the coming year this income-tax of sixpence was to be
twice repeated simply to recover arrears of taxation.
What should we think of a government which should
propose to exact from the day-labourer, by direct
taxation, a tax equal to between two and three weeks'
wages !

The selfishness of Tudor legislation—or, perhaps it

---

[1] 6 Henry VIII. c. 24.   [2] Ibid. c. 26.

might be more just to say of *Wolsey's* legislation, for he was the presiding spirit of this Parliament—was shown no less clearly in its manner of dealing with the social evils which came under its notice.

Thus the Act of Apparel, with its pains and penalties, was obviously more likely to give a handle to unscrupulous ministers to be used for purposes of revenue, than to curb those tastes for grandeur in attire which nothing was so likely to foster as the example of Wolsey himself.[1]

Legal interference with wages.

Thus, too, not content with carrying their income-tax down to the earnings of the peasant, this and the previous Parliament attempted to interfere with the wages of the labouring classes solely for the benefit of employers of labour. The simple fact was that the drain upon the labour market to keep the army supplied with soldiers had caused a temporary scarcity of labour, and a natural rise in wages. Complaints were made, according to the chronicles, that ' labourers ' would in nowise work by the day, but all by task, and ' in great,' and that therefore, ' especially in harvest ' time, the husbandmen [i.e. the farmers and land- ' owners] could scarce get workmen to help in their ' harvest.' [2] The agricultural interest was strongly represented in the House of Commons—the labourers not at all. So, human nature being the same then as now, the last Parliament had attempted virtually to re-enact the old statutes of labourers, as against the labourers, whilst repealing all the clauses which might

---

[1] 6 Henry VIII. c. 1. The draft of this Act in the final form in which it was adopted when Parliament met again in the autumn, is in

Wolsey's handwriting.—Brewer.

[2] Grafton, p. 104. Holinshed, ii. 835, under date 6 Henry VIII.

possibly prove inconvenient to employers. This
Parliament of 1515 completed the work; re-enacted
a rigid scale of wages, and imposed pains and penalties
upon ' artificers who should leave their work except
' for the King's service.' [1] Here again was oppression
of the poor to spare the pockets of the rich.

Again, the scarcity of labour made itself felt in the *Increase*
increased propensity of landowners to throw arable *of pasture*
farming.
land into pasture, involving the sudden and cruel
ejection of thousands of the peasantry, and the enactment of statutory provisions [2] to check this tendency
was not to be wondered at; but the rumour that
many by compounding secretly with the Cardinal
were able to exempt themselves [3] from the penalties
of inconvenient statutes, leads one to suspect that
Wolsey thought more of the wants of the exchequer
than of the hardship and misery of ejected peasants.

It was natural that the result of wholesale ejections, and the return of deserting or disbanded soldiers
(often utterly demoralised),[4] should still show itself
in the appalling increase of crime. Perhaps it was *Increase*
equally natural that legislators who held the comforts *of crime*
and of
and lives of the labouring poor so cheap, should think *execu-*
tions.
that they had provided at once a proper and efficient
remedy, when by abolishing benefit of clergy in the
case of felons and murderers, and by abridging the
privilege of sanctuary, they had multiplied to a
terrible extent the number of executions.[5]

---

[1] 4 Henry VIII. c. 5, and 6 Henry VIII. c. 3.
[2] 6 Henry VIII. c. 5.
[3] Lord Herbert's History, under date 1521, ed. 1649, p. 108; and

Grafton, pp. 1016–1018.
[4] Brewer, i. Nos. 4019 and 4020.
[5] 4 Henry VIII. c. 2, and 6 Henry VIII. c. 6.

If the labouring classes were thus harshly dealt with, so also the mercantile classes did not find their interests very carefully guarded.

The breach of faith with Prince Charles in the matter of the marriage of the Princess Mary had caused a quarrel between England and the Nether-
lands, and this Parliament of 1515 had followed it up by prohibiting the exportation of Norfolk wool to Holland and Zealand,[1] thus virtually interrupting commercial intercourse with the Hanse Towns of Belgium at a time when Bruges was the great mart of the world.

It was not long before the London merchants expressed a very natural anxiety that the commercial intercourse between two countries so essential to each other should be speedily resumed. They saw clearly that whatever military advantage might be gained by the attempt to injure the subjects of Prince Charles by creating a wool-famine in the Netherlands, would be purchased at their expense. It was a game that two could play at, and it was not long before retaliative measures were resorted to on the other side, very injurious to English interests.

When therefore it was rumoured that Henry VIII. was about to send an embassy to Flanders, to settle international disputes between the two countries, it was not surprising that London merchants should complain to the King of their own special grievances, and pray that their interests might not be neglected. It seems that they pressed upon the King to attach ' Young More,' as he was still called, to the embassy, specially to represent themselves. So, according to

---

[1] 6 Henry VIII. c. 12.

Roper, it was at the suit and instance of the English merchants, ' and with the King's consent,' that in May 1515 More was sent out on an embassy with Bishop Tunstal, Sampson, and others, into Flanders.

The ambassadors were appointed generally to obtain a renewal and continuance of the old treaties of intercourse between the two countries, but More, aided by a John Clifford, ' governor of the English ' merchants,' was specially charged with the *commercial* matters in dispute : Wolsey informing Sampson of this, and Sampson replying that he ' is ' pleased with the honour of being named in the King's ' commission with Tunstal and " Young More." ' [1]

The party were detained in the city of Bruges about four months.[2] They found it by no means easy to allay the bitter feelings which had been created by the prohibition of the export of wool, and other alleged injuries.[3] In September they moved on to Brussels,[4] and in October to Antwerp,[5] and it was not till towards the end of the year that More, having at last successfully terminated his part in the negotiations, was able to return home.

II. COLET'S SERMON ON THE INSTALLATION OF CARDINAL WOLSEY (1515).

During the absence of More, on his embassy to Flanders, Wolsey, quit of a Parliament which, however selfish and careless of the true interests of the Commonweal, and especially of the poorer classes,

---

[1] Brewer, ii. 422 (7 May), 480, and 534 ; also Roper, 10.

[2] Brewer, ii. 672, 679, 733, 782, 807.

[3] Ibid. 672 and 733.

[4] Ibid. 904 and 922.

[5] Ibid. 1067.

had shown some symptoms of grumbling at Royal demands, had pushed on more rapidly than ever his schemes of personal ambition.

His first step had been to procure from the Pope, through the good offices of Henry VIII., a cardinal's hat. It might possibly be the first step even to the papal chair ; at least it would secure to him a position within the realm second only to the throne. It chafed him that so unmanageable a man as Warham should take precedence of himself.

Let us try to realise the magnificent spectacle of the installation of the great Cardinal, for the sake of the part *Colet* took in it.

Installation of Cardinal Wolsey. It was on Sunday, November 18, 1515, that the ceremony was performed in Westminster Abbey. Mass was sung by Archbishop Warham (with whom Wolsey had already quarrelled), Bishop Fisher acting as crosier-bearer. The Bishop of Lincoln read the Gospel, and the Bishop of Exeter the Epistle. The Archbishops of Armagh and Dublin, the Bishops of Winchester, Durham, Norwich, Ely, and Llandaff, the Abbots of Westminster, St. Alban's, Bury, Glastonbury, Reading, Gloucester, Winchcombe, and Tewkesbury, and the Prior of Coventry, were all in attendance ' in pontificalibus.' All the magnates of the realm were collected to swell the pomp of the ceremony. Before this august assemblage and crowds of spectators Dean Colet had to deliver an address to Wolsey.

Colet preaches the sermon. As was usual with him, he preached a sermon suited to the occasion, more so perhaps than Wolsey intended. First speaking to the people, he explained the meaning of the title of ' Cardinal,' the high honour

and dignity of the office, the reasons why it was conferred on Wolsey, alluding, first, to his merits, naming
some of his particular virtues and services ; secondly,
to the desire of the Pope to show, by conferring this
dignity on one of the subjects of Henry VIII., his
zeal and favour to his grace. He dwelt upon the
great power and dignity of the rank of cardinal, how
it corresponded to the order of ' Seraphim ' in the
celestial hierarchy, ' which continually burneth in the
' love of the glorious Trinity.' [1] And having thus
magnified the office of cardinal in the eyes of the
people, he turned to Wolsey—so proud, ambitious, and
fond of magnificence—and addressed to him these
few faithful words :

    ' Let not one in so proud a position, made most
' illustrious by the dignity of such an honour, be
' puffed up by its greatness. But remember that our
' Saviour, in his own person, said to his disciples,
' " I came not to be ministered unto, but to minister,"
' and " He who is least among you shall be greatest
' " in the kingdom of heaven ; " and again, " He who
' " exalts himself shall be humbled, and he who
' " humbles himself shall be exalted." ' And then, with
reference to his secular duties, and having perhaps in
mind the rumours of Wolsey's partiality and the un-
fairness of recent legislation to the poorer classes, he
added—' My Lord Cardinal, be glad, and enforce
' yourself always to do and execute righteousness to
' rich and *poor*, with mercy and truth.'

    Then, addressing himself once more to the people,

---

[1] 'First after the Trinity come the ' *Seraphic* spirits, *all flaming and on* ' *fire.* . . . They are *loving* beings of ' the highest order, &c.' Colet's abstract of the *Celestial Hierarchy of Dionysius.* Mr. Lupton's translation, p. 20.

he desired them to pray for the Cardinal, that ' he ' might observe these things, and in accomplishing the ' same receive his reward in the kingdom of heaven.'

This sermon ended, Wolsey, kneeling at the altar, had the formal service read over him by Warham, and the cardinal's hat placed upon his head. The ' Te ' Deum ' was then sung, and, surrounded by dukes and earls, Wolsey left the Abbey and passed in gorgeous procession to his own decorated halls, there to entertain the King and Queen, in all pomp and splendour, bent upon pursuing his projects of self-exaltation, regardless of Colet's honest words so faithfully spoken, and little dreaming that they would ever find fulfilment in his own fall.[1]

Wolsey made Lord Chancellor

Five weeks only after this event, on December 22, Warham resigned the great seal into the King's hands, and the Cardinal Archbishop of York assumed the additional title of Lord Chancellor of England.[2] On the same day, Parliament, which had met again on November 12 to grant a further subsidy, was dissolved, and Wolsey commenced to rule the kingdom, according to his own will and pleasure, for eight years, without a Parliament, and with but little regard to the opinions of other members of the King's council.

III. MORE'S 'UTOPIA' (1515).

It was whilst More's keen eye was anxiously watching the clouds gathering upon the political horizon, and during the leisure snatched from the

---

[1] Fiddes' *Life of Wolsey.* Collections, p. 252, quoted from MS. in Heralds' office. Cerem. vol. iii.

p. 219, &c. Brewer, ii. 1153.
[2] Brewer, ii. 1335.

business of his embassy, that he conceived the idea of
embodying his notions on social and political questions
in a description of the imaginary commonwealth
of the Island of ' Utopia '—' Nusquama '—or ' No-
' where.' [1]

It does not often happen that two friends, engaged
in fellow-work, publish in the same year two books,
both of which take an independent and a permanent
place in the literature of Europe. But this may be
said of the ' Novum Instrumentum ' of Erasmus and
the ' Utopia ' of More.

Still more remarkable is it that two such works,
written by two such men, should, in measure, be trace-
able to the influence and express the views of a more
obscure but greater man than they. Yet, in truth,
much of the merit of both these works belongs indirectly to Colet.

As the ' Novum Instrumentum,' upon careful examination, proves to be the expression, on the part of
Erasmus, not merely of his own isolated views, but of
the views held in common by the little band of Oxford
Reformers, on the great subject of which it treats ; so
the ' Utopia ' will be found to be in great measure the
expression, on More's part, of the views of the same
little band of friends on social and political questions.
On most of these questions Erasmus and More, in the
main, thought alike : and they owed much of their
common convictions indirectly to the influence of
Colet.

The first book of the ' Utopia ' was written after the
second, under circumstances and for reasons which
will in due course be mentioned.

---

[1] Eras. Epist. ccli. and App. lxxxvii.

The second book was complete in itself, and contained the description, by Raphael, the supposed traveller, of the Utopian commonwealth. Erasmus informs us that More's intention in writing it was to point out where and from what causes European commonwealths were at fault, and he adds that it was written with special reference to *English* politics, with which More was most familiar.[1]

Whilst, however, we trace its close connection with the political events passing at the time in England, it must not be supposed that More was so gifted with prescience that he knew what course matters would take. He could not know, for instance, that Wolsey was about to take the reins of government so completely into his own hands, as to dispense with a Parliament for so many years to come. As yet, More and his friends, in spite of Wolsey's ostentation and vanity, which they freely ridiculed, had a high opinion of his character and powers. It was not unnatural that, knowing that Wolsey was a friend to education, and, to some extent at least, inclined to patronise the projects of Erasmus, they should hope for the best. Hence the satire contained in 'Utopia' was not likely to be directed personally against Wolsey, however much his policy might come in for its share of criticisms along with the rest.

The point of the 'Utopia' consisted in the contrast presented by its ideal commonwealth to the condition and habits of the European commonwealths of the period. This contrast is most often left to be drawn by the reader from his own knowledge of contem-

---

[1] Erasmus to Hutten, Epist. ccccxlvii. Eras. *Op.* iii. p. 476, F.

porary politics, and hence the peculiar advantage of
the choice by More of such a vehicle for the bold satire
it contained.   Upon any other hypothesis than that
the evils against which its satire was directed were
admitted to be *real*, the romance of ' Utopia ' must
also be admitted to be harmless.   To pronounce it to
be dangerous was to admit its truth.

Take, *e.g.*, the following passage relating to the
international policy of the Utopians :—

' While other nations are always entering into
' leagues, and breaking and renewing them, the
' Utopians never enter into a league with any nation.
' For what is the use of a league ? they say. As
' though there were no natural tie between man and
' man ! and as though any one who despised this
' natural tie would, forsooth, regard mere words !
' They hold this opinion all the more strongly, because
' in that quarter of the world the leagues and treaties
' of princes are not observed as faithfully as they
' should be. For in *Europe*, and especially in those
' parts of it where the Christian faith and religion are
' professed, the sanctity of leagues is held sacred and
' inviolate ; partly owing to the justice and goodness
' of princes, and partly from their fear and reverence
' of the authority of the Popes, who, as they them-
' selves never enter into obligations which they do not
' most religiously perform [!], command other princes
' under all circumstances to abide by *their* promises,
' and punish delinquents by pastoral censure and dis-
' cipline. For indeed, with good reason, it would be
' thought a most scandalous thing for those whose
' peculiar designation is " the faithful," to be wanting
' in the faithful observances of treaties. But in those
' distant regions. . . no faith is to be placed in leagues,

' even though confirmed by the most solemn cere-
' monies. Some flaw is easily found in their wording
' which is intentionally made ambiguous so as to leave
' a loophole through which the parties may break both
' their league and their faith. Which craft—yes,
' *fraud* and *deceit*—if it were perpetrated with respect
' to a contract between private parties, they would
' indignantly denounce as sacrilege and deserving the
' gallows, whilst those who suggest these very things
' to princes, glory in being the authors of them.
' Whence it comes to pass that justice seems altogether
' a plebeian and vulgar virtue, quite below the dignity
' of royalty ; or at least there must be two kinds
' of it, the one for common people and the poor, very
' narrow and contracted, the other, the virtue of
' princes, much more dignified and free, so that *that*
' only is unlawful to *them* which they don't *like*. The
' morals of princes being such in that region, it is not,
' I think, without reason that the Utopians enter into
' no leagues at all. Perhaps they would alter their
' opinion if they lived amongst us.' [1]

Its bitter
sa[t]ire on
the policy
of princes.
Read without reference to the international history
of the period, these passages appear perfectly harmless.
But read in the light of that political history which,
during the past few years, had become so mixed up
with the personal history of the Oxford Reformers,
recollecting ' *how* religiously ' treaties had been made
and broken by almost every sovereign in Europe—
Henry VIII. and the Pope included—the words in
which the justice and goodness of European princes
is so mildly and modestly extolled, become almost as
bitter in their tone as the cutting censure of Erasmus

---

[1] *Utopia*, 1st ed. T. Martins. Louvain [1516], chap. ' De Fœderibus.' Leaf k, ii.

in the ' Praise of Folly,' or his more recent and open
satire upon kings.

Again, bearing in mind the wars of Henry VIII.,
and how evidently the love of military glory was the
motive which induced him to engage in them, the
following passage contains almost as direct and
pointed a censure of the King's passion for war as
the sermon preached by Colet in his presence :—

' The Utopians hate war as plainly brutal, although
' practised more eagerly by man than by any other
' animal. And contrary to the sentiment of nearly
' every other nation, they regard nothing more in-
' glorious than glory derived from war.' [1]

Turning from international politics to questions of
internal policy, and bearing in mind the hint of Erasmus, that More had in view chiefly the politics of his
own country, it is impossible not to recognise in the
' Utopia ' the expression, again and again, of the *sense
of wrong* stirred up in More's heart, as he had witnessed how every interest of the commonwealth had
been sacrificed to Henry VIII.'s passion for war ; and
how, in sharing the burdens it entailed, and dealing
with the social evils it brought to the surface, the
interests of the poor had been sacrificed to spare the
pockets of the rich ; how, whilst the very wages of
the labourer had been taxed to support the long-
continued war expenditure, a selfish Parliament,
under colour of the old ' statutes of labourers,' had
attempted to cut down the amount of his wages, and
to rob him of that fair rise in the price of his labour
which the drain upon the labour market had produced.

---

[1] Utopia, 1st ed. ' De Re Militari.' Leaf k, iii.

It is impossible not to recognise that the recent statutes of labourers was the target against which More's satire was specially directed, in the following paragraph :—

'Let any one dare to compare with the even justice 'which rules in Utopia, the justice of other nations ; 'amongst whom, let me die, if I find any trace at all 'of equity and justice. For where is the justice, that 'noblemen, goldsmiths, and usurers, and those classes 'who either do nothing at all, or, in what they do, are 'of no great service to the commonwealth, should live

'a genteel and splendid life in idleness or unproductive 'labour ; whilst in the meantime the servant, the wag-'goner, the mechanic, and the peasant, toiling almost 'longer and harder than the horse, in labour so neces-'sary that no commonwealth could endure a year 'without it, lead a life so wretched that the condition 'of the horse seems more to be envied ; his labour 'being less constant, his food more delicious to his 'palate, and his mind disturbed by no fears for the 'future ? . . .

'Is not that republic unjust and ungrateful which 'confers such benefits upon the gentry (as they are 'called) and goldsmiths and others of that class, whilst 'it cares to do nothing at all for the benefit of peasants, 'colliers, servants, waggoners, and mechanics, without 'which no republic could exist ? Is not that republic 'unjust which, after these men have spent the spring-'time of their lives in labour, have become burdened 'with age and disease, and are in want of every com-'fort, unmindful of all their toil, and forgetful of all 'their services, rewards them only by a miserable death?

'Worse than all, the rich constantly endeavour to 'pare away something further from the daily wages of

' the poor, by private fraud, *and even by public laws*, so
' that the already existing injustice (that those from
' whom the republic derives the most benefit should
' receive the least reward), is made still more unjust
' *through the enactments of public law!* Thus, after
' careful reflection it seems to me, as I hope for mercy,
' that our modern republics are nothing but a con-
' spiracy of the rich, pursuing their own selfish interests
' under the name of a republic. They devise and in-
' vent all ways and means whereby they may, in the
' first place secure to themselves the possession of what
' they have amassed by evil means; and, in the
' second place, secure to their own use and profit the
' work and labour of the poor at the lowest possible
' price. And so soon as the rich, in the name of the
' public (*i.e.* even in the name of the poor), choose to
' decide that these schemes shall be adopted, then they
' become *law!*' [1]

Chap. XII.

A.D. 1515.

Modern governments a conspiracy of the rich against the poor.

The whole framework of the Utopian commonwealth bears witness to More's conviction, that what
should be aimed at in his own country and elsewhere,
was a true *community*—not a rich and educated aris-
tocracy on the one hand, existing side by side with a
poor and ignorant peasantry on the other—but *one
people, well-to-do and educated throughout.*

The Utopian Commonwealth a true *community*.

Thus More's opinion was, that in England in his
time, ' far more than four parts of the whole [people],
' divided into ten, could never read English,' [2] and
probably the education of the other six-tenths was
anything but satisfactory. He shared Colet's faith in
education, and represented that in Utopia *every child
was properly educated.*[3]

Every child educated.

---

[1] *Utopia*, 1st ed. Leaves m, iv. v.
[2] More's English Works: *The*
Apology, p. 850.
[3] *Utopia*, 1st ed. Leaf h, i.

A A

Reduction of the hours of labour.

Again the great object of the social economy of Utopia was not to increase the abundance of luxuries, or to amass a vast accumulation in few hands, or even in national or royal hands, but to *lessen the hours of labour to the working man.* By spreading the burden of labour more evenly over the whole community— by taking care that there shall be no idle classes, be they beggars or begging friars—More expressed the opinion that the hours of labour to the working man might probably be reduced to *six*.[1]

General sanitary arrangements.

Again : living himself in Bucklersbury, in the midst of all the dirt and filth of London's narrow streets ; surrounded by the unclean, ill-ventilated houses of the poor, whose floors of clay and rushes, never cleansed, were pointed out by Erasmus as breeding pestilence, and inviting the ravages of the sweating sickness ; himself a commissioner of sewers, and having thus some practical knowledge of London's sanitary arrangements ; More described the towns of Utopia as well and regularly built, with wide streets, waterworks, hospitals, and numerous common halls ; all the houses well protected from the weather, as nearly as might be fireproof, three stories high, with plenty of windows, and doors both back and front, the back door always opening into a well-kept garden.[2] All this was Utopian doubtless, and the result in Utopia of the still more Utopian abolition of private property ; but the gist and point of it consisted in the contrast it presented with what he saw around him in Europe, and especially in England, and men could hardly fail to draw the lesson he intended to teach.

---

[1] *Utopia*, 1st ed. Leaf f, iii.   [2] *Ibid.* chap. 'De Urbibus,' Leaf f, i.

It will not be necessary here to dwell further upon the details of the social arrangements of More's ideal commonwealth,[1] or to enter at length upon the philosophical opinions of the Utopians ; but a word or two will be needful to point out the connection of the latter with the views of that little band of friends whose joint history I am here trying to trace.

One of the points most important and characteristic is the *fearless faith in the laws of nature combined with a profound faith in religion*, which runs through the whole work, and which may, I think, be traced also in every chapter of the history of the Oxford Reformers. Their scientific knowledge was imperfect, as it needs must have been, before the days of Copernicus and Newton ; but they had their eyes fearlessly open in every direction, with no foolish misgivings lest science and Christianity might be found to clash. They remembered (what is not always remembered in this nineteenth century), that if there be any truth in Christianity, Nature and her laws on the one hand and Christianity and her laws on the other, being framed and fixed by the same Founder, must be in harmony, and that therefore for Christians to act contrary to the laws of Nature, or to shut their eyes to facts, on the ground that they are opposed to Christianity, is—to speak plainly—to fight against one portion of the Almighty's laws under the supposed sanction of another ; to fight, therefore, without the least chance of success, and with every prospect of doing harm instead of good.

---

[1] I may be allowed to refer the reader to the valuable mention of 'Utopia' in the preface to Mr. Brewer's *Calendar of the Letters, &c. of Henry VIII.* vol. ii. cclxvii *et seq.*, where its connection with the political and social condition of Europe at the time is well pointed out.

Hence the moral philosophy of the Utopians was both Utilitarian and Christian. Its distinctive features, according to More, were—1st, that they placed *pleasure* (in the sense of ' utility ') as the chief object of life ; and 2ndly, that they drew their arguments in support of this as well from the principles of religion as from natural reason.[1]

---

[1] In support of the abstract here given of the moral philosophy of the Utopians, see *Utopia*, 1st ed. Leaf h, ii. *et seq.*

For the following careful translation of the most material part of it, I am indebted to the Rev. W. G. Rouse, M.A.

' The same points of moral philosophy are discussed by the Utopians as by us. They inquire what ' is " *good* " in respect as well of the ' mind as of the body, as also of ex- 'ternal things; also, whether the title ' " *good* " be applicable to all these, ' or to the mental qualities alone. ' They discuss " *virtue* " and " *plea-* ' " *sure.*" But their first and prin- ' cipal topic of debate is concerning ' human " *happiness* "—on what ' thing or things they consider it ' to depend.

'But here they seem more inclined ' than they should be to that party ' which advocates " *pleasure,*" as be- ' ing that which they define as either ' the whole, or the most important ' part of human happiness. And, ' what is more surprising, they even ' draw arguments in support of so ' nice an opinion from the principles ' of religion, which is usually sombre ' and severe, and of a stern and me- ' lancholy character. For they never ' dispute about happiness without ' joining some principles drawn from ' religion to those derived from ra- ' tional philosophy; without which, ' reason is, in their opinion, defective ' and feeble in the search for true ' happiness.' Their religious princi- ' ples are as follow. The soul is im- ' mortal, and, by the goodness of ' God, born to happiness. He has ' appointed rewards after this life ' for man's virtues and good deeds ' —punishment for his sins. Now, ' though these principles appertain ' to *religion*, yet they think that they ' are led by *reason* to believe and ' assent to them. Apart from these ' principles, they unhesitatingly de- ' clare that no man can be so foolish ' as not to see that pleasure is to be ' pursued for its own sake through ' thick and thin ; so long as he ' takes care only not to let a less ' pleasure stand in the way of a ' greater, and not to pursue any ' pleasure which is followed in its ' turn by pain.

' For they consider " *virtue* " aus- ' tere and hard to strive after ; and ' they deem it the greatest madness ' for a man not only to exclude all ' " *pleasure* " from life, but even ' voluntarily to suffer pain without ' prospect of future profit (for what ' profit can there be, if you gain ' nothing after death, after having ' spent the whole of your life with- ' out pleasure, that is, in misery ?).

They defined ' pleasure ' as ' every emotion or state ' of body or mind in which nature leads us to take

'But now they do not place happi-'ness in the enjoyment of every kind 'of pleasure, but in that only which 'is honest and good. For they think 'that our nature is attracted to 'happiness, as to its supreme good, 'by that very " *virtue* " to which 'alone the opposite party ascribes 'happiness. For they define " *vir-*'*tue*," the living in accordance with 'nature ; inasmuch as, to this end, 'we are created by God. They 'believe that he follows the guid-'ance of nature who obeys the 'dictates of reason in the pursuit or 'avoidance of anything ; and they 'say that reason first of all inflames 'men with a love and reverence for 'the Divine Majesty, to whom we 'owe it both that we exist, and that 'we are capable of happiness ; and 'secondly, that reason impresses 'upon us and urges us to pass our 'lives with the least amount of care 'and the greatest amount of pleasure 'ourselves ; and, as we are bound to 'do by the natural ties of society, 'to give our assistance to the rest of 'mankind towards attaining the 'same ends. For never was there a 'man so stern a follower of *"virtue,"* 'or hater of pleasure, who, whilst thus 'enjoining upon you labours, watch-'ings, and discomfort, would not 'tell you likewise to relieve the want 'and misfortunes of others to the 'utmost of your ability, and would 'not think it commendable for men 'to be of mutual help and comfort 'to one another in the name of hu-'manity. If, then, it be in human 'nature (and no virtue is more pe-'culiar to man) to relieve the misery

'of others, and, by removing their 'troubles, to restore them to the en-'joyment of life, that is, to pleasure '—does not nature, which prompts 'men to do this for others, urge 'them also to do it for themselves ? 'For a joyful life—that is, a life of 'pleasure—is either an evil—in 'which case, not only should you 'not help others to lead such a life, 'but, as far as you can, prevent 'them from leading it, as being 'hurtful and deadly ; or, if it be a 'good thing, and if it be not only 'lawful, but a matter of duty to 'enable others to lead such a life— 'why should it not be good for your-'self first of all, who ought not to 'be less careful of yourself than of 'others ? For when nature teaches 'you to be kind to others, she does 'not bid you to be hard and severe 'to yourself in return. Nature her-'self then, in their belief, enjoins a 'happy life—that is " *pleasure* "— 'as the end of all our efforts ; and to 'live by this rule, they call *"virtue."*

' But, since nature urges men to 'strive together to make life more 'cheerful (which, indeed, she rightly 'does ; for no man is so much raised 'above the condition of his fellows 'as to be the only favourite of 'nature, which cherishes alike all 'whom she binds together by the tie 'of a common shape), she surely 'bids you urgently to beware of 'attending so much to your own 'interest as to prejudice the interest 'of others. They think, therefore, 'that not only all contracts between 'private citizens should be kept, 'but also public laws, which either

' delight.' And from reason they deduced, as modern utilitarians do, that not merely the pleasure of the moment must be regarded as the object of life, but what will produce the greatest amount and highest kind of pleasure in the long run ; that, *e.g.* a greater pleasure must not be sacrificed to a lesser one, or a pleasure pursued which will be followed by pain. And from reason they also deduced that, nature having bound men together by the ties of Society, and no one in particular being a special favourite of nature, men are bound, in the pursuit of pleasure, to regard the pleasures of others as well as their own—to act, in fact, in the spirit of the golden rule; which course of action, though it may involve some immediate sacrifice, they saw clearly never costs so much as it brings back, both in the interchange of mutual benefits, and in the mental pleasure of conferring kindness on others. And thus they arrived at the same result as modern

---

' a good prince has legally enacted, ' or a people neither oppressed by ' tyranny, nor circumvented by ' fraud, has sanctioned by common ' consent for the apportionment of ' the conveniences of life ; that is, ' the material of pleasure. Within ' the limits of these laws, it is com- ' mon prudence to look after your ' own interests ; it is a matter of ' duty to have regard for the public ' weal also. But to attempt to ' deprive another of pleasure in ' favouring your own, is to do a ' real injury. On the other hand, ' to deprive yourself of something ' in order that you may give it to ' another, that is indeed an act of ' humanity and kindness which in ' itself never costs so much as it ' brings back. For it is not only

' repaid by the interchange of kind- ' nesses; but also the very conscious- ' ness of a good action done and ' the recollection of the love and ' gratitude of those whom you have ' benefited, afford more pleasure to ' the mind, than the thing from ' which you have abstained would ' have afforded to the body. And, ' lastly, God repays the loss of these ' small and fleeting pleasures with ' vast and endless joy; a doctrine of ' the truth of which religion easily ' convinces a believing mind.
'Thus, on these grounds, they ' determine that, all things being ' carefully weighed and considered, ' all our actions, and our very virtues ' among them, regard pleasure and ' happiness after all as their object.' *Utopia*, 1st ed. Leaf h, ii. *et seq.*

utilitarians, that, while ' nature enjoins *pleasure* as the ' end of all men's efforts,' she enjoins such a reasonable and far-sighted pursuit of it that ' to live by this rule ' is "*virtue*." '

In other words, in Utopian philosophy, ' *utility* ' was recognised as *a* criterion of right and wrong ; and from experience of what, under the laws of Nature, is man's real far-sighted interest, was derived *a* sanction to the golden rule. And thus, instead of setting themselves against the doctrine of utility, as some would do on the ground of a supposed opposition to Christianity, they recognised the identity between the two standards. They recognised, as Mr. Mill urges that Christians ought to do now, ' in the golden rule of Jesus of ' Nazareth, the complete spirit of the ethics of ' utility.' [1]

The Utopians had no hesitation in defining ' virtue ' as ' living according to nature ' ; for, they said, ' to ' this end we have been created by God.' Their religion itself taught them that ' God in his goodness ' created men for happiness ; ' and therefore there was nothing unnatural in his rewarding, with the promise of endless happiness hereafter, that ' virtue ' which is living according to those very laws of nature which He Himself established to promote the happiness of men on earth.

Nor was this, in More's hands, a merely philosophical theory. He made the right practical use of it, in correcting those false notions of religion and piety which had poisoned the morality of the middle ages, and soured the devotion even of those mediæval mystics whose mission it was to uphold the true religion of the heart. Who does not see that the deep devotion even

---

[1] J. S. Mill's *Essay on Utilitarianism*, p. 24.

of a Tauler, or of a Thomas à Kempis, would have been
deepened had it recognised the truth that the religion
of Christ was intended to add heartiness and happiness to daily life, and not to draw men out of it ; that
the highest ideal of virtue is, not to stamp out those
feelings and instincts which, under the rule of selfishness, make a hell of earth, but so, as it were, to tune
them into harmony, that, under the guidance of a
heart of love, they may add to the charm and the
perfectness of life ?   The ascetic himself who, seeing
the vileness and the misery which spring out of selfish
riot in pleasure, condemns natural pleasure as almost
in itself a sin, fills the heaven of his dreams with
white robes, golden crowns, harps, music and angelic
songs.   Even *his* highest ideal of perfect existence is
the unalloyed enjoyment of pleasure.   He is a Utilitarian in his dreams of heaven.

More, in his ' Utopia,' dreamed of this celestial
morality as practised under earthly conditions.   He
had banished selfishness from his commonwealth.   He
was bitter as any ascetic against vanity, and empty
show, and shams of all kinds, as well as all sensuality
and excess ; but his definition of ' virtue ' as ' living
' according to nature ' made him reject the ascetic
notion of virtue as consisting in crossing all natural
desires, in abstinence from natural pleasure, and
stamping out the natural instincts.   The Utopians,
More said, ' gratefully acknowledged the tenderness
' of the great Father of nature, who hath given us
' appetites which make the things necessary for our
' preservation also agreeable to us.   How miserable
' would life be if hunger and thirst could only be re-
' lieved by bitter drugs.' [1]   Hence, too, the Utopians

---

[1] *Utopia*, 1st ed. Leaf i, ι.

esteemed it not only ' madness,' but also ' *ingratitude*
' *to God,*' to waste the body by fasting, or to reject the
delights of life, unless by so doing a man can serve
the public or promote the happiness of others.[1]

Hence also they regarded the pursuit of natural
science, the ' searching out the secrets of nature,' not
only as an agreeable pursuit, but as ' peculiarly accept-
' able to God.'[2] Seeing that they believed that ' the
' first dictate of reason is love and reverence for Him
' to whom we owe all we have and all we can hope
' for,'[3] it was natural that they should regard the
pursuit of science rather as a part of their religion
than as in any way antagonistic to it. But their
science was not likely to be speculative and dogmatic
like that of the Schoolmen ; accordingly, whilst they
were said to be very expert in the mathematical
sciences (*numerandi et metiendi scientia*), they knew
nothing, More said, ' of what even boys learn here in
' the "*Parva logicalia*" ; ' and whilst, by long use and
observation, they had acquired very exact knowledge
of the motions of the planets and stars, and even of
winds and weather, and had invented very exact
instruments, they had never dreamed, More said, of
those astrological arts of divination ' which are now-
' a-days in vogue among Christians.'[4]

From the expression of so fearless a faith in the
consistency of Christianity with science, it might be
inferred that More would represent the religion of the
Utopians as at once broad and tolerant. It could not
logically be otherwise. The Utopians, we are told,
differed very widely ; but notwithstanding all their

---

[1] Leaf i, ii.   [2] Leaf i, iii.   [3] Leaf h, ii.   [4] Leaves h, i. and ii.

different objects of worship, they agreed in thinking that there is one Supreme Being who made and governs the world. By the exigencies of the romance, the Christian religion had only been recently introduced into the island. It existed there side by side with other and older religions, and hence the difficulties of complete toleration in Utopia were much greater hypothetically than they would be in any European country. Still, sharing Colet's hatred of persecution, More represented that it was one of the oldest laws of Utopia 'that no man is to be punished for his religion.' Everyone might be of any religion he pleased, and might use argument to induce others to accept it. It was only when men resorted to other force than that of persuasion, using reproaches and violence, that they were banished from Utopia ; and *then*, not on account of their religion, and irrespective of whether their religion were true or false, but for sowing sedition and creating a tumult.[1]

> No man punished for his religion.

This law Utopus founded to preserve the public peace, and for the interests of religion itself. Supposing only one religion to be true and the rest false (which he dared not rashly assert), Utopus had faith that in the long run the innate force of truth would prevail, if supported only by fair argument, and not damaged by resort to violence and tumult. Thus, he did not punish even avowed atheists, although he considered them unfit for any public trust.[2]

> Priests of both sexes selected by ballot.

Their priests were very few in number, of either sex,[3] and, like all their other magistrates, elected by ballot (*suffragiis occultis*) ;[4] and it was a point of dispute even with the Utopian *Christians*, whether *they*

---

[1] Leaf l, iv.   [2] Ibid.   [3] Leaf m, ii.   [4] Leaf m, i.

could not elect their own Christian priests in like
manner, and qualify them to perform all priestly
offices, without any apostolic succession or authority
from the Pope.[1] Their priests were, in fact, rather
conductors of the public worship, inspectors of the
public morals, and ministers of education, than
'priests' in any sacerdotal sense of the word. Thus
whilst representing *Confession* as in common use
amongst the Utopians, More significantly described
them as confessing not to the priests but to the heads
of families.[2] Whilst also, as in Europe, such was the
respect shown them that they were not amenable to
the civil tribunals, it was said to be on account of
the extreme fewness of their number, and the high
character secured by their mode of election, that no
great inconvenience resulted from this exemption in
Utopian practice.

If the diversity of religions in Utopia made it more
difficult to suppose perfect toleration, and thus made
the contrast between Utopian and European practice
in this respect all the more telling, so also was this
the case in respect to the conduct of *public worship*.

The hatred of the Oxford Reformers for the endless
dissensions of European Christians ; the advice Colet
was wont to give to theological students, ' to keep to
' the Bible and the Apostles' Creed, and let divines,
' if they like, dispute about the rest '; the appeal of
Erasmus to Servatius, whether it would not be better
for ' all Christendom to be regarded as one monastery,
' and all Christians as belonging to the same religious
' brotherhood,'—all pointed, if directed to the practical
question of public worship, to a mode of worship in
which all of every shade of sentiment could unite.

---

[1] Leaf l, iii.　　　[2] Leaf m, iii.

This might be a dream even then, while as yet Christendom was nominally united in one Catholic Church ; and still more practically impossible in a country like Utopia, where men worshipped the Supreme Being under different symbols and different names, as it might be now even in a Protestant country like England, where religion seems to be the source of social divisions and castes rather than a tie of brotherhood, separating men in their education, in their social life, and even in their graves, by the hard line of sectarian difference. It might be a dream, but it was one worth a place in the dream-land of More's ideal commonwealth.

All sects unite in public worship.

Temples, nobly built and spacious, in whose solemn twilight men of all sects meet, in spite of their distinctions, to unite in a public worship avowedly so arranged that nothing may be seen or heard which shall jar with the feelings of any class of the worshippers— nothing in which all cannot unite (for every sect performs its own *peculiar* rites in *private*) ;—no images, so that every one may represent the Deity to his own thoughts in his own way ; no forms of prayer, but such as every one may use without prejudice to his own private opinion ;—a service so expressive of their common brotherhood that they think it a great impiety to enter upon it with a consciousness of anger or hatred to any one, without having first purified their hearts and reconciled every difference ; incense and other sweet odours and waxen lights burned, not from any notion that they can confer any benefit on God, which even men's prayers cannot, but because they are useful aids to the worshippers ; [1] the men occupying

---

[1] It is impossible not to see in this a ritualism rather of the *Dionysian* than of the modern sacerdotal type.

one side of the temple, the women the other, and all clothed in white ; the whole people rising as the priest who conducts the worship enters the temple in his beautiful vestments, wonderfully wrought of birds' plumage, to join in hymns of praise, accompanied by music ; then priest and people uniting in solemn prayer to God in a set form of words, so composed that each can apply its meaning to himself, offering thanks for the blessings which surround them, for the happiness of their commonwealth, for their having embraced a religious persuasion which they *hope* is the most true one ; praying that if they are mistaken they may be led to what is *really* the true one, so that all may be brought to unity of faith and practice, unless in his inscrutable will the Almighty should otherwise ordain ; and concluding with a prayer that, as soon as it may please Him, He may take them to Himself ; lastly, this prayer concluded, the whole congregation bowing solemnly to the ground, and then, after a short pause, separating to spend the remainder of the day in innocent amusement,—this was More's ideal of public worship ! [1]

Such was the second book of the ' Utopia,' probably written by More whilst on the embassy, towards the close of 1515, or soon after his return. Well might he conclude with the words, ' I freely confess that ' many things in the commonwealth of Utopia I ' rather *wish* than *hope* to see adopted in *our own* ! '

IV. THE ' INSTITUTIO PRINCIPIS CHRISTIANI ' OF ERASMUS (1516).

Some months before More began to write his ' Utopia,' Erasmus had commenced a little treatise

---

[1] *Utopia*, 1st ed. ' De Religionibus Vtopiensium.'

with a very similar object. In the spring of 1515, while staying with More in London, he had mentioned, in a letter to Cardinal Grimanus [1] at Rome, that he was already at work on his ' Institutes of the Christian ' Prince,' designed for the benefit of Prince Charles, into whose honorary service he had recently been drawn.

Connection between the ' Utopia ' and the ' Christian Prince.'

The similarity in the sentiments expressed in this little treatise and in the ' Utopia ' would lead to the conclusion that they were written in concert by the two friends, as their imitations of Lucian had been under similar circumstances. Political events must have often formed the topic of their conversation when together in the spring ; and the connection of the one with the Court of Henry VIII. and the other with that of Prince Charles, would be likely to give their thoughts a practical direction. Possibly they may have parted with the understanding that, independently of each other, both works should be written on the common subject, and expressing their common views. Be this as it may, while More went on his embassy to Flanders, and returned to write his ' Utopia,' Erasmus went to Basle to correct the proof-sheets of the ' Novum Instrumentum,' and to finish the ' Institutio Principis Christiani.'

On his return from Basle in the spring of the following year Erasmus brought his manuscript with him, and left it under the care of the Chancellor of Prince Charles,[2] to be printed by Thierry Martins, the

---

[1] Epist. clxvii. Eras. *Op.* iii. p. 144, A.

[2] Erasmus to Savage : Epist.

clxxvi. June 1, 1516. Brewer, 1976.

printer of Louvain, whilst he himself proceeded to
England. Thus it was being printed while Erasmus
was in England in August 1516, and while the manuscript of the second book of More's ' Utopia ' was
still lying unpublished, waiting until More should
find leisure to write the Introductory Book which he
was intending to prefix to it.

The publication by Erasmus of the ' Christian
' Prince ' so soon after the ' Novum Instrumentum '
that the two came before the public together was
not without its significance. It gave to the public
expression of the views of Erasmus that wideness and
completeness of range which More had given to his
views by embracing both religious and political
subjects in his as yet unpublished ' Utopia.'

By laying hold of the truth that the laws of nature Chris-
and Christianity owe their origin to the same great tianity
Founder, More had adopted the one standpoint from laws of
which alone, in the long run, the Christian in an age nature.
of rapid progress can look calmly on the discoveries of
science and philosophy without fears for his faith. He
had trusted his bark to the current, because he was
sure it must lead into the ocean of truth ; while other
men, for lack of that faith, were hugging the shore,
mistaking forsooth, in their idle dreams, the shallow
bay in which they had moored their craft for the
fathomless ocean itself ! This faith of More's had been
shared by Colet—nay, most probably More had
caught it from him. It was Colet who had been the
first of the little group of Oxford Reformers to pro-
claim that Christianity had nothing to fear from the
' new learning,'—witness his school, and the tone
and spirit of his Oxford lectures. Erasmus, too, had

shared in this same faith. In his ' Novum Instrumen-
' tum ' he had placed Christianity, so far as he was
able, in its proper place—at the head of the advanced
thought of the age.

But More had gone one step further. The man who
believes that Christianity and the laws of nature were
thus framed in perfect harmony by the same Founder
must have faith in *both*. As he will not shrink from
accepting the results of science and philosophy, so he
will not shrink, on the other hand, from carrying out
Christianity into practice in every department of
social and political life.

Accordingly More had fearlessly done this in his
' Utopia.' And this Colet also had done in his own practical way ; preaching Christian politics to Henry VIII.
and Wolsey, from his pulpit as occasion required,
believing Christianity to be equally of force in the
sphere of international policy as within the walls of
a cloister. And now, in the ' Institutio Principis
' Christiani,' Erasmus followed in the same track for
the special benefit of Prince Charles, who, then sixteen
years old, had succeeded, on the death of Ferdinand
in the spring of 1516, to the crowns of Castile and
Aragon, as well as to the kingdoms of Naples and
Sicily and of the island of Sardinia.

The full significance of this joint action of the three
friends will only be justly appreciated if it be taken
into account that probably, at the very moment when
Erasmus was writing his ' Christian Prince ' and More
his ' Utopia,' the as yet unpublished manuscript of
' *The Prince* ' of *Machiavelli* was lying in the study of
its author. The semi-pagan school of Italy was not
only drifting into the denial of Christianity itself, but
it had already cast aside the Christian standard of

' The Prince' of Machia-velli.

morals as one which would not work in practice at least in political affairs. The Machiavellian theory was already avowedly accepted and acted upon in international affairs by the Pope himself ; and indeed, as I have said, it was not a theory invented by Machiavelli ; what that great philosopher had achieved was rather the codification of the current practice and traditions of the age.[1] A revolution had to be wrought in public feeling before the Christian theory of politics could be established in place of the one then in the ascendant—a revolution to attempt which at that time might well have seemed like a forlorn hope. But placed as the Oxford Reformers were, so close to the ears of royalty, in a position which gave them some influence at least with Henry VIII., with Prince Charles, and with Leo X., it was their duty to do what they could. And possibly it may have been in some measure owing to their labours that a century later Hugo Grotius, the father of the modern international system, was able in the name of Europe to reject the Machiavellian theory as one that would not work, and to adopt in its place the Christian theory as the one which was sanctioned by the laws of nature, and upon which alone it was safe to found the polity of the civilised world.[2]

---

[1] 'There is certainly a steadiness ' of moral principle and Christian ' endurance, which tells us that it is ' better not to exist at all than to ' exist at the price of virtue; but few ' indeed of the countrymen and con- ' temporaries of Machiavel had any ' claim to the practice, whatever ' they might have to the profession, ' of such integrity. *His crime in the* ' *eyes of the world, and it was truly* ' *a crime, was to have cast away* ' *the veil of hypocrisy, the profession* ' *of a religious adherence to maxims* ' *which at the same moment were* ' *violated.*'—Hallam's *Literature of the Middle Ages*, chap. vii. s. 31.

[2] ' Whatever may be thought of ' the long-disputed question as to ' Machiavelli's motives in writing, ' his work certainly presents to us ' a gloomy picture of the state of

B B

It may be worth while to notice also one other point which may be said to turn upon this perception of the relation of Christianity to the laws of nature.

To the man who does not recognise the harmony between them, religion and the world are divorced, as it were. Religion has no place in politics or business, and scarcely even in family life. These secular matters begin to be considered as the devil's concerns. A man must choose whether he will be a monk or man of the world, or still more often he tries to live at the same time two separate lives, the one sacred, the other secular, trusting that he shall be able to atone for the sins of the one by the penances and devotions of the other. This was the condition into which the dogmatic creed of the Schoolmen had, in fact, brought its adherents. It is a matter of notorious history that there *had* grown up this vicious severance between the clergy and the laity, and between things religious and secular, and that in consequence religion had lost its practical and healthy tone, while worldly affairs were avowedly conducted in a worldly spirit. The whole machinery of confession, indulgences, and penances bore witness as well to the completeness of the severance as to the hopelessness of any reunion.

'public law and European society 'in the beginning of the sixteenth 'century: one mass of dissimulation, 'crime, and corruption, which called 'loudly for a great teacher and re- 'former to arise, who should speak 'the unambiguous language of 'truth and justice to princes and 'people, and stay the ravages of 'this moral pestilence.

'Such a teacher and reformer 'was *Hugo Grotius,* who was born 'in the latter part of the same 'century and flourished in the be- 'ginning of the seventeenth. . . . . 'He was one of those powerful 'minds which have paid the 'tribute of their assent to the truth 'of Christianity.' — Wheaton's *Elements of International Law*: London, 1836, pp. 18, 19.

But to the man who *does* recognise in the laws of
nature the laws of the Giver of the golden rule, the
distinction between things religious and things secular
begins to give way. In proportion as his heart
becomes Christian, and thus catches the spirit of the
golden rule, and his mind becomes enlightened and
begins to understand the laws of social and political
economy, in that proportion does his religion lose its
ascetic and sickly character, and find its proper
sphere, not in the fulfilment of a routine of religious
observances, but in the honest discharge of the daily
duties which belong to his position in life.

The position assumed by Erasmus in these respects
will be best learned by a brief examination of the
' Institutes of the Christian Prince.'

First he struck at the root of the notion that a
prince having received his kingdom *jure Divino* had
a right to use it for his own selfish ends. He laid
down at starting the proposition that the one thing
which a ' prince ought to keep in view in the admini-
' stration of his government is that same thing
' which a people ought to keep in view in choosing a
' prince, viz. *the public good.*' [1]

Christianity in his view was as obligatory on a
prince as on a priest or monk. Thus he wrote to
Prince Charles :—

' As often as it comes into your mind that you are
' a prince, call to mind also that you are a *Christian*
' prince.' [2]

But the Christianity he spoke of was a very different
thing from what it was thought to be by many. ' Do

---

[1] 1st ed. leaf c, i.   [2] 1st ed. leaf d, ii.   Eras. *Op.* iv. p. 567.

' not think,' he wrote, ' that Christianity consists in ' ceremonies, that is, in the observance of the decrees ' and constitutions of the Church, The Christian is ' not he who is baptized, or he who is consecrated, or he ' who is present at holy rites ; but he who is united to ' Christ in closest affection, and who shows it by his ' holy actions. . . . . Do not think that you have ' done your duty to Christ when you have sent a fleet ' against the Turks, or when you have founded a ' church or a monastery. There is no duty by the per-' formance of which *you* can more secure the favour ' of God *than by making yourself a prince useful to* ' *the people.*' [1]

Duties
of a
Christian
Prince
to his
people.

Having taken at the outset this healthy and practical view of the relations of Christianity to the conduct of a prince, Erasmus proceeded to refer everything to the Christian standard. Thus he continued :—

' If you find that you cannot defend your kingdom, ' without violating justice, without shedding much ' human blood, without much injury to religion, ' rather lay it down and retire from it.'

But he was not to retire from the duties of his kingdom merely to save himself from trouble or danger. ' If you cannot defend the interests of your people ' without risk to your life, prefer the public good ' even to your own life.' [2] . . . The Christian prince should be a true father to his people.[3]

The good of the people was from the Christian point of view to override everything else, even royal prerogatives.

' If princes were perfect in every virtue, a pure and

---

[1] 1st ed. leaf d, iii. Eras. *Op.* iv. p. 567. [2] Leaf d, iii.   [3] 1st ed. leaf f, ii. Eras. *Op.* iv. p. 574.

' simple monarchy might be desirable ; but as this can
' hardly ever be in actual practice, as human affairs
' are now, a *limited monarchy*[1] is preferable, one in
' which the aristocratic and democratic elements are
' mixed and united, and so balance one another.'[2]
And lest Prince Charles should kick against the pricks,
and shrink from the abridgment of his autocratic
power, Erasmus tells him that ' if a prince wish well
' to the republic, his power will not be restrained, but
' aided by these means.'[3]

After contrasting the position of the pagan and
Christian prince, Erasmus further remarks :—

' He who wields his empire as becomes a Christian,
' does not *part* with his right, but he holds it in a dif-
' ferent way ; both more gloriously and more safely.
' . . . Those are not your subjects whom you *force* to
' obey you, for it is *consent* which makes a prince, but
' those are your true subjects who serve you volun-
' tarily. . . . The duties between a prince and people
' are *mutual.*   The people owe *you* taxes, loyalty, and
' honour ; you in your turn ought to be to the people
' a good and watchful prince.   If you wish to levy
' taxes on your people as of right, take care that you
' first perform your part—first in the discharge of
' your duties pay *your* taxes to them.'[4]

Proceeding from the general to the particular, there
is a separate chapter, ' De Vectigalibus et Exaction-
' ibus,' remarkable for the clear expression of the
views which More had advanced in his ' Utopia,' and

CHAP. XII.

A.D. 1516.

Limited
monarchy
the best.

Consent of
the people
makes a
Prince.

---

[1] ' Monarchia temperata,' in the marginal reading.

[2] Abridged quotation, 1st ed. leaf f, iv. Eras. *Op.* iv. p. 576.

[3] *Ibid.*

[4] 1st ed. leaf g, iii.   Eras. *Op.* iv. p. 579.

which the Oxford Reformers held in common, with regard to the unchristian way in which the interests of the poor were too often sacrificed and lost sight of in the levying of taxes. The great aim of a prince, he contended, should be to reduce taxation as much as possible. Rather than increase it, it would be better, he wrote, for a prince to reduce his unnecessary expenditure, to dismiss idle ministers, to avoid wars and foreign enterprises, to restrain the rapacity of ministers, and rather to study the right administration of revenues than their augmentation. If it should be really necessary to exact something from the people, then, he maintained, it is the part of a good prince to choose such ways of doing so as should cause as little inconvenience as possible to those of *slender means.* It may perhaps be expedient to call upon the rich to be frugal ; but to reduce the *poor* to hunger and crime would be both most inhuman and also hardly *safe*. . . It requires care also, he continued, lest the inequality of property should be too great. ' Not that I would ' wish to take away any property from any one by force, ' but that means should be taken to prevent the wealth ' of the multitude from getting into few hands.' [1]

Taxes should not oppress the poor.

Erasmus then proceeded to inquire what mode of taxation would prove least burdensome to the people. And the conclusion he came to was, that ' a good ' prince will burden with as few taxes as possible such ' things as are in *common use amongst the lowest classes,* ' such things as corn, bread, beer, wine, clothes, and ' other things necessary to life. Whereas these are ' what are now most burdened, and that in more than ' one way ; first by heavy taxes which are farmed out, ' and commonly called *assizes* ; then by *customs,*

Necessaries of life should not be taxed.

---

[1] Leaf l, i.

' which again are farmed out in the same way ; lastly
' by *monopolies*, from which little revenue comes to the
' prince, while the poor are mulcted with great charges.
' Therefore it would be best, as I have said, that a
' prince should increase his revenue by contracting his
' expenditure ; . . . and if he cannot avoid taxing
' something, and the affairs of the people require it, let
' those foreign products be taxed which minister not
' so much to the necessities of life as to *luxury and
' pleasure, and which are used only by the rich* ; as, for
' instance, fine linen, silk, purple, pepper, spices, oint-
' ments, gems, and whatever else is of that kind.' [1]

Erasmus wound up this chapter on taxation by
applying the principles of common honesty to the
question of *coinage*, in connection with which
many iniquities were perpetrated by princes in the
sixteenth century.

' Finally, in coining money a good prince will main-
' tain that good faith which he owes to both God and
' man, . . . in which matter there are four ways in
' which the people are wont to be plundered, as we
' saw some time ago after the death of Charles, when a
' long anarchy more hurtful than any tyranny afflicted
' your dominions. First the metal of the coins is de-
' teriorated by mixture with alloys, next its weight is
' lessened, then it is diminished by clipping, and lastly
' its nominal value is increased or lowered whenever
' such a process would be likely to suit the exchequer
' of the prince.' [2]

In the chapter on the ' *Making and Amending of
' Laws,*' [3] Erasmus in the same way fixes upon some

---

[1] 1st ed. leaf l, i. Eras. *Op.* iv. pp. 593, 594.
[2] *Ibid.* Charles the Bold was the prince alluded to.
[3] Eras. *Op.* iv. p. 595, *et seq.*

of the points which are so prominently mentioned in the 'Utopia.'

Thus he urges that the greatest attention should be paid, not to the punishment of crimes when committed, but to the prevention of the commission of crimes worthy of punishment. Again, there is a paragraph in which it is urged that just as a wise surgeon does not proceed to amputation except as a last resort, so all remedies should be tried before *capital punishment* is resorted to.[1] This was one of the points urged by More.

Prevention of crime rather than punishment.

Thus also in speaking of the removal of occasions and causes of crime, he urged, just as More had done, that idle people should either be set to work or banished from the realm. The number of priests and monasteries should be kept in moderation. Other idle classes—especially soldiers—should not be allowed. As to the nobility, he would not, he said, detract from the honour of their noble birth, if their character were noble also. 'But if they are such as 'we see plenty nowadays, softened by ease, made 'effeminate by pleasure, unskilled in all good arts, 'revellers, eager sportsmen, not to say anything 'worse ; . . . . why should this race of men be pre-'ferred to shoemakers or husbandmen ? '[2] The next chapter is '*De Magistratibus et Officiis*,' and then follows one, '*De Fœderibus*,'[3] in which Erasmus takes the same ground as that taken by More, that Christianity itself is a bond of union between Christian nations which ought to make leagues unnecessary.[4]

The nobility.

---

[1] 1st ed. leaf l, iv.
[2] Leaf m, i.
[3] Eras. *Op.* iv. 603.

[4] 1st ed. leaf o, i. Eras. *Op.* iv. pp. 607 *et seq.*

In the chapter '*De Bello suscipiendo*,' he expressed
his well-known hatred of war. 'A good prince,' he
said, 'will never enter upon any war at all unless after
' trying all possible means it cannot be avoided. If
' we were of this mind, scarcely any wars would ever
' occur between any nations. Lastly, if so pesti-
' lential a thing cannot be avoided, it should be the
' next care of a prince that it should be waged with as
' little evil as possible to his people, and as little ex-
' pense as possible of Christian blood, and as quickly
' as possible brought to an end.' It was natural that,
holding as he did in common with Colet and More such
strong views against war, he should express them as
strongly in this little treatise as he had already done
elsewhere. It is not needful here to follow his
remarks throughout. It would involve much repetition. But it may be interesting to inquire what
remedy or substitutes for war be proposed. He
mentioned two. First, the reference of disputes between princes to arbitrators ; second, the disposition
on the part of princes rather to concede a point in
dispute than to insist upon it at far greater cost than
the thing is worth.[1]

He concludes this, the last chapter of the book,
with a personal appeal to Prince Charles. 'Christ
' founded a bloodless empire. He wished it always
' to be bloodless. He delighted to call himself the
' "Prince of *Peace*." May He grant likewise that
' by *your* good offices and by *your* wisdom there may
' be a cessation at last from the maddest of wars. The
' remembrance of past evils will commend peace to
' our acceptance, and the calamities of former times
' redouble the honour of the benefits conferred by *you*.'

---

[1] 1st ed. leaf o, iii.

This was the 'Institutio Principis Christiani' of Erasmus ; a work written, as I have said, while More was writing his 'Utopia,' but printed in August 1516, at Louvain, while Erasmus was in England, and while the manuscript of the 'Utopia' was lying unpublished, waiting for the completion of More's Introduction.

V. MORE COMPLETES HIS 'UTOPIA'—THE INTRODUCTORY BOOK (1516).

More's Introduction was still unwritten, and the 'Utopia' thus in an unfinished state, when Erasmus arrived in England in the autumn of 1516. Erasmus seems on this occasion to have spent more time with Fisher at Rochester than with More in London ; but he at least paid the latter a short visit on his way to Rochester,[1] and repeated it before leaving England. The latter visit seems also to have been more than a flying one, for we find him writing to Ammonius, that he might possibly stay a few days longer in England, were he not ' afraid of making himself a stale guest to ' More's wife.' [2] Encouraged as More doubtless was by Erasmus, and spurred on by the knowledge that the 'Institutio Principis Christiani' was already in the press, he still does not seem to have been able to find time to complete his manuscript before Erasmus

---

[1] On August 5 he seems to have been in London, and to have written a letter from thence to Leo X. Eras. Epist. clxxxi. Brewer, ii. 2257.

On August 17 he writes from Rochester to Ammonius, that he is spending ten days there. Eras. Epist. cxlvi. Brewer, ii. 2283. And again on August 22. Eras. Epist. cxlvii. Brewer, ii. 2290. On the 31st he writes to Boville from the same place. Eras. Epist. cxlviii. Brewer, ii. 2321.

[2] Erasmus to Ammonius : Epist. cxxxiii. Brewer, ii. 2323, without date.

left England. Probably, however, it was arranged

between them that it should be completed and printed

with as little delay as possible at the same press and
in the same type and form as Erasmus's work.

The manuscript was accordingly sent after Eras-

mus in October,[1] and by him and Peter Giles at once
placed in the hands of Thierry Martins for publication at Louvain.[2]

This long delay in the completion of the ' Utopia '
had been caused by a concurrence of circumstances.
More had been closely occupied by public matters,
in addition to his judicial duties in the city, and a
large private practice at the bar—a combination of
pressing engagements likely to leave him but little
leisure for literary purposes. Even when the daily
routine of public labours was completed, there were
domestic duties which it was not in his nature to
neglect. He was passionately fond of his home, and
' reckoned the enjoyment of his family a necessary
' part of the business of the man who does not wish
' to be a stranger in his own house.' [3]

Nor did the ' Utopia ' itself suffer from the delay
in its publication. Instead of losing its freshness it
gained in interest and point ; for, as it happened, the
introductory book was written under circumstances
which gave it a peculiar value which it could not
otherwise have had.

On More's return to England from his foreign mission, he had been obliged to throw himself again into

---

[1] Eras. Epist. lxxxvii. App. and
ccxviii. Brewer, ii. 2409.

[2] Erasmus Ægidio: Epist. cccxlv.
November 18, 1518. The mention
of St. Jerome as not yet finished

(see Epist. ccxviii. ; Brewer, 2409)
fixes the date 1516. Brewer, ii.
2558.

[3] Letter from More to Peter
Giles, prefixed to ' Utopia.'

the vortex of public business.   The singular discretion
and ability displayed by him in the conduct of the
delicate negotiations entrusted to his charge on this
and another occasion, had induced Henry VIII. to try
to attach him to his court.

More
declines
to enter
the Royal
service.
Hitherto he had acted more on behalf of the London
merchants than directly for the King.   Now Wolsey
was ordered to retain him in the King's service.   More
was unwilling, however, to accede to the proposal, and
made excuses.   Wolsey, thinking no doubt that he
shrank from relinquishing the emoluments of his position as under-sheriff, and the income arising from his
practice at the bar, offered him a pension, and suggested that the King could not, consistently with his
honour, offer him less than the income he would re-
linquish by entering his service.[1]   More wrote to Erasmus that he had declined the pension, and thought
he should continue to do so ; he preferred, he said,
his present judicial position to a higher one, and
was afraid that were he to accept a pension without
relinquishing it, his fellow-citizens would lose their
confidence in his impartiality in case any questions
were to arise, as they sometimes did, between them
and the Crown.   The fact that he was indebted to the
King for his pension might make them think him a
little the less true to their cause.[2]   Wolsey reported
More's refusal to the King, who it seems honourably
declined to press him further at present.[3]   Such, however, was More's popularity in the city, and the rising
estimation in which he was held, that it was evident

---

[1] Roper, pp. 9, 10.   Eras. *Op.*
iii. pp. 474, 476.

[2] More to Erasmus : Eras. Epist.
ccxxvii.   [3] Roper, 10.

the King would not rest until he had drawn him into his service—yes, ' *dragged*,' exclaims Erasmus, ' for no ' one ever tried harder to get admitted to court than ' he did to keep out of it.' [1]

As the months of 1516 went by, More, feeling that his entry into Royal service was only a question of time, determined, it would seem, to take the opportunity, while as yet he was free and unfettered, to insert in the introduction to his unfinished ' Utopia ' still more pointed allusion to one or two matters relating to the social condition of the country and the policy of Henry VIII. ; also at the same time to make some public explanation of his reluctance to enter the service of his sovereign.

The prefatory book which More now added to his description of the commonwealth of Utopia was arranged so as to introduce the latter to the reader in a way likely to attract his interest, and to throw an air of reality over the romance.

More related how he had been sent as an ambassador to Flanders in company with Tunstal, to compose some important disputes between Henry VIII. and Prince Charles. They met the Flemish ambassadors at Bruges. They had several meetings without coming to an agreement. While the others went back to Brussels to consult their prince, More went to Antwerp to see his friend Peter Giles. One day, coming from mass, he saw Giles talking to a stranger—a man past middle age, his face tanned, his beard long, his cloak hanging carelessly about him, and wearing altogether the aspect of a seafaring man.

---

[1] Erasmus to Hutten: Epist. ccccxlvii. Eras. *Op.* iii. p. 476, B.

More then related how he had joined in the conversation, which turned upon the manners and habits
of the people of the new lands which Raphael (for that
was the stranger's name) had visited in voyages he
had recently taken with Vespucci. After he had told
them how well and wisely governed were some of these
newly-found peoples, and especially the Utopians,
and here and there had thrown in just criticisms
on the defects of European governments, Giles asked
the question, why, with all his knowledge and judgment, he did not enter into Royal service, in which
his great experience might be turned to so good an
account? Raphael expressed in reply his unwilling-
ness to enter into Royal servitude. Giles explained
that he did not mean any '*servitude*' at all, but
honourable service, in which he might confer great
public benefits, as well as increase his own happiness.
The other replied that he did not see how he was to be
made happier by doing what would be so entirely
against his inclinations. Now he was free to do as he
liked, and he suspected very few courtiers could say
the same.

Here More put in a word, and urged that even
though it might be against the grain to Raphael, he
ought not to throw away the great influence for good
which he might exert by entering the council of some
great prince. Raphael replied that his friend More
was doubly mistaken. His talents were not so great
as he supposed, and if they were, his sacrifice of rest
and peace would be thrown away. It would do no
good, for nearly all princes busy themselves far more
in military affairs (of which, he said, he neither had,
nor wished to have, any experience), than in the good
arts of peace. They care a great deal more how, by

fair means or foul, to acquire new kingdoms, than how Chap. XII.
to govern well those which they have already.　Be-A.D. 1516.
sides, their ministers either are, or think that they are,
too wise to listen to any new counsellor ;　and, if they
ever do so, it is only to attach to their own interest
some one whom they see to be rising in their prince's
favour.

After this, Raphael having made a remark which
showed that he had been in England, the conversation
turned incidentally upon *English* affairs, and Raphael
proceeded to tell how once at the table of Cardinal
Morton he had expressed his opinions freely upon the
social evils of England.　He had on this occasion, he Raphael
said, ventured to condemn the system of the wholesale on the
number of
execution of thieves, who were hanged so fast that thieves in
England.
there were sometimes twenty on a gibbet.[1]　The seve-
rity was both unjustly great, and also ineffectual.　No
punishment, however severe, could deter those from
robbing who can find no other means of livelihood.

Then Raphael is made to allude to three causes
why the number of thieves was so large :—

1st.　There are numbers of wounded and disbanded
soldiers who are unable to resume their old employ-
ments, and are too old to learn new ones.

2nd.　The gentry who live at ease out of the labour
of others, keep around them so great a number of idle
fellows not brought up to any trade, that often, from
the death of their lord or their own illness, numbers
of these idle fellows are liable to be thrown upon the
world without resources, to steal or starve.　Raphael
then is made to ridicule the notion that it is needful
to maintain this idle class, as some argue, in order to
keep up a reserve of men ready for the army, and

---

[1] Leaf b, 4.

still more severely to criticise the notion that it is necessary to keep a standing army in time of peace. France, he said, had found to her cost the evil of keeping in readiness these human wild beasts, as also had Rome, Carthage, and Syria, in ancient times.

3rd. Raphael pointed out as another cause of the number of thieves—an evil peculiar to England—the

rage for sheep-farming, and the ejections consequent upon it. 'For,' he said, 'when some greedy and 'insatiable fellow, the pest of his county, chooses to 'enclose several thousand acres of contiguous fields 'within the circle of one sheepfold, farmers are 'ejected from their holdings, being got rid of either 'by fraud or force, or tired out by repeated injuries 'into parting with their property. In this way it 'comes to pass that these poor wretches, men, women, 'husbands, wives, orphans, widows, parents with 'little children—households greater in number than 'in wealth, for arable-farming requires many hands '—all these emigrate from their native fields without 'knowing where to go. Their effects are not worth 'much at best; they are obliged to sell them for 'almost nothing when they are forced to go. And 'the produce of the sale being spent, as it soon must 'be, what resource then is left to them but either to 'steal, and to be hanged, justly forsooth, for stealing, 'or to wander about and beg? If they do the latter, 'they are thrown into prison as idle vagabonds 'when they would thankfully work if only some one 'would give them employment. For there is no 'work for husbandmen when there is no arable-'farming. One shepherd and herdsman will suffice 'for a pasture-farm, which, while under tillage, em-

'ployed many hands. Corn has in the meantime
'been made dearer in many places by the same cause.
'Wool, too, has risen in price, owing to the rot
'amongst the sheep, and now the little clothmakers
'are unable to supply themselves with it. For the
'sheep are falling into few and powerful hands; and
'these, if they have not a *monopoly*, have at least an
'*oligopoly*, and can keep up the price.

'Add to these causes the increasing luxury and
'extravagance of the upper classes, and indeed of all
'classes—the tippling houses, taverns, brothels, and   On beer-
'other dens of iniquity, wine and beer houses, and   houses,
'places for gambling. Do not all these, after rapidly   &c.
'exhausting the resources of their devotees, educate
'them for crime?

'Let these pernicious plagues be rooted out. Enact   Practical
'that those who destroy agricultural hamlets or towns   remedies
'should rebuild them, or give them up to those who   suggested.
'will do so. Restrain these engrossings of the rich,
'and the license of exercising what is in fact a
'monopoly. Let fewer persons be bred up in idleness.
'Let tillage farming be restored. Let the woollen
'manufacture be introduced, so that honest employ-
'ment may be found for those whom want has already
'made into thieves, or who, being now vagabonds or
'idle retainers, will become thieves ere long. Surely
'if you do not remedy these evils, your rigorous
'execution of justice in punishing thieves will be in
'vain, which indeed is more specious than either just
'or efficacious. For verily if you allow your people to
'be badly educated, their morals corrupted from child-
'hood, and then, when they are men, punish them for
'the very crimes to which they have been trained

' from childhood, what is this, I ask, but first to make
' the thieves and then to punish them ? ' [1]

Raphael then went on to show that, in his opinion,
it was both a bad and a mistaken policy to inflict the
same punishment in the case of both theft and murder,
such a practice being sure to operate as an encouragement to the thief to commit murder to cover his crime,
and suggested that hard labour on public works would
be a better punishment for theft than hanging.

After Raphael had given an amusing account of the
way in which these suggestions of his had been received at Cardinal Morton's table, More repeated his
regret that his talents could not be turned to practical
account at some royal court, for the benefit of mankind. Thus the point of the story was brought round
again to the question whether Raphael should or
should not attach himself to some royal court—the
question which Henry VIII. was pressing upon More,
and which he would have finally to settle, in the course
of a few months, one way or the other. It is obvious
that, in framing Raphael's reply to this question,
More intended to express his own feelings, and to do so
in such a way that if, after the publication of the
' Utopia,' Henry VIII. were still to press him into his
service, it would be with a clear understanding of his
strong disapproval of the King's most cherished
schemes, as well as of many of those expedients which
would be likely to be suggested by courtiers as the
best means of tiding over the evils which must of
necessity be entailed upon the country by his per-
sistence in them.

Raphael, in his reply, puts the supposition that the

---

[1] Leaves b, iv to c, ii. These extracts are somewhat abridged
and condensed.

councillors were proposing schemes of international
intrigue, with a view to the furtherance of the King's
desires for the ultimate extension of his empire :—

What if Raphael were then to express his own
judgment that this policy should be entirely changed,
the notion of extension of empire given up, that the
kingdom was already too great to be governed by one
man, and that the King had better not think of adding
others to it ? What if he were to put the case of the
' Achorians,' neighbours of the Utopians, who some
time ago waged war to obtain possession of another
kingdom to which their king contended that he was
entitled by descent through an ancient marriage alliance [just as Henry VIII. had claimed France as ' *his*
' *very true patrimony and inheritance* '], but which
people, after conquering the new kingdom, found
the trouble of keeping it a constant burden [just as
England was already finding Henry's recent conquests
in France], involving the continuance of a standing
army, the burden of taxes, the loss of their property,
the shedding of their blood for another's glory, the
destruction of domestic peace, the corrupting of their
morals by war, the nurture of the lust of plunder and
robbery, till murders became more and more auda-
cious, and the laws were treated with contempt ?
What if Raphael were to suggest that the example of
these Achorians should be followed, who under such
circumstances refused to be governed by half a king,
and insisted that their king should choose which of
his two kingdoms he would govern, and give up the
other ; how, Raphael was made to ask, would such
counsel be received ?

And further : what if the question of ways and

means were discussed for the supply of the royal exchequer, and one were to propose tampering with the
currency ; a second, the pretence of imminent war to
justify war taxes, and the proclamation of peace as
soon as these were collected ; a third, the exaction of
penalties under antiquated and obsolete laws which
have long been forgotten, and thus are often trans-
gressed ; a fourth, the prohibition under great penalties of such things as are against public interest, and
then the granting of dispensations and licenses for
large sums of money ; a fifth, the securing of the
judges on the side of the royal prerogative ;—' What
' if here again I were to rise ' [Raphael is made to say]
' and contend that all these counsels were dishonest
' and pernicious, that not only the king's honour, but
' also his safety, rests more upon his people's wealth
' than upon his own, who (I might go on to show)
' choose a king for their own sake and not for his, viz.
' that by his care and labour they might live happily
' and secure from danger ; . . . that if a king should
' fall into such contempt or hatred of his people that he
' cannot secure their loyalty without resort to threats,
' exactions, and confiscations, and his people's im-
' poverishment, he had better abdicate his throne,
' rather than attempt by these means to retain the
' name without the glory of empire ? . . . What if I
' were to advise him to put aside his sloth and his
' pride, . . . that he should live on his own revenue,
' that he should accommodate his expenditure to his
' income, that he should restrain crime, and by good
' laws prevent it, rather than allow it to increase and
' then punish it, that he should repeal obsolete laws
' instead of attempting to exact their penalties ? . . .

' If I were to make such suggestions as these to men ' strongly inclined to contrary views, would it not be ' telling idle tales to the deaf ? ' [1]

Thus was Raphael made to use words which must have been understood by Henry VIII. himself, when he read them, as intended to convey to a great extent More's own reasons for declining to accept the offer which Wolsey had been commissioned to make to him.

The introductory story was then brought to a close by the conversation being made again to turn upon the laws and customs of the Utopians, the detailed particulars of which, at the urgent request of Giles and More, Raphael agreed to give after the three had dined together. A woodcut in the Basle edition, probably executed by Holbein, represents them sitting on a bench in the garden behind the house, under the shade of the trees, listening to Raphael's discourse, of which the second book of the ' Utopia ' proposed to give, as nearly as might be, a verbatim report.

With this bold and honest introduction the ' Utopia ' was published at Louvain by Thierry Martins, with a woodcut prefixed, representing the island of Utopia, and with an imaginary specimen of the Utopian language and characters. It was in the hands of the public by the beginning of the new year.[2]

Utopia published at Louvain.

Such was the remarkable political romance, which, from its literary interest and merit, has been translated into almost every modern language—a work which, viewed in its close relations to the history of the times

---

[1] Leaves d, ii. *et seq.* These extracts are somewhat abridged and condensed.

[2] Eras. Epist. App. xliv. (Brewer, ii. 2748), in which Lord Mountjoy acknowledges the receipt of a copy sent by Erasmus, dated Jan. 4, 1516; i.e. 1517 in modern reckoning.

in which it was written, and the personal circumstances of its author when he wrote it, derives still greater interest and importance, inasmuch as it not only discloses the visions of hope and progress floating before the eyes of the Oxford Reformers, but also embodies, as I think I have been able to show, perhaps one of the boldest declarations of a political creed ever uttered by an English statesman on the eve of his entry into a king's service.[1]

---

[1] The extracts from the 'Utopia,' translations of which are given in this chapter, have in all cases been taken from the first edition (Louvain, 1516), but very few alterations were made in subsequent editions. The first edition was published in Dec. 1516. I am indebted to Mr. Lupton for the suggestion that the publication of some letters of Vespucci at Florence, in 1516, may have suggested More's use of that voyager's name in his introductory book.

Erasmus, writing from Antwerp to More, March 1 [1517], says: 'Utopiam tuam recognitam, huc 'quam primum mittito, et nos ex'emplar, aut Basilium mittemus 'aut Lutetiam.'—Epist. ccviii.

Erasmus sent it to Froben of Basle, by whom a corrected edition was published in March 1518, and another in November of the same year. See Appendix F.

CHAPTER XIII.

I. WHAT COLET THOUGHT OF THE 'NOVUM INSTRUMENTUM' (1516).

HAVING traced the progress and final publication of these works by Erasmus and More, the enquiry suggests itself, how were they received ?

And first it may naturally be asked, What did Colet think of them, especially of the 'Novum Instru-'mentum'?

An early copy had doubtless been sent to him, and with the volume itself, it would seem, came a letter from Erasmus, probably from Antwerp, by the hand of Peter Meghen—'Unoculus,' as his friends called him.[1] In this letter Erasmus had consulted him about his future plans. After the labours of the past, and suffering as he was from feeble and precarious health, he had indulged, it would seem, in the expression of longings that he could share with Colet his prospects of rest. He knew how often Colet had mentioned the wish to spend his old age in retirement and peace, with one or two congenial companions, such as Erasmus ; and now, just escaped from his monotonous labours at Basle, he was for the moment inclined to take Colet at his word. Still, much as he talked of rest, his mind would not stop working.

---

[1] Eras. Epist. cclvi.   Brewer, ii. 2000 ; from St. Omer ; and see ccxxv. Brewer, ii. 1976.

Witness, for instance, his ' Institutio Principis Chris-
' tiani.' In fact, while the ' Novum Instrumentum '
and the works of St. Jerome had been passing through
the press the number of other works of his had
increased rather than lessened. During the very
intervals of travel he was sure to be writing some book.
On his way to Basle he had written his letter to Dorpius, and he had published with it a commentary on
the first Psalm, ' *Beatus est vir,*' &c., which, by the
way, he had dedicated to his gentle friend, *Beatus*
Rhenanus, because, said he, ' *blessed is* the man who is
' such as the Psalm describes.' New editions, also,
of the ' De Copia,' of the ' Praise of Folly,' and of the
' Adagia,' were constantly being issued from the press
of Froben, Martins, Schurerius, or some other printer ;
for whatever bore the name of Erasmus now found
so ready a sale, that printers were anxious for his
patronage. Visions, too, of future work kept rising up
before him. He wanted to write a commentary on
the Epistle to the Romans ; and in writing to Colet it
would seem that he had confided to him his project of
adding to his Latin version of the New Testament an
honest exposition of its meaning in the form of a

simple *paraphrase*—a work which it took him years to
complete. Thus it came to pass that he had mentioned these literary projects in the same letter in
which he had expressed himself as envious of Colet's
anticipated rest, and that freedom from the cares of
poverty to which he himself was so constantly a prey.
Doubtless for a moment it had seemed to him easier to
wish himself in Colet's place than with renewed energy
to toil on in his own.

But every heart knoweth its own bitterness. Colet
had his share of troubles, which made him, in his turn,

almost envy Erasmus. He felt as keenly as Erasmus and More did, how the mad rush of princes to arms had blasted the happy visions of what had seemed like a golden age approaching, and he had been the first to speak out what he thought ; but now, while More and Erasmus could speak boldly and get Europe to listen to what they had to say, he was thwarted and harassed by his bishop, and obliged to crawl into retirement. His work was almost done. He could not use his pulpit as he used to do. He had spent his patrimony in the foundation of his school, and he had not another fortune to spend, for his uncle's quarrel and other demands upon the residue had reduced his means even below his wants. Nor had he much of bodily strength and energy left. The sole survivor of a family of twenty-two, his health was not likely to be robust, and now, at fifty, he spoke of himself as growing old, and alluded with admiration to the high spirits of his still surviving mother, and the beauty of her happy old age.

Still Colet had his heart in the work as much as ever. We do not hear much of his doings, but what we *do* hear is all in keeping with his character. Thus we find him incidentally exerting himself to get some poor prisoner released from the royal prison, and Erasmus exclaiming, ' I love that Christian spirit of Colet's, for ' I hear that it was all owing to him, and him alone, ' that N. was released, notwithstanding that N., ' though always treated in the most friendly way by ' Colet, and professing himself as friendly to Colet, had ' sided with Colet's enemies at the time that he was ' accused by the calumnies of the bishops.' [1]

Colet driven into retirement.

He procures the release from prison of one who had injured him.

---

[1] Epist. clviii. Erasmus to Ammonius : June 5, 1514; in error for 1516.

It was about the time that he was thus returning good for evil to this unfortunate prisoner, that the letter of Erasmus and the copy of the ' Novum In-' strumentum ' came to his hands.

Colet's de-
light in the
success of
Erasmus.

In spite of his own troubles he could hail the labours and success of Erasmus with delight. Twenty years ago, while alone and single-handed, he had longed for fellowship ; now he could rejoice that in Erasmus he had not only found a fellow-worker, but a successor who would carry on the work much further than he could do. He had looked forward with eager expectation to the appearance of the ' Novum ' Instrumentum,' and, anticipating its perusal, had for months past [1] been working hard to recover the little knowledge of Greek which, during the active business of life, he had almost lost. And the more he felt that his own work was drawing to a close, the more was he disposed to encourage Erasmus to go on with his. He looked upon Erasmus now as the leader of the little band, forgetting that Erasmus owed, in one sense, almost everything to him.

This is the beautiful letter he wrote after reading the ' Novum Instrumentum ' :—

Colet to Erasmus.

' You cannot easily believe, my dear Erasmus, how ' much joy your letter gave me, which was brought to ' me by our " one-eyed friend." For I learned from it ' where you are (which I did not know before), and ' also that you are likely to return to us, which would

---

[1] More to Erasmus : Eras. Epist. lii. App.   London, Feb. 25, 1516.

' be very delightful both to me and to your other
' friends, of whom you have a great many here.

: What you say about the New Testament I can
' understand. The volumes of your new edition of
' it [the " Novum Instrumentum "] are here both
' eagerly bought and everywhere read. By many,
' your labours are received with approval and ad-
' miration. There are a few, also, who disapprove and
' carp at them, saying what was said in the letter of
' Martin Dorpius to you. But these are those divines
' whom you have described in your " Praise of Folly "
' and elsewhere, no less truly than wittily, as men
' whose praise is blame, and by whom it is an honour
' to be censured.

What
Colet
thought
of the
' Novum
Instru-
mentum.'

' For myself, I so love your work, and so clasp to
' my heart this new edition of yours, that it excites
' mingled feelings. For at one time I am seized with
' sorrow that I have not that knowledge of Greek,
' without which one is good for nothing ; at another
' time I rejoice in that light which you have shed
' forth from the sun of your genius.

' Indeed, Erasmus, I marvel at the fruitfulness of
' your mind, in the conception, production, and daily
' completion of so much, during a life so unsettled,
' and without the assistance of any large and regular
' income.

' I am looking out for your " Jerome," who will
' owe much to you, and so shall *we* also when able to
' read him with your corrections and explanations.

' You have done well to write " De Institutione
' " Principis Christiani." I wish Christian princes
' would follow good institutes ! By their madness
' everything is thrown into confusion. . . . .

' As to the " peaceful resting-place " which you say

' you long for, I also wish for one for you, both
' peaceful and happy ; both your age and your studies
' require it.   I wish, too, that this your final resting-
' place may be with us, if you think us worthy of
' so great a man ; but what we are you have often
' experienced.   Still · you have here some who love
' you exceedingly.

' Our friend, the Archbishop of Canterbury, when I
' was with him a few days ago, spoke much of you, and
' desired your presence here very much.   Freed from
' all business cares, he lives now in quiet retirement.

' What you say about " Christian philosophising "
' is true.   There is nobody, I think, in Christendom
' more fit and suited for that profession and work than
' you are, on account of the wide range of your know-
' ledge.   *You* do not say so, but I say so because I
' think so.

Treatise of
Erasmus
on the
First
Psalm.

' I have read what you have written on the First
' Psalm, and I admire your eloquence.   I want to
' know what you are going to write on the Epistle to
' the Romans.

The
projected
' Para-
phrases '
of
Erasmus.

' Go on, Erasmus.   As you have given us the New
' Testament in Latin, illustrate it by your expositions,
' and give us your commentary most at length on
' the Gospels.   Your length is brevity ; the appetite
' increases if only the digestive organs are sound.   You
' will confer a great boon upon those who delight to
' read your writings if you will explain the meaning
' [of the Gospels], which no one can do better than
' you can.   And in so doing, you will make your name
' immortal—*immortal* did I say ?—the name of Eras-
' mus never can perish ; but you will confer eternal
' *glory* on your name, and, toiling on in the name of
' Jesus, you will become a partaker of his eternal life.

' In deploring your fortune you do not act bravely.
' In so great a work—in making known the Scriptures
' —your fortune cannot fail you.   Only put your trust
' in God, who will be the first to help you, and who
' will stir up others to aid you in your sacred labours.

' That you should call me happy, I marvel !   If you
' speak of fortune, although I am not wholly without
' any, yet I have not much, hardly sufficient for my
' expenses.   I should think myself happy if, even in
' extreme poverty, I had a thousandth part of that
' learning and wisdom which you have got without
' wealth, and which, as it is peculiar to yourself, so also
' you have a way of imparting it, which I don't know
' how to describe, unless I call it that " Erasmican "
' way of your own.

' If you will let me, I will become your disciple, even
' in learning Greek, notwithstanding my advanced
' years (being almost an old man), recollecting that
' Cato learned Greek in his old age, and that you
' yourself, of equal age with me, are studying Hebrew.

' Love me as ever ; and, if you should return to us,
' count upon my devotion to your service.—Farewell.

' From the country at Stepney, with my mother,
' who still lives, and wears her advancing age beauti-
' fully ; often happily and joyfully speaking of you.
' On the Feast of the Translation of St. Edward.' [1]

Colet's
mother.

---

[1] Eras. Epist. lxxxiv. App. Brewer, ii. 2941, dated ' in die ' sancti Edwardi, in festo *suæ* ' [? secundæ] translationis, sive 13 ' Octobris, 1516.' Probably ' *second* ' translation of St. Edward,' on June 20, 1516. The words ' sive ' 13 Oct.' are not found in the copy of this letter in *Aliquot Epistolæ, &c.* (Basle, 1518, pp. 249, 252), nor in the ed. of 1640. The earlier date seems to harmonise more with the contents of the letter than the later date.

II. RECEPTION OF THE 'NOVUM INSTRUMENTUM' IN OTHER QUARTERS (1516).

CHAP.
XIII.

A.D. 1516.
Reception
of the
' Novum
Instru-
mentum '
in Eng-
land.

Colet was not alone in his admiration of the ' Novum ' Instrumentum ' and its author.

William Latimer, of Oxford, one of the earliest Greek scholars in England, expressed his ardent approval of the new Latin translation, and would have been glad, he said, if Erasmus had gone still further, and translated even such words as ' sabbatum ' and the like into classical Latin.[1]

Warham had all along encouraged Erasmus in his labours, both by presents of money and constant good offices, and now he recommended the ' Novum Instru- ' mentum ' to some of his brother bishops and divines, who, he wrote to Erasmus, all acknowledged that the work was worthy of the labour bestowed upon it.[2]

Fox, the Bishop of Winchester, in a large assembly of magnates, when the conversation turned on Erasmus and his works, declared that his new version threw so much light on the New Testament, that it was worth more to him than ten commentaries, and this remark was approved by those present.[3] The Dean of Salisbury used almost the same words of commendation.[4]

In fact, it would appear that in England it was received coldly only by that class of pseudo-orthodox divines, now waning both in numbers and influence, who had consistently opposed the progress of the new

---

[1] Eras. Epist. lxxxvii. App. Brewer, ii. 2492.

[2] Eras. Epist. Waramus Erasmo, cclxi. *Aliquot Epistolæ, &c.* Basle, 1518, p. 231.

[3] Eras. Epist. ccxxi. App.

[4] Thomæ Mori ad Monachum Epistola: *Epistolæ aliquot Eruditorum Virorum.* Basle, 1520, p. 122.

learning, ‘ blasphemed ’ Colet's school, and censured the heretical tendencies of Erasmus as soon as their blind eyes had been opened to them by the recent edition of the ‘ Praise of Folly.’

Thus while Erasmus was in England in the autumn, enjoying at Rochester the hospitality of Bishop Fisher, who was Chancellor of the University of Cambridge, he was informed that his ‘ Novum Testamentum ’ had encountered no little opposition in some circles at that centre of learning.

In one of his letters from the Bishop's palace to his friend Boville, who was resident at Cambridge, he mentions a report that a decree had been formally issued in one of the colleges, forbidding anyone to bring ‘ that book ’ within the precincts of the college, ‘ by horse or by boat, on wheels or on foot.’ He hardly knew, he said, whether to laugh at or to grieve over men ‘ so studiously blind to their own interests ; ‘ so morose and implacable, harder to appease even ‘ than wild beasts ! How pitiful for men to condemn ‘ and revile a book which they have not even read, or, ‘ having read, cannot understand ! They had pos- ‘ sibly heard of the new work over their cups, or in ‘ the gossip of the market, ... and thereupon ex- ‘ claimed “ O heavens ! O earth ! Erasmus has cor- ‘ “ rected the Gospels ! ” when it is they themselves ‘ who have *depraved* them. . . . .

‘ Are they indeed afraid,’ Erasmus continued, ‘ lest ‘ it should divert their scholars, and empty their lec- ‘ ture-rooms ? Why do they not examine the facts ? ‘ Scarcely thirty years ago, nothing was taught at ‘ Cambridge but the “ parva logicalia ” of Alexander, ‘ antiquated exercises from Aristotle, and the “ Quæs-

' " tiones " of Scotus. In process of time improved
' studies were added—mathematics, a new, or, at all
' events, a *renovated* Aristotle, and a knowledge of
' Greek letters. . . . What has been the result of all
' this ? Now the University is so flourishing, that it can
' compete with the best universities of the age. It con-
' tains men, compared with whom, theologians of the
' old school seem only the *ghosts* of theologians. These
' men grieve because more and more students study
' with more and more earnestness the Gospels and the
' apostolic Epistles. They had rather that they spent
' all their time, as heretofore, in frivolous quibbles.
' Hitherto there have been theologians who so far
' from having read the Scriptures, had never read even
' the " *Sentences*," or touched anything beyond the
' collections of questions. Ought not,' exclaimed
' Erasmus, such men to be called back to the very
fountain-head ? ' He then told Boville that he
wished his works to be useful to *all*. He looked to
Christ for his chief reward ; still he was glad to have
the approval of wise men. He hoped too, that what
now was approved by the *best* men, would ere long
meet with *general* approval. He felt sure that posterity would do him justice.[1]

Nor was the opposition to the ' Novum Instrumen-
' tum ' by any means confined to Cambridge. A few
weeks later, very soon after Erasmus had left England
—in October—More wrote to inform him that a set of
acute men had determined to scrutinise closely, and
criticise remorselessly, what they could discover to find
fault with. A party of them, with a Franciscan divine

[1] Erasmus to Boville, from the Bishop's palace at Rochester, pridie calendas Septembris. *Aliquot Epistolæ, &c.* Basle, 1518, pp. 234– 246. Eras. Epist. cxlviii. Brewer, ii. 2321. The above is only an abstract of this letter, and some of the quotations are abridged.

at their head, had agreed to divide the works of Erasmus between them, and to pick out all the faults they
could find as they read them.   But, More added, he
had heard that they had already given up the project.
The labour of reading was more laborious and less
productive than the ordinary work of mendicants,
and so they had gone back again to that.[1]

The work was indeed full of small errors which
might easily give occasion to adverse critics to exercise their talents.   But Erasmus was fully conscious
of this, and within a year of the completion of the
first edition, he was busily at work making all the
corrections he could, with a view to a second edition.

The reception of the 'Novum Instrumentum' on
the Continent was much the same as in England.   It
had some bitter enemies, especially at Louvain and
Cologne.[2]   But, on the other hand, letters poured in
upon Erasmus from all sides of warm approval and
congratulation,[3] and so great a power had his name
become, that ere long princes competed for his residence within their dominions ; and if their numerous
promises had but been faithfully performed, Erasmus
need have had little fear for the future respecting
'ways and means.'

Amongst the numerous tributes of admiration received by Erasmus, was one forwarded to him by
Beatus Rhenanus, in Greek verse,[4] from the pen of an

Reception
of the
'Novum
Instru-
mentum'
on the
Continent.

[1] More to Erasmus : Epist.
lxxxvii. App. dated Oct. 31, 1516.

[2] Erasmus to Ammonius, from
Brussels, December 29, 1516.
Brewer, ii. 2709.

[3] Epist. cclvi. June 1517; should
be 1516.   Brewer, ii. 2000.

[4] Bearing date, Tubingen, Aug.
21, 1516.   Eras. *Op.* iii. p. 1595.
It was first printed probably at
the back of the titlepage of ' *Epigrammata Des. Erasmi Roterodami.*'   Basle, March 1518.

accomplished and learned youth at the University of Tubingen, already known by name to Erasmus, and mentioned with honour in the ' Novum Instrumen-' tum '—a student devoted to study, and reported to be working so hard that his health was in danger of giving way, whom another correspondent introduced as worthy of the love of ' Erasmus the first,' inasmuch as he was likely to prove ' Erasmus the second.' His name—then little known beyond the circle of his intimate friends—was *Philip Melanchthon.*[1]

III. MARTIN LUTHER READS THE ' NOVUM INSTRUMENTUM ' (1516).

In the winter of 1516-17, Erasmus received a letter from George Spalatin, whose name he may have heard before, but to whom he was personally a stranger. It was dated from the castle of the Elector of Saxony. It was a letter full of flattering compliments. The writer introduced himself as acquainted with a friend of Erasmus, and as being a pupil of one of his old schoolfellows at Deventer. He mentioned his intimacy with the Elector, whom he reported to be a diligent and admiring reader of the works of Erasmus, and informed him that these had honourable places on the shelves of the ducal library. It was, in fact, a letter evidently written with a definite object ; but beating about the bush so long, that one begins to wonder what matter of importance could require so roundabout an introduction.

At length the writer disclosed the object of his letter :—' A friend of his,' whose name he did not give, had written to him suggesting that Erasmus in

---

[1] Œcolampadius Erasmo : Eras. Epist. ccxxxviii. ; also cxix. App. and ccccxi.

his Annotations on the Epistle to the Romans, in the
'Novum Instrumentum,' had misinterpreted St.
Paul's expression, *justicia operum*, or *legis*, and also had
not spoken out clearly respecting ' original sin.' He
believed that if Erasmus would read St. Augustine's
books against Pelagius, &c., he would see his mistake.
His friend interpreted *justicia legis*, or the ' righteous-
' ness of works,' not as referring only to the keeping of
the ceremonial law, but to the observance of the whole
decalogue. The observance of the latter might make
a Fabricius or a Regulus, but without Christian faith
it would no more savour of ' righteousness ' than a
medlar would taste like a fig. This was the weighty
question upon which his friend had asked him to
consult the oracle, and a response, however short,
would be esteemed a most gracious favour.[1]

This unnamed friend of Spalatin was in fact *Martin
Luther.* The singular coincidence, that not only this
letter of Spalatin to Erasmus, but also the letter of
Luther to Spalatin,[2] have been preserved, enables us to
picture the monk of Wittemberg sitting in his room in
a corner of the monastery, pondering over the pages
of the ' Novum Instrumentum,' and ' moved,' as he
reads it, with feelings of grief and disappointment,
because his quick eye discerns that the path in which
Erasmus is treading points in a different direction
from his own.

In truth, Luther, though as yet without European
fame—not having yet nailed his memorable theses to
the Wittemberg church-door—had for years past fixed,
if I may use the expression, the cardinal points of his

Martin
Luther
reads the
' Novum
Instru-
mentum.'

---

[1] Spalatinus Erasmo : Eras.
Epist. xciv. App.

[2] Luther's *Briefe*. De Wette, i.
40, No. xxii.

theology. He had already clenched his fundamental convictions with too firm a grasp ever to relax. He had chosen his permanent standpoint, and for years had made it the centre of his public teaching in his professorial chair at the university, and in his pulpit also.

The standpoint which he had so firmly taken was *Augustinian.*

During the four years spent by him in the Augustinian monastery at Erfurt, into which he had fled to escape from the terrors of conscience, he had deeply studied, along with the Scriptures, the works of St. Augustine. It was from the light which these works had shed upon the Epistles of St. Paul that he had mainly been led to embrace those views upon ' justifi- ' cation by faith ' which had calmed the tumult and disarmed the lightnings of his troubled conscience. This statement rests upon the authority of Melanchthon, and is therefore beyond dispute.[1]

Eight years had passed since he had left Erfurt to become a professor in the Wittemberg University, and four or five years since his return from his memorable visit to Rome. During these last years his teaching and preaching had been full of the Augustinian theology. Melanchthon states that during this period he had written commentaries on the ' Romans,' and that in them and in his lectures and sermons he had laboured to refute the prevalent error, that it is possible to merit the forgiveness of sins by good works, pointing men to the Lamb of God, and throwing great light upon such questions as ' penitence,' ' remission of ' sins,' ' faith,' the difference between the ' Law ' and the ' Gospel,' and the like. He also mentions that

---

[1] Philippi Melanchthonis *Vita Martini Lutheri,* chap. v. ' Vita ejus ' monastica.'

Luther, catching the spirit which the writings of Erasmus had diffused, had taken to the study of Greek and Hebrew.[1]

We may therefore picture the Augustinian monk—deeply read in the works of St. Augustine, and, as Ranke expresses it,[2] ' *embracing even his severer views*,' having for years constantly taught them from his pulpit and professorial chair, clinging to them with a grasp which would never relax, looking at everything from this immovable Augustinian standpoint—now in 1516 with a copy of the ' Novum Instrumentum ' before him on his table in his room in the cloisters of Wittemberg, reading it probably with eager expectation of finding his own views reflected in the writings of a man who was looked upon as the great restorer of Scriptural theology.

He reads the Annotations on the Epistle to the Romans. He does not find Erasmus using the watchwords of the Augustinian theology. He does not find the words *justicia legis* understood in the Augustinian sense, as referring to the observance of the whole moral law, but, rather, explained as referring to the Jewish ceremonial.

Luther detects the Anti-Augustinian tendencies of Erasmus.

He turns as a kind of touchstone to Chapter V., where the Apostle speaks of death as ' having reigned ' from Adam to Moses over those who had not sinned ' after the similitude of Adam's transgression.' He finds Erasmus remarking that he does not think it needful here to resort to the doctrine of ' *original sin*,' however true in itself; he finds him hinting at the possibility ' of hating Pelagius more than enough,' and

---

[1] Philippi Melanchthonis *Vita Martini Lutheri*, chap. vi. vii.

[2] Ranke refers to the period before 1516. See *Hist. of Reformation*, vol. i. bk. ii. ch. i.

of resorting too freely to the doctrine of ' original sin '
as a means of getting rid of theological difficulties, in
the same way as astrologers had invented a system of
epicycles to get them out of their astronomical ones.[1]

The Augustinian doctrine of ' original sin ' compared to the *epicycles* of the astrologers ! No wonder
that Luther was *moved* as he traced in these Annotations symptoms of wide divergence from his own
Augustinian views. In writing to Spalatin, he told
him that he was ' moved ' ; and in asking him to
question Erasmus further on the subject, he added
that he felt no doubt that the difference in opinion
between himself and Erasmus was a real one, because
that, as regards the interpretation of Scripture, he saw
clearly that Erasmus preferred Jerome to Augustine,
just as much as he himself preferred Augustine to
Jerome. Jerome, evidently on principle, he said,
follows the *historical* sense, and he very much feared
that the great authority of Erasmus might induce
many to attempt to defend that *literal,* i.e. *dead,* understanding [of the Scriptures] of which the commentaries of Lyra and almost all after Augustine are full.[2]

Still Luther went on with his study of the ' Novum
' Instrumentum,' and we find him writing again from
his ' hermitage ' at Wittemberg, that every day as he
reads he loses his liking for Erasmus. And again the
reason crops out. Erasmus, with all his Greek and
Hebrew, is lacking in Christian wisdom ; ' just as
' Jerome, with all his knowledge of five languages,
' was not a match for Augustine with his one.' . . . .
' The judgment of a man who attributes *anything* to

---

[1] *Novum Instrumentum,* folio,
433.

[2] Luther to Spalatin : Luther's
Briefe. De Wette, No. xxii.

' the human will ' [which Jerome and Erasmus did] is
' one thing, the judgment of him who recognises *no-*
' *thing but grace* ' [which Augustine and Luther did] ' is
' quite another thing.' . . . ' Nevertheless [continues
' Luther] I carefully keep this opinion to myself, lest I
' should play into the hands of his enemies. May God
' give him understanding in his own good time ! ' [1]

Chap.
XIII.
———
A.D. 1516.

This is not the place to discuss the rights of the
question between Luther and Erasmus. It is well,
however, that by the preservation of these letters the
fact is established to us, which as yet was unknown to
Erasmus, that this Augustinian monk, as the result of
hard-fought mental struggle, had years before this
irrevocably adopted and, if we may so speak, welded
into his very being that Augustinian system of religious convictions, a considerable portion of which
Erasmus made no scruple in rejecting ; that at the
root of their religious thought there was a divergence
in principle which must widen as each proceeded on
his separate path—unknown as yet, let me repeat it,
to Erasmus, but already fully recognised, though
wisely concealed, by Luther.

Differ-
ence in
principle
between
Erasmus
and
Luther.

IV. THE ' EPISTOLÆ OBSCURORUM VIRORUM ' (1516–17).

In the meantime symptoms had appeared portend-
ing that a storm was brewing in another quarter
against Erasmus. It was not perhaps to be wondered
at that the monks should persist in regarding him as a
renegade monk. His bold reply to the letter of
Servatius, and the unsubdued tone in which he had
answered the attack of Martin Dorpius, must have
made the monastic party hopeless of his reconversion to

---

[1] Luther an Joh. Lange : De Wette, No. **xxix.** p. 52.

orthodox views.   At the same time, neither his letter
to Servatius nor his reply to Dorpius had at all converted them to his way of thinking.   Men perfectly
self-satisfied, blindly believing in the sanctity of their
own order, and arrogating to themselves a monopoly of
orthodox learning, were in a state of mind, both intel-
lectually and morally, beyond the reach of argument,
however earnest and convincing.   They still really did
believe, through thick and thin, that the Latin of the
Vulgate and the Schoolmen was the sacred language.
They still did believe that Hebrew and Greek were the
languages of heretics ; and that to be learned in these,
to scoff at the Schoolmen and to criticise the Vulgate,
were the surest proofs of *ignorance* as well as impiety.

' Epistolæ
Obscu-
rorum
Virorum.'

It was in the years 1516 and 1517 that the ' Epistolæ
' Obscurorum Virorum ' were published.   They were
written in exaggerated monkish Latin, and professed
to be a correspondence chiefly between monks, con-
veying their views and feelings upon current events
and the tendencies of modern thought.   Of course the
picture they gave was a caricature, but nevertheless it
so nearly hit the truth that More wrote to Erasmus
that ' in England it delighted every one.   To the
' learned it was capital fun.   Even the ignorant, who
' seriously took it all in, smiled at its style, and did
' not attempt to defend it ; but they said the *weighty*
' *opinions* it contained made up for that, and under
' a rude scabbard was concealed a most excellent
' blade.' [1]

The first part was full of the monks' hatred of
Reuchlin and the Jews.   One monk writes to his
superior to consult him in a difficulty.   Two Jews were

[1] More to Erasmus : Epist. lxxxvii. App. Eras. *Op.* iii. p. 1575, A and B.

walking in the town in a dress so like that of monks
that he bowed to them by mistake. To have made
obeisance to a Jew! Was this a venial or a mortal
sin? Should he seek absolution from episcopal
authority, or would it require a dispensation from the
Pope? [1]

Side by side with scrupulosity such as this were hints
of secret immorality and scandal. Immense straining
at gnats was put in contrast with the ease with which
camels were swallowed within the walls of the cloister.

In the appendix to the first part Erasmus at length
makes his appearance. The writer of the letter, a
medical graduate, informs his learned correspondent
that, being at Strasburg, he was told that a man who
was called ' Erasmus Roterdamus ' (till then unknown
to him) was in the city—a man said to be most learned
in all branches of knowledge. This, however, he did
not believe. He could not believe that so small a man
could have so vast a knowledge. To test the matter,
he laid a scheme with one or two others to meet
Erasmus at table, get him into an argument, and con-
fute him. He thereupon betook himself to his ' vade-
' mecum,' and crammed himself with some abstruse
medical questions, and so armed entered the field.
One of his friends was a lawyer, the other a speculative
divine. They met as appointed. All were silent.
Nobody would begin. At length Erasmus, in a low
tone of voice, began to sermonise (*sermonizare*), and
when he had done, another began to dispute *de ente et
essencia.* To which the writer himself responded in a
few words. Then a dead silence again. They could
not draw the lion out. At length their host started

---

[1] Vol. i. Epist. 2.

another hare—praising both the deeds and writings of Julius Cæsar. The writer here again put in. He knew something of *poetry*, and did not believe that Cæsar's ' Commentaries ' were written by Cæsar at all. Cæsar was a warrior, and always engaged in military affairs. Such men never are learned men, therefore Cæsar cannot have known Latin. ' I think,' he continued, ' that *Suetonius* (!) wrote those " Commen-
' " taries," because I never saw anyone whose style was
' so like Cæsar's as his. When I had said this,' he continued, ' Erasmus laughed, and said nothing, because
' the subtlety of my argument had confounded him.
' So I put an end to the discussion. I did not care to
' propound my question in medicine, because I knew he
' knew nothing about it, since, though himself a poet,
' he did not know how to solve my argument in poetry.
' And I assert before God that there is not as much in
' him as people say. He does not know more than other
' men, although I concede that in poetry he knows how
' to speak pretty Latin. But what of that ! ' [1]

In the second part, published in 1517, Erasmus makes a more prominent figure. One correspondent had met him at Basle, and ' found many perverse
' heretics in Froben's house.' [2]   Another writes that he hears Erasmus has written many books, especially a letter to the Pope, in which he commends Reuchlin :—
' That letter, you know, I have seen. One other
' book of his also I have seen—a great book—entitled
' " Novum Testamentum," and he has sent this book
' to the Pope, and I believe he wants the Pope's au-
' thority for it, but I hope he won't give it. One holy
' man told me that he could prove that Erasmus was
' a heretic ; because he censured holy doctors, and

---

[1] Vol. i. App. 1.   [2] Vol. ii. Ep. 9.

' thought nothing of divines. One of his things, called
' " Moria Erasmi," contained,' he said, ' many scan-
' dalous propositions and open blasphemies. On this
' account the book would be burned at Paris. There-
' fore I do not believe that the Pope will sanction his
' " great book." ' [1]

Another reports that his edition of St. Jerome has
been examined at Cologne ; that in this work Erasmus
says that Jerome was not a Cardinal ; that he thinks
evil of St. George and St. Christopher, the relics of the
saints and candles, and the sacrament of confession ;
that many passages contain blasphemy against the
holy doctors.[2]

These ' Epistolæ Obscurorum Virorum ' were widely
read, and proved like an advertisement, throughout
the monasteries of Europe, of the heresy of Erasmus
and his hatred of monks. As by degrees the latter
began to understand that these allusions to Erasmus
were intended to bring ridicule on themselves, instead
of, as they thought at first, to censure Erasmus, it
was likely that their anger should know no bounds.[3]

V. THE ' PYTHAGORICA ' AND ' CABALISTICA ' OF REUCHLIN (1517).

Reuchlin in his zeal for Hebrew had been led to
study along with the Old Testament Scriptures, other
Hebrew books, especially the ' Cabala,' and, after the
fashion of his Jewish teachers, had lost himself in the
' mystical value of words ' and in the Pythagorean
philosophy. He believed, writes Ranke, that by
treading in the footsteps of the ' Cabala,' he should

*Studies of
Reuchlin.*

---

[1] Vol. ii. Ep. 49.
[2] Ibid. Ep. 68.
[3] One of the best and most valuable essays on the *Epistolæ Obscu-*
rorum Virorum will be found in
No. cv. of the *Edinburgh Review,*
March 1831.

ascend from symbol to symbol, from form to form, till
he should reach that last and purest form which rules
the empire of mind, and in which human mutability
approaches to the Immutable and Divine [1]—whatever
that might mean.

Reuchlin had embodied his speculations on these
subjects in a work upon which he wished for the
opinion of Erasmus and his friends.

Erasmus accordingly sent a copy of this book to
Bishop Fisher, with a letter asking his opinion thereupon.[2] He sent it, it seems, by More, who, *more suo*,
as Fisher jokingly complained, purloined it,[3] so that it
did not reach its destination. What had become of it
may be learned from the following letter from Colet to
Erasmus, playful and laconic as usual, and beaming
with that true humility which enabled him to unite
with his habitual strength of conviction an equally
habitual sense of his own fallibility and imperfect
knowledge. It is doubly interesting also as the last
letter written by Colet which time has spared.

Colet to Erasmus.[4]

' I am half angry with you, Erasmus, that you send
' messages to me in letters to others, instead of writing
' direct to myself ; for though I have no distrust of our
' friendship, yet this roundabout way of greeting me
' through messages in other people's letters makes me
' jealous lest others should think you loved me less
' than you do.

' Also, I am half angry with you for another thing—
' for sending the " Cabalistica " of Reuchlin to Bishop
' Fisher and not to me. I do not grudge your sending

---

[1] Ranke's *History of the Reformation*, bk. ii. chap. 1.

[2] Epist. cxxxiii. App.

[3] Ibid. ccccxxviii. App.

[4] Ibid. ccxlvi. App.

' *him* a copy, but you might have sent *me* one also.
' For I so delight in your love, that I am jealous when
' I see you more mindful of others than of myself.

  ' That book did, however, after all come into my
' hands first. I read it through before it was handed
' to the bishop.

  ' I dare not express an opinion on this book. I am
' conscious of my own ignorance, and how blind I am
' in matters so mysterious, and in the works (opibus—
' *operibus ?*) of so great a man. However, in reading
' it, the chief miracles seemed to me to lie more in
' the words than the things ; for, according to him,
' Hebrew words seem to have no end of mystery in
' their characters and combinations.

  ' O Erasmus ! of books and of knowledge there is
' no end. There is no thing better for *us* in this
' short life than to live holily and purely, and to
' make it our daily care to be purified and enlightened,
' and really to practise what these " Pythagorica " and
' " Cabalistica " of Reuchlin promise ; but, in my
' opinion, there is no other way for us to attain this
' than by the earnest love and imitation of *Jesus.*
' Wherefore leaving these wandering paths, let us go
' the short way to work. I long, to the best of my
' ability, to do so.[1] Farewell.—*From London*, 1517.'

---

[1] ' Sed, meo judicio, nulla via
' assequemur, quam ardenti amore
' et imitatione Jesu. Quare relictis
' ambagibus, ad brevitatem brevi
' compendio eamus : ego pro viri-
' bus volo.' These sentences remind
one of the conversation between
Tauler and Nicholas of Basle, in the
beautiful story of the *Master and
the Man*, where the master says,
' Verum est, charissime fili, quod
' ais. Adhuc enim durior mihi
' videtur esse hic sermo tuus.' And
the layman replies, ' Et tamen ipse
' me rogasti, Domine Magister, ut
' compendiosissimum ad supremam
' hujus vitæ perfectionem iter tibi
' demonstrarem. Et certe securio-
' rem ego, quam sit ista, viam ad
' imitandum exemplar sacratissimæ
' humanitatis Christi nullam novi.'
Thauleri Opera, p. 16. Paris, 1623.

VI. MORE PAYS A VISIT TO COVENTRY (1517 ?).

It chanced about this time that More had occasion to go to Coventry to see a sister of his there.

Coventry was a very nest of religious and monastic establishments. It contained, shut up in its narrow streets, some six thousand souls. On the high ground in the heart of the city the ancient Monastery and Cathedral Church of the monks of St. Benedict lifted their huge piles of masonry above surrounding roofs. By their side, and belonging to the same ancient order, rose into the air like a rocket the beautiful spire of St. Michael's, lightly poised and supported by its four flying buttresses, whilst in the niches of the square tower, from which these were made to spring, stood the carved images of saints, worn and crumbled by a century's storms and hot suns. There, too, almost within a stone's throw of this older and nobler one, and as if faintly striving but failing to outvie it, rose

the rival spires of Trinity Church, and the Church of the Grey Friars of St. Francis ; while in the distance might be seen the square massive tower of the College of Babbelake, afterwards called the Church of St. John ; the Monastery of the Carmelites or White Friars ; and the Charterhouse, where Carthusian monks were supposed to keep strict vigils and fasts in lonely and separate cells. And beneath the shadow of the spire of St. Michael's stood the Hall of St. Mary, chased over with carved work depicting the glory of the Virgin Mother, and covered within by tapestry representing her before the Great Throne of Heaven, the moon under her feet, and apostles and choirs of angels doing her homage. Other hospitals and religious houses which have left no trace behind them, were to be found within the walls of this old city. Far and wide had spread the fame of the annual processions and festivals, pageants and miracle plays, which even royal guests were sometimes known to witness. And from out the babble and confusion of tongues produced by the close proximity of so many rival monastic sects, rose ever and anon the cry for the martyrdom of honest Lollards, in the persecution of whom the Pharisees and Sadducees of Coventry found a temporary point of agreement. It would seem that, not many months after the time of More's visit, *seven* poor gospellers were burned in Coventry for teaching their children the paternoster and ten commandments in their own English tongue.[1]

This was Coventry—its citizens, if not ' wholly given ' up to idolatry,' yet ' in all things too superstitious,' and, like the Athenians of old, prone to run after ' some new thing.' At the time of which we speak, they were the subjects of a strange religious frenzy— a fit of *Mariolatry.*

The doctrine of the Immaculate Conception of the Blessed Virgin had not yet been finally settled. It was the bone of contention between the rival monastic orders. The Franciscans or Grey Friars, following Scotus, waged war with the Dominicans, who followed Aquinas. Pope Sixtus IV. had in 1483 issued a bull favouring the Franciscans and the doctrine of the Immaculate Conception, and Foxe tells us that it was in consequence ' holden in their schools, written in ' their books, preached in their sermons, taught in

---

[1] Foxe, ed. 1597, p. 887.

'their churches, and set forth in their pictures.' On the other side had occurred the tragedy of the weeping image of the Virgin, and the detection and burning of the Dominican monks who were parties to the fraud.

It chanced that in Coventry a Franciscan monk made bold to preach publicly to the people, that *whoever should daily pray through the Psalter of the Blessed Virgin could never be damned.* The regular pastor of the place, thinking that it would soon blow over, and that a little more devotion to the Virgin could do no harm, took little notice of it at first. But when he saw the worst men were the most religious in their devotion to the Virgin's Psalter, and that, relying on the friar's doctrine, they were getting more and more bold in crime, he mildly admonished the people from his pulpit not to be led astray by this new doctrine. The result was he was hissed at, derided, and publicly slandered as an enemy of the Virgin. The friar again mounted his pulpit, recounted miraculous stories in favour of his creed, and carried the people away with him.

More shall tell the rest in his own words :—

' While this frenzy was at its height, it so happened
' that I had to go to Coventry to visit a sister of mine
' there. I had scarcely alighted from my horse when
' I was asked the question, " Whether a person who
' " daily prayed through the Psalter of the Blessed
' " Virgin could be damned ? " I laughed at the ques-
' tion as absurd. I was told forthwith that my answer
' was a dangerous one. A most holy and learned
' father had declared the contrary. I put by the whole
' affair as no business of mine. Soon after I was asked
' to supper. I promised, and went. Lo and behold !

' in came an old, stooping, heavy, crabbed friar ! A
' servant followed with his books. I saw I must
' prepare for a brush. We sat down, and lest any
' time should be lost, the point was at once brought
' forward by our host. The friar made answer as he
' already had preached. I held my tongue, not
' liking to mix myself up in fruitless and provoking
' disputations. At last they asked me what view I
' took of it. And when I was obliged to speak, I
' spoke what I thought, but in few words and off-hand.
' Upon this the friar began a long premeditated
' oration, long enough for at least two sermons, and
' bawled all supper time. He drew all his argument
' from the miracles, which he poured out upon us in
' numbers enough from the " Marial ; " and then from
' other books of the same kind, which he ordered to
' be put on the table, he drew further authority for
' his stories. Soon after he had done I modestly
' began to answer ; first, that in all his long discourse
' he had said nothing to convince those who perchance
' did not admit the miracles which he had recited,
' and *this might well be, and a man's faith in Christ be*
' *firm notwithstanding.* And even if these were mostly
' true, they proved nothing of any moment ; for
' though you might easily find a prince who would con-
' cede something to his enemies at the entreaty of his
' mother, yet never was there one so foolish as to
' publish a law which should provoke daring against
' him by the promise of impunity to all traitors who
' should perform certain offices to his mother.
' Much having being said on both sides, I found
' that he was lauded to the skies while I was laughed
' at as a fool. The matter came at last to that pass,

E E

' by the depraved zeal of men who cloaked their own
' vices under colour of piety, that the opinion could
' hardly be put down, though the Bishop with all his
' energy tried all the means in his power to do so.' [1]

---

[1] Thomæ Mori ad Monachum
Epistola. *Epistolæ aliquot Eruditorum Virorum* : Basle, 1520, pp.
128, 129. The letter does not state
exactly the date of this singular
occurrence.

CHAPTER XIV.

I. THE SALE OF INDULGENCES (1517–18).

WHILE Erasmus in 1517 was hard at work at the revision of his New Testament, publishing the first instalment of his Paraphrases,[1] recommending the 'Utopia' and the 'Christian Prince' to the perusal of princes and their courtiers,[2] expressing to his friends at the Papal Court his trust that under Leo X. Rome herself might become the centre of peace and religion,[3]—while Erasmus was thus working on hopefully, preparing the way, as he thought, for a peaceful reform, Europe was suddenly brought, by the scandalous conduct of princes and the Pope, to the very brink of revolution.

Leo X. was in want of money. He had no scruple to tax the Christian world for selfish family purposes any more than his predecessors in the Papal chair; but times had altered, and he thought it prudent, instead of doing so openly, to avoid scandal, by cloaking his crime in double folds of imposture and deception. It mattered little that a few shrewd men might suspect the dishonesty of the pretexts put forth, if

---

[1] *On the Romans*: 'Louvain, 1517, at the press of Martins.

[3] Erasmus to Cope, ccv. Brewer, ii. p. 2962. See also cciii. and cciv. and Erasmus to Henry VIII.

cclxviii.

[3] Erasmus to Cardinal Grymanus, prefixed to the *Paraphrases on the Romans*. Dated, Id. Nov. 1517.

CHAP.
XIV.
———
A.D. 1517.
Tenths
and in-
dulgences.

only the multitude could be sufficiently deluded to make them part with their money.

A war against the Turks could be proposed and abandoned the moment the 'tenths' demanded to pay its expenses were safe in the Papal exchequer. If *indulgences* were granted to all who should contribute towards the building of St. Peter's at Rome, the profits could easily be devoted to more pressing uses. So, in the spring of 1517, the payment of a tenth was demanded from all the clergy of Europe, and commissions were at the same time issued for the sale of indulgences to the laity. Some opposition was to be expected from disaffected princes ; but experience on former occasions had proved that these would be easily bribed to connive at any exactions from their subjects by the promise of a share in the spoil.[1]

Hence the project seemed to the Papal mind justified on Machiavellian principles, and, judged by the precedents of the past, likely to succeed.

But the seeds of opposition to Machiavellian projects of this kind had recently been widely sown. More in his ' Utopia,' and Erasmus in his ' Christian ' Prince,' had only a few months before spoken plain words to people and princes on taxation and unjust exactions. Erasmus, too, in his ' Praise of Folly,' had spoken contemptuously of the *crime of false pardons*, in other words, of Papal *indulgences*.[2] And though Lystrius, in his recent marginal note on this passage,

---

[1] Mountjoy to Wolsey: Brewer, ii. p. 1259 ; and Bishop of Worcester to Wolsey: ibid. No. 4179. Ranke's *Hist. of the Reformation*, bk. ii. chap. 1.

[2] One early edition, without date, has in the margin, ' Fictæ pontifi-

' cum condonationes vel indulgen-' tiæ ;' and Lystrius, in his note on this passage, says ' Has vulgo ' vocant indulgentias.' The marginal note in the Argent. edition of 1511 reads ' indulgentias taxat.'

had explained that Papal indulgences are not included
in this sweeping censure, ' *unless they be false,* it being
' no part of our business to dispute of the pontifical
' power,' yet he had almost made matters worse by
adding :—

   ' This one thing I know, that what Christ promised
' concerning the remission of sins is more certain than
' what is promised by men, especially since this whole
' affair [of indulgences] is of recent date and inven-
' tion.   Finally a great many people, relying on these
' pardons, are encouraged in crime, and never think
' of changing their lives.' [1]

   How eagerly the ' Praise of Folly ' was bought and
read by the people has already been seen.   New editions had recently been exceedingly numerous, for
the notes of Lystrius had opened the eyes of many
who had not fully caught its drift before.   An edition
in French had moreover appeared, and (Erasmus
wrote) it was thereby made intelligible even to monks,
who hitherto had been too deeply drowned in sensual
indulgence to care anything about it, whose ignorance
of Latin was such that they could not even understand the Psalms, which they were constantly mum-
bling over in a senseless routine.[2]

   Silently and unseen the leaven had been working ;
and when, on October 31, Luther posted up his theses
on the church-door at Wittemberg, defying Tetzel
and his wicked trade, he was but the spokesman,
perhaps unconsciously to himself, of the grumbling
dissent of Europe.

   Discontent against the proceedings of the Papal
Court was not by any means confined to Wittemberg.
It had got wind that the tenths and indulgences were

---

[1] Basle, ed. 1519, p. 141.   [2] Eras. Epist. cclxiv. Aug. 29, 1517.

resorted to for private family purposes of the Pope's ;
that they were part of a system of imposture and deception ; and hence they encountered opposition, political as well as religious, in more quarters than one.

Unhappily, the Pope had reckoned with reason on
the connivance of princes. Their exchequers were
more than usually empty, and they had proved for
the most part glad enough to sell their consciences,
and the interests of their subjects, at the price of a
share in the spoil. Had it been otherwise the Papal
collectors would have been forbidden entrance into
the dominions of many a prince besides Frederic of

Saxony ! The Pope offered Henry VIII. a fourth of
the moneys received from the sale of indulgences in
England, and the English Ambassador suggested that
one-third would be a reasonable proportion.[1] When
in December 1515 the Pope had asked for a tenth
from the English clergy, he had found it needful to
abate his demand by one-half, and even this was refused by Convocation on the ground that they had
already paid six-tenths to enable the King to defend
the patrimony of St. Peter, and that the victories of
Henry VIII. had removed all dangers from the Roman
See ; [2] and no sooner was there any talk of the new
tenth of 1517, than the Papal collector in England
was immediately sworn, probably as a precautionary
measure, not to send any money to Rome.[3] Prince
Charles, in anticipation of the amount to be collected
in his Spanish dominions, obtained a loan of 175,000
ducats. The King of France made a purse for him-

---

[1] Bishop of Worcester to Wolsey : Brewer, ii. p. 4179.

[2] Papers relating to the Convocation : Brewer, ii. p. 1312.

[3] Ranke's *History of the Reformation,* London, 1845, i. p. 333.
Brewer, ii. p. 3160 and 3688.

self out of the collections in France,[1] and by the Pope's express orders paid over a part of what was left direct to the Pope's nephew Lorenzo,[2] for whom it was rumoured in select circles that the money was required. The Elector of Maintz also received a share of the spoil taken from his subjects.[3] The Emperor had made common cause with the Pope, in hopes of attaining thereby the realisation of long-indulged dreams of ambition, and all Europe would have been thus bought over ;[4] had not the princes of the empire unexpectedly refused to follow his leading, and to grant any taxes on their subjects without their consent.[5]

These facts will be sufficient to show that the question of Papal taxation was becoming a serious political question. The ascendency of ecclesiastics in the courts of princes had, moreover, again and again been the subject of complaint on the part of the Oxford Reformers. These Papal scandals revealed a state not only of ecclesiastical, but also of political rottenness surpassing anything which had yet been seen. Church and State, the Pope and the Emperor, princes and their ecclesiastical advisers, were seen wedded in an unholy alliance against the rights of the people. Ecclesiastical influence, and the practice of Machiavellian principles, had brought Christendom into a condition of anarchy in which every man's hand was against his neighbour. The politics of Europe were in greater confusion than ever. Not only was the Emperor in league with the Pope against the interests of Europe, but he was obtaining money from England

CHAP.
XIV.

A.D. 1517.

Opposition of German princes.

Political condition of Europe.

---

[1] Brewer, ii. p. 3818, and preface, ccv.

[2] Ranke, p. 332.

[3] Ibid. p. 333.

[4] Ibid. p. 350.

[5] Ibid. p. 356.

under the pretext of siding with England against France and Prince Charles, while he was at the same moment making a secret treaty with France and preparing the way for the succession of Charles to the empire. The three young and aspiring princes— Henry, Francis, and Charles—were eyeing one another with shifting suspicions, and jealously plotting against one another in the dark. Europe in the meantime was kept in a chronic state of warfare. Scotland was kept by France always on the point of quarrelling

Political scandals.

with England. The Duke of Gueldres and his ' black ' band ' were committing cruel depredations in the Netherlands to the destruction of the peace and prosperity of an industrious people.[1] Franz von Sickingen was engaged in what those who suffered from it spoke of as ' inhuman private warfare.' [2] Such was the state of Germany, that, to quote the words of Ranke, ' there was hardly a part of the country which ' was not either distracted by private wars, troubled ' by internal divisions, or terrified by the danger of ' an attack from some neighbouring power.' [3] The administration of civil and criminal law was equally bad. Again, to quote from the same historian, ' The ' criminal under ban found shelter and protection ; ' and as the other courts of justice were in no better ' condition—in all, incapable judges, impunity for ' misdoers, and abuses without end—disquiet and ' tumult had broken out in all parts. Neither by land ' nor water were the ways safe : . . . the husband- ' man, by whose labours all classes were fed, was ' ruined ; widows and orphans were deserted ; not a

---

[1] Erasmus to Beatus Rhenanus : Epist. clxiv. App. Brewer, ii. p. 3614. Ranke, p. 378.

[2] Ranke, pp. 239 and 379.
[3] Ibid. p. 35.

' pilgrim or a messenger or a tradesman could travel
' along the roads . . . . ' [1] Such, according to Ranke,
were the complaints of the German people in the Diet
of Maintz in 1517, and the Diet separated without
even suggesting a remedy.[2]

It was from a continent thus brought, by the madness of the Pope and princes, to the very brink of
both a civil and a religious revolution, that Erasmus
looked longingly to England as ' out of the world, and
' perhaps the least corrupted portion of it ' [3]—as that
retreat in which, after one more journey southwards,
to print the second edition of his New Testament and
' some other works,' he hoped at length to spend his
declining years in peaceful retirement.   The following
portion of a letter to Colet will also show how fully
he saw through the policy of Leo X., hated the madness of princes, and shared the indignation of Luther
at the sale of indulgences.

Erasmus meditates a journey southward, and then returning to England.

Erasmus to Colet.

' I am obliged, in order to print the New Testament
' and some other books, to go either to Basle, or, more
' probably, I think, to *Venice :* for I am deterred from
' Basle partly by the plague and partly by the death
' of Lachnerus, whose pecuniary aid was almost indis-
' pensable to the work.   " What," you will say, " are
' " you, an old man, in delicate health, going to un-
' " dertake so laborious a journey !—in these times,
' " too, than which none worse have been seen for
' " six hundred years ; while everywhere lawless rob-
' " bery abounds ! "   But why do you say so ?   I was

---

[1] Ranke, p. 239.
[2] Ibid. p. 241.

[3] Erasmus to Fisher: cccvi. App.
Brewer, ii. p. 3989.

' *born* to this fate ; if I *die*, I die in a work which,
' unless I am mistaken, is not altogether a bad one.
' But if, this last stroke of my work being accom-
' plished according to my intention, I should chance
' to return, I have made up my mind to spend the re-
' mainder of my life with you, in retirement from a
' world which is everywhere rotten. Ecclesiastical

Erasmus
on indul-
gences.

' hypocrites rule in the courts of princes. The court
' of Rome clearly has lost all sense of shame ; for *what*
' *could be more shameless than these continued indul-*
' *gences ?* Now a war against the Turks is put forth

He sees
through
the Pope's
pretexts.

' as a pretext, when the real purpose is to drive the
' Spaniards from Naples ; for Lorenzo, the Pope's
' nephew, who has married the daughter of the King
' of Navarre, lays claim to Campania. If these tur-
' moils continue, the rule of the Turks would be easier
' to bear than that of these Christians.' [1]

Erasmus wrote to Warham in precisely the same
strain,[2] and shortly afterwards, on March 5, 1518, in
a letter to More, he exclaimed, ' The Pope and some
' princes are playing a fresh game under the pretext
' of a horrid war against the Turks. Oh, wretched
' Turks ! unless this is too much like bluster on the

' Julius
de Cœlo
exclusus.'

' part of us Christians.' And he added, ' They write
' to me from Cologne that a book has been printed by
' somebody, describing "Pope Julius disputing with
' "Peter at the gate of paradise." The author's
' name is not mentioned. The German press will not
' cease to be violent until some law shall restrain their

---

[1] Eras. Epist. App. cccv. Brewer,
ii. p. 3992.

[2] Eras. Epist. App. cclxix.

'boldness, to the detriment also of us, who are labour-
'ing to benefit mankind.'[1]

This satire, entitled ' Julius de Cœlo exclusus,' was
eagerly purchased and widely read,[2] and was one of
a series of satirical pamphlets upon the Papacy and
the policy of the Papal party, for which the way had
been prepared by the ' Praise of Folly ' and the
' Epistolæ Obscurorum Virorum.' It was one of the
signs of the times.

II. MORE DRAWN INTO THE SERVICE OF HENRY VIII.— ERASMUS LEAVES GERMANY FOR BASLE (1518).

It was at this juncture—at this crisis it may well be
called—in European politics, that More was induced
at length, by the earnest solicitations of Henry VIII.,
to attach himself to his court under circumstances
which deserve attention.

In the spring of 1517, a frenzy more dangerous than
that in which the men of Coventry indulged had seized
the London apprentices. Not wholly without excuse,
they had risen in arms against the merchant strangers,
who were very numerous in London, and to some of
whom commercial privileges and licenses had, perhaps,
been too freely granted by a minister anxious to increase his revenue. Thus had resulted the riots of
' the evil May-day,' and More had some part to play
in the restoration of order in the city.

Then, in August 1517, he was sent on an embassy
to Calais with Wingfield and Knight. Their mission
ostensibly was to settle disputes between French and

'Evil
May-day.'

More's
embassy
to Calais.

---

[1] Epist. App. cclxv. Brewer, ii.
p. 3991.

[2] Ægidius to Erasmus: Epist.
ccccxxxvi. Brewer, ii. p. 4238.

English merchants, but probably its real import was quite as much to pave the way for more important negotiations.

No sooner had English statesmen opened their eyes to the fact that Maximilian had been playing into the hands of the French King against the interests of England, than, with the natural perversity of men who had no settled principles to guide their international policy, they began themselves, out of sheer jealousy, once more to court the favour of the sovereign against whom they had so long been fruitlessly plotting. They began secretly to seek to bring about a French alliance with England, which should out-manœuvre the recent treaty of the Emperor with France. Thus, by a sudden and unlooked-for turn in continental politics, was brought about the curious fact that, within a few months of the publication of the ' Utopia,' in which More had advocated such a policy, the surrender of Henry's recent conquests in France was under discussion. By February in the following year (1518) not only was Tournay restored to France, but a marriage had been arranged between the infant Dauphin of France and the infant Princess Mary of England. This of course involved the abandonment, at all events for a time, of Henry's personal claims on the crown of France.[1] What share More had in the conversion of the King to this new policy remains untold ; but it is remarkable that within so short a time his Utopian counsels should have been so far practically followed, and that he himself should have been chosen as one of the ambassadors to Calais to prepare the way for it.

It would be impossible here to enter into a detailed

Henry
VIII.
meditates
giving up
his French
conquests.

---

[1] See Brewer's preface to vol. ii. pp. cxlvii-clvii.

examination of the political relations of England;
suffice it to say, that a pacific policy seems to have
gained the upper hand for the moment, and that even
Wolsey himself seems to have admitted the necessity
of so far following More's Utopian counsels as to cut
down the annual expenditure of the kingdom, and
to husband her resources.[1]

It may have been only a momentary lull in the
King's stormy passion for war, but it lasted long
enough to admit of the renewal of the King's endeavours to draw More into his service, and of More's
yielding at last to Royal persuasions.

Roper tells us that the immediate occasion of his
doing so was the great ability shown by him in the
conduct of a suit respecting a ' great ship ' belonging
to the Pope, which the King claimed for a forfeiture.
In connection with which, Roper tells us that More, ' in
' defence on the Pope's side, argued so learnedly, that
' both was the aforesaid forfeiture restored to the
' Pope, and himself among all the hearers, for his
' upright and commendable demeanour therein, so
' greatly renowned that for no entreaty would the
' King from henceforth be induced any longer to
' forbear his service.' [2]

What passed between the King and his new courtier
on this occasion, and upon what conditions More
yielded to the King's entreaties, Roper does not mention in this connection; but that he maintained his
independence of thought and action, may be inferred
from the fact that eighteen years after, when in peril of
his life from Royal displeasure, he had occasion upon
his knees to remind his sovereign of ' the most godly
' words that his Highness spake unto him at his first

---

[1] See Brewer, ii. cxlii–clxi (preface).　　[2] Roper, p. 11.

' coming into his noble service—the most virtuous
' lesson that ever a prince taught his servant—willing
' him *first to look to God, and after God unto him !* ' [1]

Now that Henry VIII. had apparently changed his
policy, now that he was giving up his pretensions to
the crown of France, and no longer talking of invading
her shores, now that he seemed to be calling to his
counsels the very man who, next to Colet, had spoken
more plainly than anyone else in condemnation of
that warlike policy in which Henry VIII. had so long
indulged, now that Henry VIII. himself seemed to be
returning to his first love of letters and the ' new
' learning,' the hopes of Erasmus began once more to
rely upon *him* rather than upon any other of the
princes of Europe.   Erasmus had lost his confidence
in Leo X.   Prince Charles was now going to Spain,
leaving the Netherlands in a state of confusion and
anarchy, a prey to the devastations of the ' black
' band,' and for the present little could reasonably be
expected from him, notwithstanding all the good advice Erasmus had given him in the ' Christian Prince.'

While Henry VIII. had been wild after military
glory, and had seemed ready to sacrifice everything
to this dominant passion, Erasmus had thought it
useless to waste words upon him which he would not
heed ; but the war being over in September 1517, he
had sent him a copy of the ' Christian Prince,' and encouraged his royal endeavours to still the tempests
which during the past few years had so violently raged
in human affairs.   Nor is it without significance that

Henry
VIII. rises
again in
the favour
of Eras-
mus.

---

[1] Roper, p. 48.

in this letter to Henry VIII. we find him using warm words in commendation of a trait of the King's character, which Erasmus said he admired above all others; viz. this,—that he delighted 'in the converse of 'prudent and learned men, *especially of those who did* 'not know how to speak just what they thought would 'please.' [1]

Under other circumstances such words written to Henry VIII. might have seemed like satire or perhaps empty adulation, but written as they were while Henry was as yet unsuccessfully trying to induce More to enter his service, and only a few months after the publication of the ' Utopia,' they do not read like words of flattery.

When in writing to Fisher he had spoken of England as ' out of the world, or perhaps the least corrupted ' portion of it,' he had honestly expressed his real feelings at a time when, whilst continental affairs were in hopeless confusion and anarchy, there were at least some hopeful symptoms that a better policy would be adopted for the future by Henry VIII.

It was strictly in accordance with the same feelings that, on hearing that More had yielded to the King's wishes, he wrote to him on April 24, 1518, not to congratulate him on the step he had taken, but to tell him that the only thing which consoled him in regard to it was the consideration that he would serve under ' the best of kings.' And from this remark he passed by a natural train of thought to speak of the dangers which would attend his own projected journey southwards through Germany, and bitterly to allude to the ' *novel clemency* ' of the Dukes of Cleves, Juliers, and

---

[1] Epist. cclxviii.

Nassau, who had been secretly conspiring to disperse in safety the ' black band ' of political ruffians, at whose depredations they had too long connived. Had their scheme been successful, it would have cast loose these lawless ruffians upon society without even the control of their robber leaders. But, as it was, the people took the matter into their own hands, and disconcerted the conspiracy of their princes. The peasantry, exasperated by constant depredations, and thirsting for the destruction of the robbers, had risen in a body and surrounded them. A chance blast from a trumpet had revealed their whereabouts, and in the *mêlée* which followed, more than a thousand were cut to pieces ; the rest escaped to continue their work of plunder.[1] It was not remarkable if, living in the midst of anarchy such as this, Erasmus should envy the comparative security of England, and even for the moment be inclined to praise the harsh justice with which English robbers, instead of being secretly protected and encouraged, were sent to the gallows.[2]

Erasmus
going to
Basle.

Erasmus had decided upon going to Basle, and in writing to Beatus Rhenanus [3] to inform him that he intended to do so in the course of the summer, ' if it ' should be safe to travel through Germany,' he spoke of the condition of Germany as ' *worse than that of the* ' *infernal regions,*' on account of the numbers of robbers ; and asked what princes could be about to allow such a state of things to exist.

' All sense of shame,' he wrote, ' has vanished alto-

---

[1] Epist. App. cccxi. and cclxxxii.
Brewer, ii. p. 4111.
[2] Erasmus to Henry VIII. :

Brewer, iii. No. 226.
[3] March 13, 1518. Eras. Epist.
App. cclxxiv. Brewer, ii. p. 4005.

' gether from human affairs. I see that the very
' height of tyranny has been reached. The Pope and
' kings count the people not as men, but *as cattle in the*
' *market.*'

Once more, on May 1, Erasmus wrote to Colet
before leaving for Basle, to tell him that he really
was going, in spite of the dangers of travel through
a country full of disbanded ruffians ; to complain of
the cruel clemency of princes who spare scoundrels
and cut-throats, and yet do not spare their own subjects, to whom those who oppress their people are
dearer than the people themselves ; and to reiterate
his intention to fly back to his English friends as
soon as his work at Basle should be accomplished.
And then he ventured on the journey.[1]

Erasmus
leaves
Louvain
for Basle.

---

[1] Epist. ccxlvii. Brewer, ii. p. 4138.   Eras. Epist. Basle, 1521, p. 217.

CHAPTER XV.

I. ERASMUS ARRIVES AT BASLE—HIS LABOURS THERE (1518).

Erasmus reaches Basle and falls ill.

His reply to Dr. Eck.

Erasmus arrived at Basle on Ascension Day, May 13, 1518.[1]

But though he had escaped the robbers, and survived the toils of the journey, he reached Basle in a state of health so susceptible of infection, that, in the course of a day or two, he found himself laid up with that very disease which he had mentioned in his letter to Colet as prevalent at Basle, and as one great reason why he had shrunk from going there.[2]

But even an attack of this 'plague' did not prevent him from beginning his work at once.

Whilst suffering from its early symptoms, during intervals of pain and weakness,[3] he wrote a careful reply to a letter he had received from Dr. Eck, Professor of the University of Ingolstadt in Bavaria, complaining, as Luther had already done, indirectly through Spalatin, of the anti-Augustinian proclivities of the 'Novum Instrumentum.'[4]

Luther and Eck had already had communications

---

[1] Eras. Epist. App. cclxxxiv.–v.
[2] Ibid. App. cccv.
[3] Eras. Op. iii. 401 E.
[4] Eras. Epist. ccciii. first printed in *Auctarium selectarum Epistolarum Erasmi, &c.* Basle, 1518, p. 39.

on theological subjects. The Wittemberg theologian
had sent to his Ingolstadt brother for his approval,
through a mutual friend, a set of propositions aimed
against the Pelagian tendencies of the times.[1]

But Eck and Luther, whilst both admirers of
St. Augustine, and both jealous of Erasmus and his
anti-Augustinian proclivities, rested their objections
on somewhat different grounds.

Luther looked coldly on the ' Novum Instrumentum ' mainly because he thought he found in its
doctrinal statements traces of Pelagian heresy. Dr.
Eck objected not so much to any error in doctrine Dr. Eck
which it might contain, as *to the method of Biblical criti-* holds to
plenary in-
cism which it adopted throughout. He objected to the spiration.
suggestion it contained, that the Apostles quoted the
Old Testament from memory, and, therefore, not
always correctly. He objected to the insinuation that
their Greek was colloquial, and not strictly classical.

With regard to the first point, he referred to the
well-known, and, as he thought, ' most excellent
' argument of St. Augustine ' against the admission of
any error in the Scriptures, lest the authority of the
whole should be lost. And with regard to the second,
he charged Erasmus with making himself a preceptor
to the Holy Spirit, as though the Holy Spirit had been
wanting in attention or learning, and required the
defects resulting from his negligence to be now, after
so many centuries, supplied by Erasmus.

He made these criticisms, he wrote, not in the spirit
of opposition, but because he could not agree with the
preference shown by Erasmus to Jerome over Augustine. It was the one point in which the Erasmian

---

[1] Luther's *Briefe.* De Wette. Epist. No. xxxvii.

creed was at fault. Nearly all the learned world was Erasmian already, but this one thing all Erasmians complained of in Erasmus—that he would not study the works of St. Augustine. If he would but do this, Eck was sure he would acknowledge that it would be rash indeed to assign to St. Augustine any other than the highest place amongst the fathers of the Church.[1]

Reply of Erasmus.

Erasmus replied [2] to the first objection, that, in his judgment, the authority of the whole Scriptures would *not* fall with any slip of memory on the part of an Evangelist—*e.g.* if he put ' Isaiah ' by mistake for ' Jeremiah '—because no point of importance turns upon it. We do not forthwith think evil of the whole life of Peter because Augustine and Ambrose affirm that even after he had received the Holy Ghost he fell into error on some points ; and so our faith is not altogether shaken in a whole book because it has some defects.

With regard to the colloquial Greek of the Apostles, he took the authority of Jerome, and Origen, and the Greek fathers as good evidence on that point.

With respect to his preference for Jerome over Augustine, he knew what he was about. His preference for Jerome was deliberate, and rested on good grounds. When he came to the passage in Eck's letter, where he stated that all Erasmians complained of his one fault—not reading Augustine—he could not read it without laughing. ' I know of nothing in ' me,' he wrote, ' why anyone should wish to be *Eras-* ' *mian,* and I altogether hate that term of division. ' We are all *Christians,* and labour, each in his own

---

[1] Eras. Epist. ccciii.

[2] Epist. ccclxxvi. dated May 15, 1518, and first printed at p. 45 of the *Auctarium selectarum Episto- larum, &c.* Basle, 1518.

' sphere, to advance the glory of Christ.' But that he had not read the works of Augustine ! Why, they were the very first that he did read of the writings of the fathers. He had read them over and over again. Let his critics examine his works, they would find that there was scarcely a work of St. Augustine which was not there quoted many hundred times. Let him compare Augustine and Jerome on their merits. Jerome was a pupil of Origen, and one page of Origen teaches more Christian philosophy than ten of Augustine. Augustine scarcely knew Greek ; at all events was not at home in Greek writers. Besides this, by his own confession, he was busied with his bishopric, and could hardly snatch time to learn what he taught to others. Jerome devoted *thirty-five years* to the study of the Scriptures.

In the meantime, in conclusion, he observed that the difference of opinion between himself and Eck upon these points need not interrupt their friendship, any more than the difference of opinion upon the same point between Jerome and Augustine interrupted theirs.

Having despatched this reply to Eck, and recovered from what proved a short but sharp attack of illness, Erasmus wrote to More on the 1st of June ·to advise him of his safe arrival at Basle, of his illness and recovery, and to express the hope that a few months would see his labours there accomplished. If the Fates were propitious, he hoped to return to Brabant in September.[1]

What were the works which he had come to Basle to publish during these tumultuous times ?

[1] Erasmus to More, App. cclxxxv. Brewer, ii. p. 4204 ; and in App. cclxxxiv. Ibid. ii. p. 4203.

CHAP. XV.

A.D. 1518.

New
editions of
works of
Erasmus.

The second edition of the New Testament will
require a separate notice by-and-by. A new and
corrected edition of More's 'Utopia' was already in
hand, and waiting only for a letter which Budæus
was writing to be prefixed to it.[1] A new edition of
the 'Institutio Principis Christiani' was also to come
forth from the press of Froben.[2]

It might seem hopeless to put forth works such as
these, expressing views so far in advance of the practices of the times, but the fact that new editions were
so rapidly called for proved that they were eagerly
read. In the same letter in which Erasmus ridiculed
to More the projected expedition against the Turks,
and spoke of the violence of the German press and
the satire which had just appeared, '*Julius de Cœlo
'exclusus,*' he spoke of his having seen another edition
of the 'Utopia' just printed at Paris.[3]

In the previous year, 1517, Froben had printed a
sixth edition of the 'Adagia,' which had now expanded
into a thick folio volume, and become a receptacle for
the views of Erasmus on many chance subjects. In
this edition he had expressed his indignant feelings
against the political anarchy and Papal scandals of
the period, and he told More to look particularly at
what he had written on the adage, '*Ut fici oculis in-
'cumbunt;*'[4] in which was an allusion to the 'insatiable
'avarice, unbridled lust, most pernicious cruelty, and
'great tyranny' of princes ; and to the evil influence
of those ecclesiastics who, ever ready to do the dirty

---

[1] Brewer, ii. p. 3991. Eras. Epist.
App. cclxv.

[2] *Lucubrationum Erasmi Index :*
Frobenius, Basle, 1519.

[3] Epist. cclxv. App. Brewer, ii.
p. 3991. Dated March 5, 1518.

[4] Eras. Epist. App. cccxi.
Brewer, ii. p. 4110.

work of princes and popes, abetted and mixed themselves up with the worst scandals.[1] And again it is remarkable to find how rapidly this ponderous edition of the ' Adagia ' must have been sold to admit of another following in 1520, still further increased in bulk—a large folio volume of nearly 800 pages.

In addition to these reprints, two separate collections of some of his letters were printed by Froben in 1518,[2] evidently intended to aid in spreading more widely those plain-spoken views on various subjects which he had expressed in his private letters to his friends during the last few years. Another edition was also called for of the ' Enchiridion ; ' and Erasmus, on his arrival at Basle, burning as well he might with increased indignation against the scandals of the times, wrote a new preface, in the form of a letter to Volzius, the Abbot of a monastery at Schelestadt— a letter which, containing in almost every line of it pointed allusion to passing events, was eagerly devoured by thinking men all over Europe, and passed through several editions in a very short space of time.

Collections of letters printed.

Letter to Volzius.

It was a letter in which he repeated the conviction which he had learned twenty years before from Colet, that the true Christian creed was exceedingly simple, adapted not for the learned alone, but for *all* men.

---

[1] *Adagia* : Basle, 1520–21, p. 494. I have not seen the edition of 1517, but it is mentioned in *Lucubrationum Erasmi Index* ; Basle, 1519.

[2] *Auctarium selectarum aliquot Epistolarum Erasmi*, &c. : Basle, with preface by Beatus Rhenanus, dated xi. Calendas Septembris, 1518, and ' *Aliquot Epistolæ sane*

' *quam elegantes Erasmi Rotero-* ' *dami, et ad hunc aliorum eruditis-* ' *simorum hominum.*' Basle, Jan. 1518. The latter includes Colet's letter to Erasmus on the *Novum Instrumentum.* An edition, containing some of the letters of Erasmus and others, had also been printed by Martins at Louvain in April 1517.

And upon this ground he defended the simplicity of his little handy-book, contrasting it with the ' *Summa* ' of Aquinas. ' Let the great doctors, which ' must needs be but few in comparison with other men, ' study and busy themselves in those great volumes.' The ' unlearned and rude multitude, which Christ died ' for, ought to be provided for also.' ' Christ would ' that the way should be plain and open to every man,' and therefore, we ourselves ought to endeavour, with all ' our strength to make it as easy as can be.' [1]

He then alluded to the war against the Turks, and hinted that it would be better to try to convert them. Do we wonder, he urged, that Christianity does not spread? that we cannot convert the Turks? What is the use of laying before them the ponderous tomes of the Schoolmen, full of ' thorny and cumbrous and ' inextricably subtle imaginations of instants, form-' alities, quiddities,' and the like ? We ought to place before them the simple philosophy of Christ contained in the *Gospels* and *Apostolic Epistles*, simplifying even their phraseology; giving them in fact the pith of them *in as simple and clear a form as possible.* And of what use would even this be if our lives belied our creed ? They must see that we ourselves are servants and imitators of Jesus Christ, that we do not covet anything of theirs for ourselves, but that we desire their salvation and the glory of Christ. This was the true, pure, and powerful theology which in olden time subjected to Christ the pride of philosophers and the sceptres of kings.

Erasmus then, after a passing censure of the scan-dals brought upon Christianity by the warlike policy

---

[1] English translation. London : Jno. Byddell, 1522.

of priests and princes, the sale of indulgences, and so CHAP. XV.
forth, proceeded to criticise the religion of modern A.D. 1518.
monks, their reliance on ceremonies, their degeneracy,
and worldliness.

' . . . Once the monastic life was a *retreat* or *retire-*
' *ment* from the world, of men who were called out of
' idolatry to Christ : now those who are called monks
' are found in the very vortex of worldly business,
' exercising a sort of tyrannical rule over the affairs
' of men.   They alone are holy, other men are scarcely
' Christians.   *Why should we thus narrow the Christian*
' *profession, when Christ wished it to be as broad as pos-*
' *sible?* [1]   Except the big name, what is a *state* but one
' great monastery ?   Let no one despise another
' because his manner of life is different. . . .   In every
' path of life let all strive to attain to the mind of
' Christ [*scopum Christi*].   Let us assist one another,
' neither envying those who surpass us, nor despising
' those who may lag behind.   And if anyone should
' excel another, let him beware lest he be like the
' Pharisee in the Gospel, who recounted his good deeds
' to God ; rather let him follow the teaching of Christ,
' and say " I am an unprofitable servant."   No one
' more truly has faith than he who distrusts himself.
' No one is really further from true religion than he
' who thinks himself most religious.   Nothing is worse
' for Christian piety than for what is really of the
' world to be misconstrued to be of Christ—for
' human authority to be preferred to Divine.' [2]

It was a letter firm and calm in its tone, and well

---

[1] ' Cur sic arctamus Christi pro-
' fessionem quam ille latissime-
' voluit patere ? '

[2] These passages are condensed
in the translation.

adapted to the end in view. It was dated from Basle, in August 1518.

The ' Enchiridion,' with this prefatory letter, was published in September, together with some minor works, amongst which was the ' Discussion on the ' Agony in the Garden,' including Colet's reply, in which he had expressed his views on the theory of the ' manifold senses ' of Scripture, the whole forming an elegant quarto volume printed in the very best type of Froben. Another beautiful edition was published at Cologne in the following year.

II. THE SECOND EDITION OF THE NEW TESTAMENT (1518–19).

The time had come for Erasmus more fully and publicly to reply to the various attacks which had been made upon the ' Novum Instrumentum.'

Its most bitter opponents had been the ignorant Scotists and monks who were caricatured in the ' Epistolæ Obscurorum Virorum.' ' There are none,' wrote Erasmus to a friend, ' who bark at me more ' furiously than they who have never seen even the ' outside of my book. Try the experiment upon any ' of them, and you will find what I tell you is true. ' When you meet any one of these brawlers, let him ' rave on at my New Testament till he has made him- ' self hoarse and out of breath, then ask him gently ' whether he has read it. If he have the impudence ' to say " *yes*," urge him to produce one passage that ' deserves to be blamed. You will find that he ' cannot.' [1]

---

[1] Erasmus to Laurinus : Epist. ccclvi. See Jortin, i, 140.

To opponents such as these, Erasmus has sufficiently replied by the re-issue of the ' Enchiridion '
with the new prefatory letter to Volzius.

But there was another class of objectors to the
' Novum Instrumentum ' who were not ignorant and
altogether bigoted, and who honestly differed from
the views of Erasmus ; some of them, like Luther,
because he did not follow the Augustinian theology ;
others, like Eck, who adhered to Augustine's theory of
verbal inspiration ; others, again, who were jealous of
the tendencies of the ' new learning,' and saw covert
heresies in all departures from the beaten track.

The reply of Erasmus to these was a second edition
of his New Testament ; and this was already in course
of publication at Froben's press.[1]

Erasmus took pains in the second edition to correct
an immense number of little errors which had crept
into the first. But in those points in which it was
the expression of the views of the Oxford Reformers,
he altered nothing, unless it were to express them
more clearly and strongly, or to defend what he had
said in the ' Novum Instrumentum.'

Thus the passage condemned by Luther, in which
the resort by theologians to the doctrine of ' original
' sin ' was compared to the invention of epicycles by
mediæval astronomers, was retained in all essential
particulars without modification.[2]

So, too, the passages censured by Eck, as inimical
to the Augustinian theory of the inspiration of the
Scriptures, were not only retained but amplified,
while opportunity was taken to strengthen the argu-

---

[1] The Epistle at the beginning
from Leo X. to Erasmus, bears
date Sept. 1518. March 1519 is
the date printed at the end.
[2] *Novum Testamentum,* 2nd ed,
p. 266.

ments in favour of the freer view of inspiration held by the Oxford Reformers.[1]

Again ; the main drift and spirit of the body of the work remained unchanged. Its title, however, was altered from ' Novum Instrumentum ' to ' Novum ' Testamentum.'

In speaking of the ' Novum Instrumentum ' it was observed, that perhaps the most remarkable portion of the work was the prefatory matter, especially the ' Paraclesis.'

' Para-
clesis.'

This ' Paraclesis ' remained the same in the second edition as in the ' Novum Instrumentum,' including the passages quoted in a former chapter, urging the translation of the New Testament into every language, so that it might become the common property of the ploughman and the mechanic, and even of Turks and Saracens, and ending also with the passage in which Erasmus had so forcibly summed up the value of the Gospels and Epistles, by pointing out how ' living ' and breathing a picture ' they presented of Christ ' speaking, healing, dying, and rising again, bringing ' his life so vividly before the eye, that we almost ' seem to have seen it ourselves.'

Next to the ' Paraclesis,' in the first edition, had followed a few paragraphs treating of the ' method of ' theological study.' This in the second edition was so greatly enlarged as to become an important feature of the work. It was also printed separately, and passed through several editions under the title, ' *Ratio Veræ Theologiæ.*'

' Ratio
Veræ
Theo-
logiæ.'

Erasmus in this treatise pointed out, as he had done before, the great advantages of the study of the New

---

[1] *Novum Testamentum*, pp. 209, 93, 82, 83.

Testament in its original language, and urged that
all branches of knowledge, natural philosophy,
geography, history, classics, mythology, should be
brought to bear upon it, again assigning the reason
which he had before given,—' that we may follow
' the story, and seem not only to read it but to *see*
' it ; for it is wonderful how much light—how much
' *life*, so to speak—is thrown by this method into
' what before seemed dry and lifeless.'

Contrasting the results of this method with that
commonly in use in lectures and sermons, he exclaimed
' How these very things which were meant to warm
' and to enliven, themselves lie cold and without any
' life ! ' And then, to give an example of the true
method, he recommended the student to study the
homily of Origen on ' Abraham commanded to sacri-
' fice his son,' in which a type or example is set before
our eyes, to show that the power of faith is stronger
than all human passions. The object [of Origen] is to
point out, dwelling on each little circumstance, by
what and how many ways the trial struck home over
and over again to the heart of the father. ' Take, he
' said, thy *son*. What parent's heart would not soften
' at the name of son ? But that the sacrifice might
' be still greater, it is added—thy *dearest* son—and
' yet more empathic—*whom thou lovest*. Here, surely,
' was enough for a human heart to grapple with. . . .
' But Isaac was more than merely a son, he was the
' son of promise. The good man longed for posterity,
' and all his hope depended on the life of this one
' child. He was commanded to ascend a high moun-
' tain, and it took him *three days* to get there. During
' all the time, what conflicting thoughts must have
' rent the heart of the parent ! his human affections

' on the one side, the Divine command on the other.
' As they are going, the boy carrying the wood calls
' to his father who bears the fire and the sword,
' " Father ! " and he replies " What dost thou want,
' " my son ? " How must the heart of the old man
' have throbbed with the pulsations of his love! Who
' would not have been moved with loving pity for the
' simplicity of the obedient boy, when he said " Here
' " is the fire and the wood, but where is the victim ? "
' In how many ways was the faith of Abraham tried !
' And now mark with what firmness, with what con-
' stancy, did he go on doing what he was commanded
' to do. He did not reply to God, he did not argue
' with him concerning his promised faithfulness, he did
' not even mourn with his friends and relations over
' his childlessness, as most men would have done to
' lighten their grief. Seeing the place afar off, he told
' his servants to stop, lest any of them should hinder
' his carrying out what was commanded. . . . He
' himself built the altar ; he himself bound the boy and
' put him on the wood ; the sword quivered in his
' grasp, and would have slain his only son, on whom all
' his cherished hope of posterity depended, had not
' suddenly the voice of an angel stayed the old man's
' hand.' [1]

Thus (continued Erasmus), but more at length and
more elegantly, are these things related by Origen,
I hardly know whether more to the pleasure or profit
of the reader ; although, be it observed, they are construed *altogether according to the historical sense* ; nor
does he apply any other method to the Holy Scriptures
than that which Donatus applies to the comedies of
Terence when elucidating the meaning of the classics.

---

[1] *Novum Testamentum*, 2nd ed. pp. 19, 20.

It would almost seem that Erasmus might have read
Luther's letter to Spalatin in which he complained of
St. Jerome's adhering upon principle to the *historical*
sense, and mourned over the tendency he had seen in
Erasmus to follow his example.   Luther spoke of this
literal historical method of interpretation as the reason
why, in the hands of commentators since St. Augustine, the Bible had been a *dead* book.   Erasmus
thought, on the other hand, that the only way to restore the position of the Bible as a *living* book was to
apply to it the same method which common sense
applied to all other books; to resume, in fact, that
literal and historical method which had been neglected
since the days of St. Jerome, and which Origen had so
successfully applied to the story of Abraham in the
passage he had cited.   It is singular also that, in
quoting from Origen this example of the skilful
application of the historical method, he was quoting
from the father whose rich imagination was mainly
responsible for the theory of ' the manifold senses.'

The adoption of the common sense historical method
of interpreting the Scriptures made it possible and
needful to rest faith in Christianity on its own evi-
dences rather than upon the dogmatic authority of the
Church, her fathers, doctors, schoolmen, or councils.
To this Erasmus seems to have been fully alive. He
was not prepared to throw aside the authority of the
general consent of Christians, especially of the early
fathers, as a thing of naught, but he was too conscious
of the fallibility of all such authority to rest wholly
upon it.   Besides, one evident object he had in view
was to gain back again to Christianity those disciples
of the new learning who, in revulsion from

the Christianity of Alexander VI., Cæsar Borgia,
and Julius II., were trying to satisfy themselves
with a refined semi-pagan philosophy. And no
ecclesiastical authority could avail to undo what
ecclesiastical scandal had done in that quarter.

The stress which in this little treatise Erasmus laid
upon internal evidence will be best illustrated by a
few examples.

Take first the following argument for the truth of
Christianity.

He recommends the student ' attentively to observe,
' in both New and Old Testaments, the wonderful
' compass and consistency of the whole story, if I may
' so speak, of Christ becoming a man for our sake.
' This will help us not only more rightly to understand
' what we read, but also to read with greater faith.
' For no *lie* was ever framed with such skill as in
' everything to comport with itself. Compare the
' types and prophecies of the Old Testament which
' foreshadowed Christ, and these same things happen-
' ing as they were revealed to the eye of faith. Next
' to them was the testimony of angels—of Gabriel
' to the Virgin at his conception, and again of a choir
' of angels at his birth. Then came the testimony of
' the shepherds, then that of the Magi, besides that of
' Simeon and Anna. John the Baptist foretold his
' coming. He pointed him out with his finger when
' he came as he whose *coming* the prophets predicted.
' And lest we should not know what to hope for from
' him, he added "Behold him who taketh away the
' " sin of the world ! "   .   .   .

' Next observe the whole course of his life, how he
' grew up to youth, always in favour with both God

'and man. . . . At twelve years of age, teaching and
'listening in the temple, he first gave a glimpse of
'what he was.   Then by his first miracle, at the mar-
'riage feast, in private, he made himself known to a
'few.   For it was not until after he had been baptized
'and commended by the voice of his Father and the
'sign of the dove ; lastly, not until after he had been
'tried and proved by the forty days' fast and the
'temptation of Satan, that he commenced the work
'of *preaching*.   Mark his birth, education, preaching,
'death ; you will find nothing but a perfect example
'of poverty and humility, yea of innocence.   The
'whole range of his doctrine, as it was consistent with
'itself, so it was consistent with his life, and also con-
'sistent with his nature.   He taught innocence ; he
'himself so lived that not even suborned witnesses,
'after trying in many ways to do so, could find any-
'thing that could plausibly be laid to his charge.   He
'taught gentleness : he himself was led as a lamb to the
'slaughter.   He taught poverty, and we do not read
'that he ever possessed anything.   He warned against
'ambition and pride : he himself washed his disciples'
'feet.   He taught that this was the way to true glory
'and immortality : he himself, by the ignominy of the
'cross, has obtained a name which is above every
'name ; and whilst he sought no earthly kingdom, he
'earned the empire both of heaven and earth.   When
'he rose from the dead, he taught what he had taught
'before.   He had taught that death is not to be feared
'by the good, and on that account he showed himself
'risen again.   In the presence of the same disciples he
'ascended into heaven, that we might know whither we
'are to strive to follow.   Lastly, that heavenly Spirit

' descended which by its inspiration made his apostles
' what Christ wished them to be. You may perhaps
' find in the books of Plato or Seneca what is not in-
' consistent with the teaching of Christ ; you may find
' in the life of Socrates some things which are certainly
' consistent with the life of Christ ; but this wide
' range, and all things belonging to it in harmonious
' agreement *inter se*, you will find in *Christ* alone.
' There are many things in the prophets both divinely
' said and piously done, many things in Moses and
' other men famous for holiness of life, but this com-
' plete range you will not find in any *man*.' [1] . . .

From this general view of the ' wonderful compass
' and consistency of the whole story ' let us pass with
Erasmus to details. We shall find him following the
same method in treating of each point, taking pains
to rest his belief rather on the evidence of *facts* than
upon mere dogmatic authority.

Proofs of
the inno-
cence of
Christ.

Thus in treating of the ' *innocence* of Christ,' it
would have been easy to have quoted a few authori-
tative passages from the Apostolic epistles, and to
have relied upon these, but Erasmus chose rather to
rest on the variety of evidence afforded by the many
different kinds of witnesses whose testimony is recorded in the New Testament. After alluding to the
testimony of the voice from heaven, of John the Baptist, and of the *friends* of Jesus, he thus proceeds :—

' . . . . The men who were sent to take him bore
' witness that " never man spake as this man." . . .
' *Pilate* also bore witness, " I am pure from the blood
' " of this *just man* ; see ye to it." Pilate's *wife* also

---

[1] *Novum Testamentum*, 2nd ed. pp. 28, 29.

' bore witness, " have nothing to do with that *just*
' " *person.*" . . . Hostile judges recognised his inno-
' cence, rejecting the evidence of the many witnesses.
' They declared, and themselves were witnesses, that
' the suborned men *lied* : they had nothing to object
' but the saying about the destruction and rebuilding
' of the temple. . . . The wretched *Judas* confessed,
' " I have sinned, in betraying *innocent* blood." The
' centurion at the cross confessed, " truly this was the
' " Son of God." The wicked Pharisees confessed that
' they had nothing to lay to his charge why he should
' be crucified, but the saying about the temple. Thus
' was he so guiltless, that nothing could even be
' *invented* against him with any show of *probability.*' [1]

In the same way, in order to show that Christ was
truly a *man,* instead of quoting texts to prove it, he
pointed to the facts ' that he called himself the " Son
' " of man ; " that he grew up through the usual stages
' of growth, that he slept, ate, hungered, and thirsted ;
' that he was wearied by travel ; that he was touched
' by human passions. We read in Matthew, that he
' pitied the crowd ; in Mark, that he was angry and
' grieved and groaned in spirit ; in John, that his mind
' was moved before his passion ; that such was his
' anguish in the garden that his sweat was like drops
' of blood ; that he thirsted on the cross, which was
' what usually happened during crucifixion ; that he
' wept over the city of Jerusalem ; that he wept and
' was moved at the grave of Lazarus.' [2]

And in the same way to prove Christ's divinity,
Erasmus pointed to his miracles, and their consistency

CHAP. XV.

A.D. 1518.

Proofs of
Christ's
humanity.

Proofs
of the
divinity
of Christ.

---

[1] *Novum Testamentum,* 2nd ed. pp. 34, 35.   [2] *Ibid.* p. 32.

with his own declarations. Again he wrote, 'Who 'indeed would look for true salvation from a mere 'man ? . . . He said that he was sent from heaven, that 'he was the Son of God, that he had been in heaven. 'He called God his Father ; and the Jews understood 'what he meant by it, for they said " Thou, a man, '" makest thyself God." Lastly, he rose from the dead, 'ascended into heaven, and sent down the Paraclete, 'by whom the Apostles were suddenly refreshed.' [1]

The mode by which Christ influenced the world.

Another subject upon which Erasmus dwelt was 'the way which was adopted by Christ to draw the 'world under his influence.' He showed how the prophets and the preaching of John had prepared the way for him. 'He did not seek suddenly to change 'the world ; for it is difficult to remove from men's 'minds what they have imbibed in childhood, and 'what has been handed down to them by common con-'sent from their ancestors. First, John went before 'with the baptism of repentance ; then the Apostles 'went forth, not yet announcing the coming Messiah, 'but only that the kingdom of heaven was at hand. 'By means of poor and unlearned men the thing began, '. . . and for a long while he bore with the rudeness 'and distrust of even these, that they might not seem 'to have believed rashly. Thomas pertinaciously dis-'believed, and not until he had touched the marks of 'the nails and the spear did he exclaim " My Lord '" and my God ! " When about to ascend to heaven, 'he upbraided all of them for their hardness of heart 'and difficulty in believing what they had seen. . . . . 'He added the evidence of miracles, but even these

---

[1] *Novum Testamentum,* 2nd ed. p. 32. These passages are abridged in the translation.

' were nothing but acts of kindness. He never worked
' a miracle for anyone who had not faith. The crowd
' were witnesses of nearly all he did. He sent the
' lepers to the priests, not that they might be healed
' but that it might be more clearly known that they
' were healed. . . . And for all the benefits he ren-
' dered, he never once took any reward, nor glory, nor
' money, nor pleasure, nor rule, so that the suspicion
' of a corrupt motive might not be imputed to him.
' And it was not till after the Holy Spirit had been sent
' that the Gospel trumpet was sounded through the
' whole world, *lest it should seem that he had sought any-*
' *thing for himself while alive.* Moreover, there is no
' testimony held more efficacious amongst mortals
' than blood. By his own death, and that of his
' disciples, he set a seal to the truth of his teaching.
' I have already alluded to the consistency of his
' whole life.' [1]

These passages will serve as examples of the means
by which, in this treatise, Erasmus sought to bring out
the facts of the life of Christ as the true foundation of
the Christian faith, instead of the dogmas of scholastic
theology. After thus thoughtfully dwelling upon the
facts of the life of Christ, he proceeds to examine his
teaching, and he concludes that there were two things
which he peculiarly and perpetually inculcated—faith
and love—and, after describing them more at length,
he writes, ' Read the New Testament through, you will
' not find in it any precept which pertains to *cere-*
' *monies.* Where is there a single word of meats or
' vestments? Where is there any mention of fasts
' and the like? *Love* alone He calls *His* precept. Cere-

---

[1] *Novum Testamentum*, 2nd ed. pp. 35, 36.

' monies give rise to differences ; from love flows peace.
' . . . And yet *we* burden those who have been made
' free by the blood of Christ with all these almost
' senseless and more than Jewish constitutions ! ' [1]

Finally, turning from the New Testament and its
theology to the Schoolmen and theirs, he exclaimed,
' What a spectacle it is to see a divine of eighty years
' old knowing nothing but mere sophisms ! ' [2] and
ended with the sentences which have already been
quoted as the conclusion of the shorter treatise prefixed to the ' Novum Instrumentum.'

This somewhat lengthy examination of ' the method
' of true theology ' will not have been fruitless, if it
should place beyond dispute what was pointed out
with reference to the ' Novum Instrumentum,' that its
value lay more in its prefaces, and its main drift and
spirit as a whole, than in the critical exactness of its
Greek text or the correctness of its readings. If it
could be said of the ' Novum Instrumentum ' that
much of its value lay in its preface—in its beautiful
' *Paraclesis* '—it may also be said that the importance
of the second edition was greatly enhanced by the
addition of the ' *Ratio Veræ Theologiæ.*'

And as, like its forerunner, this second edition went
forth under the shield of Leo X.'s approval, with the
additional sanction of the Archbishops of Basle and of
Canterbury, and with all the prestige of former success,
it must have been felt to be not only a firm and dignified, but also a triumphant reply to the various attacks
which had been made upon Erasmus—a reply more
powerful than the keenest satire or the most bitter in-

---

[1] *Novum Testamentum,* 2nd ed. p. 42.   [2] *Ibid.* p. 61.

vective could have been—a reply in which the honest Chap. XV.
dissentient found a calm restatement of what perhaps A.D. 1518.
he had only half comprehended ; the candid critic, the
errors of which he complained corrected ; and the blind
bigot, the luxury of something further to denounce.[1]

III. ERASMUS'S HEALTH GIVES WAY (1518).

After several months' hard and close labour in Fro- Erasmus
ben's office in the autumn of 1518, Erasmus left Basle, leaves Basle.
jaded and in poor health. As he proceeded on his
journey to Louvain his maladies increased. Car-
buncles made their appearance, and added to the pains
of travel. He reached Louvain thoroughly ill ; and Reaches Louvain ill.
turned into the house of the hospitable printer, Thierry
Martins, almost exhausted. A physician was sent for.
He told Martins and his wife that Erasmus had the
plague, and never came again for fear of contagion.
Another was sent for, but he likewise did not repeat
his visit. A third came, and pronounced it not to be
the plague. A fourth, at the first mention of ulcers,
was seized with fear, and though he promised to call
again, sent his servant instead. And thus for weeks
lay Erasmus, ill and neglected by the doctors, in the
house of the good printer at Louvain.[2]

Some monks were drinking together at Cologne, a
city where Erasmus had many bigoted enemies. One

---

[1] When, after the 3rd edition had
been published and a 4th was in
preparation, in 1526, a Doctor of
the Sorbonne attacked the New
Testament of Erasmus, he was able
triumphantly to ask him, ' what he
' wanted ? ' His New Testament

had already been ' scattered abroad
' by the printers in thousands of
' copies over and over again.' His
critic ' *should have written in time !* '
—Erasmus to the Faculty of Paris.
Jortin, ii. App. No. xlix. p. 492.

[2] Eras. *Op.* iii. pp. 374, 375.

CHAP. XV.   of the fraternity of preaching friars brought to them

A.D. 1518.   the news that Erasmus was dead at Louvain! The

Joy of the   intelligence was received with applause by the con-
monks at
the report   vivial monks, and again and again was the applause
of the
death of   repeated, when the preacher added, in his monkish
Erasmus.   Latin, that Erasmus had died, like a heretic as he was,
'*sine lux, sine crux, sine Deus.*' [1]

---

[1] Eras. *Op.* iii. p. 432, D and E.

CHAPTER XVI.

I. ERASMUS DOES NOT DIE (1518).

THE monks of Cologne were disappointed. Erasmus did not die. His illness turned out not to be the plague. After four weeks' nursing at the good printer's house, he was well enough to be removed to his own lodgings within the precincts of the college. Thence he wrote to Beatus Rhenanus in these words :—

Erasmus to Beatus Rhenanus.[1]

. . . . .

' My dear Beatus,—Who would have believed that
' this frail delicate body, now weaker from increasing
' age, after the toils of so many journeys, after the
' labours of so many studies, should have survived
' such an illness ? You know how hard I had been
' working at Basle just before. . . . . A suspicion
' had crossed my mind that this year would prove
' fatal to me, one malady succeeded so rapidly upon
' another, and each worse than the one which pre-
' ceded it. When the disease was at its height, I
' neither felt distressed with desire of life, nor did
' I tremble at the fear of death. All my hope was in
' Christ alone, and I prayed for nothing to him except

---

[1] Eras. Epist. ccclvii.

' that he would do what he thought best for me.
' Formerly, when a youth, I remember I used to
' tremble at the very name of death ! .... '

Had Erasmus fallen a victim to the plague and
died at the house of Martins the printer, as the friar
had reported, and the convivial monks had too readily
believed, it does not seem likely that his death would
have been as dark and godless as they fancied it
might have been. As it was, instead of dying without
lighted tapers and crucifix and transubstantiated
wafer, or in monkish jargon, ' *sine lux, sine crux, sine*
' *Deus*,' their enemy *still lived*, and the disappointed
monks, instead of ill-concealed rejoicings over his
death, were obliged to content themselves for many
years to come with muttering in quite another tone,
' It were good for that man if he had never been
' born.' [1]

II. MORE AT THE COURT OF HENRY VIII. (1518)

While the plague had been raging in Germany, the
sweating sickness had been continuing its ravages in
England. Before More left for Calais it had struck

down, after a few days' illness, Ammonius, with whom
Erasmus and More had long enjoyed intimate friendship. Wolsey also had narrowly escaped with his life,
after repeated attacks. When More returned from
the embassy he found the sickness still raging. In
the spring of 1518 the court was removed to Abingdon, to escape the contagion of the great city ; and
whilst there, More, who now was obliged to follow
the King wherever he might go, had to busy himself

---

[1] Eras. *Op.* iii. 1490, D.   Brewer, ii. Nos. 3670, 3671, dated Sept. 1517.

with precautionary measures to prevent its spread in Oxford, where it had made its appearance.[1]

Whilst at Abingdon, he was called upon, also, to interfere with his influence to quiet a foolish excitement which had seized the students at Oxford. It was not the spread of the sweating sickness which had caused their alarm ; but the increasing taste for the study of Greek had roused the fears of divines of the old school. The enemies of the ' new learning ' had raised a faction against it. The students had taken sides, calling themselves Greeks and Trojans, and, not content with wordy warfare, they had come to open and public insult. At length, the most virulent abuse had been poured upon the Greek language and literature, even from the university pulpit, by an impudent and ignorant preacher. He had denounced all who favoured Greek studies as ' heretics ; ' in his coarse phraseology, those who taught the obnoxious language were ' *dia-* ' *bolos maximos* ' and its students ' *diabolos minutulos.*'

More, upon hearing what had been passing, wrote a letter of indignant but respectful remonstrance to the university authorities.[2] He and Pace interested the King also in the affair, and at their suggestion he took occasion to express his royal pleasure that the students ' would do well to devote themselves with energy and ' spirit to the study of Greek literature ; ' and so, says Erasmus, ' silence was imposed upon these brawlers.'[3]

On another occasion the King and his courtiers had attended Divine service. The court preacher had, like the Oxford divine, indulged in abuse of Greek litera-

---

[1] Brewer, preface, ccxi.
[2] Jortin's *Life of Erasmus*, App.

pp. 662–667.
[3] Eras. *Op.* iii. p. 408, b.

ture and the modern school of interpretation—having
Erasmus and his New Testament in his eye. Pace
looked at the King to see what he thought of it. The
King answered his look with a satirical smile. After
the sermon the divine was ordered to attend upon the
King. It was arranged that More should reply to
the arguments he had urged against Greek literature.
After he had done so, the divine, instead of replying
to his arguments, dropped down on his knees before
the King, and simply prayed for forgiveness, urging,
however, by way of extenuating his fault, that he was
carried away by the spirit in his sermon when he
poured forth all this abuse of the Greek language.
'But,' the King here observed, 'that spirit was not
'the spirit of *Christ*, but the spirit of *foolishness*.' He
then asked the preacher what works of Erasmus he

had read. He had not read any. 'Then,' said the
King, 'you prove yourself to be a fool, for you con-
'demn what you have never read.' 'I read once,'
replied the divine, 'a thing called the "Moria."' . . .
Pace here suggested that there was a decided con-
gruity between that and the preacher. And finally
the preacher himself relented so far as to admit :—
'After all I am not so *very* hostile to Greek letters,
'because they were derived from the Hebrew.' The
King, wondering at the distinguished folly of the man,
bade him retire, but with strict injunctions never
again to preach at Court ! [1]

So far, then, from More's new position having extinguished his own opinions or changed his views, he
had the satisfaction of being able now and then to

---

[1] *Eras. Op.* iii. p. 408.

advance the interests of the 'new learning,' and to act the part of its 'friend at court.'

III. THE EVENING OF COLET'S LIFE (1518–19).

The sweating sickness continued its ravages in England, striking down one here and another there with merciless rapidity. It was generally fatal on the first day. If the patient survived twenty-four hours he was looked upon as out of danger. But it was liable to recur, and sometimes attacked the same person four times in succession. This was the case with Cardinal Wolsey ; whilst several of the royal retinue were attacked and carried off at once, Wolsey's strong constitution carried him through four successive attacks.[1]

During the period of its ravages Colet was three times attacked by it and survived, but with a constitution so shattered, and with symptoms so premonitory of consumptive tendencies, as to suggest to him that the time might not be far distant when he too must follow after his twenty-one brothers and sisters, and leave his aged mother the survivor of all her children.

Meanwhile an accidental ray of light falls here and there upon the otherwise obscure life of Colet during these years of peril, revealing little pictures, too beautiful in their simple consistency with all else we know of him to be passed by unheeded.

The first glimpse we get of Colet reveals him engaged in the careful and final completion of the rules and statutes by which his school was to be governed after his own death. Having spent a good part of his life and his fortune in the foundation of this school, as the

---

[1] *Four Years at the Court of Henry VIII.* ii. p. 127.

best means of promoting the cause which he had so deeply at heart, one might have expected that he would have tried, in fixing his statutes, to give permanence and perpetuity to his own views. This is what most people try to do by endowments of this kind.

No sooner do most reformers clear away a little ground, and discover what they take to be truths, than they attempt, by organising a sect, founding endowments, and framing articles and trust-deeds, to secure the permanent tradition of their own views to posterity in the form in which they are apprehended by themselves. Hence, in the very act of striking off the fetters of the past, they are often forging the fetters of the future. Even the Protestant Reformers, whilst on the one hand bravely breaking the yoke under which their ancestors had lived in bondage, ended by fixing another on the neck of their posterity. Those who remained in the old bondage found themselves, as the result of the Reformation, bound still tighter under Tridentine decrees; whilst those who had joined the exodus, and entered the promised land of the Reformers, found it to be a land of almost narrower boundaries than the one they had left. Freed from Papal thraldom it might be, but bound down by an Augustinian theology as rigid and dogmatic as that from which they had escaped.

If Colet did not do likewise, he resisted with singular wisdom and success a temptation which besets every one under his circumstances. That Colet strove to found no sect of his own has already been seen. If the movement which he had done so much to set agoing had produced its fruits—if a school or party had been the result—he had not called it, or felt it to be, in any way his *own*; he might call it ' Erasmican ' in joke, and leave Erasmus indignantly to repudiate ' that

' name of division ; ' but Erasmus expressed the view of Colet as well as his own when he said to the abbot, ' Why should we try to narrow what Christ intended ' to be broad ? '

Perfectly consistent with this feeling, Colet did not now show any anxiety to perpetuate his own particular views by means of the power which, as the founder of the endowment, he had a perfect right to exercise. The truth was, I think, that he retained the spirit of free enquiry—the mind open to light from whatever direction—to the last, in full faith that the facts of Christianity—in so far as they are facts—must have everything to gain and nothing to lose from the discovery of other facts in other fields of knowledge. As I have before pointed out, the Oxford Reformers felt that they were living in an age of discovery and progress ; they never dreamed that they had reached finality either in knowledge or creed ; it would have been a sad blow to their hopes if they had been told that they had. They took a humble view of their own attainments, and had faith in the future.

In this spirit do we find Colet in these days of peril from the sweating sickness, and conscious that his shattered health must soon give way, settling the statutes of his school with a wisdom seldom surpassed even in more modern times.

First with great practical shrewdness, instead of putting his school under the charge of ecclesiastics or clergymen, he intrusted it entirely ' to the most honest ' and faithful fellowship of the *Mercers* of London.' As Erasmus expressed it, ' of the whole concern, he set ' in charge, not a bishop, not a chapter, not dignitaries, ' but married citizens of established reputation.' [1]

---

[1] Eras. *Op.* iii. p. 457, E. See also Mr. Lupton's *Introduction* to his edition of *Dean Colet on the Sacraments of the Church*, pp. 19 and 26.

Time had been when Colet had regarded ' marriage '
as almost an unholy thing.   But he had seen much
both of the church and the world since then ; and
as perhaps his faith in Dionysian speculations had
lessened, his English common sense had more and
more asserted its own.   He had, as already mentioned,
wisely advised Thomas More to marry.   In his ' Right
' fruitful Admonition concerning the Order of a good
' Christian Man's Life,' from which I have quoted before, he had said, ' If thou intend to marry, or be
' married, and hast a good wife, thank our Lord there-
' for, for she is of his sending.'   So now he intrusted
his school to ' married citizens ; ' and Erasmus adds,
' when he was asked the reason, he said, that nothing
' indeed is certain in human affairs, but that yet
' amongst *these* he had found the least corruption.[1] . . .
' He used to declare that he had nowhere found less
' corrupt morals than among married people, because
' natural affection, the care of their children, and
' domestic duties, are like so many rails which keep
' them from sliding into all kinds of vice.' [2]

In defining the duties and salaries of the masters of
his school, he provided expressly that they might be
married men (and those chosen by him actually were
so) ;[3] but they were to hold their office ' in no rome of
' continuance and perpetuity, but upon their duty in
' the school.'   The chaplain was to be ' some good,
' honest, and virtuous man, and to help to teach in the
' school.'

---

[1] Eras. *Op.* iii. p. 457, E.
[2] *Ibid.* p. 459, A and B.
[3] William Lilly was married and
had several children. The sur-mas-
ter, John Rightwyse, married his
daughter.   Mr. Lupton informs me,
that in vol. iv. of Stow's *Historical*

Collections (Harleian, No. 450), fol.
58 *b*, is a Latin epitaph, in ten lines,
by Lilly on his wife.   Her name is
spelt ' Hagnes,' and (if the reading
be correct) they appear to have had
fifteen children.

Respecting the children he expressed his desire to be that they should not be received into the school until they could read and write fairly, and explained ' what they shall be taught ' in general terms ; ' for,' said he, ' it passeth my wit to devise and determine ' in particular.'

Then, last of all, he added the following clause, headed ' Liberty to Declare the Statutes : '—

' And notwithstanding these statutes and ordi-
' nances before written, in which I have declared my
' mind and will ; yet because in time to come many
' things may and shall survive and grow by many
' occasions and causes which at the making of this
' book was not possible to come to mind ; in conside-
' ration of the assured truth and circumspect wisdom
' and faithful goodness of the most honest and sub-
' stantial fellowship of the Mercery of London, to
' whom I have committed all the care of the school,
' and trusting in their fidelity and love that they
' have to God and man and to the school ; and also be-
' lieving verily that they shall always dread the great
' wrath of God :—*Both all this that is said, and all that is*
' *not said, which hereafter shall come into my mind while*
' *I live to be said, I leave it wholly to their discretion and*
' *charity* : I mean of the wardens and assistances of the
' fellowship, with such other counsel as they shall call
' unto them—good lettered and learned men—*they to*
' *add and diminish of this book and to supply it in every*
' *default* ; and also to declare in it every obscurity and
' darkness as time and place and just occasion shall
' require ; calling the dreadful God to look upon them
' in all such business, and exhorting them to fear the
' terrible judgment of God, which seeth in darkness,

CHAP.
XVI.

A.D. 1518.

Colet
wisely
gives
power to
alter the
statutes.

H H

' and shall render to every man according to his works ;
' and finally, praying the great Lord of mercy, for their
' faithful dealing in this matter, now and always
' to send unto them in this world much wealth and
' prosperity, and after this life much joy and glory.' [1]

This done, he wrote in the Book of Statutes the
following memorandum :—' This book I, John Colet,
' delivered into the hands of Master Lilly the 18th day
' of June 1518, that he may keep it and observe it in
' the school.' [2]

Having completed the statutes of his school, Colet
turned his attention to a few other final arrangements,
including certain reforms in the church of St. Paul's.[3]

He had already prepared a simple tomb for himself at
the side of the choir of the great cathedral with which
his labours had been so closely connected, and the
simple inscription, ' Johannes Coletus,' was already
carved on the plain monumental stone which was to
cover his grave.   Thus he was ready to depart whenever the summons should arrive.   But the pale
messenger came not yet.

Meanwhile Colet retained his interest in passing
events.   If he seemed to take little part in public
affairs, it was not owing to his want of interest in them.
It would almost seem that he sympathised much
during this quiet season with Luther's attack upon
Indulgences, and was a reader of those of his works—
chiefly pamphlets—which had reached England.
This, however, rests only upon the remark of Erasmus,
that he was in the habit of reading heretical books,

---

[1] Knight's *Life of Colet. Miscellanies,* No. v.

[2] The original of this book with
Colet's signature is still preserved
at the Mercers' Hall.

[3] Knight, p. 227.   He drew up
a body of statutes, which, however, were never accepted by the
chapter.—Milman's *Annals of St.
Paul's,* p. 124.

declaring that he often got more good from them than
from the Schoolmen ; [1] and the further statement
made incidentally by Erasmus to Luther, that there
were in England some men in the highest position who
thought well of his works. [2] His close retirement may
be accounted for as well by his shattered health as
by the circumstance that Bishop Fitzjames still lived
in his grey hairs to harass him.

It was probably to secure a safe retreat in emergency
beyond the jurisdiction of this bigoted bishop that
Colet was building his ' nest,' as he called it, within
the precincts of the Charterhouse—not in London, but
at Sheen, near Richmond. Whether he ever really
entered this ' nest,' so long in course of preparation,
does not appear. Perhaps there was no need for it.

Little as of late he had mixed himself up with public
affairs, he was still looked up to by those who, through
the report of Erasmus, recognised his almost apostolic
piety and wisdom. Thus, in his quiet retirement, he
received a letter from Marquard von Hatstein, one of
the canons of Maintz, a connection of Ulrich von
Hutten's, [3] mentioned by Erasmus as ' a most excellent
' young man ; ' [4] one of the little group of men who,
under the lead of the Archbishop of Maintz, had boldly
taken the side of Reuchlin against his persecutors—a
letter which shows so true an appreciation of Colet's
character and relation to the movement which was
now known as ' Erasmian,' that it must have been
exceedingly grateful to the feelings of Colet, now that
he had set his house in order, and was ready to leave

Colet
receives a
letter from
Marquard
von Hat-
stein.

---

[1] *Eras. Op.* iii. p. 460, A.
[2] *Ibid.* p. 445, B.
[3] *Ibid.* p. 751, E.

[4] Strausz. Leipzig, 1858, vol. i.
p. 123.

in other hands the work which he himself had commenced.

Marquard von Hatstein to John Colet.[1]

' I have often thought with admiration of *your*
' blessedness, who born to wealth and of so illustrious
' a family have added to these gifts of fortune man-
' ners and intellectual culture abundantly correspond-
' ing therewith.   For such is your learning, piety, and
' manner of life, such lastly your Christian constancy,
' that notwithstanding all these gifts of fortune, you
' seem to care for little but that you may run in the
' path of Christ in so noble a spirit, that you are not
' surpassed by any even of those who call themselves
' " mendicants."   For they in many things simulate
' and dissimulate for the sake of sensual pleasures.

' When recently the trumpet of cruel war sounded
' so terribly, how did you hold up against it the image
' of Christ ! the olive-branch of peace !   You exhorted
' us to tolerance, to concord, to the yielding up of our
' goods for the good of a brother, instead of invading
' one another's rights.   You told us that there was no
' cause of war between Christians, who are bound to-
' gether by holy ties in a love more than fraternal.
' And many other things of a like nature did you urge,
' with so great authority, that I may truly say that the
' virtue of Christ thus set forth by Colet was seen from
' afar.   And thus did you discomfit the dark designs
' of your enemies.   Men raging against the truth, you
' conquered with the mildness of an apostle.   You
' opposed your gentleness to their insane violence.

---

[1] *Epistolæ aliquot Eruditorum, &c.*   Appended to *Apologia Erasmi,*
&c. Basil. 1520, pp. 139, 140.

' Through your innocence you escaped from any harm,
' even though by their numbers (for there is always
' the most abundant crop of what is bad) they were
' able to override your better opinion. With a skill
' like that with which Homer published the praises of
' Achilles, Erasmus has studiously held up to the ad-
' miration of the world and of posterity the name of
' England, and especially of Colet, whom he has so
' described that there is not a good man of any nation
' who does not honour you. I seem to myself to see
' that each of you owes much to the other, but which
' of the two owes most to the other I am doubtful.
' For he must have received good from you : seeing
' that you are hardly likely to have been magnified by
' his colouring pen. You, however, if I may freely say
' what I think, do seem to owe some thanks to him for
' making publicly known those virtues which before
' were unknown to us. Still I fancy you are not the
' less victor in the matter of benefits conferred, since
' you have blessed Erasmus, a stranger to England,
' otherwise an incomparable man, with so many
' friends—Mountjoy, More, Linacre, Tunstal, &c. . . . .

   ' Having commenced my theological studies, I have
' learned from the conversation and writings of Eras-
' mus to regard you as my examplar. I wish I could
' really follow you as closely as I long to do. I long,
' not only to improve myself in letters, but to lead a
' holier life. Farewell in Christ. VI. Cal. Maii, Anno
' MDXX.' (should be probably 1519).[1]

---

[1] This letter possibly may not have reached England before Colet's death ; but it is most likely that the date is wrong, as so often is the case with these letters—the year not being often added by the writer himself at the time, but by some copyist subsequently.

IV. MORE'S CONVERSION ATTEMPTED BY THE
MONKS (1519).

Erasmus was as much hated by the monks in England as by the monks at Cologne; but they found
their attempts to stir up ill-feeling against him check-
mated by the influence of More and his friends.

More's father was known to be a good Catholic, and
probably to belong, as an old man with conservative
tendencies was likely to do, to the orthodox party.
He himself was now too near the royal ear to be a
harmless adherent of the new learning—as they had
learned to their cost before now. He was so popular,
too, with all parties! If only he could be detached
from Erasmus and brought over to their own side,
what a triumph it would be!

More
receives a
letter from
a monk.

So an anonymous letter was written by a monk to
More, expressing great solicitude for his welfare, and
fears lest he should be corrupted by too great intimacy
with Erasmus; lest he should be led astray, by too
great love of his writings, into the adoption of his
new and foreign doctrines!

The good monk was particularly shocked at the
hints thrown out by Erasmus in his writings, that,
after all, the holy doctors and fathers of the Church
were fallible.

He took up the vulgar objections which the letter of
Dorpius, and a still more recent attack upon Erasmus,
by an Englishman named Edward Lee, had put into
every one's mouth, and tried to persuade More to be
wise in time, lest he should become infected with the
Erasmian poison,

More's letter in reply to the over-anxious monk h'as been preserved.[1]

He indignantly repelled the insinuation that he was in danger of contamination from his intimacy with Erasmus, whose New Testament the very Pope had sanctioned, who lived in the nearest intimacy with such men as Colet, Fisher, and Warham; to say nothing of Mountjoy, Tunstal, Pace, and Grocyn. Those who knew Erasmus best, loved him most.

Then turning to the charge made against Erasmus, that he denied the infallibility of the fathers, More wrote :—

'Do *you* deny that they ever made mistakes ? I
' put it to you—when Augustine thought that Jerome
' had mistranslated a passage, and Jerome defended
' what he had done, was not *one of the two* mistaken ?
' When Augustine asserted that the Septuagint is to be
' taken as an indubitably faithful translation, and
' Jerome denied it, and asserted that its translators
' had fallen into errors, was not one of the two mis-
' taken ? When Augustine, in support of his view,
' adduced the story of the wonderful agreement of the
' different translations produced by the inspired trans-
' lators writing in separate cells, and Jerome laughed
' at the story as absurd, was not one of the two mis-
' taken ? When Jerome, writing on the Epistle to the
' Galatians, translated its meaning to be that Peter
' was blamed by Paul for dissimulating, and Augustine
' denied it, was not one of them mistaken ? . . .

---

[1] ' Epistola clarissimi viri Thomæ ' Mori, qua refellit rabiosam maledi- ' centiam monachi cujusdam juxta ' indocti atque arrogantis.'—*Epi-* *stolæ aliquot Eruditorum Virorum, &c.* Basileæ, MDXX. pp. 92–138. Also Jortin's *Life of Erasmus,* Appendix.

' Augustine asserts that demons and angels also have
' material and substantial bodies. I doubt not that
' even *you* deny this ! He asserts that infants dying
' without baptism are consigned to physical torments
' in eternal punishment—how many are there who be-
' lieve this now ? unless it be that Luther, *clinging by*
' *tooth and nail to the doctrine of Augustine*, should be
' induced to revive this antiquated notion. . . .' [1]

Alludes to
Luther's
clinging
by tooth
and nail
to Augus-
tine.

I have quoted this passage from More's letter because it shows clearly, not only how fully More had
adopted the position taken up by Erasmus, but also
how fully his eyes were open to the fact, that the rising
reformer of Wittemberg did ' *cling by tooth and nail to*
' *the doctrine of Augustine*,' and was likely, by doing so,
to be led astray into some of the harsh views, and, as
he thought, obvious errors of that Holy Father.

At the same time the following passage may be
quoted as proof that, in rejecting the Augustinian
creed, More and his friends did not run into the other
extreme of Pelagianism.

He had told the monk at the beginning of his letter,
that after he had shown how safe was the ground upon
which Erasmus and he were walking in the valley, he
would turn round and assail the lofty but tottering
citadel, from which the monk looked down upon them
with so proud a sense of security. So after he had
disposed of the monk's arguments, he began :—

' Into what factions—into how many sects is the
' order cut up ! Then, what tumults, what tragedies
' arise about little differences in the colour or mode of
' girding the monastic habit, or some matter of cere-
' mony which, if not altogether despicable, is at all

---

[1] ' Nisi quod Lutherus fertur Augustini doctrinam mordicus tenens
' antiquatam sententiam rursus instaurare.'—p. 99.

' events not so important as to warrant the banish-
' ment of all charity. How many, too, are there (and
' this is surely worst of all) who, relying on the
' assurances of their monastic profession, inwardly
' raise their crests so high that they seem to themselves
' to move in the heavens, and reclining among the
' solar rays, to look down from on high upon the people
' creeping on the ground like ants, looking down thus,
' not only on the ungodly, but also upon all who are
' without the circle of the enclosure of their order, so
' that for the most part nothing is holy but what they
' do themselves. . . . . They make more of things
' which appertain specially to the religious order than
' of those valueless and very humble things which are
' in no way peculiar to them but entirely common to
' all Christian people, such as the vulgar virtues—
' faith, hope, charity, the fear of God, humility, and
' others of the kind.   Nor, indeed, is this a new thing.
' Nay, it is what Christ long ago denounced to his
' chosen people, " Ye make the word of God of none
' " effect through your traditions." . . . .

' There are multitudes enough who would be afraid
' that the devil would come upon them and take them
' alive to hell, if, forsooth, they were to set aside their
' usual garb, whom nothing can move when they are
' grasping at *money.*

' Are there only a few, think you, who would deem
' it a crime to be expiated with many tears, if they
' were to omit a line in their hourly prayers, and yet
' have no fearful scruple at all, when they profane
' themselves by the worst and most infamous lies ? . . . .

' Indeed, I once knew a man devoted to the religious
' life—one of that class who would nowadays be
' thought " most religious."   This man, by no means

'a novice, but one who had passed many years in
'what they call regular observances, and had advanced
'so far in them that he was even set over a convent—
'but, nevertheless, more careless of the precepts of
'God than of monastic rites—slid down from one
'crime to another, till at length he went so far as to
'meditate the most atrocious of all crimes—a crime
'execrable beyond belief—and what is more, not a
'simple crime, but one pregnant with manifold guilt,
'for he even purposed to add sacrilege to murders
'and parricide. When this man thought himself in-
'sufficient without accomplices for the perpetration of
'so many crimes, he associated with himself some
'ruffians and cutpurses. They committed the most
'horrible crimes which I ever heard of. They were all
'of them thrown together into prison. I do not wish
'to give the details, and I abstain from the names of
'the criminals, lest I should renew anything of past
'hatred to an innocent order.

'But to proceed to narrate the circumstances on
'account of which I have mentioned this affair. I
'heard from those wicked assassins that, when they
'came to that religious man in his chamber, they had
'not spoken of the crime ; but being introduced into
'his private chapel, they appeased the sacred Virgin
'by a salutation on their bent knees according to
'custom. *This being properly accomplished, they at
'length rose purely and piously to perpetrate their
'crime !* . . . . .

'Now, I have not mentioned this with the view
'either to defame the religion of the monks with these
'crimes, since the same soil may bring forth useful
'herbs and pestiferous weeds, or to condemn the rites
'of those who occasionally salute the sacred Virgin,

' than which nothing is more beneficial ; but because
' people trust so much in such things that under the
' very security which they thus feel they give them-
' selves up to crime.

' From reflections such as these you may learn the
' lesson which the occasion suggests. That you should
' not grow too proud of your own sect—nothing could
' be more fatal. Nor trust in private observances.
' That you should *place your hopes rather in the Chris-*
' *tian faith than in your own* ; and not trust in those
' things which you can do *for yourself*, but in those
' which you cannot do *without God's help*. You can
' fast by yourself, you can keep vigils by yourself, you
' can say prayers by yourself—and you can do these
' things by the devil ! But, verily, Christian faith,
' which Christ Jesus truly said to be in spirit ; Chris-
' tian hope, which, despairing of its own merits, con-
' fides only in the mercy of God ; Christian charity,
' which is not puffed up, is not made angry, does not
' seek its own glory,—none, indeed, can attain these
' except by the grace and gracious help of God alone.

' By how much the more you place your trust in
' those virtues which are common to Christendom,
' by so much the less will you have faith in private
' ceremonies, whether those of your order or your
' own ; and by how much the less you trust in them
' by so much the more will they be useful. For then
' at last God will esteem you a faithful servant, when
' you shall count yourself good for nothing.'

That these passages prove that More and his friends
had not set aside monasticism, or even Mariolatry, as
altogether wrong, cannot be too clearly recognised.
In an age of transition it is the *direction* of the thoughts

and aims of men which constitutes the radical difference or agreement between them, rather than the
exact distance that each may have travelled on the
same road.   Luther himself had not yet in his hatred
of ceremonies travelled so far as the Oxford Reformers,
though in after years he went farther, because he
travelled faster than they did.   Upon these questions
they were very much practically at one.   And if here
and there the three friends observed in Luther an
impetuosity which carried him into extremes, much
as they might differ from some of his statements, and
the tone he sometimes adopted, their respect for his
moral earnestness, and their perception of the amount
of exasperation to which his hot nature was exposed,
made them readily pardon what they could not approve.   They had as yet little idea—though More's
letter showed that they had *some*—much less than
Luther himself had—how practically important was
the difference between them.   For the moment their
two orbits seemed almost to coincide.   They seemed
even to be approaching each other.   They seemed to
meet in their common hatred of the formalism of the
monks, in their common attempt to grasp at the spirit
—the reality—of religion through its forms and
shadows.   They had little idea that they were crossing
each other's path, and that ere long, as each pursued
his course, the divergence would become wider and
wider.

V. ERASMUS AND THE REFORMERS OF WITTEMBERG
(1519).

In the summer of 1518 Melanchthon had joined
Luther at Wittemberg.   During the remainder of
that year the controversy on Indulgences was going

on. Rome had taken the matter up. Luther had
appeared before the Papal legate Cajetan, and from
his harsh demand of simple recantation, had shrunk
with horror and fled back into Saxony. The legate
had threatened that Rome would never let the matter
drop, and urged the Elector of Saxony to send
Luther to Rome. But he had made common cause
with the poor monk, and refused to banish him. Leo
X. was afraid to quarrel with Frederic of Saxony, and
under the auspices of Miltitz, aided by the moderation
of Luther and the firmness of his protector, a little oil
was thrown on the troubled waters. But in the spring
of 1519, when the Papal tenths came to be exacted,
murmurs were heard again on all sides. Hutten commenced his series of satirical pamphlets, and it became
evident that the storm was not permanently laid, the
lull might last for a while, but fresh tempests were
ahead. [1]

It was during this interval of uncertainty that the
first intercourse took place between Erasmus and the
Wittemberg Reformers.

Letters had already passed between Melanchthon
and Erasmus; they had been known to one another
by name for some years, and were on the best of
terms. Thus Melanchthon, in writing to a friend of
his in January 1519, spoke of Erasmus as ' the first to
' call back theology to her fountain-head,' [2] and of
Luther as belonging to the same school. He freely
admitted how much greater was the learning of
Erasmus than that of Luther, and when in March he
received from Froben a copy of the ' Method of True

---

[1] For the above particulars see Ranke's *History of the Reformation*, bk. ii. c. iii.

[2] *Melanchthonis Epistolæ* : Bret-schneider, i. p. 63, and p. 66.

'Theology,' told Spalatin that 'this illustrious man 'seemed to have touched upon many points in the 'same strain as Luther, for in these things,' he said, 'they agreed;' adding, that Erasmus was 'freer than 'Luther, because he had the assistance of real and 'sacred learning;' and he mentioned this as an illustration of what he had just been saying, 'that 'every good man thought well of their cause.' [1]

Erasmus's opinion of Melanchthon.

Erasmus, on his side, also spoke in the highest possible terms of Melanchthon. He had great hopes from his youth that he might long survive himself, and if he did, he predicted that his name would throw that of Erasmus into the shade. [2]

Whilst, however, Erasmus thus freely acknowledged the friendship and merits of Melanchthon, he was careful not to commit himself to an approval of all that Luther was doing. And surely it was wise; for that his strong Augustinian tendencies were well know to the Oxford Reformers, has already been seen in More's letter to the anonymous monk.

What he says of Luther to Melanchthon.

On April 2, 1519, in reply to a letter from Melanchthon [3] mentioning Luther's desire of his approval, Erasmus wrote, that 'while every one of his friends 'honoured Luther's private life, *as to his doctrine there 'were different opinions*. He himself had not read 'Luther's books. Luther had censured some things 'deservedly, but he wished that he had done so as 'happily as he had freely.' At the end of this letter he expressed his affectionate anxiety lest Melanchthon should be wearing himself out by too hard study. [4]

---

[1] March 1519, Bretschneider, i. p. 75.

[2] Erasmus to Œcolampadius, 1518, Epist. cccliv.

[3] Dated January 5, from Wittemberg. Bretschneider, i. p. 59.

[4] Epist. ccccxi.

On March 28, Luther had written a letter to Erasmus, which probably crossed this on the way between Wittemberg and Louvain. It was a letter in which he had not made the slightest allusion to any difference of opinion between himself and Erasmus. On the contrary, he had spoken as though he held Erasmus in the greatest possible honour. He had spoken of his having a place, and ' reigning ' in the hearts of all who really loved literature. He had been reading the new preface to the ' Enchiridion,' and from it and from his friend Fabricius Capito he had learned that Erasmus had not only heard but approved of what he had done respecting indulgences. And with much genuine humility he had begged Erasmus to acknowledge him, however ignorant and unknown to fame, buried as it were in his cell, *as a brother in Christ*, by whom he himself was held in the greatest affection and regard.[1]

To this Erasmus, on May 30, replied, in a letter in which he *did* address Luther as a ' brother in Christ.' He said he had not yet read the books which had created so much clamour, and therefore could not judge of them. He had looked into his Commentaries on the Psalms, was much pleased with them, and hoped they would prove useful. Some of the best men in England, even some at Louvain, thought well of him and his writings. As to himself, he devoted himself, as he had done all along, to the revival of good literature [including first and foremost the Scriptures]. And it seemed to him, he said, that more good would come of courteous modesty than of impetuosity. It was by this that Christ drew the world under his

CHAP.
XVI.
———
A.D. 1519.
Luther
writes to
Erasmus.

---

[1] Luther's *Briefe*. De Wette, vol. i. Epist. cxxx. p. 249.

influence. It was thus that Paul abrogated that Judaical law, treating it all as typical. It were better to exclaim against *abuses* of pontifical authority than against the Popes themselves. ' May the Lord Jesus ' daily impart to you abundantly ' (he concluded) ' of ' his own Spirit to his own glory and the public good.' [1]

Thus he seems to have said the same things to both Melanchthon and Luther.

In the same strain, also, he wrote to others *about* them.

To the exasperated monks, who charged him with aiding and abetting Luther in writing the books which had caused such a tumult, he replied that, as he had not read them, he could not even express a decided opinion upon them.[2]

To Cardinal Wolsey he wrote, that he had only read a few pages of Luther's books, not because he disliked them, but because he was so closely occupied with his own. Luther's life was such that even his enemies could not find anything to slander. Germany had young men of learning and eloquence who would, he foretold, bring her great glory. Eobanus, Hutten, and Beatus Rhenanus were the only ones he knew personally. If these German students were too free in their criticisms, it should be remembered to what constant exasperation they had been submitted in all manner of ways, both public and private.[3]

To Hutten, who was perhaps the most hot-headed of these German young men, and whose satire had already proved itself more trenchant and bitter than any in which Erasmus had ever indulged, he urged

---

[1] Louvain, May 30, 1519. Eras. Epist. ccccxxvii.

[2] Eras. *Op.* iii. p. 444, E and F.
[3] Epist. cccxvii. May 8, 1519.

moderation, and said that for himself he had rather spend a month in trying to explain St. Paul or the Gospels than waste a day in quarrelling.[1]

Erasmus was, in fact, working hard at his 'Para-'phrases.' That on the Epistle to the Romans had been already printed in 1517, in the very best type of Thierry Martins, and forming a small and very readable octavo volume. Those on the next seven epistles [2] now followed in quick succession in the spring of 1519. How fully the heart of Erasmus was in his work is incidentally shown by the fact that, being obliged to write a pamphlet in defence of a former publication of his, he cut it short by saying that he had rather be working at the Paraphrase on the 'Galatians,' which he was just completing.[3] And Erasmus was preparing, in addition to these Paraphrases on the Epistles, others, at Colet's desire, more lengthy, on the Gospels. Here was work enough surely on hand to excuse him from entering into the Lutheran controversy—work precisely of that kind, moreover, which he had told Luther that he was devoting himself to. It was the work which, when he was longing for rest, and his zeal for the moment was threatening to flag, Colet had urged him to go on with through good and evil fortune; and which he himself, in his letter to Servatius, had said he was determined to work at to the day of his death. It is clear that he was in earnest when he told Hutten that he 'had rather spend a 'month in expounding St. Paul than waste a day in 'quarrelling.'

It seems to me, therefore, that the attitude of

Erasmus is writing his 'Paraphrases.'

---

[1] Epist. ccccxiii. Ap. 23, 1519.
[2] Eras. Epist. Laurentio: Louvain, Feb. 1519, prefixed to the Basle edition of the Five Epistles, 1520.
[3] *Apologia pro Declamatione de Laude Matrimonii*: Basil. 1519.

Erasmus towards Luther was that, not of a coward, but of a man who knew what he was about.

VI. ELECTION OF CHARLES V. TO THE EMPIRE (1519).

On January 12, 1519, Maximilian had died. It is not within the scope of this history to trace the steps and countersteps, the plots and counterplots, the bribery and treachery—the Machiavellian means and devices—in which nearly every sovereign in Europe was implicated, to the detriment of both conscience and exchequer, and which ended in placing Charles V., then absent in Spain, at the head of the German empire. With the accession of the new emperor commenced a new political era, which belongs to the history of the Protestant Reformation, and not to that of the Oxford Reformers.

Election of
Charles V.

Erasmus was too hard at work at his Paraphrases to admit of his meddling in politics, even though he himself had an honorary connection with the court of the prince who was the successful candidate, and had written his ' *Christian Prince* ' expressly for his benefit.

Colet was living in retirement, suffering from shattered health, too closely watched by the restless eye of his bishop to take any part in public affairs.[1]

Even More, though now a constant attendant upon Henry VIII., was probably not initiated into continental secrets, and even had he shared all the counsels of Wolsey, any part which he might play would be purely executive, and belong rather to the history of his own political career than to that of the fellow-work

---

[1] Colet seems even to have retired from the office of preacher before the King on Good Friday, which he had filled in 1510, 1511, 1512, 1513, 1515, 1516, and 1517. Brewer, ii. pp. 1445–1474. In 1518 the sermon was preached by the Dean of Sarum, p. 1477.

of the three friends. He probably had little or nothing really to do with Wolsey's plottings to secure the empire for his master, in order that he might, on the death of Leo X., secure the Papal chair for himself. But there was one circumstance connected with the election of the Emperor of too much significance to be passed over in this history without distinct mention— the part which Duke Frederic of Saxony played in it ; and this shall simply be alluded to in the words of Erasmus himself.

'The Duke Frederic of Saxony has written twice ' to me in reply to my letter. Luther is supported ' solely by his protection. He says that he has acted ' thus for the sake rather of the *cause* than of the ' person [of Luther]. He adds that he will not lend ' himself to the oppression of innocence in his domi- ' nions by the malice of those who seek their own, and ' not the things of Christ.' And Erasmus goes on to say, that ' when the imperial crown was offered to ' Frederic of Saxony by all [the electors], with great ' magnanimity he had refused it, the very day before ' Charles was elected. And ' (he writes) ' Charles ' never would have worn the imperial title had it not ' been declined by Frederic, whose glory in refusing ' the honour was greater than if he had accepted it. ' When he was asked who he thought should be elected, ' he said that no one seemed to him able to bear the ' weight of so great a name but Charles. In the same ' noble spirit he firmly refused the 30,000 florins offered ' him by our people [*i.e.* the agents of Charles]. When ' he was urged that at least he would allow 10,000 ' florins to be given to his servants, " They may take ' " them " (he said) " if they like, but no one shall

CHAP.
XVI.
———
A.D. 1519.

Noble
conduct
of the
Elector of
Saxony.

' " remain my servant another day who accepts a
' " single piece of gold." ' ' The next day ' (continues
' Erasmus) ' he took horse and departed, lest they
' should continue to bother him. This was related to
' me as entirely reliable, by the Bishop of Liège, who
' was present at the Imperial Diet.' [1]

Well did the conduct of the Elector of Saxony merit
the admiration of Erasmus. Would that Charles V.
had merited as fully the patronage of the wise Elector !

It was a significant fact that, after all the bribery
and wholesale corruption by which this election was
marked, the only prince who in the event had a chance
of success, other than Charles, was the one man who
was superior to corruption, and would not allow even
his servants to be bribed, who did not covet the
imperial dignity for himself, but firmly refused it
when offered to him—the protector of Luther against
the Pope and the empire—the hope and strength of
the Protestant Revolution which was now so rapidly
approaching.

VII. THE HUSSITES OF BOHEMIA (1519).

While the election of the Emperor was proceeding
the famous disputation at Leipzig took place, which
commenced between Carlstadt and Eck, upon the
question of grace and free-will, and was continued
between Eck and Luther on the primacy of the Pope—
that remarkable occasion on which, after pressing Eck
into a declaration that all the Greek and other Christians who did not acknowledge the primacy of the
Pope were heretics and lost, Luther himself was finally
driven to assert, probably as much to his own surprise
as to that of his auditors, ' that among the articles on

---

[1] Epist. cccclxxiv. Erasmus to Fisher: Louvain, Oct. 17, 1519.

'which the Council of Constance grounded its con-
'demnation of John Huss, were some fundamentally
'Christian and evangelical.'

Well might Duke George mutter in astonishment
'*a plague upon it.*' A few months later Luther himself, after pondering the matter over and over with
his New Testament and Melanchthon, was obliged to
exclaim, ' I taught Huss's opinions without knowing
'them, and so did Staupitz : we are all of us Hussites
'without knowing it ! Paul and *Augustine* are Hus-
'sites ! I do not know what to think for amazement.' [1]

Meanwhile, before Luther had come to the conclusion *that he himself*, with St. Augustine, was a *Hussite*,
Erasmus had been in correspondence with Johannes
Schlechta, a Bohemian,[2] on the religious dissensions
which existed in Bohemia and Moravia, and with
special reference to the *Hussite* sect of the ' *Pyghards*,'
or United Brethren.[3] Schlechta had informed

Luther
finds he is
a Hussite.

Letter
from
Schlechta
to
Erasmus.

---

[1] Ranke, bk. ii. c. iii. De Wette,
i. No. ccviii. p. 425. That Luther
had found a point of unison between
himself and the Hussites, not only
in their common opposition to
Papal authority, but also in their
common adoption of the severest
views of St. Augustine, see ' *As-*
'*sertio omnium articulorum M.*
' *Lutheri per Bullam Leonis X. no-*
'*vissimam damnatorum.*' Mense
Martio M.DXXI. Leaves Kk, ii. and
iii. ' Habes, miserande Papa, quid
'hic oggannias. Unde et hunc
'articulum necesse est revocare,
'male enim dixi quod liberum ar-
'bitrium ante gratiam sit res de
'solo titulo, sed simpliciter debui
'dicere, lib. arb. est figmentum in
'rebus, seu titulus sine re. Quia

'nulli est in manu sua quippiam
'cogitare mali aut boni, sed omnia
'(ut Viglephi articulus *Constantiæ*
'damnatus recte docet) de neces-
'sitate absoluta eveniunt.' These
articles were condemned as a part
of the heresy of John Huss, of
whom Luther in the same treatise
had said :—' Et in faciem tuam,
'sanctissime Vicarie Dei, tibi libere
'dico, omnia damnata JoannisHuss
'esse evangelica et Christiana,' &c.
(*Ibid.* leaf Hh, iii.)

[2] See Epist. ccccxii. Louvain,
April 23, 1519.

[3] *History of the Protestant
Church of the United Brethren.*
By the Rev. John Holmes. Lon-
don, 1825, vol. i. chaps. i. and ii.

CHAP.
XVI.

A.D. 1519.

The
Pyghards
of
Bohemia.

Erasmus that, setting aside Jews and unbelieving philosophers who denied the immortality of the soul, the people were divided into three sects :—First, the Papal party, including most of the magistrates and nobility. Secondly, a party to which he himself belonged, who acknowledged the Papacy, but differed from other good Catholics in dispensing the Sacrament in both kinds to the laity, and in chanting the Epistle and Gospel at mass, not in Latin, but in the vulgar tongue ; to which customs they most pertinaciously adhered, on the ground that they were confirmed and approved in the Council of Basle (1431).[1] Thirdly, the sect of the ' Pyghards ' [or ' United Brethren '], who since the times of John Zisca [2] had maintained their ground through much bloodshed and violence. These, he said, regarded the Pope and clergy as manifest ' Anti' christs ' ; the Pope himself sometimes as the ' Beast,' and sometimes as the ' Harlot ' of the Apocalypse. They chose rude and ignorant and even married laymen as their priests and bishops. They called each other ' brothers and sisters.' They acknowledged no writings as of authority but the Old and New Testaments. Fathers and Schoolmen they counted nothing by. Their priests used no vestments, and no forms of prayer but ' the Lord's Prayer.' They thought lightly of the sacraments ; used no salt or holy water—only

[1] This middle party were called ' Calixtines.' See introduction to Holmes's *History*, vol. i. p. 21, where the facts mentioned in this letter are detailed, very much in accordance with Schlechta's account.

[2] John Zisca was a Hussite. He died in 1424, nine years after the death of Huss, and on his monument was inscribed, ' Here ' lies John Zisca, who having de' fended his country against the ' encroachments of Papal tyranny, ' rests in this hallowed place in ' spite of the Pope.'—Ibid. p. 20.

pure water—in baptism, and rejected extreme unction. They saw only simple bread and wine, no divinity, in the Sacrament of the Altar, and regarded these only as signs representing and commemorative of the death of Christ, who they said was in heaven. The suffrages of the saints and prayers for the dead they held to be vain and absurd, and also auricular confession and penance. Vigils and fasts they looked upon as hypocritical. The festivals of the Virgin, Apostles, and Saints, they said, were invented by the idle ; Sunday, Christmas, Good Friday, and Pentecost they observed. Other pernicious dogmas of theirs were not worthy of mention to Erasmus. If, however (his Bohemian friend added), the first two of these three sects could but be united, then perhaps this vicious sect, now much on the increase, owing to recent ecclesiastical scandals, might, by the aid of the King, be either *exterminated* or forced into a better form of creed and religion. Erasmus, he concluded, had now the whole circumstances of these Bohemian divisions before him.[1]

Here, then, Erasmus was brought into direct contact with the opinions of the very sect to which Luther was gradually approaching, but had not yet discovered his proximity.

The reply of Erasmus may be regarded, therefore, as evidence of his views, not only on the opinions and practices of the Hussites of Bohemia, but also as foreshadowing what would be his views with regard to the opinions and practices of Luther and the Protestant Reformers so soon as they should publicly profess themselves Hussites.

---

[1] Epist. cccclxiii. Dated Oct. 10, 1519.

' You point out ' (Erasmus wrote) ' that Bohemia ' and Moravia are divided up into three sects.   I wish, ' my dear Schlechta, that some pious hand could unite ' the three into one ! '

The second party (Erasmus said) erred, in his opinion, more in scornfully rejecting the judgment and custom of the Roman Church than in thinking it right to take the Eucharist in both kinds, which was not an unreasonable practice in itself, though it might be better to avoid singularity on such a point.   As to the ' Pyghards,' he did not see why it followed that the Pope was Antichrist, because there had been some bad popes, or that the Roman Church was the ' harlot,' because she had often had wicked cardinals or bishops. Still, however bad the ' Pyghards ' might be, he would not advise a resort to violence.   It would be a dangerous precedent.   As to their electing their own priests and bishops, that was not opposed to primitive practice.   St. Nicholas and St. Ambrose were thus elected, and in ancient times even kings were elected by the people.   If they were in the habit of electing ignorant and unlearned men, that did not matter much, if only their *holy life* outweighed their ignorance.   He did not see why they were to be blamed for calling one another ' brothers and sisters.'   He wished the practice could obtain amongst all Christians, if only the fact were consistent with the words.   In thinking less highly of the Doctors than of the Scriptures—that is, in preferring God to man—they were in the right ; but altogether to reject them was as bad as altogether to accept them.   Christ and the Apostles officiated in their everyday dress ; but it is impious to condemn what was instituted, not without good reason, by the fathers.   Vigils and fasts, in moderation, he did not

see why they rejected, seeing that they were com- Chap.
XVI.
mended by the Apostles ; but he had rather that men
were *exhorted* than *compelled* to observe them. Their A.D. 1519.
views about festivals were not very different from
Jerome's. Nowadays the number of festivals had
become enormous, and on no days were more crimes
committed. Moreover, the labourer was robbed by so
many festivals of his regular earnings.

As to the cure for these diseases of Bohemia : he
desired *unity,* and expressed his views how unity could
be best attained.

' In my opinion ' (he wrote) ' many might be recon- Erasmus
' ciled to the Church of Rome if, instead of everything thinks the
Church
' being defined, we were contented with what is should be
broad and
' evidently set forth in the Scriptures or necessary to tolerant.
' salvation. And these things are *few* in number, and
' the *fewer* the easier for *many* to accept. Nowadays
' out of one article we make six hundred, some of which
' are such that men might be ignorant of them or doubt
' them without injury to piety. It is in human nature
' to cling by tooth and nail to what has once been
' defined. The sum of the philosophy of Christ ' (he
continued) ' lies in this—that we should know that all
' our hope is placed in God, who freely gives us all things
' through his son Jesus ; that by his death we are re-
' deemed ; that we are united to his body in baptism
' in order that, dead to the desires of the world, we may
' so follow his teaching and example as not only not to
' admit of evil, but also to deserve well of all ; that if
' adversity comes upon us we should bear it in the hope
' of the future reward which is in store for all good men
' at the advent of Christ. Thus we should always
' be progressing from virtue to virtue, and whilst

' assuming nothing to ourselves, ascribe all that is
' good to God. If there should be anyone who would
' inquire into the Divine nature, or the nature (*hypo-*
' *stasis*) of Christ, or abstruse points about the sacra-
' ments, let him do so ; only let him not try to force
' his views upon others. In the same way as very
' verbose instruments lead to controversies, so too
' many definitions lead to differences. Nor should we
' be ashamed to reply on some questions : " God
' " knows how this should be so, it is enough for me to
' " believe that it is." I know that the pure blood and
' body of Christ are to be taken purely by the pure, and
' that he wished it to be a most sacred sign and pledge
' both of his love to us and of the fellowship of Chris-
' tians amongst themselves. Let me, therefore, exa-
' mine myself whether there be anything in me incon-
' sistent with Christ, whether there be any difference
' between me and my neighbour. As to the rest, *how*
' the same body can exist in so small a form and in so
' many places at once, in my opinion such questions
' can hardly tend to the increase of piety. I know
' that I shall rise again, for this was promised to all by
' Christ, who was the first who rose from the dead. As
' to the questions, with what body, and how it can be
' the same after having gone through so many changes,
' though I do not disapprove of these things being
' inquired into in moderation on suitable occasions,
' yet it conduces very little to piety to spend too
' much labour upon them. Nowadays men's minds
' are diverted, by these and other innumerable sub-
' tleties, from things of vital importance. Lastly it
' would tend greatly to the establishment of concord,
' if secular princes, and especially the Roman Pontiff,
' would abstain from all tyranny and avarice. For

' men easily revolt when they see preparations for en-
' slaving them, when they see that they are not to be
' invited to piety but caught for plunder. If they saw
' that we were innocent and desirous to do them good,
' they would very readily accept our faith.' [1]

It will be seen that the point of this letter turns not
directly upon the difference which Luther had dis-
cerned between himself and Erasmus (viz. that the one
rejected and the other accepted the doctrinal system
of St. Augustine), but rather upon questions involving
the duty and object of ' *the Church.*' From More's
delineation of the Church of Utopia, it has been seen
that the notion of the Oxford Reformers was that the
Church was intended to be broad and tolerant, not to
define doctrine and enforce dogmas, but to afford a
practical bond of union whereby Christians might be
kept united in one Christian brotherhood, in spite
of their differences in minor matters of creed. In
full accordance with this view, Erasmus had blamed
Schlechta and his party, in this letter, not for holding
their peculiar views respecting the ' Supper,' but for
making them a ground for separation from their fellow-
Christians. So also he blamed Schlechta (himself a
dissenter from Rome) for his harsh feelings towards
the ' Pyghards ' and his wish ' to exterminate ' them.
So, too, whilst sympathising strongly with the poor
' Pyghards ' in many of the points in which they
differed from the Church of Rome, he blamed them
for jumping to the conclusion that the Church was
' Antichrist,' and for flying into extremes. So, too, he
blamed the Church herself, as he always had blamed

---

[1] Epist. cccclxxviii. Dated Nov. 1, 1519. The letter is a long one,
and these quotations are somewhat abridged in translation.

her, for so narrowing her boundaries as to shut out
these ultra-dissenters of Bohemia from her communion.

Now it is obvious that at the foundation of the
position here assumed by Erasmus, and elsewhere by
the Oxford Reformers, lay the conviction that many
points of doctrine were in their nature uncertain
and unsettled—that many attempted definitions of
doctrine, on such subjects as those involved in the
Athanasian Creed, in the Augustinian system, and in
scholastic additions to it, were, after all, and in spite
of all the ecclesiastical authority in the world, just as
unsettled and uncertain as ever ; in fact, mere hypotheses, which in their nature never *can* be verified.

The point
at issue
between
the Oxford
Reformers
and those
who held
by the Au-
gustinian
system.
Here again, therefore, was *indirectly* involved the
point at issue between Erasmus and Luther ; between
the Oxford and the Wittemberg Reformers.   For the
latter in accepting the Augustinian system still adhered, in spirit, to the scholastic or dogmatic system
of theology.   To treat questions such as those above
mentioned as open and unsettled seemed to them to be
playing the part of the sceptic.   Luther was honestly
and naturally shocked when he found Erasmus hinting
that the doctrine of ' original sin ' was in some measure
analogous to the epicycles of the astrologer.   He was
equally shocked again when Erasmus, a few years
after, treated the question of the Freedom of the Will
as one insoluble in its nature, involving the old philosophical questions between free-will and fate.[1]   And
why was he shocked ?   Because the Augustinian

---

[1] Luther replied :—' Absint a
' nobis Christianis Sceptici. . . .
' Nihil apud Christianos notius et
' celebratius, quam assertio. Tolle
' assertiones et Christianissimum
' tulisti. . . . Spiritus Sanctus non
' est scepticus, nec dubia aut opinio-
' nes in cordibus nostris scripsit, sed
' assertiones, ipsa vita, et omni ex-
' perientia, certiores et firmiores.'
—*De Servo Arbitrio* Mar. Lutheri.
Wittembergæ, 1526, pp. 7–12.

system which he had adopted, treated these questions as finally concluded. And how were they concluded? By the judgment of the Church based upon a verbally inspired and infallible Bible.

Luther did not indeed assert so strongly the verbal inspiration of the Bible, much less of the Vulgate version, as Dr. Eck and other Augustinian theologians had done; yet his standing-point obliged him practically to assume the truth of this doctrine, as it obliged his successors more and more strongly to assert it as the years rolled on. And so, whilst rejecting, even more thoroughly than Erasmus ever did, the ecclesiastical authority of the Church of Rome, yet it is curious to observe that, in doing so, Luther did not reject the notion of ecclesiastical authority in itself, but rather, amidst many inconsistencies, set up the authority of what he considered to be the *true* church against that of the church which he regarded as the *false* one. As a consistent Augustinian he was driven to assume, in replying to the Wittemberg prophets on the one hand and the scepticism of Erasmus on the other, that there is a true church somewhere, and that somewhere in the true church there is an authority capable of establishing theological hypotheses. He was not willing that the Scriptures should be left simply to the private judgment of each individual for himself. He even allowed himself to claim for the public ministers of his own church—' the leaders of the ' people and the preachers of the Word '—authority ' not only for themselves but also for others, and for ' the salvation of others, to judge with the greatest ' certainty the spirit and dogmas of all men.' [1]

---

[1] ' Ideo alterum est judicium externum, quo non modo pro nobis ' ipsis, sed et pro aliis et propter aliorum salutem, certissime judi-

Not that Luther always consistently upheld this
doctrine any more than Erasmus consistently upheld
its opposite. Luther was often to be found asserting
and using the right of private judgment against the
authority of Rome, as Erasmus was often found
upholding the authority of the Catholic Church and
her authorised councils against the rival authority of
Luther's schismatic and unauthorised church. In
times of transition, men *are* inconsistent ; and regard
must be had rather to the direction in which they are
moving than the precise point to which at any particular moment they may have attained. And what I
wish to impress upon the reader is this—that not only
Luther, but all other Reformers, from Wickliffe down
to the modern Evangelicals, who have adopted the
Augustinian system and founded their reform upon it,
have practically assumed as the basis of their theology,
first, the plenary inspiration of each text contained in
the Scriptures ; and, secondly, the existence of an
ecclesiastical authority of some kind capable of establishing theological hypotheses ; so that, *in this respect*,
Luther and other Augustinian reformers, instead of
advancing beyond the Oxford Reformers, have lagged
far behind, seeing that they have contentedly remained
under a yoke from which the Oxford Reformers had
been labouring for twenty years to set men free.

The power
of St.
Augus-
tine.

In saying this I am far from overlooking the fact,
that the Protestant Reformers, in reverting to a purer
form of Augustinian doctrine than that held by the
Schoolmen, did practically by it bring Christianity to

'camus spiritus et dogmata om-
'nium. Hoc judicium est publici
'ministerii in verbo et officii ex-
'terni, et maxime pertinet ad

'duces et præcones verbi &c.'—*De
Servo Arbitrio* Mar. Lutheri. Wittembergæ, 1526, p. 82.

bear upon men with a power and a life which contrasted strangely with the cold dead religion of the Thomists and Scotists. I am as far also from underrating the force and the fire of St. Augustine. What, indeed, must not that force and that fire have been to have made it possible for him to bind the conscience of Western Christendom for fourteen centuries by the chains of his dogmatic theology! And when it is considered, on the one hand, that the greatest of the Schoolmen were *so loyal* to St. Augustine, that some of their subtlest distinctions were resorted to expressly to mitigate the harshness of the rigid results of his system, and thus were attempts, not to get from under its yoke, but *to make it bearable* ; [1] and, on the other hand, that the chief *reactions* against scholastic formalism—those of Wickliffe, Huss, Luther, Calvin, the Portroyalists, the Puritans, the modern Evangelicals—were *Augustinian* reactions ; so far from *under*estimating the power of the man whose influence was so diverse and so vast, it may well become an object of ever-increasing astonishment to the student of Ecclesiastical History.

At the same time, these considerations must raise also our estimate of the need and the value of the firm stand taken 350 years ago by the Oxford Reformers

---

[1] See Mozley's *Augustinian Doctrine of Predestination.* Chap. x. *Scholastic Doctrine of Predestination.* And see the particular instance there given on the subject of infants dying in original sin, p. 307. ' Being by nature reprobate, and ' not being included within the ' remedial decree of predestination, ' they were . . . [according to the ' pure Augustinian doctrine] . . . ' subject to the sentence of eternal ' punishment. . . . The Augustinian ' schoolman [Aquinas] could not ' expressly contradict this position, ' but what he could not contradict ' he could explain. Augustine had ' laid down that the punishment of ' such children was the mildest of ' all punishment in hell.' . . . Aquinas ' laid down the further ' hypothesis, that this punishment ' was not pain of body or mind, but ' *want of the Divine vision.*'

against this dogmatic power so long dominant in the realm of religious thought. It has been seen in every page of this history, that they had taken their standpoint, so to speak, *behind* that of St. Augustine ; behind even the schism between Eastern and Western Christendom ; behind those patristic hypotheses which grew up into the scholastic theology ; behind that notion of Church authority by which these hypotheses obtained a fictitious verification ; behind the theory of 'plenary inspiration,' without which the Scriptures could not have been converted, as they were, into a mass of raw material for the manufacture of any quantity of hypotheses—behind all these—on the foundation of *fact* which underlines them all.

The essential difference between the standpoints of the Protestant and Oxford Reformers Luther had been the first to perceive. And the correctness of this first impression of Luther's has been singularly confirmed by the history of the three-and-a-half centuries of Protestant ascendency in Western Christendom. The Protestant movement, whilst accomplishing by one revolutionary blow many objects which the Oxford Reformers were striving and striving in vain to compass by constitutional means, has been so far antagonistic to their work in other directions as to throw it back—not to say *to wipe it out of remembrance*—so that in this nineteenth century those Christians who have desired, as they did, to rest their faith upon honest facts, and not upon dogmas—upon evidence, and not upon authority—instead of taking up the work where the Oxford Reformers left it, have had to begin it again at the beginning, as Colet did at Oxford in 1496. They have had, like the Oxford Reformers, to combat at the outset the theory of ' plenary inspiration,' and the tendency inherited along with it from St. Augustine, by both Schoolmen and Protestant Reformers, to build up a theology, as I have said, upon unverified hypotheses, and to narrow the boundaries of Christian fellowship by the imposition of dogmatic creeds so manufactured. They have had to meet the same arguments and the same blind opposition ; to bear the same taunts of heresy and unsoundness from ascendant orthodox schools ; to be pointed at by their fellow-Christians as insidious enemies of the Christian faith, because they have striven to present it before the eyes of a scientific age, as what they think it really is—*not* a system of unverified hypotheses, but a faith in *facts* which it would be unscientific even in a disciple of the positive philosophy to pass by unexplored.

VIII. MORE'S DOMESTIC LIFE (1519).

By the aid of a letter from Erasmus to Ulrich Hutten,[1] written in July 1519, one more lingering look may be taken at the beautiful picture of domestic happiness presented by More's home. This history would be incomplete without it.

The ' young More,' with whom Colet and Erasmus had fallen in love twenty years ago, was now past forty.[2] The four motherless children, Margaret, Elizabeth, Cicely, and John, awhile ago nestling round their widowed father's knee, as the dark shadow of sorrow passed over the once bright home in Bucklersbury, were now from ten to thirteen years old. The good stepmother, Alice Middleton, is said to have ruled

More forty years old.

---

[1] Epist. ccccxlvii.   [2] See note on the date, More's birth, Appendix C.

her household well, and her daughter had taken a place in the family circle as one of More's children. There was a marked absence of jarring or quarrelling,[1] which in such a household bore witness to the good-nature of the mistress. She could not, indeed, fill

His first
wife.

altogether the void left in More's heart by the loss of his first wife—the gentle girl brought up in country retirement with her parents and sisters, whom he had delighted to educate to his own tastes, in letters and in music, in the fond hope that she would be to him a lifelong companion,[2] and respecting whom, soon after his second marriage, in composing the epitaph for the family tomb, in which *she* was already laid, he had written this simple line :—

'Cara Thomæ jacet hic Joanna uxorcula Mori !'[3]

His second
wife.

The 'dame Alice,' though somewhat older than her husband and matronly in her habits, 'nec bella nec 'puella,' as he was fond of jokingly telling her, out of deference to More's musical tastes, had learned to sing and to play on the harp ;[4] but, after all, she was

---

[1] Eras. *Op.* iii. p. 475, E.

[2] *Ibid.* C. and D. One is tempted to think that More intended to describe his first wife in the epigram, 'Ad Candidum qualis uxor 'deligenda,' very freely translated into English verse by Archdeacon Wrangham as follows :—

* * * * *

Far from her lips' soft door
  Be noise or silence stern,
And hers be learning's store,
  Or hers the power to learn.

With books she'll time beguile,
  And make true bliss her own,
Unbuoyed by Fortune's smile,
  Unbroken by her frown.

So still thy heart's delight,
  And partner of thy way,
She'll guide thy children right,
  When myriads go astray.

So left all meaner things,
  Thou'lt on her breast recline,
While to her lyre she sings
  Strains, Philomel, like thine ;

While still thy raptured gaze
  Is on her accents hung,
As words of honied grace
  Steal from her honied tongue.

· · · · · ·

Quoted from *Philomorus*, p. 42.

[3] More's English *Works*, p. 1420.

[4] Eras. *Op.* iii. p. 745, D and E.

more of the housekeeper than of the wife. It was
not to her but to his daughter Margaret that his
heart now clung with fondest affection.

More himself, Erasmus described to Hutten as
humorous without being foolish, simple in his dress
and habits, and, with all his popularity and success,
neither proud nor boastful, but accessible, obliging,
and kind to his neighbours.[1] Fond of liberty and ease
he might be, but no one could be more active or more
patient than he when occasion required it.[2] No one
was less influenced by current opinion, and yet no man
had more common sense.[3] Averse as he was to all
superstition, and having shown in his ' Utopia ' what
were regarded in some quarters as freethinking tendencies, he had to share with Colet the sneers of the
' orthodox,' yet a tone of unaffected piety pervaded
his life. He had stated times for devotion, and when
he prayed, it was not as a matter of form, but from
his heart. When, too, as he often did, he talked to
his intimate friends of the life to come, Erasmus tells
Hutten that he evidently spoke from his heart, and
not without the brightest hope.[4]

More's
true piety.

He was careful to cultivate in his children not only
a filial regard to himself, but also feelings of mutual
interest and intimacy. He made himself one of them,
and took evidently as much pleasure as they did in
their birds and animals—the monkey, the rabbits, the
fox, the ferret, and the weasel.[5] Thus when Erasmus
was a guest at his house, More would take him into
the garden to see the children's rabbit hutches, or to

The
children's
animals.

---

[1] Eras. *Op.* iii. p. 476, D, &c.
[2] *Ibid.* p. 474, B. .
[3] *Ibid.* p. 474, E.

[4] *Ibid.* p. 477, B.
[5] *Ibid.* p. 474, E and F.

CHAP
XVI.

A.D. 1519.
Their
celebrated
monkey.

watch the sly ways of the monkey; which on one
occasion so amused Erasmus by the clever way in
which it prevented the weasel from making an assault
upon the rabbits through an aperture between the
boards at the back of the hutch, that he rewarded
the animal by making it famous all over Europe,
telling the story in one of his ' Colloquies.' [1] Whereupon so important a member of the household did
this monkey become, that when Hans Holbein some
years afterwards painted his famous picture of the
household of Sir Thomas More, its portrait was taken
along with the rest, and there to this day it may be
seen nestling in the folds of dame Alice's robes.

If More thus took an interest in the children's
animals, so they were trained to take an interest in his
pictures, his cabinet of coins and curiosities, and his
literary pursuits. He did everything he could to
allure his children on in acquiring knowledge. If an
astronomer came in his way he would get him to stay
awhile in his house, to teach them all about the stars
and planets.[2] And it surely must have been More's
children whom Erasmus speaks of as learning the
Greek alphabet by shooting with their bows and
arrows at the letters.[3]

Unhappily of late More had been long and frequently absent from home. Still, even when away
upon an embassy, trudging on horseback dreary stages
along the muddy roads, we find him on the saddle com-

posing a metrical letter in Latin to his ' sweetest chil-
' dren, Margaret, Elizabeth, Cicely, and John,' which,
when a second edition of his ' Epigrams ' was called
for, was added at the end of the volume and printed

---

[1] Colloquy entitled *Amicitia.*
[2] Stapleton's *Tres Thomœ*, p.257

[3] Eras. *Op.* i. p. 511, E.

with the rest by the great printer of Basle [1]—a letter in
which he expresses his delight in their companionship,
and reminds them how gentle and tender a father he
has been to them, in these loving words :—

Kisses enough I have given you forsooth, but stripes hardly ever,
If I have flogged you at all it has been with the tail of a peacock !

. . . .

Manners matured in youth, minds cultured in arts and in know-
    ledge,
Tongues that can speak your thoughts in graceful and elegant
    language :—
These bind my heart to yours with so many ties of affection
That now I love you far more than if you were merely my
    children.

. . . .

Go on (for you can !), my children, in winning your father's
    affection,
So that as now your goodness has made me to feel as though
    never
I really had loved you before, you may on some future occasion,

. . . .

Make me to love you so much that my present love may seem
    nothing !

What a picture lies here, even in these roughly
translated lines, of the gentle relation which during
years of early sorrow had grown up between the
widowed father and the motherless children !

It is a companion-picture to that which Erasmus
drew in colours so glowing, of More's home at Chelsea
many years after this, when his children were
older and he himself Lord Chancellor. What a gleam
of light too does it throw into the future, upon that
last farewell embrace between Sir Thomas More and

---

[1] *Mori Epigrammata* : Basle, | the *Utopia* in 1518, and does not
1520, p. 110. The first edition | contain these verses.
was printed at Basle along with |

Margaret Roper upon the Tower-wharf, when even
stern soldiers wept to behold their ' fatherly and
' daughterly affection ! '

More's
character.

  This was the man whom Henry VIII. had at last
succeeded in drawing into his court ; who reluctantly,
this summer of 1519,[1] in order that he might fulfil his
duties to the King, had laid aside his post of under-
sheriff in the city and his private practice at the bar ;
' who now,' to quote the words of Roper, ' was often
' sent for by the King into his traverse, where some-
' times in matters of astronomy, geometry, divinity,
' and such other faculties, and sometimes of his
' worldly affairs, he would sit and confer with him.
' And otherwhiles in the night would he have him up
' into the leads there to consider with him the diver-
' sities, courses, motions, and operations of the stars
' and planets.

  ' And because he was of a pleasant disposition, it
' pleased the King and Queen after the Council had
' supped for their pleasure commonly to call for him
' to be merry with them.   Till he,' continues Roper,
' perceiving them so much in his talk to delight that
' he could not once in a month get leave to go home
' to his wife and his children (whose company he most
' desired), and to be absent from court two days
' together but that he should be thither sent for
' again ; much misliking this restraint of his liberty,
' began thereupon somewhat to dissemble his nature,
' and so by little and little from his former mirth to
' disuse himself.'

  This was the man who, after ' trying as hard to

---

[1] Mackintosh's *Life of Sir Thomas*   [2] Roper, p. 12.
More, p. 73, quoting ' City Records.'

'keep out of court as most men try to get into it,' had accepted office on the noble understanding that he was 'first to look unto God, and after God to the 'King,' and who under the most difficult circumstances, and in times most perilous, whatever may have been his faults and errors, still

Reverenced his conscience as his King,

and died at last upon the scaffold, a martyr to integrity!

IX. THE DEATH OF COLET (1519).

Erasmus was working hard at his Paraphrases at Louvain, when the news reached him that *Colet was dead!* On the 11th September Pace had written to Wolsey that 'the Dean of Paul's had lain continually 'since Thursday *in extremis*, but was not yet dead.'[1] He had died on the 16th of September 1519.

When Erasmus heard of it, he could not refrain from weeping. 'For thirty years I have not felt the death of 'a friend so bitterly,'[2] he wrote to Lupset, a young disciple of Colet's. 'I seem,' he wrote to Pace, 'as 'though only half of me were alive, Colet being dead. 'What a *man* has *England* and what a *friend* have I 'lost!' To another Englishman he wrote, 'What 'avail these sobs and lamentations? They cannot 'bring him back again. In a little while we shall 'follow him. In the meantime we should rejoice for 'Colet. He now is safely enjoying *Christ*, whom he 'always had upon his lips and at his heart.'[3] To Tunstal, 'I should be inconsolable for the death of

---

[1] Ellis, *Original Letters*, 3rd series, letter lxxx.

[2] Epist. cccclxvii.

[3] Ibid. cccclxx.

' Colet did I not know that my tears would avail no-
' thing for him and for me ; '[1] and to Bishop Fisher,
' I have written this weeping for Colet's death. . . .
' I know it is all right with him who, escaped from this
' evil and wretched world, is in present enjoyment of
' that Christ whom he so loved when alive. I cannot
' help mourning in the public name the loss of so
' rare an example of Christian piety, so remarkable
' a preacher of Christian truth ! '[2] And, in again
writing to Lupset, a month or two afterwards, a long
letter, pouring his troubles, on account of a bitter controversy which Edward Lee had raised up against him,
into the ears of Lupset, instead of, as had hitherto
been his wont, into the ears of Colet, he exclaimed in
conclusion, ' O true theologian ! O wonderful preacher
' of evangelical doctrine ! With what earnest zeal
' did he drink in the philosophy of Christ ! How
' eagerly did he imbibe the spirit and feelings of
' St. Paul ! How did the purity of his whole life corre-
' spond to his heavenly doctrine ! How many years
' following the example of St. Paul, did he teach the
' people without reward ! '[3] ' You would not hesitate,'
finally wrote Erasmus to Justus Jonas, ' to inscribe
' the name of this man in the roll of the saints although
' uncanonised by the Pope.'

' For generations,' wrote More, ' we have not had
' amongst us any one man more learned or holy ! '[4]

The inscription on the leaden plate laid on the coffin
of Dean Colet [5] bore witness that he died ' to the great

---

[1] Epist. cccclxxi.

[2] Ibid. cccclxxiv.

[3] Eras. *Op.* iii. Epist. cccclxxxi.
and *Epistolæ aliquot Eruditorum
Virorum* : Basil. 1520, p. 46.

[4] Ibid. p. 122. ' Coletum nomino,

' quo uno viro neque doctior neque
' sanctior apud nos aliquot retro
' seculis quisque fuit.'

[5] Ashmolean MSS. Oxford 77–
141a. I have to thank Mr. Coxe
for the following copy of the

' grief of the whole people, by whom, for his integrity
' of life and divine gift of preaching, he was the most
' beloved of all his time ; ' and his remains were laid in
the tomb prepared by himself in St. Paul's Cathedral.

X. CONCLUSION.

With the death of Colet this history of the Oxford
Reformers may fitly end. Erasmus and More, it is
true, lived on sixteen years after this, and retained
their love for one another to the last. But even *their*
future history was no longer, to the same extent as
it had been, a joint history. Erasmus never again
visited England, and if they did meet during those
long years, it was a chance meeting only, on some
occasion when More was sent on an embassy, and
their intercourse could not be intimate.

The fellow-work of the Oxford Reformers was to a
great extent accomplished when Colet died. From
its small beginnings during their college intercourse
at Oxford it had risen into prominence and made its
power felt throughout Europe. But now for three
hundred years it was to stop and, as it were, to
be submerged under a new wave of the great tide of
human progress. For, as has been said, the Protestant Reformation was in many respects a new
movement, and not altogether a continuation of that
of the Oxford Reformers.

The fellow-work of the Oxford Reformers accomplished.

The Protestant Reformation a new movement under which theirs was submerged.

---

inscription : ' Joannes Coletus,
' Henrici Coleti iterum prætoris
' Londini filius, et hujus templi
' decanus, magno totius populi
' mœrore, cui, ob vitæ integritatem
' et divinum concionandi munus,
' omnium sui temporis fuit chariss.,
' decessit anno a Christo nato 1519
' et inclyti regis Henrici Octavi 11,
' mensis Septembris 16. Is in cœme-
' terio Scholam condidit ac magis-
' tris perpetua stipendia contulit.'

As yet the ' tragedy of Luther ' had appeared only like the little cloud no bigger than a man's hand rising above the horizon.   But scarcely had a year passed from Colet's death before the whole heavens were overcast by it, and Christendom was suddenly involved, by the madness of her rulers, in all the terrors of a religious convulsion, which threatened to shake social and civil, as well as ecclesiastical, institutions to their foundations.

The future
course
of the
survivors
could not
alter the
fellow-
work of
the past.

How Erasmus and More met the storm—how far they stood their ground, or were carried away by natural fears and disappointment from their former standing-point—is well worthy of careful inquiry ; but it must not be attempted here.   In the meantime, the subsequent course of the two survivors could not alter the spirit and aim of the fellow-work to which for so many years past the three friends had been devoting their lives.

Their fellow-work had been to urge, at a critical period in the history of Christendom, the necessity of that thorough and comprehensive reform which the carrying out of Christianity into practice in the affairs of nations and of men would involve.

Nature
of the
Reform
urged by
the Oxford
Reform-
ers.

Believing Christianity to be true, they had faith that it would work.   Deeply imbued with the spirit of Christianity as the true religion of the heart, they had demanded, not so much the reform of particular ecclesiastical abuses, as that the whole Church and the lives of Christians should be reanimated by the

Christian spirit.   Instead of contenting themselves with urging the correction of particular theological errors, and so tinkering the scholastic creed, they had sought to let in the light, and to draw men's attention from dogmas to the facts which lay at their root. Having faith in free inquiry, they had demanded freedom of thought, tolerance, education.

Believing that Christianity had to do with secular as well as with religious affairs, they had urged the necessity, not only of religious but also of political reform. And here again, instead of attacking particular abuses, they had gone to the root of the matter, and laid down the *golden rule* as the true basis of political society. They not only had censured the tyranny, vices, and selfishness of princes, but denied the divine right of kings, assuming the principle that they reign by the consent and for the good of the nations whom they govern. Instead of simply asserting the rights of the people against their rulers in particular acts of oppression, they had advocated, on Christian and natural grounds, the equal rights of rich and poor, and insisted that the good of the *whole people as one community* should be the object of all legislation.

Believing lastly in the Christian as well as in the natural brotherhood of nations, they had not only condemned the selfish wars of princes, but also claimed that the golden rule, instead of the Machiavellian code, should be regarded as the true basis of international politics.

Such was the broad and distinctively *Christian* Reform urged by the Oxford Reformers during the years of their fellow-work.

And if ever any reformers had a fair chance of a hearing in influential quarters, surely it was they. They had direct access to the ears of Leo X., of Henry VIII., of Charles V., of Francis I. ; not to mention multitudes of minor potentates, lay and ecclesiastical, as well as ambassadors and statesmen, whose influence upon the politics of Europe was scarcely less than that of princes. But though they were courted and patronised by the potentates of Europe, *their reform was refused.*

The destinies of Christendom, by a remarkable concurrence of circumstances, were thrown very much into the hands of the young Emperor Charles V. ; and, unfortunately for Christendom, Charles V. turned out to be the opposite of the ' Christian Prince' which Erasmus had done his best to induce him to become. Leo X. also had bitterly disappointed the hopes of Erasmus. When the time for final decision came, in the Diet of Worms the Emperor and the Pope were found banded together in the determination to refuse reform.

Reform of
Luther.

In the meantime the leadership of the Reform movement had passed into other and sterner hands. Luther, concentrating his energies upon a narrower point, had already, in making his attack upon the abuse of Indulgences, raised a definite quarrel with the Pope. Within fifteen months of the death of Colet, he had astonished Europe by defiantly burning the Bull issued against him from Rome. And summoned by the Emperor to Worms, to answer for his life, he still more startled the world by boldly demanding, in the name of the German nation from the Emperor and Princes, that Germany should throw off the Papal yoke from her neck. For this was practically what Luther did at Worms.[1]

---

[1] Luther in his famous speech at the Diet, after alluding to his doc- | trinal and devotional works, and offering to retract whatever in them

The Emperor and Princes had to make up their minds, whether they would side with the Pope or with the nation, and they decided to side with the Pope. They thought they were siding with the stronger party, but they were grievously mistaken. Their defiance of Luther was engrossed on parchment. Luther's defiance of *them*, and assertion of the rights of conscience against Pope and Emperor, rang through the ages. It stands out even now as a watershed in history dividing the old era from the new.

CHAP. XVI.

A.D. 1519. Luther's battle-cry at the Diet of Worms.

In the history of the next three centuries, it is impossible not to trace the onward swell, as it were, of a great revolutionary wave, which, commencing with the Peasant War and the Sack of Rome, swept on through the Revolt of the Netherlands, the Thirty Years' War, the Puritan Revolution in England, and the foundation of the great American Republic, until it culminated and broke in the French Revolution. It is impossible not to see, in the whole course of the events of this remarkable period, an onward movement as irresistible and certain in its ultimate progress as that of the great geological changes which have passed over the physical world.

The refusal of Reform followed by a period of Revolution.

It is in vain to speculate upon what might have been the result of the concession of broad measures

---

was contrary to Scripture, emphatically refused to retract what he had written against the Papacy, on the ground that were he to do so, it would be ' like throwing both doors ' and windows right open ' to Rome to the injury of the German nation. And in his German speech he added an exclamation, most characteristic, at the very idea of the absurdity of its being thought possible, that he could retract anything on this point :—' Good God, what a great ' cloak of wickedness and tyranny ' should I be ! ' See Förstermann's *Urkundenbuch zur Geschichte der evangelischen Kirchen-Reformation*, vol. i. p. 70 : Hamburg, 1842.

of reform whilst yet there was time ; but in view of
the bloodshed and misery, which, humanly speaking,
might have been spared, who can fail to be impressed
with the terrible responsibility, in the eye of History,
resting upon those by whom, in the sixteenth century,
the reform was refused ? They were utterly power-
less, indeed, to stop the ultimate flow of the tide,
but they had the terrible power to turn, what might
otherwise have been a steady and peaceful stream,
into a turbulent and devastating flood. They had the
terrible power, and they used it, of involving their
own and ten succeeding generations in the turmoils
of revolution.

APPENDIX A.

———◦◇◦———

EXTRACTS FROM MS. Gg. 4, 26, IN THE CAMBRIDGE UNIVERSITY
LIBRARY, TRANSLATIONS OF WHICH ARE GIVEN AT PAGES
37, 38 OF THIS WORK.

Fol. 4 *b.* ' Quapropter concludit Paulus justificatos ex fide,
' et soli deo confidentes per Jesum reconciliatos esse deo,
' restitutosque ad gratiam ; ut apud deum stent et maneant
' ipsi filii dei, et filiorum dei certam gloriam expectent. Pro
' qua adipiscenda interim ferenda sunt omnia patienter : ut
' firmitas spei declaretur. Quæ quidem non falletur. Siqui-
' dem ex dei amore et gratia erga nos ingenti reconciliati
' sumus, alioquin ejus filius pro nobis etiam impiis et con-
' trariis deo non interiisset. Quod si alienatos a se dilexit,
' quanto magis reconciliatos et diligit et dilectos conservabit.
' Quamobrem firma et stabili spe ac letitia esse debemus,
' confidereque deo indubitanter per Jesum Christum ; per
' quem unum hominem est ad deum reconciliatio. Nam ab
' illo ipso primo homine, et diffidentia, impietateque, et scelere
' ejusdem, totum humanum genus deperiit.

f. 5 *b.* ' Sed hic notandum est, quod hec gracia nichil est
' aliud, quam dei amor erga homines ; eos videlicet, quos
' vult amare, amandoque inspirare spiritu suo sancto, qui ipse
' est amor, et dei amor, qui (ut apud Joannem evangelistam
' ait salvator) ubi vult spirat. Amati autem et inspirati a
' deo vocati sunt, ut, accepto amore, amantem deum red-
' ament et eundem amorem desiderent et expectent. Hec
' exspectacio et spes, ex amore est. Amor vero noster est,
' quia ille nos amat, non (ut scribit Joannes in secunda
' epistola) quasi nos prius dilexerimus deum : sed quia ipse
' prior dilexit nos, eciam nullo amore dignos, siquidem im-
' pios et iniquos, jure ad sempiternum interitum destinatos.
' Sed quosdam, quos ille novit et voluit, deus dilexit, dili-

' gendo vocavit, vocando justificavit, justificando magnificavit.
' Hec in deo graciosa dileccio et caritas erga homines, ipsa
' vocacio et justificacio et magnificacio est : nec quicquid
' aliud tot verbis dicimus quam unum quiddam, scilicet
' amorem dei erga homines eos quos vult amare. Item cum
' homines gracia attractos, vocatos, justificatos, et magnifi-
' catos dicimus, nichil significamus aliud, quam homines
' amantem deum redamare.

f. 18. . . . 'aperte videas providente et dirigente deo res
' duci, atque ut ille velit in humanis fieri ; non ex vi quidem
' aliqua illata, quum nichil est remotius a vi quam divina
' actio : sed cum hominis natura voluntate et arbitrio, divina
' providentia et voluntate latenter et suaviter et quasi natu-
' raliter comitante, atque una et simul cum eo incedente tam
' mirabiliter, ut et quicquid velis egerisque agnoscatur a deo,
' et quod ille agnoverit statuitque fore simul id necessario
' fiat.

ff. 79, 80. 'Hominis anima constat intellectu et voluntate.
' Intellectu sapimus. Voluntate possumus. Intellectus sa-
' pientia, fides est. Voluntatis potentia, charitas. Christus
' autem dei virtus, i.e. potentia, est, et dei sapientia. Per
' christum illuminantur mentes ad fidem : qui illuminat
' omnem hominem venientem in hunc mundum, et dat
' potestatem filios dei fieri, iis qui credunt in nomine ejus.
' Per christum etiam incenduntur voluntates in charitatem :
' ut deum, homines, et proximum ament : in quibus est com-
' pletio legis. A deo ergo solo per christum et sapimus et
' possumus ; eo quod in christo sumus. Homines autem ex
' se intellectum habent cæcum, et voluntatem depravatam
' in tenebrisque ambulant et nesciunt quid faciunt. . . .

' Christus autem (ut modo dixi) dei virtus, et dei sapientia
' est. Qui sunt calidis radiis illius divinitatis acciti ut illi in
' societate adhereant, hii quidem sunt *tercii* [1. Jews ; 2.
' Gentiles ; 3. Christians], illi quos Paulus vocatos et electos
' in illam gloriam, appellat : quorum mentes presentia divini-
' tatis illustrantur ; voluntates corriguntur ; qui fide cernunt
' clare sapientiam christi, et amore ejusdem potentiam fortiter
' apprehendunt.'

APPENDIX B.

———◆———

(a) 'Deus autem ipse animi instar totus in toto est, et
'totus in qualibet parte: verumtamen non omnes partes simi-
'liter deificat (dei enim animare deificare est), sed varie, vide-
'licet, ut convenit ad constructionem ejus, quod est in eo
'unum, ex pluribus. Hoc compositum eciam ex deo et homi-
'nibus, modo templum dei, modo ecclesia, modo domus,
'modo civitas, modo regnum, a *dei* prophetis appellatur. . . .
'In quo quum Corinthei erant, ut videri voluerunt et pro-
'fessi sunt: sapienter sane Paulus animadvertens si quid
'laude dignum in illis erat, inde exorditur, et gracias agit
'de eo quod præ se ferunt boni, quodque adhuc fidei et ec-
'clesiæ fundamentum tenent; ut hoc leni et molli principio
'alliciat eos in lectionem reliquæ epistolæ, faciatque quod re-
'prehendit in moribus eorum facilius audiant. Nam si sta-
'tim in initio asperior fuisset graviusque accusasset, profecto
'teneros adhuc animos et novellos in religione, presertim in
'gente illa Greca, arrogante et superba, ac prona in dedigna-
'tionem, a se et suis exhortationibus discussisset. Prudenter
'igitur et caute agendum fuit pro racione personarum, loco-
'rum et temporum: in quibus observandis fuit Paulus certe
'unus omnium consideratissimus, qui proposito fini ita novit
'media accommodare: ut quum nihil aliud quesierat nisi gloriam
'Jesu christi in terris, et amplificationem fidei ac charitatis,
'homo divina usus solertia nihil nec egit nec omisit unquam
'apud aliquos, quod ejusmodi propositum vel impediret vel
'retardaret. Itaque jam necessario correcturus quamplurima
'per literas in Corinthiis, qui, post ejus ab eis discessum,
'obliqua acciderant, acceptiore utitur principio et quasi quen-
'dam aditum facit ad reliqua, quæ non nihil amara cogitur

L L

' adhibere, ut salutaris medicinæ poculum, modo ejus os sac-
' charo illiniatur, Corinthii libenter admittant et hauriant.
' Quanquam vero Corinthii omnes qui fuerunt ex ecclesia
' christum professi sunt, in illiusque doctrina et nomine glo-
' riati sunt : tamen super hoc fundamento nonnullorum erant
' malæ et pravæ edificationes partim ignorantia partim malicia
' superintroductæ. Fuerunt enim quidam parum modesti,
' idemque non parum arrogantes, qui deo et christo et christi
' apostolis non nihil posthabitis, ceperunt de lucro suo cogi-
' tare, ac freti sapientia seculari, quæ semper plurimum potuit
' apud Grecos, in plebe sibi authoritatem quærere, simulque
' opinionem apostolorum, maxime Pauli, derogare ; cujus
' tamen adhuc apud Corinthios (ut debuit) nomen plurimum
' valuit. At illi nescio qui invidi et impatientes laudis
' Pauli, et suam laudem ac gloriam amantes, attentaverunt
' aliquid institutionis in ecclesia, ut eis venerat in mentem,
' utque sua sapientia et opibus probare potuerint, voluerunt-
' que in populo videri multa scire et posse ac quid ex-
' poscit christiana religio nihil ignorare, facileque quid
' venerat in dubium posse solvere et sententiam ferre.
' Qua insolentia nimirum in molli adhuc et nascente
' ecclesia molliti sunt multa, multa passi eciam sunt quæ
' ab institutis Pauli abhorruere. Item magna pars populi
' jamdudum et vix a mundo tracti in eam religionem quæ
' mundi contemptum edocet et imperat, facile retrospexit ad
' mundanos mores : et oculos in opes, potentiam, et sapientiam
' secularem conjecit. Unde nihil reluctati sunt, quin qui
' opibus valuerunt apud eos iidem authoritate valeant. Immo
' ab illis illecti prompti illorum nomina sectati sunt, quo fac-
' tum fuit ut partes nascerentur et factiones ac constitutiones
' sibi diversorum capitum : ut quæque conventicula suum
' caput sequeretur. Ex quo dissidio contentiosæ altercationes
' proruperunt et omnia simul misere corruerunt in deterius.
' Quam calamitatem Corinthiensis ecclesiæ quorundam impro-
' bitate inductam, illius primus parens Paulus molestissime
' tulit, non tam quod conati sunt infringere suam authorita-
' tem, quam quod sub malis suasoribus qui bene ceperint
' navigare in christi archa periclitarentur. Itaque quantum
' est ausus et licuit insectatur eos qui volunt videri sapientes,
' quique in christiana republica plus suis ingeniis quam ex

'deo moliuntur. Quod tamen facit ubique modestissime,
'homo piissimus, magis querens reformationem malorum
'quam aliquorum reprehensionem. Itaque docet omnem et
'sapientiam et potentiam a deo esse hominibus per Jesum
'christum, qui dei sui patris eterni virtus et sapientia est,
'cujus virtute sapiat oportet et possit quisque qui vere sapiat
'aliquid et recte possit ; hominum autem sapientiam inanem
'et falsam affirmat : Item potentiam vel quanquumque quan-
'dam enervationem et infirmitatem : atque hec utraque
'deo odiosa et detestabilis, ut nihil possit fieri nec stultius
'nec impotentius, neque vero quod magis deo displiceat,
'quam quempiam suis ipsius viribus conari aliquid in ecclesia
'christiana : quam totam suum solius opus esse vult deus ;
'atque quenquam in eo ex se solo suoque spiritu sapere, ut
'nulla sit in hominibus prorsus neque quod possunt boni-
'tate, neque quod sapiunt fide, neque denique quod sunt qui-
'dem spe, nisi ex deo in christo gloriatio, per quem sumus in
'ipso, et in deo, a quo sane solo possumus et sapimus, et sumus
'denique quicquid sumus. Hoc in tota hac epistola contendit
'Paulus asserere : verum maxime et apertissime in prima
'parte : in qua nititur eradicare et funditus tollere falsam
'illam opinionem, qua homines suis viribus se aliquid posse
'arbitrantur, qua sibi confisi, tum deo diffidunt, tum deum
'negligunt. Quæ hominum arrogantia et opinio de seipsis,
'fons est malorum et pestis, ut impossibile sit eam societatem
'sanam et incolumem esse, in qua possunt aliquid, qui suis
'se viribus aliquid posse arbitrantur. Secundum vero Pauli
'doctrinam, quæ est christi doctrina et evangeliis consona (si-
'quidem unus est author et idem spiritus) nihil quisquam ad
'se ipsum, sed duntaxat ad deum spectare debet, ei se subji-
'cere totum, illi soli servire, postremo ab illo expectare omnia
'et ex illo solo pendere : ut quicquid in christiana repub-
'lica (quæ dei est civitas) vel vere sentiat, vel recte agat ab
'illo id totum credat proficisci, et acceptum deum referat.'
—*Leaf* a 4, *et seq.*

(*b*) 'Quod si quando voluerit quempiam preditum sapi-
'entia seculari, cujusmodi Paulus et ejus discipulus Diony-
'sius Areopagita ac nonnulli alii veritates sapientiæ suæ, et
'accipere et ad alios deferre : profecto hi nunciaturi aliis quod
'a deo didicerint, dedita opera nihil magis curaverunt quam ut

' ex seculo nihil sapere viderentur ; existimantes indignum
' esse ut cum divinis revelatis humana racio commisceatur :
' nolentes eciam id committere quo putetur veritati credi
' magis suasione hominum quam virtute dei.

‘ Hinc Paulus in docta et erudita Grecia nihil veritus est,
' ex se videri stultus et impotens, ac profiteri se nihil scire nisi
' Jesum christum et eundem crucifixum : nec posse quicquam
' nisi per eundem ut per stulticiam predicationis salvos faciat
' credentes et ratiocinantes confundet.'—*Leaf* 3, 4.

(*c*) ' Idem etiam potentes non sua quidem potentia et vir-
' tute, sed solius dei per Jesum christum dominum nostrum, in
' quo illud venerandum et adorandum miraculum, quod deus
' ipse coierit cum humana natura ; quod quiddam compositum
' ex deo et homine (quod Greci vocant " Theantropon ") hic
' vixit in terris, et pro hominum salute versatus est cum ho-
' minibus, ut eos deo patri suo revocatos reconciliaret : quod
' idem præstitit in probatione et ostensione virtutis defen-
' sioneque justiciæ usque ad mortem, mortem autem crucis :
' quod deinde victa morte, fugato diabolo, redempto humano
' genere, ut liberam habeat potestatem, omnino sine adversarii
' querela, eligendi ad se quos velit, ut quos velit vocet, quos
' vocet justificet.   Quod (inquam) sic victa et prostrata morte,
' mortisque authore, ex morte idem resurrexit vivens, ac
' vivum se multis ostendit, multisque argumentis compro-
' bavit.   Quod tum postremo cernentibus discipulis sursum
' ut erat deus et homo ascendit ad patrem, illic ex celo
' progressum sui inchoati operis in terris, et perfectionem
' despecturus, ac quantum sibi videbitur continuo adjuturus.
' Quod deinde post hæc tandem opportuno tempore, rebus
' maturis, contrariis deo rationibus discussis, longe et a
' creaturis suis exterminatis injusticia videlicet et ignorantia,
' in quarum profligatione nunc quotidie dei et sapientia et
' virtus in suis ministris operatur, operabiturque usque in
' finem.   Quod tum (inquam) post satis longum conflictum
' et utrinque pugnam inter lucem et tenebras, deo et angelis
' spectantibus, tandem ille idem dux et dominus exercituum,
' qui, hic primus, bellum induxit adversariis et cum hostibus
' manum ipse conseruit, patientia et morte vincens, in sub-
' sidium suorum prelucens et prepotens, rediet, ut fugata
' malitia et stultitia, illustret et bona faciet omnia : utque

'postremo, resuscitans mortuos, ipsam mortem superet
'sua immortalitate, et absorbeat, ac victuros secum rapiat in
'celum, morituros a se longe in sempiternam mortem dis-
'cutiat in tenebras illas exteriores, ut per ipsum in reformato
'mundo sola vita deinceps in perpetuum sapientia et justitia
'regnet.'—*Leaf* b. 5.

(*d*) 'Quamobrem non ab re quidem videtur factum fuisse a
'deo, ut illo vulgo hominum et quasi fæce in fundo residente
'longe a claritate posthabita, qui in tam altam obscuritatem
'non fuerint delapsi, prius et facilius a divino lumine attinge-
'rentur, qui fuerunt qui minus in vallem mundi miserique
'descenderunt, qui altius multo extantes quam alii, merito
'priores exorto justiciæ sole illuminati fuerunt; qui supra
'multitudinem varietatem et pugnam hujus humilis mundi,
'simplices, sui similes, et quieti, extiterunt, tanto propiores
'deo quanto remotius a deo distaverint. Quod si deus ipse
'est ipsa nobilitas, sapientia, et potentia; quis non videt
'Petrum, Joannem, Jacobum, et id genus reliquos, etiam an-
'tequam veritas dei illuxerat in terras, tanto aliis sapientia et
'viribus præstitisse, quanto magis abfuerint ab illorum stultitia
'et impotentia, ut nihil sit mirum, si deus, cujus est bonis
'suis, meliores eligere et accommodare, eos habitos stultos et
'impotentes delegerit, quando quidem revera universi mundi
'nobiliores fuerunt, a vilitateque mundi magis sejuncti,
'altiusque extantes: ut quemadmodum id terræ quod altius
'eminet, exorto sole facilius et citius radiis tangitur; ita
'similiter fuit necesse prodeunte luce quæ illuminaret omnem
'hominem venientem in hunc mundum, prius irradiaret eos
'qui magis in hominibus eminuerint et quasi montes ad
'hominum valles extiterint. Ad alios autem qui sunt in imo
'in regione frigoris, nebulosa sapientia obducti, et tardius
'penetrant divini radii, et illic difficilius illuminant et citius
'destituunt, nisi forte vehementius incumbentes rarifecerint
'nubem et lenifecerint hominem ut abjectis omnibus quæ
'habet, evolet in christum. Quod si fecerit, tum emergit in
'conditionem et statum Petri ac talium parvulorum quos
'dudum contempserit, ut per eam viam ascendat ad veritatem
'qui ipse est christus qui dixit, " Nisi conversi fueritis et effi-
'" ciamini sicut parvuli non intrabitis in regnum cælorum."
'Qui parvuli, sine dubio, sunt majores illis qui magni in

' mundo reputantur, ac ideo jure a deo ad sua mysteria ante-
' positi.'—*Leaf* b. 8.

(*e*) ' Angustis sane et minutis sunt animis qui hoc non
' vident, quique sentiunt de secularibus rebus contendendum
' esse, et in hisce jus quærendum suum ; qui ignorant quæ sit
' divina justitia, quæ injustitia ; quique etiam homunciones,
' quorum stultitia haud scio ridenda ne sit magis quam de-
' flenda, sed certe deflenda ; quoniam ex ea ecclesia calamita-
' tem sentit, ac pæne eversionem. Sed illi homunciones per-
' diti (quibus hoc nostrum seculum plenum est) in quibusque
' sunt etiam qui minime debent esse ecclesiastici viri, et qui
' habentur in ecclesia primarii. Illi (inquam) ignari penitus
' evangelicæ et apostolicæ doctrinæ, ignari divinæ justitiæ,
' ignari christianæ veritatis, soliti sunt dicere causam dei, jus
' ecclesiæ, patrimonium christi, bona sacerdotii, defendi a se
' oportere et sine peccato non posse non defendi. O angustia !
' O cæcitas ! O miseria istorum, qui quum ineunt rationem
' perdendi omnia, non solum hæc secularia, sed illa quoque
' etiam sempiterna ; quumque ipsa perdunt, putant se tamen
' eadem acquirere, defendere et conservare ; qui ipso rerum
' exitu ubique in ecclesia homines, ipsis piscibus oculis
' durioribus, non cernunt quæ contentionibus judiciisque dis-
' pendia religionis, diminutio auctoritatis, negligentia christi,
' blasphemia dei, sequitur. Ea etiam ipsa denique, quæ ipsi
' vocant " bona ecclesiæ," quæque putant se suis litigationibus
' vel tenere vel recuperare ; quæ quotidie paulatim et latenter
' tum amittunt, tum ægre custodiunt, siquidem magis vi
' quam hominum liberalitate et charitate, quo nihil ecclesia
' indignius esse potest. In qua procul dubio eadem debet esse
' ratio conservandi quæ data fuerint quondam, quæ fuerit
' comparandi. Amor dei et proximi, desiderium celestium,
' contemptus mundanorum, vera pietas, religio, charitas,
' benignitas erga homines, simplicitas, patientia, tolerantia
' malorum, studium semper bene faciendi vel omnibus homi-
' nibus ut [in constanti] bono malum vincant, hominum ani-
' mos conscitavit ubique tandem ut de ecclesia christi bene
' opinarentur, ei faveant, eam ament, in eam benefici et
' liberales sint, darentque incessanter, datisque etiam data
' accumulent, quum viderant in ecclesiasticis viris nullam
' avaritiam, nullum abusum liberalitatis suæ. Quod si qui

' supremam partem teneant in christiana ecclesia (id est
' sacerdotes) virtutem (quæ acquisivit omnia) perpetuo tenu-
' issent adhucve tenerent ; profecto si staret causa, effectus
' sequeretur, vel auctus vel conservatus, hominesque ecclesi-
' astici non solum quieti possiderent sua ; sed plura etiam
' acciperent possidenda. Sed quum aquæ (ut ait David)
' intraverant usque animos nostros, quumque cupiditatis et
' avaritiæ fluctibus obruimur, nec illud audimus, Divitiæ si
' affluant, nolite cor apponere, quumque neglecta illa virtute
' et justitia et studio conservandi amplificandique regni dei in
' terris, quod sacerdotio nec exposcenti nec expectanti ejusmodi
' acquisivit omnia, animos suos (proh nephas !) in illos ap-
' pendices et pendulas divitias converterint, quod onus est
' potius ecclesiæ quam ornamentum, tunc ita illo retrospectu
' canes illi et sues ad vomitum, et ad volutabrum luti, infir-
' maverunt se amissa pulchra et placida conservatrice rerum
' virtute ; ut quum vident recidere a se quotidie quod virtus
' comparavit, impotentes dimicant et turpiter sane confligunt
' inter se et cum laicis cum sui nominis infamia et ignominia
' religionis, et ejus rei etiam quam maxime quærunt indies
' majore dispendio ac perditione non videntes cæci, si qui
' [   ] acquisierit aliquid necessario ejus contrarium idem
' auferre oportere. Contemptus mundi mundanarumque
' rerum quem docuit christus comparavit omnia ; contra
' earundem amor amittet et perdet omnia. Quis non videt
' quum virtute præstitimus, nos tunc bona mundi jure exigere
' non potuisse nisi quatenus tenuiter ad victum vestitumque
' pertineat quo jubet Paulus contenti simus. Quis (inquam)
' non videt multo minus nunc nos exigere debere, quum
' omnis virtutis expertes sumus, quumque ab ipsis laicis nihil
' fere nisi tonsa coma, et corona, capitio, et demissa toga,
' differimus, nisi hoc dicat quispiam (deridens nos), quum
' nunc sumus relapsi in mundum, quæ sunt mundi et partem
' nostram in mundo nos expostulare posse ; ut non amplius
' dicamus, Dominus pars hæreditatis nostræ ; sed nobis
' dicatur, Mercedem vestram recepistis. O bone deus, quam
' puderet nos hujus descensus in mundum, si essemus
' memores amoris dei erga nos, exempli christi, dignitatis
' religionis christianæ, professionis et nominis nostri.'—
Leaf d. 3–5.

(*f*) 'Hic obstupesco et exclamo illud Pauli mei, "O altitudo
' " divitiarum sapientiæ et scientiæ dei." O sapientia admir-
' abiliter bona hominibus et misericors, ut jure tua pia benig-
' nitas altitudo divitiarum potest appellari, qui commendans
' charitatem tuam in nobis voluisti in nos tam esse liberalis
' ut temetipsum dares pro nobis, ut tibi et deo nos reddere-
' mur. O pia, O benigna, O benefica sapientia, O os, verbum,
' et veritas dei in homine, verbum veridicum et verificans, qui
' voluisti nos docere humanitus ut nos divinitus sapiamus,
' qui voluisti esse in homine ut nos in deo essemus. Qui
' denique voluisti in homine humiliari usque ad mortem,
' mortem autem crucis, ut nos exaltaremur usque ad vitam,
' vitam autem dei.'

APPENDIX C.

The following correspondence in 'Notes and Queries' (Oct. 1868) may be considered, I think, to set at rest the date of Sir Thomas More's birth.

No. 1 (Oct. 17, 1868).

'Some months ago I found the following entries, relating 'to a family of the name of More, on two blank leaves of 'a MS. in the Gale collection, in the library of Trinity 'College, Cambridge. The class mark of the volume is '"O. 2. 21." Its contents are very miscellaneous. Among 'other things is a copy of the poem of Walter de Bibles-'worth, printed by Mr. Thomas Wright in his volume of '*Vocabularies* from the Arundel MS. The date of this is 'early fourteenth century. The names of former possessors 'of the volume are "Le: Fludd" and "G. Carew;" the 'latter being probably Sir George Carew, afterwards Earl of 'Totness. The entries which I have copied are on the last 'leaf and the last leaf but one of the volume. I have added 'the dates in square brackets, and expanded the contractions:

'"M^d quod die dominica in vigilia Sancti Marce Evange-'"liste Anno Regni Regis Edwardi quarti post conquestum '"Anglie quartodecimo Johannes More Gent. maritatus fuit '"Agneti filie Thome Graunger in parochia sancti Egidij '"extra Crepylgate london. [24 April, 1474.]
'"M^{ed} quod die sabbati in vigilia sancti gregorij pape '"inter horam primam & horam secundam post Meridiem '"eiusdem diei Anno Regni Regis Edwardi quarti post con-'"questum Anglie xv° nata fuit Johanna More filia Johannis '"More Gent. [11 March, 1474-5.]
'"M^d quod die veneris proximo post Festum purificacionis '"beate Marie virginis videlicet septimo die Februarij inter

' " horam secundam et horam terciam in Mane natus fuit
' " Thomas More filius Johannis More Gent. Anno Regni
' " Regis Edwardi quarti post conquestum Anglie decimo
' " septimo. [7 Feb. 1477-8.]

' " M^d quod die dominica videlicet vltimo die Januarij
' " inter horam septimam et horam octauam ante Meridiem
' " Anno regni Regis Edwardi quarti decimo octauo nata
' " fuit Agatha filia Johannis More Gentilman. [31 Jan.
' " 1478-9.]

' " M^d quod die Martis videlicet vj^{to} die Junij inter horam
' " decimam & horam vndecimam ante Meridiem natus fuit
' " Johannes More filius Johannis More Gent. Anno regni
' " Regis Edwardi quarti vicesimo. [6 June, 1480.]

' " Me^d quod die lune viz. tercio die Septembris inter
' " horam secundam & horam terciam in Mane natus fuit
' " Edwardus Moore filius Johannis More Gent. Anno regni
' " regis Edwardi iiij^{ti} post conquestum xxj°. [3 Sept.
' " 1481.]

' " M^d quod die dominica videlicet xxij° die Septembris
' " anno regni regis Edwardi iiij^{ti} xxij° inter horam quartam
' " & quintam in Mane nata fuit Elizabeth More filia Johan-
' " nis More Gent." [22 Sept. 1482.]

' It will be seen that these entries record the marriage of a
' John More, gent., in the parish church of St. Giles, Cripple-
' gate, and the births of his six children, Johanna, Thomas,
' Agatha, John, Edward, and Elizabeth.

' Now it is known that Sir Thomas More was born, his
' biographers vaguely say, *about* 1480 in Milk Street, Cheap-
' side, which is in the parish of St. Giles, Cripplegate ; that he
' was the son of Sir John More, afterwards Lord Chief Justice,
' who, at the time of his son's birth, was a barrister, and
' would be described as " John More, gent." ; and that he had
' two sisters, Jane or Joane (Wordsworth's *Eccl. Biog.* ii. 49),
' married to Richard Stafferton, and Elizabeth, wife to John
' Rastall the printer, and mother of Sir William Rastall
' (born 1508), afterwards Lord Chief Justice of the Queen's
' Bench.

' The third entry above given records the birth of Thomas,
' son of John More, who had been married in the church of
' St. Giles, Cripplegate, and may be presumed to have lived

' in the parish.   The date of his birth is Feb. 7, 1477–8 ; that
' is, according to modern reckoning, 1478, and therefore
' " *about* 1480."   Oddly enough, the day of the week in this
' entry is wrong.   It is Friday, which in 1477–8 was Feb. 6.
' But Thomas was born between two and three in the morn-
' ing of Saturday, Feb. 7.   The confusion is obvious and
' natural.

' The second and last entries record the births of his sisters
' Johanna and Elizabeth.   The former of these names ap-
' pears to have been a favourite in the family of Sir John
' More, and was the name of his grandmother, the daughter
' of John Leycester.

' I may add, that the entries are all in a contemporary
' hand, and their formal character favours the supposition
' that they were made by some one familiar with legal docu-
' ments, and probably by a lawyer.

' This remarkable series of coincidences led me at first to
' believe that I had discovered the entry of the birth of Sir
' Thomas More.   But, upon investigation, I was met by a
' difficulty which at present I have been unable to solve.   In
' the life of the Chancellor by Cresacre More, his great-
' grandson, the name of Sir Thomas More's mother is said to
' have been " Handcombe of Holliwell in Bedfordshire."   This
' fact is not mentioned by Roper, who lived many years in
' his house, and married his favourite daughter, or by any
' other of his biographers.   The question, therefore, is whether
' the authority of Cresacre More on this point is to be
' admitted as absolute.   He was not born till nearly forty
' years after Sir Thomas More's death, and his book was not
' written till between eighty and ninety years after it.   We
' must take into consideration these facts in estimating the
' amount of weight to be attached to his evidence as to the
' name of his great-great-grandmother.

' Were there then two John Mores of the rank of gentle-
' men, both apparently lawyers, living at the same time, in
' the same parish, and both having three children bearing
' the same names ; or was John More, who married Agnes
' Graunger, the future Chief Justice and father of the future
' Chancellor ?   To these questions, in the absence of Cresacre
' More's statement, the accumulation of coincidences would

' have made it easy to give a very positive answer. Is his
' authority to be weighed against them ?

' Stapylton's assertion that Sir Thomas More had no
' brothers presents no difficulty, as they may have died in
' infancy. The entries which I have quoted would explain
' why he was called Thomas, after his maternal grandfather.

' If any heraldic readers of " Notes and Queries " could
' find what are the arms quartered with those of More upon
' the Chancellor's tomb at Chelsea, they would probably throw
' some light upon the question. Mr. Hunter describes them
' as " three bezants on a chevron between three unicorns'
' " heads."

' WILLIAM ALDIS WRIGHT.

' Trinity College, Cambridge.'

No. 2 (Oct. 31, 1868).

' There can, I think, be no reasonable doubt that Mr.
' Wright's discovery has set at rest the perplexing question
' of the true date of Sir Thomas More's birth. In the note in
' the Appendix to my " Oxford Reformers " I was obliged to
' leave the question undecided, whilst inclined to believe that
' the weight of evidence preponderated in favour of the re-
' ceived date—1480. What appeared almost incontrovertible
' evidence in favour of 1480 was the evidence of the pictures
' of Sir Thomas More's family by Holbein. The most cer-
' tainly authentic of these is the original pen-and-ink sketch
' in the Basle Museum. Upon Mechel's engraving of this
' (dated 1787), Sir Thomas's age is marked " 50," and at the
' bottom of the picture is the inscription, " Johannes Holbein
' " ad Vivum delin. : Londini : 1530." This seemed to be
' almost conclusive evidence that he was born in 1480. If
' Sir Thomas was born in Feb. 1478, according to the newly
' discovered entries, and was fifty when the picture was
' sketched by Holbein, the sketch obviously cannot have been
' made in 1530, but two or three years earlier.

' Now if it may be supposed that the sketch was made
' during the summer or autumn of 1527, I think it will be
' found that all other chronological difficulties will vanish
' before the newly discovered date.

' 1. More himself would be in his fiftieth year in 1527.

' 2. Ann Cresacre, marked on the sketch as " 15," would
' have only recently completed her fifteenth year, as, accord-
' ing to her tombstone, she was in her sixty-sixth year in
' Dec. 1577 ; and according to the inscription on the Burford
' picture she was born in 3 Henry VIII.

' 3. Margaret Roper, marked on the sketch " 22," would
' be born in 1505 or 1506, and this would allow of More's
' marriage having taken place in 20 Henry VII. 1505, as
' stated on the Burford picture.

' 4. Sir Thomas would be forty-one in July, 1519, and this
' accords with Erasmus's statement in his letter to Hutten
' of that date (*Epist.* ccccxlvii.)—" ipse novi hominem, non
' " majorem annis *viginti tribus*, nam *nunc non multum*
' " *excessit quadragesimum.*" He would be only one year past
' forty. Erasmus first became acquainted with More pro-
' bably in the course of 1498, when (being born in February)
' he was in his twentieth year. The " viginti tribus " must
' in any case be an error.

' 5. John More, jun., marked " 19 " in the sketch, would
' be " more or less than thirteen " as reported by Erasmus in
' 1521. (*Epist.* dcv.)

' 6. More's epigram, which speaks of " quinque lustra "
' (*i.e.* twenty-five years) having passed since he was " quater
' " quatuor " (sixteen), and thus makes him forty-one when
. ' he wrote it, would (if he was born in 1478) give 1519 as the
' date of the epigram ; and this corresponds with the fact,
' that the Basle edition of 1518 (*Mori Epigrammata*, Froben)
' did not contain it, while it was inserted in the second
' edition of 1520.

' 7. There is a passage in More's " History of Richard
' " III.," in which the writer speaks of having himself over-
' heard a conversation which took place in 1483.

' Mr. Gairdner, in his " Letters, &c. of Richard III. and
' " Henry VII." (vol. ii. preface, p. xxi), rightly points out
' that, if born in 1480, More, being then only three years old,
' could not have remembered overhearing a conversation.
' But if born in Feb. 1478, he would be in his sixth year,
' and could easily do so.

' On the whole, therefore, the newly discovered date

'dispels all the apparent difficulties with which the received
'date is beset, if only it may be assumed that the true date
'of the Basle sketch was 1527, and not (as inscribed upon
'Mechel's engraving and upon the English pictures of the
'family of Sir Thomas More) 1530.

'Since I published my "Oxford Reformers" I have
'obtained a photograph of the Basle sketch itself, which dis-
'pels this difficulty also, as it bears upon it *no date at all.*

'The date, 1530, on the pictures appears to rest upon
'no good authority. Holbein, in fact, had left England
'the year before. I therefore have little doubt that the
'remarkable document discovered by Mr. Wright is perfectly
'genuine.

'Should the arms quartered with those of More upon the
'Chancellor's tomb at Chelsea prove to be the arms of
'"Graunger," the evidence would indeed be complete.

'Hitchin.   'FREDERIC SEEBOHM.'

No. 3 (Oct. 31, 1868).

'Mr. Wright will find the lineage of Sir Thomas More and
'his father discussed at some length in my "Judges of Eng-
'"land," vol. v. pp. 190-206 ; and I have very little doubt
'that the John More whose marriage is recorded in the first
'entry was the person who afterwards became a Judge (not
'Chief Justice, as Mr. Wright by mistake calls him), and
'that Thomas More, whose birth is recorded in the third
'entry, was the illustrious Lord Chancellor. The only diffi-
'culty arises from John More's wife being named "Agnes
'"daughter of Thomas Graunger ;" but this difficulty is
'easily discarded, since Cresacre More, who wrote between
'eighty and ninety years after the Chancellor's death, is the
'only author who gives another name, and his other bio-
'grapher, who wrote immediately after his death, gives the
'lady no name at all.

'John More married three times ; and he must have been
'a very young man on his first marriage with Agnes Graunger
'(supposing that to be the name of his first wife), by whom
'only he had children.

'I have stated in my account that there were two John

'Mores who were contemporaries at a period considerably
'earlier, one of Lincoln's Inn and the other of the Middle
'Temple. Of the lineage of the latter there is no account;
'but of the former I have stated my conviction that he was
'the father of the John More whose marriage is here recorded,
'and consequently the grandfather of Sir Thomas More; and
'thus, as both the John Mores had originally filled dependent
'employment in Lincoln's Inn, the modest description of his
'origin given by Sir Thomas in his epitaph, "familiâ non
'"celebri, sed honestâ natus," is at once accounted for.

'EDWARD FOSS.'

No. 4 (Oct. 31, 1868).

'Permit me to set your correspondent right in a minor
'particular, which he looks to as confirming his theory, though
'I trust he may be able to substantiate it otherwise. Mr.
'Wright says—"Milk Street, Cheapside . . . . . is in the
'"parish of St. Giles, Cripplegate:" it is not so, as several
'parishes intervene; Milk Street is *within* the walls, where-
'as St. Giles's is *without*. Mr. Wright might have seen this
'by the wording of his first quotation :—" in parochia Egidij
'"extra Crepylgate;" the word "extra" implies beyond the
'walls. Milk Street is in the *ward* of Cripplegate Within,
'not in the *parish* of St. Giles Without, Cripplegate—
'a distinction not obvious to strangers.

'A great part of the district now called Cripplegate *With-*
'*out* was originally moor or fen: we have a Moorfields,
'now fields no more; and a "More" or Moor Lane. I cannot
'suppose the latter to have been named after the author of
'"Utopia;" but as he really emanated from this locality,
'possibly his family was named from the neighbouring moor.
'The Chancellor bore for his crest "a Moor's head affrontée
'"sable." I would not wish to affront his memory by adding
'more, but your readers will find something on this subject
'*antè*, 3rd S. xii. 199, 238.   'A. H.'

No. 5 (Nov. 5, 1868).

' I am indebted to your correspondents, Mr. Foss and A. H.,
' for their corrections of two inaccuracies in my paper on Sir
' Thomas More. Fortunately, neither of these affects the
' strength of my case. It is sufficient that Milk Street and
' the church of St. Giles', Cripplegate, are so near as to render
' it probable that a resident in the one might be married at
' the other. If, therefore, for " the same parish " I substitute
' " the same ward," my case remains substantially as strong
' as before. My mistake arose from not observing that the
' map in Strype's edition of Stow's *Survey*, which I consulted,
' was a map of Cripplegate Ward, and not of the parish of
' St. Giles'.

' Before writing to you, I had, of course, consulted Mr.
' Foss's *Judges of England*, but found nothing there bearing
' upon the point on which I wanted assistance, viz., the name
' and arms of Sir Thomas More's mother.

' WILLIAM ALDIS WRIGHT.

' Trinity College, Cambridge.'

APPENDIX D.

ECCLESIASTICAL TITLES AND PREFERMENTS OF DEAN COLET, IN ORDER OF TIME.*

Date of Appointment	Description of Preferment, &c.	Authority	Date of Avoidance
Aug. 6, 1485	Rectory of St. Mary, Denington, Suffolk	Reg. Norw. xii. f. 116, quoted by Kennett	Sept. 16, 1519, per mortem
(?)	Prebend of Goodeaster, in Collegiate Church of St. Martin-le-Grand	Wharton, *de Decanis*, p. 234	Jan. 26, 1503, per resign.
(?)	Vicarage of St. Dunstan and All Saints, Stepney	Reg. Hill, Lond., quoted by Kennett	Sept. 21, 1505, per resign.
Sept. 30, 1490	Rectory of St. Nicholas, Thyrning, Hunts and Northampton	Reg. Episcop. apud aedes Buodenae, quoted by Kennett	End of 1493
March 5, 1493-4	Prebend of Botevant, in Cathedral Church of York	Le Neve's *Fasti* (1854), vol. iii. p.176	
	[During this interval, Colet was apparently on the Continent]		
Dec. 17, 1497	Deacon	Reg. Savage, Lond. quoted by Kennett	
March 25, 1497-8	Priest (by Knight said to be on Feast of 'St Ann,' i.e. July 26, in error probably for 'Annunciation,' i.e. March 25)	Memorand. a Willi. Smyth, Lincoln, quoted by Kennett	
1501 (?)	S.T.B. (Bachelor of Divinity)	Anthony à Wood (sub anno 1501, on mere conjecture, apparently dating back from the assumed date of the D.D.), quoted by Kennett	
1502	Prebend of Durnesford, in Cathedral Church of Salisbury	Wharton, *de Decanis*, p. 234	
1504	S.T.P. (Doctor of Divinity)	Ant. à Wood, sub anno 1504 (probably only conjectured by Wood, as there appears to be no record at Oxford), quoted by Kennett	
May 5, 1505	Prebend of Mora, in Cathedral Church of St. Paul, London	Reg. Hill. f. 51, quoted by Le Neve, *Fasti*, ii. 411	Sept. 16, 1519, per mortem
1505 (?)	Deanery of St. Paul's, London	Le Neve, ib. p. 411	Ditto ditto
1516	Treasurership of Chichester Cathedral (Dean Colet ?)	Reg. Cicestrense, quoted by Le Neve, i. 268	

* I am mainly indebted to Mr. Lupton for this list.

APPENDIX E.

———◦◦———

CATALOGUE OF EARLY EDITIONS OF THE WORKS OF
ERASMUS IN MY POSSESSION.

A.D.

1506. D. Erasmi &c. Adagiorum Collectanea, Rursus ab
eodem recognita atque aucta . . . [also] Erasmi
varia epigrammata.

In ædibus Joannis Barbier xviii. Martij M.DVI.

1506. D. Erasmi &c. Adagiorum Collectanea, Rursus ab eodem
recognita atque aucta . . . [but without the epi-
grams].

Ex ædibus Ascensianis pridie natalis dominici M.DVI.

1508. Erasmi Rot. Adagiorum chiliades tres, ac centuriæ fere
totidem.

Venetiis in ædibus Aldi, mense Sept. MDVIII.

1511. Moriæ Encomium Erasmi Roterodami Declamatio.

Argentorati in ædibus M. Schurerii, mense augusto anno M.D.XI.

1512. Collectanea Adagiorum &c. Erasmi. Ex Tertia Recognitione. (With prefatory letter of Schurerius dated
xiiii. Calendas Julii MDIX.)

Argentorati [Strasburg] stanneis calamis denuo exscripta in
officina Matthiæ Schurerii, mense Junio M.D.XII.

1512. De ratione studii, &c.

Officium discipulorum ex Quintiliano.

Concio de puero Jesu, &c.

Expostulatio Jesu ad mortales.

Carmina scholaria.

Argentorati, Ex ædibus Schurerianis mense Julio M.D.XII.

1513. De Duplici Copia rerum ac verborum Commentarii duo.
[A reprint of the first edition of Paris.]

Argentorat. M. Schurerius exscripsit, mense Januario M.D.XIII.

1514. De ratione studii, &c.

A.D.

Officium discipulorum ex Quintiliano.

Concio de puero Jesu ad mortales.

Carmina scholaria.

> Argentorati ex ædibus M. Schurerii, mense Augusto, anno M.D.XIIII.

1514. Parabolarum sive Similium liber. (Prefatory letter of Erasmus to Ægidius dated MDXIIII. Idibus Octobreis.)

> Argentorati ex ædibus Schurerianis, mense Decembri MD.XIIII. (First edition ?)

1514. Opuscula aliquot, Erasmo Rot. castigatore et interprete. Cato . . amplectens præcepta Mimi Publiani, Septem Sapientum celebria dicta, Institutum Christiani hominis, &c.

> Colonie in edibus Martini Werdenensis, XII. KalendasDecembres.

1514(?). De duplici Copia Verborum ac rerum commentarii duo. Ab Authore ipso diligentissime recogniti et emaculati atque in plerisque locis aucti.

Item Epistola Erasmi ad Jacobum Vuymphelingium Selestatinum.

Item Parabolæ, &c.

> Argentorat. Schurerius.

1515. Enchiridion Militis Christiani. (Without the letter to Volzius.)

> Lypsiæ in ædibus Valentini Schumans. . Sexto Calendæ Septembris, M.D.XV.

1515. Enchiridion Militis Christiani. (Without the letter to Volzius.)

Disputatio de Tedio et Pavore Christi.

Exhortatio ad virtutem, &c.

Precatio ad Virginis filium Jesum.

Pæan virgini Matri, &c.

Obsecratio ad Mariam . . .

Oratio in laudem pueri Jesu.

Enarratio allegorica in Primum Psalmum.

Carmen de casa natalitia pueri Jesu.

Carmina complura de puero Jesu.

Carmina de angelis.

Carmen Græcanicum Virgini sacrum Mariæ.

> Argentorati apud M. Schurerium, mense Septembri, M.D.XV.

1515. Erasmi Roterodami Enarratio in Primum Psalmum Davidicum.

Martini Dorpii ad eundem Epistola, de Moriæ Encomio, &c.

Erasmi ad Dorpium Apologia.

Louanii Theodoricus Martinus excudebat, Mense Octobr.MDXV.

1515. Cato Erasmi. Opuscula aliquot : Precepta Mimi Publiani ; Septem sapientum celebria dicta ; Institutum christiani hominis, &c.

Colonie in edibus Quentell. M.CCCCC.XV.

1516. Novum Instrumentum.

Basileæ in ædibus Joannis Frobenii Hammelburgensis, Mense Februario Anno M.D.XVI.

1516. Collectanea Adagiorum, &c.

Argentorati M. Schurerius . . . exscripsit, Mense Maio M.D.XVI.

1516. Enchiridion, &c. (containing the same matter as the Strasburg edition of 1515).

Argentorati apud M. Schurerium, Mense Junio, M.D.XVI.

1516. Institutio Principis Christiani . . . cum aliis nonnullis, viz. :—Precepta Isocratis, &c. ; Panegyricum gratulatorium, &c. ad Principem Philippum ; Libellus Plutarchi de discrimine adulatoris et amici.

Louanii apud Theodoricum Martinum Alustensem, Mense Augusto, MDXVI.

1516. Erasmi Roterodami Epistolæ ; ad Leonem X, ad Cardinalem Grimannum, ad Cardinalem S. Georgii, ad Martinum Dorpium. Ejusdem in laudem urbis Selestadii Panegyricum Carmen.

Lypsiæ impressit Valentinus Schuman. A.D. M.CCCC.XVI.

1517. Aliquot Epistole saneque elegantes Erasmi Roterodami, et ad hunc aliorum eruditissimorum hominum, antehac nunquam excusæ præter unam et alteram. (Containing 39 letters.)

Lovanii apud Theodoricum Martinum, anno M.D.XVII. mense Aprili.

1517. Scarabeus, cum scholiis.

Basileæ apud Joannem Frobenium, Mense Maio, M.D.XVII.

1517. Bellum.

Basileæ apud Joannem Frobenium, Mense Aprili, M.D.XVII.

1517. De Octo Orationis Partium constructione Libellus. . . Erasmo autore.

Basileæ ; In officina Adæ Petri, mense Augusto, M.D.XVII.

A.D.

1517. Enchiridion, &c. (containing the same matter as the Strasburg edition of 1515).

> Argentorati apud M. Schurerium mense Novembri, M.D.XVII.

1517. In epistolam Pauli ad Romanos Paraphrasis. (First edition.)

> Louanii Ex officina Theodo. Martin. Mense Novembri, M.D.XVII.

1518. Aliquot Epistolæ saneque elegantes Erasmi Roterodami, et ad hunc aliorum eruditissimorum hominum. (Containing 56 letters.)

> In Ædibus Frobenianis apud inclytam Germaniæ Basiliam; mense Januario, Anno M.D.XVIII.

1518. De Optimo Reip. Statu deque nova insula Vtopia libellus vere aureus . . . Thomæ Mori.

Epigrammata . . . Thomæ Mori.

Epigrammata Des. Erasmi Rot.

> Basiliæ apud Joannem Frobenium, mense Martio M.D.XVIII.

1518. Enchiridion militis Christiani. (With prefatory letter to Volzius.)

Disputatiuncula de Pavore, &c. Jesu.

Jo : Coleti Responsio.

Basilius in Esaiam e Græco versus.

Epistola exhortatoria, &c.

Precatio . . . ad Jesum.

Pæan . . . virgini matri, &c.

Concio de puero Jesu.

Enarratio primi Psalmi.

Ode de casa natalitia pueri Jesu.

Expostulatio Jesu.

Hymni de Michaele, &c.

> Basileæ apud Jo. Frobenium, M.D.XVIII. Quintili mense.

1518. Auctarium selectarum aliquot Epistolarum Erasmi Roterodami ad Eruditos, et horum ad illum.

> Apud inclytam Basileam (Prefatory letter of Beatus Rhenanus dated XI. Calendas Septembreis M.D.XVIII.)

1518. Institutio boni et Christiani principis, &c.

Præcepta Isocratis, &c.

Panegyricus &c. ad Principem Philippum.

Libellus Plutarchi, &c.

> Basileæ apud J. Frobenium, mense Julio MDXVIII.

Also, Plutarchi opuscula quædam D. Erasmo Rot. . . Philippo Melanchthone &c. interpretibus.

> Basileæ apud J. Frobenium, mense Septembri M.D.XVIII.

1518. Querela Pacis undique gentium ejectæ . . . also :—
In genere Consolatorio de Morte declamatio.

Lipsiæ ex ædibus Valentini Schumann, 1518.

1519. Ratio seu Compendium veræ Theologiæ.

Basileæ apud Jo. Frobenium, mense Januario M.D.XIX.

1519. Paraclesis.

Basileæ apud Jo. Frobenium, mense Februario M.D.XIX.

1519. Novum Testamentum omne, multo quam antehac
diligentius ab Erasmo Rot. recognitum, &c. (Second
edition.)

Basileæ in ædibus Joannis Frobenii, M.D.XIX. mense Martio.

1519. D. Erasmi Rot. in Novum Testamentum ab eodem
denuo recognitum Annotationes.

Basileæ apud Joannem Frobenium, mense Martio M.D.XIX.

1519. Collectanea Adagiorum, &c.

Argentorati M. Schurerius . . . exscripsit mense Martio 1519.

1519. In Hymnum Aviæ Christi Annæ dictum ab Erasmo
Roterodamo Scholia Jacobi Spiegel Selestadiensis.

In officina excusoria Segismundi Grim. Medici et Marci Vuyr-
sung, Augustæ Vindelicorum [Augsburg] M.D.XIX. quarto
Non. Mar.

1519. D. Erasmi Rot. Apologia pro declamatione de laude
matrimonii.

Apud Joannem Frobenium, mense Maio M.D.XIX.

1519. De ratione studii, &c. (Containing the same pieces as
the edition of 1512.)

Argentorati Ex ædibus M. Schurerii, mense Junio M.D.XIX.

1519. In Epistolam Pauli ad Galatas Paraphrasis per Erasmum Rot. recens ab illo conscripta et nunc primum
typis excusa . . .

Basileæ apud Jo. Frobenium, mense Augusto M.D.XIX.

1519. Ex Novo Testamento Quatuor Evangelia jam denuo ab
Erasmo Roter. recognita, emendata ac liberius versa,
&c.

Lipsiæ ex officina industrii Valentini Schumanni. 1519.
15 Kalendas Novembris.

1519. Moriæ encomium iterum, pro castigatissimo castigatius,
una cum Listrii commentariis, &c.

Basileæ in ædibus Jo. Frobenii, mense Novembri, M.D.IX.

1519 (?). Erasmi Rot. Apologia, refellens suspiciones quorundam dictitantium dialogum D. Jacobi Latomi. . . . (To which is added, but in different type, the 'Dialogus' of Latomus.)

Basle. Froben. (The woodcut on the title-page has the inscription, HANS HOLB.)

1519. Enchiridion, &c. (Containing the same matter as the Basle edition of 1518.)

Coloniæ, apud Eucharium Cervicornum, MDXIX.

1519. D. Erasmi Rot. Opuscula, containing Paraclesis, Ratio seu Compendium veræ theologiæ, and Argumenta in omneis Apostolorum epistolas.

Lipsiæ apud Melchiorem Lottheaum. 1519.

1519. In Epistolam Pauli ad Galatas Paraphrasis per Erasmum Roterodamum, recens ab illo conscripta, et nunc primum typis excusa.

Lypsiæ ex officina Schumanniana. 1519.

1520. Enchiridion Militis Christiani (with letter to Volzius). (At the end is added the Letter of Erasmus to John Colet, from Oxford, Eras. *Op.* v. p. 1263, and referred to supra, p. 133.)

Moguntiæ, apud Joannem Schœffer, M.D.XX. mense Januario.

1520. Paraphrases D. Erasmi in Epistolas Pauli Apostoli ad Rhomanos, Corinthios, et Galatas . . .

Basileæ, in æd. Frob. per Hieronymum Frob. Joan. Filium. Mense Januario MDXX.

1520. Paraphrases in Epistolam Pauli ad Ephesios, Philippenses et Colossenses et in duas ad Thessalonicenses . . .

Basileæ in ædibus Joannis Frobenii, mense Martio MDXX.

1520. Paraphrases in Epistolas Pauli ad Timotheum duas, ad Titum unam et ad Philemonem unam.

Basileæ in ædibus Joannis Frobenii, mense Martio MDXX.

1520. Annotationes Edovardi Leei in Annotationes Novi Testamenti D. Erasmi. (With the replies of Erasmus.)

Basileæ ex ædibus Joannis Frobenii, mense Maio M.D.XX.

1520. Annotationes Edovardi Leei in Annotationes Novi Testamenti D. Erasmi.

Basileæ ex ædibus Joannis Frob. xii. Calendas Augustas M.D.XX.

1520. De Ratione Studii, &c.
Officium Discipulorum ex Quintiliano.

Concio de puero Jesu, &c.

Expostulatio Jesu ad Mortales.

Carmina Scholaria.

> Selestadii in ædibus Lazari Schurerii, mense Augusto, anno M.D.XX.

1520. Apologia Erasmi . . . de ' In principio erat Sermo.'

> Basileæ apud Jo. Frobenium, M.D.XX.

And also, with continuous paging,

Epistolæ aliquot eruditorum virorum ex quibus perspicuum quanti sit Eduardi Leeí virulentia.

> Basileæ ex ædibus Joannis Frobenii, MDXX. mense Augusto.

1520. Parabolarum sive Similium Liber. Ex secunda recognitione.

> Selestadii in ædibus Lazari Schurerii, mense Augusto M.D.XX.

1520. Adagia. Ex quarta Autoris recognitione.

> Basileæ ex ædibus Joannis Frobenii, mense Octobri M.D.XX.

1520. Antibarbarorum D. Erasmi Rot. Liber unus.

> Basileæ apud Jo. Frobenium, M.D.XX.

1520. D. Erasmi Rot. Epistola ad Cardinalem Moguntinum, qua commonefacit illius celsitudinem de causa Doctoris Martini Lutheri.

> Selestadii in officina Schureriana, sumptu Nicolai Cuferii bibliopolæ Selestadiensis, M.D.XX.

1521. De duplici copia verborum ac rerum Commentarii duo. De ratione studii.
De laudibus literariæ societatis, reipublicæ ac magistratuum urbis Argentinæ.

> Basileæ apud Jo. Frobenium, mense Februario, M.D.XXI.

1521. Parabolæ sive similia.

> Basileæ apud Joannem Frobenium, mense Julio M.D.XXI.

1521. De duplici Copia verborum ac rerum commentarii duo. De laudibus literariæ societatis, &c.
Epistola ad Wimphelingum.

> Moguntiæ ex ædibus Joannis Schœffer, mense Augusto MD.XXI.

1521. Epistolæ D. Erasmi Roterodami ad diversos, et aliquot aliorum ad illum per amicos eruditos, ex ingentibus fasciculis schedarum collectæ.

> Basileæ apud Jo. Frobenium, M.D.XXI. Pridie Cal. Septembris.

1522. Collectanea Adagiorum, &c.

> Moguntiæ in ædibus Joannis Schœffer, Anno supra sesquimillesimum XXII. mense Februario.

1522. Enchiridion militis Christiani.

> Argentinæ apud Joannem Knoblochium mense Februario MDXXII.

1522. Novum testamentum omne tertio jam recognitum.

> Anno MDXXII. (Basle).

1522. D. Erasmi Rot. in novum testamentum ab eodem tertio recognitum Annotationes.

> Basileæ M.D.XXII. mense Februario.

1522. Paraphrasis in Evangelium Matthæi, nunc primum nata et ædita, &c.

> Basileæ apud Jo. Frob. mense Martio MDXXII.

1522. Querela Pacis.

> Argentinæ apud Joannem Knoblouchum, mense Martio M.D.XXII.

1522. Ratio seu Methodus Compendio perveniendi ad veram Theologiam, postremum ab ipso autore castigata et locupletata. Paraclesis. (Also Letter from Hutten to Erasmus.)

> Basileæ in ædibus Joannis Frobenii, MDXXII. mense Junio.

1522. Moriæ Encomium, &c.

> Basileæ apud Jo. Frob. mense Julio MDXXII.

1522. De Conscribendis Epistolis, recognitum ab autore et locupletatum.

> Parabolarum sive similium liber ab autore recognitus.

> Basileæ apud Jo. Frob. M.D.XXII. mense Augusto.

1522. Familiarium Colloquiorum Formulæ. (The Prefatory Letter to Froben's Son is dated ' pridie Calendas Martias, MDXXII.')

> (A reprint of the first edition of Basle.)
> Argentorati expensis Joannis Knoblouchii et Pauli Getz. MDXXII. mense Octobri.

1522. De Conscribendis Epistolis Opus . . . recognitum ab autore et locupletatum.

> Argentorati ex ædibus Joannis Knoblouchii, MDXXII. mense Octobri.

1522. Ad Christophorum Episc. Basil. Epistola Apologetica de interdicto esu carnium, &c. cum aliis nonnullis novis, &c. (Containing Apologia contra Stunicam.)

> Argentorati ædibus Joannis Knoblouchii MDXXII. octavo calendas decemb.

1522. Ad R. Christophorum Episcopum Basiliensem, epistola apologetica de interdicto esu carnium, &c.

> In officina excusoria Sigismundi, Augustæ Vindelicorum [Augsburg], M.D.XXII.

1522. Paraclesis.

> Augustæ Vindelicorum, MDXXII.

1522. Enchiridion Militis Christiani, which may be called in Englische the Hansom Weapon of a Christen Knight replenished with many Goodly and Godly Preceptes: made by the famous Clerke Erasmus of Roterdame, and newly corrected and imprinted.

> Imprinted at London by Johan Byddell, dwellynge at the sygne of the Sonne, against the Cundyte in Fletestrete, where they be for to sell. Newly corrected in the yere of our Lorde god, M.CCCCC[X*]XII.

* This letter has evidently dropped out of its place in the printing.

1523. Enchiridion Militis Christiani.

> Apud Sanctam Ubiorum Agrippinam, M.D.XXIII. In ædibus Eucharii Œrvicorni, impensa et ære integerrimi bibliopolæ Godefridi Hittorpii civis Coloniensis, mense Martio.

1523. Paraphrasis in Evangelium Joannis Apostoli. (First edition.)

> Basileæ apud Jo. Frobenium, mense Martio MDXXIII.

1523. Catalogus omnium Erasmi Lucubrationum, ipso autore, cum aliis nonnullis. (Containing Letters of Erasmus to Botzhem, and to Marcus Laurinus.)

> Basileæ in ædibus Joannis Frobenii, mense Aprili M.D.XXIII.

1523. Enchiridion Militis Christiani.

> Parisiis in ædibus Simonis Colinæi, Pridie Calendas Maii MD.XXIII.

1523. Enchiridion Militis Christiani. (With Letter to Volzius.)

> Argentorati excudebat Joan. Knob. mense Octobri M.D.XXIII.

1523. Querela Pacis, &c.

> Argent. J. Cnoblochus excudebat apud Turturem, mense Novembri MD.XXIII.

A.D.

1523. Virginis Matris apud Lauretum Cultæ Liturgia, per Erasmum Roterodamum.

> Basileæ apud Jo. Frobenium, Anno M.D.XXIII. mense Novembri.

1523. Ratio seu methodus compendio perveniendi ad veram Theologiam, postremum ab ipso autore castigata et locupletata.

Paraclesis, and letter from Hutten to Erasmus.

> Basle. Froben. MDXXIII.

1523. Ad Christophorum episcopŭm Basiliensem epistola apologetica Erasmi Roterodami de interdicto esu carnium, &c.

> Apud Sanctam Coloniam MD.XX.III.

1523 (?). Spongia Erasmi adversus aspergines Hutteni.

> Without date or printer's name.

1523 or 4. Precatio dominica . . . opus recens ac modo natum et mox excusum. (Prefatory letter dated nono calend. Novemb. MDXXIII.)

> Froben. Basle.

1524. De Octo orationis partium constructione libellus.

> Parisiis in ædibus Simonis Colinæi, mense Januario MDXXIV.

1524. De libero Arbitrio ΔΙΑΤΡΙΒΗ. (Bound with this copy is the De servo Arbitrio Mar. Lutheri, ad D. Erasmum Roterodamum. Wittembergæ, 1526.)

> Basileæ apud Joan. Frob. mense Septemb. M.D.XXIIII.

1524. De Libero Arbitrio ΔΙΑΤΡΙΒΗ, sive Collatio, D. Erasmi Roterod.

> Antwerpiæ apud Michaelem Hillenium Hoochstratanum, mense Septemb. MD.XX.IIII.

1524. De immensa dei misericordia D. Erasmi Rot. Concio. Virginis et Martyris comparatio per eundem. Nunc primum et condita et edita.

> Basileæ apud Jo. Frob. mense Septemb. MD.XXIV.

1524. Tomus Primus Paraphraseon D. Erasmi Rot. in novum testamentum. (Containing the Paraphrases on the Four Gospels and the 'Acts.')

> Basileæ apud Joannem Frobenium MDXXIV.

1524. 1. Exomologesis sive modus Confitendi, opus nunc primum et natum et excusum.

2. Paraphrasis in tertium Psalmum.

A.D.

3. Duo diplomata Papæ Adriani sexti cum respon-
sionibus.

4. Epistola de morte.

5. Apologia ad Stunicæ conclusiones.

Basileæ apud Joannem Frob. MD.XXIIII.

1524. D. Eras. Rot. Breviores aliquot Epistolæ, studiosis
juvenibus admodum utiles. (Apparently a selection
of Letters from the Basle collection of 1521.)

Parisiis. Apud Simonem Colinæum.

1526. Familiarium Colloquiorum opus . . . recognitum, magna-
que accessione auctum. (From p. 246 to p. 750 is all
additional matter not included in the first edition.
This edition is the first which contained the Vindication of the Colloquies, ' D. Erasmus Roterodamus
De utilitate colloquiorum, ad lectorem.')

Basileæ apud Joan. Frob. mense Junio, M.D.XXVI.

1526. Erasmi Rot. Detectio præstigiarum cujusdam libelli ger-
manice scripti, ficto authoris titulo, cum hac inscrip-
tione, Erasmi et Lutheri opiniones de Cœna domini.

Norembergæ apud Joan. Petreium M.D.XXVI. mense Junio.

1526. Hyperaspistes Diatribæ adversus servum Arbitrium
Martini Lutheri.

Basileæ apud Jo. Frob. M.D.XXVI.

1526. Moriæ encomium, nunc postremum ab ipso religiose
recognitum, doctissimique Gerardi Listrii commentariis illustratum.

Eucharius Cervicornus excudebat M.D.XXVI.

1526. Lingua, opus novum et hisce temporibus aptissimum.
(Prefatory Letter of Erasmus dated Postridie Idus
Augusti 1525.)

[Cologne.] Anno M.D.XXVI.

1527. Novum Testamentum. (Fourth edition.)

Basileæ in ædibus Jo. Frobenii. M.D.XXVII. mense martio.

1527. Hyperaspistæ liber secundus.

Anno M.D.XXVII. mense Novembri. (No name of printer or
place where printed.)

1527. Hyperaspistæ liber secundus, opus nunc primum excusum.

Basileæ apud Joannem Frobenium, MD.XXVII.

1530. Utilissima consultatio de bello Turcis inferendo et obiter
enarratus Psalmum XXVIII. per Des. Erasmum Roterodamum. Opus recens et natum et æditum.

Lutetiæ Parisiorum, mense Junio MDXXX.

1530. De Civilitate morum Puerilium per Des. Erasmum Rot.
Libellus nunc primum et conditus et æditus.

Parisiis Expensis Christiani Wechel, MDXXX. mense Octobri.

1530. Lingua.

Apud sanctam Coloniam quarto Idus Novembris M.D.XXX.

1532. D. Erasmi Rot. Dilutio eorum quæ Judocus Clithoveus
scripsit adversus declamationem suasoriam matrimonii.

Epistola de delectu ciborum, &c. In elenchum Alberti
Pii brevissima scholia.

Froben, MDXXXII.

1533. De sarcienda Ecclesiæ concordia, &c (nunc primum typis
excusa).

Basileæ ex officina Frobeniana, M.D.XXXIII.

1534. De preparatione ad mortem, nunc primum et conscriptus
et æditus.

Accedunt aliquot epistolæ seriis de rebus, in quibus item
nihil est non novum ac recens. (Containing, inter alia,
Sir Thos. More's Letter to Erasmus on resigning the
chancellorship, and appended thereto his epitaph.)

Basileæ in officina Frobeniana per Hieronymum Frobenium et
Nicolaum Episcopium, MDXXXIIII.

1536. Ecclesiastæ sive de ratione concionandi libri quatuor,
opus recens, denuo ab autore recognitum.

Basileæ in officina Frobeniana per Hieronymum Frobenium et
Nicolaum Episcopium, mense Augusto MDXXXVI.

1542. D. Erasmi Rot. in Novum Testamentum Annotationes
ab ipso autore jam postremum sic recognitæ ac
locupletatæ ut propemodum novum opus videri possit.
(Reprint of the fifth and last edition.)

Basileæ in officina Frobeniana M.D.XLII.

APPENDIX F.

A.D.

1516. Utopia (First edition).—' Libellus vere aureus nec minus
(Dec.)   salutaris quam festivus de optimo reip. statu, deque
nova Insula Vtopia authore clarissimo viro Thoma
Moro inclytæ Civitatis Londinensis cive et Vicecomite,
cura M. Petri Aegidii Antuerpiensis, et arte Theodorici
Martini Alustensis, Typographi almæ Louaniensium
Academiæ, nunc primum accuratissime editus.'

> Without date, but containing a Prefatory Letter from Petrus
> Aegidius to Hier. Buslidius, dated MDXVI. cal. Novembris;
> and a Letter from Joannes Paludanus to Petrus Aegidius,
> dated calen. Decemb.

1518. Utopia (Second edition).—' De Optimo Reip. statu
deque nova Insula Vtopia, libellus vere aureus,' &c.
Also,
Epigrammata clarissimi disertissimique viri Thomæ
Mori. Also,
Epigrammata Des. Erasmi Rot.

> Basileæ apud Jo. Frobenium, mense Martio MDXVIII.

1518. Ditto ditto.

> Basileæ apud Joannem Frobenium, mense Novembri MDXVIII.
> (HANS HOLB. inscribed in the woodcut on the title-page).

1520. Epigrammata clarissimi disertissimique viri Thomæ
Mori, Britanni, ad emendatum exemplar ipsius
autoris excusa. (With some additional Epigrams,
including More's Letter to his Children.)

> Basileæ apud Joannem Frobenium, mense Decembri M.D.XX.

A.D.

1557. The Workes of Sir Thomas More, Knyght, sometime Lorde Chauncellorr of England, wrytten by him in the Englysh tongve.

Printed at London, at the costes and charges of John Cawod John Waly, and Richarde Tottell.   Anno 1557.

1563. Thomæ Mori Angliæ ornamenti eximii Lucubrationes, ab innumèris mendis repurgatæ.

Basil. apud Episcopium F.   1563.

1566. Thomæ Mori Angli . . . Omnia, quæ hucusque ad manus nostras peruenerunt, Latina opera . . .

Lovanii, apud Joannem Bogardum sub Bibliis Aureis.   Anno 1566.

1568. Doctissima D. Thomæ Mori clarissimi ac disertiss. viri Epistola, in qua non minus facetè quàm piè, respondet Literis Joannis Pomerani, hominis inter Protestantes nominis non obscuri.

Opusculum . . . ex Authoris quidem autographo emendato, dum viveret, exemplari desumptum, nunquam vero antehac in lucem editum.

Lovanii, ex officina Joannis Fouleri.   MD.LXVIII.   (Not included in any of the above collections of More's works.)

1588. Tres Thomæ . . . D. Thomæ Mori . . . Vita, authore Thoma Stapletono Anglo.

Dvaci, Ex officina Joannis Bogardi.   M.D.LXXXVIII.

1612. Ditto ditto.

Coloniæ Agrippinæ, Sumptibus Bernardi Gualteri, MDC.XII. (Stapleton had access to a collection of More's papers, made by Harris, his private secretary, and has preserved Latin translations of his letters to his children, &c., not in the collected works.)

INDEX.

N N